TAKE CHARGE OF YOUR CHILD'S HEALTH

TAKE CHARGE OF YOUR CHILD'S HEALTH

A Complete Guide to
Recognizing Symptoms
and Treating Minor
Illnesses at Home

George Wootan, M.D., and Sarah Verney

CROWN PUBLISHERS, INC. NEW YORK

The graphs on pages 239–41 are reprinted by permission of the estate of Professor T. McKeown and Blackwell Scientific Publications Ltd., Oxford, England.

Published by Crown Publishers, Inc., 201 East 50th Street, New York, New York 10022. Member of the Crown Publishing Group.

CROWN is a trademark of Crown Publishers, Inc.

Manufactured in the United States of America

Library of Congress Cataloging-in-Publication Data
Wootan, George.
Take charge of your child's health : a complete guide to recognizing symptoms and treating minor illnesses at home / by George Wootan and Sarah Verney. — 1st ed.
p.   cm.
1. Pediatrics—Popular works.   2. Children—Diseases.   I. Verney, Sarah.   II. Title.
RJ61.W93   1992
618.92—dc20   91-38761
CIP

ISBN 0-517-57365-2

Book Design by Shari deMiskey

10 9 8 7 6 5 4 3 2 1

First Edition

Contents

Contents

Part Three

THE UNSICK CHILD

Part Four

THE SICK CHILD

Acknowledgments

How do I begin to thank all of the people who have helped me put the ideas in this book into action and then into print? I must start with my parents. My mother gave me the love that I needed to be able to open myself up to new ideas. My father gave me the ability to dream the impossible.

I also want to thank my wife Pat. She has shared my vision of healthy children, and the ability to help parents achieve that goal. Together we have grown in our desire to achieve the good health of our children through self-education. She has helped provide our own private laboratory of eleven children to practice on. She has endured while I have grown, and seen that the instincts and intuition that God gave her were, in fact, more valuable than all the studies in the medical journals about child care. For more than thirty years our relationship has continued to be mutually fulfilling as we have helped each other achieve our personal goals.

I am so grateful to my children Kimberly Michele, Brian Sidney, Keith George, Eric Thomas Allen, Margo Gaye, Hope Susan, Brendan Scott, Cicely Sarah, Jared Stewart Anson, Nina Mary Caroline, and Bethany Letha. They have certainly taught me as much, or more, than I have taught them. They are really a great bunch of kids (not perfect, but really great). Each one has taught me something special, and I thank them for that.

I would also like to thank my co-author, Sarah Verney, for persevering when the going got tough; our editors, Lisa Healy and Irene Prokop, for their insight and endless patience; and my dear friend Richard Gabriel, who gave life to the words with his wonderful illustrations.

Finally, many of the ideas in this book come from parents, human beings on the front line of child-rearing that have had to deal with difficult situations and resolve them. To you I give a hearty thanks.

GEORGE WOOTAN, M.D.

• •

This book is dedicated to my parents, Jean and Richard Verney, for all they've taught me; to my husband Robert Fink, for his loving support and encouragement; and to my children, Evan, Lucas, and Abigail Verney-Fink, for the joy they bring me every day.

SARAH VERNEY

Author's Note

Medicine is an ever-changing science. As new research and clinical experience broaden our knowledge, changes in treatment and drug therapy are required. I have worked hard to ensure that the statements in this book are accurate. I have also tried to distinguish between the ideas and treatments that are widely accepted by most physicians and those that are solely my own, arrived at after years of experience and through trial and error.

Each human body is unique, and yet we are all alike in some ways. These similarities are what allow those of us in the medical profession to develop standards of treatment. My particular bias, however, is toward discovering those individual differences that cause some of us not to follow the "normal" path.

In order for you to get the most out of this book, you must take the material presented here, assimilate it, and then try to apply it to your family. If my ideas don't work for you, don't try to force them. You may be trying to fit a round peg into a square hole (my round ideas into your square child). Back off, and use the principles presented here to guide you to another therapy.

This book is not meant to take the place of a doctor. But, as I frequently stress in this book, good health is ultimately up to you.

GEORGE WOOTAN, M.D.

Introduction

This book is the culmination of a process that began about fourteen years ago. I had been practicing medicine for eleven years then, and was a fairly typical doctor, with a good-sized practice and the attitude that I knew much more about the health of my young patients than their parents ever could. Around that time I had lunch with Dr. Robert Mendelsohn, the pediatrician and author. At some point we got on to the subject of well-baby and well-child exams, and Bob asked if I performed such exams in my practice. Of course I did, I told him. What kind of doctor did he think I was? He then asked how many times, in those eleven years, I had picked up something significant that the parents of the child had not already noticed. I thought back, and came up with only one incident, several years before, where I had diagnosed a condition of which the mother was unaware. Bob informed me that my experience seemed to be about the average, and we dropped the subject.

His observation got me thinking, however, and when I returned to work I began paying closer attention to what transpired in my well-child exams. Most of the time the child would be perfectly healthy, and I would simply confirm that this was the case. If there was a problem, the mother would tell me what she thought was wrong. If, for example, the child had an ear infection, I'd whip out my otoscope, check his ears, and confirm her diagnosis. I'd then write out a prescription, charge the mother twenty dollars, and send her on her way. The mother had told me what was wrong, and she was the one who would buy the medicine and nurse the child back to health. My role in getting the child well consisted of little more than writing a prescription—and, in the case of a child who was not ill, I didn't even do that much—and yet I was the one getting paid. Not a bad deal for me, I thought, but not quite fair to the mother.

As a result of my observations I went through a crisis of confidence. If I were really a good doctor, I thought, I'd pick up more disease during my well-baby exams. My concern about my abilities led me to do my own research on the value of these exams. I read more than one hundred fifty articles in various medical journals on the subject. Not one of these articles was able to show that regular exams by a doctor gave a child any better chance for good health than he would have if the exams were not performed. The only benefit shown was that the information transmitted from the physician to the parent enabled her to recognize symptoms of disease sooner than she would have otherwise.

Now, my well-child exams at that time took approximately seven minutes, which is about average. Obviously, not much doctor-parent education can take place in a mere seven minutes. To remedy the situation, I began scheduling my patients so that parents would have plenty of time to discuss whatever was on their minds. My well-child exams jumped to forty-five minutes in length, and I soon found myself becoming very popular in the community. This really wreaked havoc with my practice: I had more patients than ever, and I was committed to spending large chunks of time with each of them. I also found myself answering the same questions over and over again. Finally, as a way of easing the demands of my time, I decided to hold a weekly class for parents. During these classes, I'd answer all questions in a group setting, then check over each of the babies who had been brought in, and send everyone on their way. This worked out great, except that every few weeks a new mother would join the class, and—understandably—ask questions about material we'd already covered. I finally set up a schedule of ten classes, which parents could attend in sequence, so that no one would have to sit through old material over and over again. At this point I was asked to speak about the sessions at a statewide La Leche League convention in New York. After the convention I was approached by several people who wanted me to teach the classes in their towns. In order to make this feasible, I compiled a two-day seminar called "Pediatrics: A Course for Parents," which included a physical exam that parents could perform on their children, as well as other information that I felt was crucial to raising healthy children. I began teaching the course around the state, and then, after speaking at a national La Leche League convention, around the country.

As I took the course to a national level, I was struck by the overwhelming number of parents who expressed a desire to take greater responsibility for their children's health care. Many felt frustrated by a medical system that refused to take into account their intuitions and observations and that often assumed they were unable to understand even basic medical procedures. Because of my own medical training and the kind of doctor I once was, I understood what they were up against. Doctors simply do not give parents enough credit when it comes to their ability to recognize physical problems in their own children.

This tendency on the part of doctors is as ironic as it is unfortunate. Parents know their children better than anyone else, and their observations are invaluable. When you bring a child to a doctor for medical treatment, ninety percent of the information used to make a diagnosis comes from what you tell the doctor about the child's symptoms and history. The physical exam provides another five percent, and lab tests, the final five percent. Nevertheless, parents often feel—or are made to feel—that they cannot adequately judge when something is wrong with their child. Perhaps more important, they are often told that they are incapable of evaluating the seriousness of any given illness or condition.

As a result, parents tend to run to the doctor at the first sign of a problem. Advanced medical technology contributes substantially to this doctor-dependency, since parents are often led to believe that they cannot evaluate their child's health status without the sophisticated equipment and tests that are now a part of every doctor's practice. However, as I've stated, *ninety percent* of the information we use to make a diagnosis comes from the parent. When cultures, X rays, blood tests, and other tests are used, they often serve only to confirm what the doctor already knows, rather than to provide him with new information. Add to this the fact that approximately ninety percent of childhood ailments will cure themselves. What we hope to illustrate in this book is how to recognize when your child's condition merits a trip to the pediatrician and when it may not.

Okay, you say, so it's unnecessary, but so what? All this running to the doctor doesn't hurt anyone, either, does it? Actually, it may. Leaving aside economic considerations, let's look at the health aspects of medical treatment. A study done and reported by the American Medical Association showed that of sixty thousand people in North Carolina who saw a doctor about a specific illness or complaint, ninety percent would have gotten better without treatment. Of the ten percent who might have benefited from a doctor's treatment, only five percent did. The remaining five percent were actually made worse. According to this study, if your child has an ailment that truly requires medical attention, she has only a fifty percent chance of benefiting from that treatment. Consider, too, that should you take her to the doctor for one of those conditions that is inherently self-correcting, you may be needlessly subjecting her to tests, procedures, or drugs that could ultimately prove more harmful than the condition they were intended to help.

Nevertheless, I'm not about to tell you you should never take your child to a doctor. Just about every child needs a physician's attention at one time or another, and there is no question that modern medical science is capable of performing minor miracles. What you need to know is how to distinguish between ailments that will heal themselves and those that will benefit from a doctor's treatment, as well as how to ensure that your child will get good medical care when she does need it. That, in a nutshell, is what this book is all about.

It is my belief that you, as a parent, are best qualified to head up your children's health care team. You know your child better than anyone else, and your intuitions concerning his health are valid. All you lack is basic medical information, which this book will provide. To ensure that your child gets the best medical care, you'll learn how to do a physical exam that will teach you to recognize what is normal for your child, how to deal with most of the common ailments of childhood at home, and how to work with your doctor, effectively communicating the information he needs. In addition, you'll learn about providing a healthy physical and emotional environment through sound nutrition and good nurturing, so that you can effectively practice preventative medicine.

Sickness, Unsickness, and Wellness

Throughout these pages you will encounter some of "Wootan's theories" on subjects as diverse as allergies, marriage, and the nature of toddlers. Let me introduce you to the first of these now: Wootan's theory of wellness, which states that on a continuum between sickness and wellness, there is a third condition that falls right in the middle: unsickness. Undoubtedly you know the difference between sickness and wellness, but the difference between wellness and unsickness may not be as clear. When you're well, your body is able to resist disease. When you're unsick, this capacity is diminished. A well person goes to the grocery store and leaves with a bag of groceries, but an unsick person goes to the grocery store and leaves with a bag of groceries and a virus, courtesy of the guy who was coughing all over her in the checkout line. When you're well, you generally stay that way (although even the healthiest person is susceptible to disease *sometimes*). When you're unsick, illness is as close as the nearest germ.

In trying to maintain a state of wellness in your children, one thing you should understand is that the Medical Doctor (M.D.) is an expert at taking people from sickness to unsickness, but it is up to the parents to take a child from unsickness to wellness. Doctors' antibiotics destroy bacteria, our decongestants drain stuffy sinuses, and our cough syrups suppress a cough. Most of the time, however, the drugs we prescribe just take care of the manifestation of the disease without really "curing" it. For example, consider the adult who has hypertension, diabetes, or arthritis. An M.D. can prescribe medications that will control the symptoms, but he can't cure the disease. Take away the drugs, and the patient's condition remains with all its symptoms. The same is true for the diseases of childhood, except that (as I've already noted) in the overwhelming number of cases, the illnesses are inherently self-correcting.

If your child has one middle ear infection in four years and your doctor prescribes an antibiotic to clear it up, you might argue, with some justification, that his drugs will take your child from sickness to wellness. It's certainly true that the penicillin will kill the bacteria in your child's ear canal. However, it won't do anything about the conditions that allowed the bacteria to grow in the first place. Maybe the child was susceptible to the disease because of fatigue, stress, poor nutrition, anemia, or allergy. Whatever the reason, it is you, the parent—not a doctor—who provides the tender loving care that will allow the child to make that leap from unsick to well again. Luckily for children, giving TLC is an area in which parents, particularly mothers, shine.

For the sake of argument, however, let's say that your child has had not one ear infection in four years, but four in six months. Your doctor repeatedly prescribes antibiotics, but the infection recurs shortly after your daughter goes off the medication. When this happens, it is not because you are a failure at giving tender loving care, but rather because you are not getting at the cause of the infections. You are effectively treating a symptom—the overgrowth of bacteria—but not eliminating the underlying problem. With your doctor's help, the child is going from sickness to unsickness, which is as far on the continuum as he can take her. In order to progress to a state of wellness, you, the parent, are going to have to make an extra effort to discover the cause of the recurring illness and eliminate it. In this case, the problem is probably a food allergy (see chapters 12 and 13 for more information), but whatever the cause, you are the one who will have to do the detective work. You can, of course, have help—perhaps from your doctor or other health practitioners, from this book, or any number of other sources—but you're the one who will have to do the footwork, coordinate the information, and then make the right thing happen to get your child truly well.

If you find the prospect of this responsibility a little daunting, keep in mind that when it comes to understanding a disease that your child has, no one can do a better job than you. True, you may not have a medical education, but you have two advantages over your doctor in this situation: You know your child better than anyone else does, and his problem is the only one you need to learn about. Your doctor can't possibly know everything about every disease. The rarer the condition, the less he's likely to know about it, since, in the interests of practicality, he has to spend most of his time learning about the illnesses he'll be treating often.

Even with common illnesses, no one doctor can keep up with every new bit of research or information that becomes available. If you're trying to understand an illness that your child has, however, you can narrow your focus and take the time to learn as much as possible about that one disease.

Several years ago, one of my patients found herself in a position where she needed to do just that. Diane brought her son to me because of a rash that would not clear up. I checked him over but was, quite frankly, completely baffled, and told her so. Diane tried another doctor, who also could not identify the rash but felt that putting the child on several different vitamins would help. The vitamins had no effect, however, and so Diane decided to take the child to a dermatologist. This doctor also could not identify the problem, but was sure that cortisone would clear it up. Because she did not feel comfortable with this treatment when she still did not know the cause of the rash, Diane rejected this doctor's advice and finally arranged a consultation with the chief of dermatology at a major medical center. This doctor was able to identify the child's condition immediately, and told her that the only way to clear up the rash was to put her son on cortisone and sulfa drugs, and that he would have to take them for the rest of his life. Diane was understandably upset at this prospect, so she came back to me to see if I could suggest another treatment. Now, I hadn't even been able to recognize the disease, so I certainly didn't have a clue as to how to treat it. However, I felt the situation was worth looking into, and suggested we do a little research. We used my computer to search a medical data bank, and came up with a stack of articles on the disease (most hospitals and some libraries are able to do this type of search). I turned them over to Diane, telling her that I would be happy to help her understand any of the technical jargon and the disease process, but that she was the one who would have to do the footwork. She took the articles home and started reading. As it turned out, two of the articles suggested the possibility of the rash being related to a wheat allergy. Following up that lead, Diane put her son on a wheat-free diet, and sure enough, the rash cleared up and has not returned, except for the rare occasions when her son eats wheat.

Now, you may wonder why the chief of dermatology at this major medical center was not aware of the possible connection between this disease and an allergy to wheat. The two articles that we found on the subject were published in obscure journals—one from Arkansas, the other from South Africa—that undoubtedly were not on that doctor's reading list. Because the treatment suggested in the two articles concerned nutrition instead of drug therapy, it was considered outside the realm of standard practice, and so was not likely to be reported in the bigger medical journals, which, no doubt, the eminent dermatologist *did* read. He was an expert in the field, but even the experts can't know everything. It was up to the child's parents to track down the information that was the key to his problem, and to take him from unsick to well. The best the doctor could do for him—clear up the rash with drugs—would still have left the child unsick.

Whether you're dealing with a common problem or an unusual one, a chronic condition or a one-time disease, remember to keep your mind open and to hold on to your common sense. Be willing to consider ideas and treatments that are outside the realm of the current medical wisdom, and to question standard practices. After all, modern medicine is constantly changing, so that today's radical new idea may be tomorrow's accepted treatment. Use your head, think things through, and follow the course that makes sense to you.

My approach to health has come from several sources: my medical education, my twenty-five years as a board-certified family practitioner, and most of all, my role as a partner with my wife in the raising of our eleven children. My experience with my own children's health care and medical problems has afforded me an opportunity to learn more than I ever could from any medical text. I've tried to convey some of the knowledge I've gained in the hope that you will benefit from my experiences. I am still learning, too, however, so that I hope you will consider what you learn here to be the foundation, not the entirety, of your medical education. Continue to learn about health care by reading other sources, attending seminars or lectures, and staying open to new ideas. Every step you take toward becoming an educated consumer of medical care and a practitioner of preventative medicine helps to ensure the continued health of your family. And when you come right down to it, that's something only you—not your doctor—can do.

Part One

Examining Your Child

The Body as a Whole

*T*his chapter and the five that follow are devoted to a physical exam that you can perform on your children at home. People are often surprised to learn that I advocate such an exam, and doctors in particular tend to oppose the idea vehemently. Typically, they comment that I couldn't possibly teach parents, in a two-day seminar or even in a book like this one, something they spent years learning. That's absolutely true, and I have no intention of trying to turn any parent into a physician. Doctors do "physical exams" on their patients, and you will learn to do a "physical exam" on your child, but they are not the same thing. Your intention in performing the exam will be to learn to recognize *what is normal* for that child, to notice *when there is a deviation from the norm*, and to judge *when an illness requires a doctor's attention.* The purpose of your doctor's physical exam is to diagnose specific diseases. While you will

learn to identify and treat some of the minor medical conditions of childhood, you will not learn to diagnose every medical condition, nor do you need to.

Let's say that while doing the exam one day, you discover a lump in your child's abdomen. Because you have been performing the physical exam on him regularly, you know that this lump is not normally there. In order to find out its cause, you will have to consult your doctor, who has had the opportunity to palpate thousands of abdomens and who spent years in medical school, learning such things as what different types of abdominal lumps feel like. By doing your physical exam you will learn to recognize and evaluate deviations from the norm, so that you will know when it is appropriate to seek a doctor's services. His physical exam, in turn, will serve to diagnose those deviations with which you are not familiar.

Obviously, then, it is not my intention to try to turn you into a doctor. In fact, you'll often find I deal less with treatment than with learning to recognize problems, and for good reason. There are many approaches to any ailment, and medical doctors provide only one. Chiropractors, osteopaths, homeopaths, naturopaths, nutritional therapists, and others all have a certain degree of success in treating various diseases and conditions. No single field in the health services has a perfect batting average. For this reason, I'd like you to learn to recognize problems, evaluate specific symptoms, and monitor the progress of whatever treatment you choose, be it traditional medicine or not. If you learn to recognize what is normal for your child, that is enough. Then, when problems arise, you can consult with your doctor, or, if you choose, another health professional, for a diagnosis and appropriate treatment.

While the information in this book will not turn you into an M.D., it *will* give you a decided advantage in taking charge of your child's health and in cutting your medical costs. One of the objections doctors raise to a home physical exam is that they fear its adherents will fail to seek appropriate medical treatment when necessary. It has been my experience that this is emphatically not the case, but the exam will allow you to avoid *unnecessary* visits to the doctor, which can substantially cut your medical costs. In fact, research supports the notion that patient education can reduce medical costs. A study reported in the *Journal of the American Medical Association* showed that for every dollar spent on educational interven-

tion, between $2.50 and $3.50 is saved in utilization of medical services.[1] This conclusion has been borne out in the experience of many of the parents who attended the seminars upon which this book is based, with some of them reducing their doctor bills by as much as eighty-five percent.

In some instances these same parents sought a doctor's advice much sooner than they would have otherwise because they were able to identify abnormalities that would have gone undetected until much later had they not performed the exam. In one case, a mother performed the exam on her baby because he seemed listless and had a slight fever, although he did not seem terribly sick. The mother discovered that the baby's fontanel was bulging and called me to report that she thought he had meningitis. Her diagnosis was, in fact, correct, even though the baby did not have any of the other clinical symptoms of the disease. The baby had to be hospitalized, but thanks to early treatment, he did survive and is thriving today. Had the mother not done the physical exam learned in my course, she might have been inclined to postpone seeking treatment, since her baby did not seem very ill. In this case, a delay could have proven fatal for her child.

Doing the physical exam is the first step in taking greater responsibility for your children's health care. I have found that parents are sometimes intimidated by the prospect of performing an exam on their children, but it is actually quite simple to do and, once you have learned the routine, should take only ten or fifteen minutes. The time you set aside for the exam can also present the ideal opportunity for a "teaching moment" with your child. You can use it to discuss personal hygiene, sexuality, nutrition, menstruation—whatever is on your (or your child's) mind. I've found that children come to view the exam as an expression of your love and will value it as such.

When you are first learning the exam, you should perform it about once a week. (If you have more than one child, you can do the exam on a different child each week during this practice period.) As you become more proficient, you can gradually stretch out the time between exams to once a month, then every three months, then six months, until finally you are performing the exam just once a year when your child is well. You will, of course, also want to do the exam any time your child is sick, to gain a clearer understanding of his symptoms and to be better able to judge the severity of the illness, so that you will know when to consult a doctor.

In order for the physical exam to be of any use to you, you must perform it regularly when your child is healthy. If you don't, the information in these five chapters will do you little good, for you will lack a frame of reference when your child is ill. For instance, if the first time you listen to your child's chest is when he is congested, you will not know whether the sounds you hear are normal, or are an indication of respiratory difficulty.

Once you have become familiar with the physical exam, I recommend that you first do all the sections that require that the child be in a sitting position, and then lay the child down to complete the parts of the exam that require that the child be supine. This routine may take some getting used to, so I suggest that you not worry about it while you are still learning the procedure. Getting the child up and down as you progress through the exam probably won't bother him a bit, but once you are able to proceed in a more organized fashion, the exam will go more quickly and smoothly for you.

As you read through these chapters, you may be alarmed to see references to serious diseases and conditions. Please don't be put off. In all likelihood, you will not discover anything seriously wrong with your child. Should you come upon a symptom that may indicate a real problem, don't assume the worst. Keep in mind an expression we have in the medical profession: When you hear hoofbeats, don't look for zebras. Common problems are common. Should you find, for example, that your child has swollen lymph nodes, the first thing that comes into your mind should not be leukemia, but rather swelling due to a cold, which is much more common. If you also discover other symptoms that don't accompany a cold, such as bleeding gums or signs of anemia, you may then be justified in thinking about leukemia, but not until then. Don't jump to conclusions. Study the information you have, consider the possibilities, and look for horses first. If your exam leads you to believe that you are dealing with something other than a common, easily treated problem, consult your doctor. In the overwhelming number of cases, however, you will be dealing with horses, not zebras.

The Physical Exam

The following is a list of the tools you will need to assemble for the exam:

THERMOMETER. A rectal or oral thermometer will do; there is no difference between the two aside from the shape of the bulb (rectal thermometers have a shorter, fatter bulb for easier insertion.) You can substitute one for the other if necessary, provided you are careful about disinfecting the thermometer with rubbing alcohol and then washing it in lukewarm water. The digital thermometers now on the market are very accurate and have the advantage of being unbreakable.

FLASHLIGHT OR PENLIGHT

OTOSCOPE. An otoscope with adjustable magnification is best; these are available by mail through Living Well Enterprises, P.O. Box 270, Hurley, N.Y. 12443

STETHOSCOPE. Available at drugstores and medical supply stores or from Living Well Enterprises (address above)

POPSICLE STICK, BUTTER KNIFE, OR SPOON. (to be used as a tongue blade)

STOPWATCH OR CLOCK

BATHROOM SCALE

MEASURING TAPE WITH METRIC UNIT, OR MEASURING TAPE PLUS METRIC RULER

EYE CHART. Available free of charge from The American Association of Ophthalmology, 1100 17th St., Washington, D.C. 20036

Also, I strongly suggest that for each of your children, you purchase a blank bound book in which to keep a health record. Ideally, this record would begin while the mother is pregnant, and would include information about her prenatal care, particularly any drugs taken and tests performed during her pregnancy. The record should also include the findings of your exams, any illnesses or accidents the child may suffer, and the outcome of any visits to his physician. (Follow the sample format on page 7.) This medical history will become an invaluable asset to your child later in life, as he takes on the responsibility for his own health care. You can imagine how significant it would have been if your own health record, kept by your parents as you were growing up, revealed that your mother had taken DES while she was pregnant. (For your own children, information on ultrasounds or X rays may prove equally important.) The record you keep for your child today may provide vital information for his health care in the future.

Health Record Format

....

PAST HISTORY

List all previous   illnesses
                            injuries
                            hospitalizations
                            accidents

List any allergies to   medications
                            foods
                            inhalants

FAMILY HISTORY

Should include siblings, parents, grandparents, aunts and uncles, with information on serious illnesses, congenital problems, allergies, etc. Should be as detailed as possible.

Past history and family history need only be recorded once, at the start of the medical record. The following information should be recorded for each exam.

SOCIAL HISTORY

List   age
        grade in school
        activities and hobbies

HISTORY

State   the current problem or reason for doing the exam (i.e., routine exam, follow-up on previous problem)

Record   significant occurrences since previous exam

REVIEW OF SYSTEMS

List any symptom associated with each of the "systems" of the body: skin, head, eyes, ears, nose, throat, mouth, neck, heart/lungs, abdomen, kidneys, urinary tract, reproductive organs, extremities, neurological. These are symptoms not obviously related to the primary complaint.

PHYSICAL EXAM

Note findings from the exam itself.

Note: If you are using the health record to present information to your doctor, the physician's standard format would place the "history" section at the beginning of the exam. I have chosen to modify this slightly to make the record more practical for use by parents.

The physical exam is divided into sections on each of the various parts of the body. Each of these, in turn, is divided into the "general exam" and a section on "characteristics, problems, and diseases." The general exam includes all the steps you should include in examination of a perfectly well child. If your child is ill or you discover problems as you do the exam, you can refer to the section on characteristics, et cetera, to find the information you need regarding his symptoms.

General Exam

....

VITAL SIGNS

The vital signs that must be checked are the pulse rate, which is the rate of the heart, the respiratory rate, and the body temperature.* The pulse rate and respiratory rate are explained in detail in the sections on the heart and the chest, respectively. You may want to wait until you arrive at those points in the exam to check the pulse and respiration, but you should record your findings at the beginning section of your child's health notebook so that they are easy to locate if you need to look them up for comparison purposes.

BODY TEMPERATURE

There are three ways to take a child's temperature: orally, under the arm (axillary), or rectally. The average normal temperature, when taken orally, is 98.6°F. When taken under the arm it is 97.6°F, and when taken rectally, 99.6°F. These are just *average* temperatures, however. Normal body temperatures vary from one child to the next.

An elevated temperature, even if slight, is an indication that something out of the ordinary is happening in the body. Fever is only one symptom of disease, however, and must be considered within the context of the child's general condition. See chapter 11 for more information on fever.

APPEARANCE

Next, note the general appearance of the child. As a parent, you are, of course, very familiar with how he looks. What I want you to pay attention to here is how he stands, walks, runs, smiles, cries, and manipulates objects. Make notes of your observations.

In addition, check the child's face for

---

*I don't recommend that you attempt to check your child's blood pressure, since this is difficult to do accurately without a range of sizes in blood pressure cuffs (if you use a cuff that is too narrow for the child's arm, you may get a reading that is falsely high, or conversely, if you use a cuff that is too wide, a reading that is falsely low). In all likelihood, you will find yourself in a position to have the blood pressure checked by a professional once or twice a year. Since blood pressure problems are unusual in children, this should be sufficient.

symmetry. When the child smiles, cries, or puckers up to kiss or whistle, the sides of the face should be symmetrical.

Changes in your child's general appearance may signal an illness or problem. For example, a sudden limp may indicate an injury, appendicitis, or a congenital hip problem, and persistent tilting of the head to one side may indicate a spasm of the neck muscles, vision problems, or brain disease (this is very rare). An asymmetrical face (e.g., only one side of the forehead wrinkles when the child cries, the smile is uneven) may signal a neurological problem, such as a problem with a facial nerve, possibly caused by an infection around or in the ear, or rarely, a tumor within the central nervous system. Any unexplained changes in your child's general appearance should be reported to your doctor.

The Well-Child Quick Checklist

···

THE BODY

1. Check and record the pulse rate, respiratory rate, and body temperature.

2. Note the child's general appearance. There should be no sudden changes in the ways he stands, walks, runs, smiles, cries, and manipulates objects.

3. The child's face should be symmetrical.

Note

1. Donald M. Vickery, "Effect of a Self-Care Education Program on Medical Visits," *Journal of the American Medical Association*, Vol. 250, No. 21 (Dec. 2, 1983): p. 2952.

Chapter 2

The Skin

The Skin

GENERAL EXAM

Observe the tone and color of the skin (make notes!). While there is no one correct skin tone, a change in skin tone may indicate illness. Also, note the condition of the skin. Is it dry, oily, sweaty, warm, or cool?

Check for moles, warts, bruises, cuts, boils, lumps, rashes, insect bites, and birthmarks. The first time you notice an abnormality, measure it with a metric ruler (this will give you greater accuracy than a ruler that measures inches). Make a note of the size, location, and color of the blemish, as well as its mobility (can you wiggle it around under the skin, or is it fixed?) and whether or not it is tender to the touch. On subsequent exams, note any changes in the abnormality.

CHARACTERISTICS/PROBLEMS/DISEASES OF THE SKIN

BIRTHMARKS. You may notice a strawberry birthmark, sometimes called a stork bite, on the eyelids, between the eyes, or most commonly, in the hairline at the base of the skull. Strawberry birthmarks are present at birth, and gradually fade in the months that follow, generally disappearing completely by the end of the first year, but sometimes persisting for as long as six years. Even after this type of birthmark has faded, it may be visible when the child strains or cries. Strawberry birthmarks do not require treatment.

Another, less common, type of birthmark is a hemangioma. A hemangioma is a tumor of the blood vessels that appears as a brilliant red raised mark. It is not usually present at birth, but develops in the first two weeks of life. Most hemangiomas will grow for a few weeks and then remain unchanged until eventually the center will begin to fade, and then the rest of the mark will disappear as well. Approximately ninety-eight percent of hemangiomas will disappear by the age of five years, and virtually all will disappear by the age of nine or ten. Surgical removal is not recommended. The surface of the hemangioma comprises only about one-tenth of the entire tumor, with the rest lying under the skin. If surgery is attempted, the result can be a large hole that requires skin grafting. If a hemangioma does not disappear spontaneously, or continues to grow, it is best treated with dry ice, liquid nitrogen, or lasers. A hemangioma that does not stop growing can outgrow its blood supply, resulting in an ulceration and, possibly, infection. Parents often worry that a hemangioma will bleed, but this rarely happens.

MOLES. Most infants are not born with moles, but some children go through a stage where they begin to get them. In the vast majority of cases these moles are harmless. Just to be on the safe side, however, you should occasionally check for the following signs of malignancy: an asymmetrical shape or an irregular edge; a size of more than six millimeters; a variety of colors, such as different shades of black, brown, tan, red, blue, or white, all in the same mole; and bleeding, oozing, or becoming hard to the touch. In addition, you should be concerned about any mole that is growing, especially if it spreads in only one direction, or one that has little "tentacles" sticking out from it. Unless a mole is malignant, there is no reason to remove it, although in some cases you may want to have one taken off for cosmetic reasons.

WARTS. A viral infection of the skin, warts tend to come and go at will, and everyone and their mother, grandmother, and uncle has a different "cure" for them. Most of these cures work some of the time, but none of them works all of the time. My favorite remedy is to apply vitamin A two or three times a day (just poke a hole in the vitamin capsule and squeeze a small amount onto the wart). After about three weeks the wart will usually disappear. Warts on the foot are more difficult to treat because the virus that causes the warts lies at the basement membrane of the skin (see fig. 1), and the skin on the feet is particularly thick. I recommend using a lava stone or pumice stone to abrade the skin and remove any dead cells. You can then apply whatever remedy you are using to attempt to eliminate the wart, and it will be better able to penetrate through to the virus.

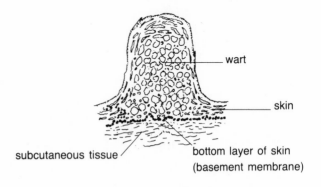

Fig. 1

BRUISES. The dark blue coloration we associate with bruises is a result of broken blood vessels bleeding into the skin. As the blood is reabsorbed into the body, a bruise turns various shades of green and yellow and appears to get larger. This is because the body is spreading the blood out over a larger area so that it can be absorbed more efficiently, in much the same way that you might break up a block of ice in order to get it to melt more quickly. A large bruise on the thigh can actually spread all the way to the ankle or even to the toes as it is reabsorbed.

BRUISES JUST BELOW THE SKIN'S SURFACE. Small hemorrhages that occur in the superficial layers of the skin and that look like small to large bruises just below the surface of the skin are called purpura. Most commonly, they appear on the legs and arms, and are usually small and rice-shaped. Purpura are rarely seen in children, but may appear in those whose blood does not clot properly or who have had problems with the spleen that have affected components of the blood. They can be seen when something is tightly wrapped around a limb, such as a sleeve that is too tight. Purpura, regardless of their nature, require further medical attention, and should always be reported to your child's doctor.

SMALL WHITE BUMPS. Small white bumps on the backs of the arms or the fronts of the thighs are called keratosis pilaris. The bumps, which are completely harmless, are caused by hair follicles that continue to produce oil after the hairs have broken off. They are especially evident in the win-

ter. You can get rid of the bumps by washing them with a Buf-Puf, loofah sponge, or a coarse washcloth to remove the dead skin and open up the pores.

SPLINTERS. The best way to approach a splinter is to clean the skin around it with lots of soap and water and then try to pull it out with a pair of sterile tweezers. Before you go digging around with the tweezers, however, sterilize a sewing needle by placing it in a flame for a few seconds. When it has cooled, gently pick open the skin directly above the splinter. Since this skin is not tender, you will be able to do this without hurting your child. Once that skin has been opened up slightly, the splinter will be much easier to lift out. Another way to open the skin is by soaking the area until the splinter floats out or until you are able to remove it by the methods stated above. Once the splinter is out, wash the area well with lots of water and cover it with an adhesive bandage. If by some chance the area gets very infected and you are unable to remove the splinter, take the child to the doctor, who will deaden the skin and then remove the splinter.

POISON IVY, OAK, AND SUMAC. Each of these plants contains a chemical that causes a type of contact dermatitis characterized by itchy blisters. The rash is easily spread to other parts of the body when minute amounts of the chemical are picked up on the fingers from the original patch of affected skin and then deposited somewhere else. The best way to treat poison ivy, oak, or sumac is to rub the affected area with the sap of a jewel weed, a tall, slender, watery plant that usually grows in and around the same area as poison ivy. If this is not possible, the next best alternative is to get the child into a bath as soon as possible to try to wash the chemical off the skin. Like sap, the chemical won't rinse right off the skin, but must be soaked and scrubbed off. I have also found that Rhus tox., a homeopathic preparation that is available in some health food stores and pharmacies, will often clear up poison ivy, oak, or sumac in about forty-eight hours. If you are unable to find Rhus tox., a mild steroid ointment may be used to cool down the skin until the reaction is over.

DRY SKIN. Technically called xerosis or xerotic eczema, this is a common problem in children as well as adults, especially in the winter. The skin is red, rough, and chapped, with tiny cracks in the surface. In severe cases, actual fissures may develop. Most people assume that dry skin is lacking in oil, so they treat it by rubbing on petroleum jelly or lotion. While a lack of oil on the skin does contribute to the problem, the skin is really mostly lacking in water. When you bathe with soap and water, you remove the protective oil on the surface of the skin, which allows the water in it to move to the surface and evaporate. This does not present much of a problem in the summer, when we sweat more—producing more of that protective oil—and when the air is more humid, so that the water evaporates more slowly. Winter, however, is a different story. To prevent dry skin, wash with plain water, or if you must use soap, choose one with a low pH. (The skin's pH balance is about 5.5; most soaps have a pH of about 11, slightly lower than that of Drāno). Keep

the water warm, not hot, and don't scrub the skin, because this removes its top layers. Immediately after the bath, rub on lotion to seal the water in the skin. Don't use bath oils, since they can make the tub very slippery, and may cause allergic reactions in some children.

SCALY, DRY SKIN. A red, scaly, dry rash that itches is probably eczema. Eczema appears primarily in the flexion creases (the front of the elbow, the front of the ankle, behind the knees, and behind the ears), but may occur anywhere on the body. I believe most eczema is caused by food allergies, which are discussed in chapter 12. However, eczema is often intensified when the pollen count is elevated.

RED, ROUND LESIONS. There are two conditions that appear on the skin as red, round lesions: ringworm and pityriasis rosea. Ringworm, which is caused by a fungus, not a worm, is transmitted from infected humans, and is highly contagious. The infection begins as a single itchy lesion with a clear center. As the lesion grows, the center continues to clear up so that it appears as an expanding circle, and more lesions appear. The treatment for ringworm is Tinactin, a topical antifungal preparation that can be purchased without a prescription. Application of Tinactin to the lesions twice a day for two weeks will usually clear up the infection. If it does not, you will need a prescription from your doctor for an oral antibiotic.

Pityriasis rosea begins with one irregular, round, red, raised lesion that usually appears on the torso. The lesion does not itch, and the center is not clear, but red. The original lesion, called the herald patch, will vary in size from one to ten centimeters. About a week to ten days after the herald patch appears, it will be followed by several more, which may show up suddenly overnight or after a hot bath, or more slowly, over the course of two to three days. These new lesions will be primarily on the torso, although there may be some on the arms and legs also. The means of transmission of pityriasis rosea is unknown (it may be a virus), and there is no treatment for it, although lotion may be helpful if the patches itch. Once the herald patch disappears, generally after two to twelve weeks, the remainder will also clear up. Pityriasis rosea is seen most often in the late winter and early spring.

SCABS, BLISTERS, OR PUSTULES THAT SPREAD. Scabs, blisters, or pustules (blisters filled with pus) that spread over the skin are probably impetigo, an infection of the skin caused by staph or strep bacteria. Impetigo is highly contagious. Lesions should be washed five to eight times a day with an antiseptic solution such as Betadine. If this is not effective, a topical antibiotic cream such as Polysporin, Neosporin, or bacitracin can be applied after each cleansing with the Betadine. Since impetigo may be caused by strep bacteria, some doctors feel that it should be treated with an oral antibiotic, and even conclude that rheumatic fever can follow a strep infection of the skin. However, the bacteria is not the same as that which causes throat infections, so antibiotic treatment is not necessary. On rare occasions when impetigo

due to strep is followed by rheumatic fever or nephritis, the patient may have two different strep infections at the same time.

SEVERE ITCHING. Severe itching may be caused by scabies, insect mites that live under the surface of the skin and leave small red lines or trails, especially between the webs of the fingers and around the elbow. (If the infestation is heavy, the trails may also appear on other parts of the body.)

Scabies burrow through the skin at about two to three millimeters per day, with the females laying eggs that hatch after about three days (although this may take as long as ten days). The life cycle is about fifteen days. The females can survive off the host for two to three days at room temperature, so that scabies can be transmitted by clothing or bed linen, although the most common means of transmission is physical contact with an infected person. Anyone, regardless of personal cleanliness, can get scabies, but they are more likely to spread in unhygienic conditions.

The recommended medical treatment for scabies is Kwell, a highly toxic lotion that is known to be carcinogenic and to cause birth defects. Most doctors recommend applying Kwell to the child's entire body, but considering the lotion's toxicity, I think it is wiser to apply it only to the affected areas so that you limit exposure to it. If you treat just the affected areas, keep in mind that the eggs hatch at approximately three-day intervals. You will probably have to re-treat these areas every three days for about twelve days to eliminate any mites hatching from eggs that were previously missed. (If you treat the entire body, you should not need to re-treat, since Kwell does kill both the eggs and the mites.) Even with this re-treatment, however, the exposure will be less than if you treat the entire body.

Doctors generally prefer to treat infants, pregnant women, and children with particularly large areas of infection with crotamitron 10 percent. Another drug that is sometimes used to combat scabies is pyrethrin, which contains piperonyl, the active ingredient in over-the-counter shampoos for head lice. Some studies have shown that piperonyl is as effective as Kwell but less toxic.

As an alternative treatment for scabies, I recommend using larkspur, an herb that is available in tincture forms. While poisonous, it is not nearly as toxic as Kwell. Larkspur can also be applied to just the affected areas. It does require re-treatment at three-day intervals, since it kills only the mites, not the eggs.

To ensure against reinfestation of scabies, you must also wash the child's sheets and whatever clothing he has worn. Use hot water and dry the items on the hottest setting of a dryer, if possible.

CHICKEN POX. Chicken pox is a highly contagious disease that most people contract before reaching adulthood. The incubation period for chicken pox is fourteen to twenty-one days, with most cases developing earlier rather than later. The child may be vaguely ill for a day or two, and then begin to break out in the rash, which appears as small, fluid-filled sacs that have a dewdrop appearance. The rash is very itchy, and most children will scratch until the lesions scab over, so you may have to look in an area the child can't reach to find one that is still filled with fluid. The spots can appear anywhere on the body, including the soles of the feet, the palms, the head, the eyelids, the penis and testicles, and the inside of the ears, throat, and vagina. The child will usually continue to develop spots for three to four days, but this stage of the disease may last as long as a week. How sick a child feels does not necessarily correlate with how many spots he has.

There is no treatment for chicken pox, although Benadryl, an over-the-counter antihistamine taken orally, will help to relieve the itching. The disease will clear up spontaneously, usually in about a week. Occasionally the lesions may become infected from excessive scratching, and in rare instances a child may develop pneumonia or encephalitis following chicken pox.

While it generally poses no risks to an otherwise healthy child, chicken pox can be dangerous, even fatal, to a child with an impaired immune system. For this reason, a vaccine has been developed for use in children who are at risk. The vaccine has not yet been put into general use, however, and there is very little information available about its possible side effects or complications. I do not recommend its use, except in cases when chicken pox poses a significant threat. It is also not advisable to give the child aspirin, because of the possibility of Reye's syndrome, a severe, often fatal complication.

ROSEOLA. Roseola (also called roseola infantum and sixth disease) is characterized by the sudden onset of a high fever that lasts for several days, and then, as the fever finally drops, the appearance of a rash. Roseola is generally seen in children from the ages of six months to three years. During the fever phase of the disease, the child will appear sick, although not as ill as you would expect, considering the height of the fever (it is not uncommon for a child with roseola to have a 105°F fever for as long as five days). The rash consists of red lesions that are usually about three to five millimeters in size and are sometimes slightly raised. If you press on the lesions, they will momentarily turn white, just as a rash from scarlet fever does. With roseola, however, there are individual, discrete lesions, while those seen with scarlet fever run together. There is no treatment for roseola, but the disease will disappear spontaneously, does not recur, and does not carry the risk of complications.

LYME DISEASE.   Lyme disease, which is carried by the tiny deer tick, is probably the most common tick-borne disease in this country. Discovered in 1975, it is rapidly on the increase, particularly in the northeastern states and Minnesota, Wisconsin, and parts of California, Oregon, and Texas. In about thirty percent of the cases, the afflicted person is aware of having been bitten by the tick. In the remaining seventy percent, the first sign of having contracted the disease is a red, round rash, sometimes slightly raised in appearance. The rash may move around and change, and as it continues to grow, the center will usually become clear. Lesions then begin to develop on other parts of the body, and symptoms

such as fever, fatigue, chills, and aching muscles may appear. The rash and other symptoms will usually disappear spontaneously, but several months later, arthritis (most commonly in the knees) and problems with the central nervous system and the heart may appear. Children with Lyme disease are sometimes misdiagnosed as having juvenile rheumatoid arthritis. (The only way to distinguish between the two is through the use of blood tests.) It is widely agreed that early treatment with antibiotics, particularly tetracycline, can prevent the later complications of Lyme disease. However, we don't really know what will happen with the disease twenty or thirty years in the future. The organism that causes Lyme disease, a spirochete, is related to the organism that causes syphilis, which can cause problems thirty years or so after it is originally contracted if it is not totally eradicated at the start. If my own child were diagnosed as having Lyme disease, I would make a point of reading all of the medical literature on the subject, and, perhaps, of talking to some of the doctors on Long Island, where most of the research is being done. I would certainly use an antibiotic, since this is the best we have to offer at present, but I would probably also try an herbal treatment as well as large doses of vitamin C.

Unfortunately, there is a lot of misinformation circulating about Lyme disease in the medical community, and most certainly, the final word on the disease is not out yet. If you live in an area where the disease is just beginning to be seen, your doctor may not immediately recognize it, and even if he does, may not be up to date on treatment. There are Lyme disease hotlines in some states that may be of help to you, or you may want to consider traveling to a medical center in an area where the infection has become more common in order to receive the best possible care.

SCARLET FEVER. Scarlet fever is strep throat accompanied by a rash. Symptoms usually appear two to seven days after contact with someone with strep throat. In addition to the rash, fever, and chills, the child usually will have a sore throat, abdominal pain, or both, although sometimes these symptoms will be absent. In most cases the rash begins on the trunk, although in small children it may first be seen under the diaper or underpants. It then spreads over most of the body, including both the fronts and backs of the hands and feet. It is very fine, with small lesions that run together, giving the skin a rough, sandpapery feel and making it appear completely red. If you press on the rash, and then pull away, it will momentarily turn white. The rash is more intense in the folds of the skin, particularly in the groin, underneath the arms, and in the flexion creases in the elbows and behind the knees. One to two weeks after the child has begun to feel well again the skin may begin to peel, particularly on the hands and feet. The diagnosis of scarlet fever is made by the appearance of the rash, rather than by the condition of the throat, although the throat culture will usually be positive for strep bacteria. Scarlet fever is no more serious than strep throat

(see chapter 3) and will usually clear up without treatment, as long as the child has had good health and sound nutrition.

FOURTH DISEASE. Fourth disease (Filatov-Dukes disease), like scarlet fever, is characterized by fever and a skin rash that eventually peels. Unlike a scarlet fever rash, however, the rash that occurs with this disease is made up of distinct lesions. Fourth disease is caused by staphylococcus, or possibly streptococcus, bacteria. (Because it may be caused by strep, some doctors actually consider fourth disease a form of scarlet fever.) Fourth disease is very contagious. For this reason, a culture should be done if it is suspected. The culture will confirm the presence of bacteria, its type, and which antibiotic will be most effective. Once the child is put on antibiotics, the symptoms will clear up very quickly. After forty-eight to seventy-two hours of treatment, the child will no longer be contagious.

FIFTH DISEASE. Fifth disease (*Erythema infectiosum*) may be caused by a virus, although the cause and means of transmission are uncertain. Most cases occur in children between the ages of three and eighteen years, but it also occurs in adults. The incubation period is one to two weeks, after which the child usually has a mild temperature and a rash on the cheeks. The rash has a "slapped-cheek" appearance. Because it becomes more pronounced when the child is exposed to heat or cold, in most cases it is first noticed immediately after the child has come in from playing outdoors. The child will then develop a fever and the rash will spread to other parts of the body. These symptoms generally last for three to four days. After this the fever will drop and the rash will tend to come and go, depending on exposure to heat or cold, until it finally fades completely. In some cases, the rash will itch. Because fifth disease occasionally affects women of childbearing age, studies have been done to determine whether or not it causes birth defects, but no problems have been found. There is no treatment for fifth disease, and no known complications.

MEASLES AND GERMAN MEASLES. Measles (rubeola) and German measles (rubella), now relatively uncommon because of the vaccine, do still occur, even in vaccinated children. For the symptoms of measles and German measles and information on the vaccine, see chapter 14.

PALENESS. Paleness may indicate anemia— a low iron or red blood cell count. In children, anemia is usually caused by an insufficient intake of iron or by some condition in the body that causes the red blood cells to be destroyed or lost through bleeding. Anemia is most accurately detected by a blood test, but doctors may look for indications of it by pulling down the lower eyelid and looking at the red blood cells on the underside. An easier and more accurate means of judging whether or not a child is anemic

is to stretch the skin on the palm of the hand by pulling it tight between the little finger and the thumb. If red lines appear in the creases of the hand, the child has a hemoglobin count of at least nine. A count of eleven to fourteen is considered normal, but if the count is at least nine, the child is not dangerously anemic.

YELLOW SKIN TONE. A yellowish cast to the skin and the whites of the eyes is called jaundice. It is caused by abnormally high levels of bilirubin, a pigment in the blood. There are several causes of jaundice, which is seen most frequently in newborns, affecting sixty percent of full-term infants and eighty percent of premature babies in the first few days after birth. (In babies of Japanese, Chinese, Korean, and American Indian ethnic origin, the rates are even higher.) Elevated bilirubin levels in full-term newborns are most commonly due to normal physiological jaundice, which is just what its name suggests. It is normal, because it occurs in perfectly healthy newborns, and is physiological because it is not caused by any disease. Physiological jaundice of the newborn usually appears around the third day after birth and may last until the seventh day, possibly longer. (If your child is found to have a high bilirubin count, you should ask to have the test repeated to be sure that it is accurate.) In a normal, full-term infant, there is no reason to treat jaundice; simply nursing the baby will help to flush out the system and allow the bilirubin to come down to normal levels (unless, of course, the baby has breast milk jaundice, which is discussed on page 22).

Unfortunately, most doctors tend to overtreat normal physiological jaundice. This happens because they do not make a distinction between jaundice that occurs normally and that which is caused by a pathological, or disease, condition. The current wisdom seems to be that jaundice is jaundice, and the same problems can occur whatever its cause. Since bilirubin levels above 20 have been shown to cause brain damage in infants with Rh incompatibility, doctors often recommend that normal, full-term infants with bilirubin levels of twelve or above be placed under fluorescent "bili" lights as treatment. (Most doctors would not consider a bilirubin level of 3–4 to be abnormal in an infant.) This is unnecessary, however. According to two pediatric textbooks, normal physiological jaundice does not require treatment,[1,2] and one review of twelve studies of bilirubin levels concluded that "[healthy, full-term] babies are not at risk of mental or physical impairment until serum bilirubin levels rise well above 20. . . ."[3] (This does not apply to premature infants, who are at a greater risk of complications as a result of jaundice and are more likely to require treatment.) Since bilirubin lights can damage the eyes if the protective coverings come off during treatment, the lights may well prove to be more dangerous to the child than the jaundice they are supposed to treat.

Doctors also sometimes recommend that a jaundiced baby be weaned, even though studies have shown that nursing more than eight times a day tends to reduce bilirubin levels. One reason for this recommendation, I think, is that a baby in a hospital nursery may be brought to his mother to nurse only every four hours. As a result, he may become slightly dehydrated, which will produce artificially high bilirubin readings. My recommendation, then, is to keep the baby with you and nurse him as often as possible. (I also feel that nursing the baby for a prolonged period immediately after birth is good preventative medicine.)

Jaundice Caused by Rh Incompatibility. If the jaundice appears on the first day after birth or persists beyond seven days, further investigation into the cause is in order. Two possible causes are Rh or ABO incompatibility. Rh incompatibility occurs when the father's blood is Rh positive and the mother's is Rh negative. The baby's blood may then be Rh positive. If it is, and some of the baby's blood enters the mother's bloodstream, the mother may produce antibodies to it. When these are passed back to the baby, they will destroy some of his red blood cells, resulting in an anemic, jaundiced newborn. When carrying her first child, the mother is not apt to develop antibodies in time to harm the baby, unless she has had a transfusion of Rh positive blood at some time during her life. However, each time she becomes pregnant with an Rh positive baby, her blood may become sensitized further, increasing the risk to the infant. Doctors now realize that if a mother receives RhoGAM (immune globulin) after the birth of each Rh positive child, her blood will not become sensitized and there will be no danger to subsequent children. Before RhoGAM was used, about thirty-five percent of mothers who were Rh negative became sensitized during their pregnancies. This figure is sufficiently high and the dangers great enough to justify routine use of RhoGAM in Rh negative mothers, especially since the RhoGAM itself poses no risk to the mother.* Because of RhoGAM, jaundice as a result of Rh incompatibility is relatively rare. However, should it occur, the bilirubin levels should not be allowed to rise above 20.

Jaundice Caused by ABO Incompatibility. ABO incompatibility may occur if the mother and father have different blood types. The baby may then have a blood type that is different from the mother's. If he does, and some of his blood mixes with the mother's blood, her body will produce antibodies that can destroy the baby's red blood cells and result in jaundice and anemia. ABO incompatibility can be diagnosed by blood tests to determine the blood types of both the mother and the baby. Although ABO incompatibility is similar to Rh incompatibility, studies have shown that full-term babies with this condition can tolerate bilirubin levels of as high as 25 without risk of brain damage. Should the level go above 25, treatment with the bili lights may become necessary.

Breast Milk Jaundice. While rare, there are several other conditions that can cause prolonged jaundice, including breast milk jaundice, blood infections, congenital malformations of the bile ducts, herpes infections, and various blood diseases that result in the breaking down of blood cells. Breast milk jaundice, which is usually diagnosed by ruling out other possible causes of prolonged jaundice, occurs in about one of every two hundred breast-fed babies, and may result in increased bilirubin levels for as long as ten weeks or more. It is a harmless condition that does not indicate a need to wean. If the bilirubin level reaches 19, however, the baby should be taken off the breast until the level falls slightly (usually after eighteen to twenty-four hours), and then be allowed to return to the breast. (It may be that it is perfectly safe to allow the levels to go higher than 19, but as no studies are available to confirm this, I feel it is best to work with this conservative figure.) While the baby is off the breast, the bilirubin level should be checked twice a day to determine when it has started to fall. During this time the baby can be fed another mother's milk, if it is available, rather than a substitute. Once the bilirubin level has begun to fall, nursing can and should be resumed. The level will rarely rise as high as 19 again, although it may remain elevated. Kernicterus, an accumulation of bilirubin in the brain and other nerve tissues that may cause brain damage, has not been reported in children with breast milk jaundice. A mother who has

*Since RhoGAM is a blood product, some people have expressed concern about the possibility of the transmission of AIDS through its use. The manufacturer has assured me that the blood from which the immune globulin is extracted is carefully screened, and that it is processed in such a way that the virus would be destroyed if it were present. There have been no cases of AIDS linked to RhoGAM.

problems with breast milk jaundice with one child will generally not encounter this condition in her other children.

Jaundice Caused by Infectious Hepatitis. Jaundice can occur in older children as a result of viral, or infectious, hepatitis. (Other symptoms of hepatitis include fever, loss of appetite, vomiting, headache, and abdominal pain.) This type of hepatitis is transmitted from one person to the next by fecal content. In other words, in order to get infectious hepatitis, you must get some of the infected person's stool into your mouth. It is therefore unlikely that very limited contact with a person who has viral hepatitis will result in your child being infected. Should he play with, eat with, and use the same bathroom as an infected child, however, his chances of exposure are greatly increased. In most cases, infectious hepatitis can be prevented by an injection of gamma globulin given within one to two weeks of exposure to the disease.

BLUE SKIN TONE. A blue coloration around the lips and in the nail beds is caused by insufficient oxygen in the system (cyanosis). Cyanosis does not indicate any specific disease or condition, but simply tells you that for some reason not enough oxygen is reaching the cells. It may be caused by insufficient oxygen in the room, a blockage that is preventing enough oxygen from reaching the lungs, or a failure of the blood to supply enough oxygen to the body. The easiest way to detect cyanosis is to hold your hand next to the child's and compare the color of the nail beds. They should appear approximately the same color. If they do (assuming you are not cyanotic also), the child's blood is receiving sufficient oxygen. A child who is cyanotic may also have symptoms of respiratory distress (see chapter 4).

The Well-Child Quick Checklist

THE SKIN

1. Observe the color, tone, and condition of the skin. There should be no deviations from the usual appearance and feel of the child's skin.

2. Examine and note any moles, warts, bruises, cuts, boils, lumps, rashes, insect bites, and birthmarks.

Notes

1.   L. Emmett Holt, Jr., and Rustin McIntosh, *Holt Pediatrics*, 12th Edition (New York: Appleton-Century-Crofts, Inc., 1940): p. 114.

2.   J. P. Crozer Griffith and A. Graeme Mitchell, *Textbook of Pediatrics*, 3rd Edition (Philadelphia: W. B. Saunders, 1941): p. 179.

3.   Thomas B. Newman and Jeffrey Maisels, "Does Hyperbilirubinemia Damage the Brain of Healthy, Full-Term Infants?," *Clinics in Perinatology*, Vol. 17, No. 2 (June 1990): p. 331.

The Head

This section of the physical exam consists of an examination of the head, hair, and scalp, and of the eyes, ears, nose, mouth, and neck.

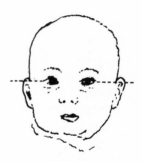

The Head

GENERAL EXAM/ALL AGES

Draw an imaginary line from the outside corner of one eye, around the head to the ear. Some portion of the ear should be above the line (see fig. 1). If it is not, there may be a congenital abnormality of the kidneys.

Look at the scalp and feel for any lumps, bumps, or tender areas. Check the hair for cleanliness, shininess, bounce, and texture, and the scalp for bald spots, flakiness or dandruff, and head lice or other insects.

Fig. 1

GENERAL EXAM/INFANTS

If you are examining an infant, also check the fontanel, or soft spot. There are actually four fontanels: one in the front of the head, one in the back, and one on each side, although we are usually only concerned with the one on the front of the head, which is easy to locate. It generally should appear flat, not sunken or bulging, although some infants do have fontanels that are normally slightly depressed.

The purpose of the fontanels is to allow

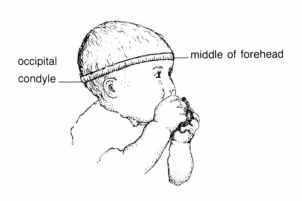

occipital condyle

middle of forehead

Fig. 2

the brain to continue growing. They close between eight and eighteen months of age, but will feel closed sooner. To judge whether or not a baby's head is growing normally (and the fontanels are closing properly) you need to measure the head. Place a tape measure across the forehead and bring it around the back of the head over the occipital condyle (the bump where the head joins the spine; see fig. 2) and back around to the forehead. As a general rule of thumb, the head measurement should roughly equal that of the circumference of the chest (measured at the nipple line) for the first eighteen months of life. If you take both these measurements shortly after birth, you will have a reference point for the future. Some babies are born with large heads, some with small, so that there may be a discrepancy between the head and chest measurement. This discrepancy should remain fairly constant through the first year and a half of life, however. An-

other formula for evaluating the head size is to take the child's length in centimeters, divide that number by two, and add 9.5 centimeters. If that measurement, plus or minus 2.5 centimeters, equals the circumference of the head, the baby falls between the fifth and ninety-fifth percentile for head growth in normal infants.[1] If it does not, or if you have any doubts concerning the growth of your baby's head, consult with your physician. He will check the measurements against tables and charts that take into account not only the head and chest sizes, but also the weight, length, and age of the child, for a more accurate assessment of growth. If you want to check the charts and tables yourself, they can be found in any pediatric textbook, available in medical libraries.

One of my pet peeves is seeing parents overreact when an older child touches a baby's head. The typical scenario involves a new baby, just home from the hospital, and his older sibling. The older child will rush over to the baby and try to put her hand on his head, and the mother or father will scream in horror. The child, meanwhile, sees Mom and Dad gently stroking the baby's head, and comes to feel that this must really be an exquisite pleasure that's being denied her. She'll then spend an inordinate amount of time trying to get at that fuzzy little head, worrying her parents half to death. All this is really quite unnecessary. Although the skull has not completely grown over the brain in the area of a fontanel, nature has actually protected the brain quite well, with several layers of skin, fat, muscle, connective tissue, and the per-

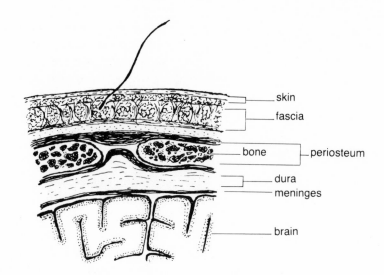

skin
fascia
bone
periosteum
dura
meninges
brain

Fig. 3

iosteum (see fig. 3). Unless she severely manhandles the new baby, an older child will not be able to damage the fontanels.

CHARACTERISTICS/PROBLEMS/DISEASES OF THE HEAD

BALD SPOTS.   The most common bald spot seen on children is something called alopecia areata, which translates from Latin as simply, "round bald spot." That's exactly what it is: a small round spot with absolutely no hair in it. There is usually one such spot on the child's head, but there may be two or three, ranging in size from about that of a dime to that of a quarter. If you consult a dermatologist about this condition, he may treat the area with cortisone injections, and the hair will grow back in approximately six months. On the other hand, you can leave the spot alone, and the hair will grow back in about six months anyway.

Bald spots in children also may be caused by ringworm of the scalp. These bald spots are also small and round, but if you examine them closely you will see that the hair has actually broken off next to the scalp, leaving a little bit of stubble. You can try to treat this type of ringworm with Tinactin, but there's a good chance it won't be entirely effective. Washing the scalp first with a dandruff shampoo will loosen any dead scales and help the Tinactin to penetrate to the affected skin, but it still may not eradicate the fungus. If it does not, the next step is to see a doctor, who will in all likelihood prescribe an oral antifungal agent called griseofulvin, which is a fairly toxic drug. Its side effects range from minor problems, such as an upset stomach or a headache, to serious ones, such as malformation of the blood or liver toxicity. Because of these possible side effects, it should be used with great caution. Concerns have been raised that the drug might also be a carcinogen, but this has not been proven.

CRADLE CAP. Cradle cap is simply infant dandruff, or seborrhea, and is generally best left alone. If the flakiness really bothers you, you can wash the baby's hair with a dandruff shampoo, which will clear it up. I don't recommend this, however, because all those toxic chemicals in the shampoo will find their way into the baby's bloodstream, and they're not the best thing for a growing child. Another approach is to apply baby oil to the scalp to loosen the scales, and then comb them out. Personally, however, I favor just leaving cradle cap alone.

HEAD LICE. If a child has head lice, there will be little white egg sacs attached to the individual hairs at the roots. The medical treatment for head lice is to wash the hair with Kwell shampoo, which, like Kwell lotion, is extremely toxic. Over-the-counter shampoos, such as RID, which are less toxic but still poisonous, will kill the lice but not the eggs, as will the herb larkspur. If you kill just the live lice, you then have to pick out the nits with a fine-tooth comb, and if any new lice manage to hatch, reuse the RID or larkspur. (If the nits are difficult to remove, rinsing the scalp with a solution of fifty percent water and fifty percent vinegar will help loosen them.) Perhaps the least toxic solution to the problem of head lice is to pick out the eggs once a day, and allow the live lice to die off, which will take about four weeks.

While it is uncommon, children with head lice occasionally also have them in the eyelashes. These can be eliminated by coating the eyelashes with petroleum jelly, which will suffocate the live lice. Fluorescein eyedrops are also highly effective against lice in the eyelashes, and will kill off most of the live lice in minutes. Fluorescein does stain the skin, however, so don't attempt to use it on the scalp.

ABNORMAL FONTANEL. A sunken fontanel can be a sign of serious dehydration (see chapter 5). A taut, bulging fontanel should never be considered normal, and can be an indication of meningitis (see page 46).

A fontanel that fails to close and actually grows larger usually indicates hydrocephalus, a condition in which cerebrospinal fluid collects within the skull. Hydrocephalus must be treated or it will lead to mental retardation and other difficulties.

A fontanel that closes too soon leads to microcephaly, a condition in which the brain is unable to grow properly, resulting in brain damage.

The Eyes

GENERAL EXAM

Note the appearance of the eyeball in relation to the whole eye. It should not appear popped out, and the eyelids should cross the eyeball in approximately the same place on both eyes. In some children there normally may be a slight difference in where the eyelid crosses the eyeball, but it should not change from one time to another.

The eyelids should not be swollen or droopy, although droopy eyelids may be a congenital family trait that is perfectly normal. When this is the case, the droopiness is usually noticeable in photos showing several members of the family lined up together.

Check the whites of the eyes. They should be clear.

The pupils should be approximately the same size; however, they may be different sizes and still be perfectly normal. It is important to note whether or not the child's pupils are normally of equal size when the child is well, since abnormally unequal pupils are a sign of cerebral hemorrhage, a serious condition (see chapter 18).

Next, shine your flashlight into one of the child's eyes. The pupil of that eye should constrict quite a bit, and as it does, the pupil of the other eye should also constrict slightly. Repeat, shining the flashlight into the other eye.

VISUAL ACUITY. Check for visual acuity with your eye chart.

LAZY EYE. It is very important to check your child for lazy eye, or amblyopia. With amblyopia, the eye muscles are not properly balanced, so that one eye becomes dominant. If the muscles are not strengthened, the weak eye will gradually see less and less and may eventually cease to function. Once this has happened, vision cannot be restored to that eye, even though it is essentially healthy.

To test for lazy eye, have the child stare straight into the light of a flashlight that is held directly out in front of the face. The reflection of the light on the cornea should fall in the center of the pupil of each eye. If it does not, but appears, for example, at the lower edge of the left pupil and at the center of the right pupil, the eyes are not aligned properly.

Another way to test for lazy eye (if the child is old enough to cooperate) is to have her sit on another adult's lap as you hold an object about eighteen inches out in front of her face. As she focuses on the object, cover her left eye with your hand, and then uncover it. Watch the right eye as she does this. It should not move. If it does, the left eye is dominant, and the right eye is shifting off of the object it has been focused on as the left eye takes over. Repeat the procedure, having the child cover the right eye. If neither eye shifts, the eyes are properly aligned.

If you have any suspicion that the child has a lazy eye, it is absolutely essential to have her checked by an eye specialist. For treatment, I recommend that you first consult an optometrist, who will treat the problem with glasses and exercises to strengthen the muscles of the weak eye. If the eye does not respond to this type of treatment, you will need to consult an ophthalmologist, who may recommend surgery.

CHARACTERISTICS/PROBLEMS/DISEASES OF THE EYE

ALLERGIC SHINERS. Dark circles under the eyes are an indication of allergy problems, and are sometimes referred to as allergic shiners. Most people attribute dark circles to lack of sleep, and, in fact, the child may sleep poorly. However, it is the allergy that causes both the sleep problems and the dark circles.

SCALING OF THE EYELID. Scaling of the eyelid, like fine dandruff, may be due to a food allergy and is often associated with seborrhea on the scalp.

PLUGGED TEAR DUCT. Plugged tear ducts are quite common in newborns, although technically the duct is not so much blocked as just undeveloped. If the whites of the eyes are clear but there is a discharge that causes the lids of one or both eyes to stick together, the tear duct of that eye is blocked. Located in the lower eyelid at the inside corner of the eye, the tear duct goes through the nose bone, so that when tears are produced, they drain into the nose. (This is why your nose runs when you cry.) When the tears are not able to drain properly, they dry up, become gummy and turn green. Given time, this type of plugged duct will open up on its own. Most will clear up by the time the baby is three to six months old, but in some children a plugged duct will persist through the first two years. Some doctors will recommend massaging the tear duct to help open it up. Since most of the duct is on the other side of the nose bone, however, this really does very little good, although it certainly does no harm. Doctors also occasionally suggest inserting a probe in the tear duct. As long as this is done without the use of general anesthesia it does not present a problem other than discomfort for the child. Often, however, doctors prefer to do the procedure with the child under general anesthesia. Since there is, overall, a one percent risk of mortality from anesthesia, I strongly recommend against this. While small, the risk is too great to take for a condition that will eventually right itself.

A child who is older than eighteen months and does not have a history of plugged tear ducts may develop one because of nasal congestion. With this type of plugged duct the mucous membrane in the nose becomes swollen, blocking the duct so that the tears cannot drain properly. As in an infant, the whites will be clear but there will be a discharge which may cause the lids to stick together. To treat this condition, keep the eyes clean by bathing them both with a warm, moist washcloth or cotton ball. If you feel you must do something more, you can also give the child a decongestant to help reduce the swelling of the mucous membranes and allow the duct to drain, but this is not really necessary.

REDDENED WHITES. When the whites of the eyes are red, this condition is called conjunctivitis. If the whites of the eyes are red but there is no mucous discharge, the cause is allergy. If you remove the child from the environment or eliminate the offending substance from the air, the redness should disappear. If the redness is accompanied by a mucous discharge, the child has pinkeye, an infection of the lining, or conjunctiva, of the eye. The best treatment for pinkeye is to place two tablespoons of fresh breast milk in each eye five times a day until the infection has cleared up. The reason breast milk is effective against pinkeye is that it contains white blood cells, which destroy bacteria and viruses, eliminating the infection. In some cultures, mothers routinely place breast milk in their babies' eyes to ward off infection, and at least one study has shown that this practice reduces the incidence of infection.[2]

If breast milk is not available, you may want to try waiting the infection out for two to three days, since most cases are caused by a virus that will clear up spontaneously in this time. If the infection persists, it is probably caused by bacteria. The medical treatment in these cases is a prescription antibiotic solution that is put directly into the eyes. A child with conjunctivitis must be kept away from other children if at all possible, since the condition is highly contagious.

STYES. Small, painful yellowish or red lumps that occur at the roots of the eyelashes are styes, which are caused by a blocked oil gland. To encourage the gland to drain, apply heat, either with a heating pad or a warm, moist washcloth. Occasional styes are perfectly normal, but if they recur frequently, they may indicate eyestrain, exposure to dust, an allergy such as hay fever, or very rarely, diabetes.

NONPAINFUL SWELLING ON THE EYELID. A yellowish swelling that occurs at the edge of the eyelid but is not painful is probably a chalazion. These swellings appear and gradually grow until they reach a certain size and then will remain unchanged. There is no need to treat a chalazion unless it becomes infected, which will usually only

happen if someone pinches or picks at it. If a chalazion does become infected, it can be treated with moist heat, or, in persistent cases, with an antibiotic intended for use on the eyes. Surgery is the only way to remove a chalazion permanently.

INFECTION OF THE EYELID. Blepharitis is an infection of the eyelid that is most often seen following an insect bite or puncture wound. Like a stye and an infected chalazion, it can be treated with moist heat.

CONDITIONS OF THE EYE THAT MAY INDICATE SERIOUS DISEASE. There are several conditions of the eye that may indicate serious disease. If the eyeball appears popped out, the child may have a thyroid problem. If the eyelids cross the eyeball in different places (and this is not normal for your child) she may have a certain type of muscular dystrophy or a thyroid problem. Swollen eyelids may indicate allergy problems or, rarely, kidney disease. Droopy eyelids, when not a family trait, may be caused by a disease such as myasthenia gravis or amyotonia. As noted above, recurrent styes may very rarely be a sign of diabetes. With the exception of swollen eyelids that are obviously due to allergy (e.g., the eyes are also watery and itchy) a child who has any of these conditions should be examined by a doctor to investigate further the possibility of disease.

Changes in the ways the pupils react to light may also be signs of serious problems. Pupils that fail to react to light at all may indicate blindness, poisoning, or severe head injury (see chapter 18). Pupils that are constricted and that do not react to light may indicate ingestion of drugs, such as opiates, or poison.

The Nose

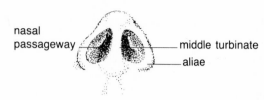

nasal passageway — middle turbinate — aliae

Fig. 4

GENERAL EXAM

Place your hand under the child's nostrils and feel her breath as she exhales. She should be breathing through both nostrils and exhaling a normal amount of air. (If you do this often enough over a short period of time, you will learn to recognize a normal exhalation of breath for your child.)

If there is any discharge, examine it and make note of the color and consistency. Then, using your otoscope, take a look at the inside of the nostrils. On the outer portion of each nostril there is a swelling called a turbinate (see fig. 4). These turbinates are the "air conditioners" of the nose: they humidify, cool or warm the air as necessary, and the mucus that covers them serves to trap dust, pollen, and other irritants so that they cannot further invade the body. Normally, the turbinates should be a healthy pink color. If they are red and inflamed, the child may have a viral or bacterial infection. However, if they are boggy (like The Pillsbury Doughboy's stomach) and pale pink, allergy problems are indicated.

As you examine the inside of the nose, check the nasal passages. They should be approximately the same size. If one passage is much smaller than the other, the child has a deviated septum. A deviated septum can occur naturally or as a result of trauma. A naturally deviated septum does not neces-

sarily require treatment, but it is good to know that that is the normal state for the child, so that the first time she falls and bangs her nose, you will not discover it and assume the nose is broken.

Press firmly on the sinus areas (just above the eyes, and on each side of the nose). They should not be tender.

CHARACTERISTICS/PROBLEMS/DISEASES OF THE NOSE

NASAL CONGESTION. If the child has a stuffy nose, you can usually just leave it alone. If the child's nose is so stuffed up and dry that you feel you must loosen the mucus, saltwater nose drops are safe and effective. To make your own solution, dissolve a pinch of salt in four ounces of boiled water that has been allowed to cool. Place a few drops in each nostril. This will cause the nose to run as the body attempts to dilute the mineral concentration you have created. The secretions will loosen the mucus, which can then be cleared out.

If the child is too young to be able to blow her nose effectively, you can remove the mucus for her with a three-ounce rubber ear syringe. There are several sizes of ear syringes available, as well as nose syringes, but I have found everything but the three-ounce blue ear syringe to be very stiff and therefore not as effective. In using the syringe, it is important to note that the nasal passages do not go straight up in the nose, but straight back into the head. Most people make the mistake of trying to use the syringe with it held parallel to the nose, which will only suck out the nasal membranes, not the nasal passages. Instead, you must place the syringe in the child's nostril and then bring it up so that it is perpendicular to her face. You can then suck out the mucus that is in the nasal passage. Another remedy for nasal congestion is to drink linden tea. For the child who is still nursing, breast milk is also very effective.

NOSEBLEEDS. Nosebleeds are a common occurrence in children. Ninety-five percent originate in the soft, forward portion of the nose, and simply applying pressure to that location will stop the bleeding. However, you must apply pressure consistently for a full fifteen minutes, by the clock. If you attempt to just pinch the nose between the thumb and forefinger, you'll find your hand tires long before the fifteen minutes is up. Instead, press your palm against the child's face with her nose between your thumb and the base of your index finger. When that hand gets tired, use the thumb and index finger of your other hand to pinch the thumb and index finger of the first hand together, so that you maintain constant pressure with the hand that is against the child's face. You can go back and forth between the two positions until the fifteen minutes are over. (If you remove your hand from the face and attempt to switch hands,

the blood clot will break and you will have to start over again.) If you are able to determine that only one side of the nose is bleeding, you can just apply pressure with your finger to that one side, and then press on the finger with your other hand when it tires. This technique is quite effective if the child is old enough to be cooperative. If, however, you attempt to carry it out on a two-year-old, you will need at least four people: one to apply pressure and three to hold the child down. Since most nosebleeds will stop of their own accord within fifteen minutes anyway, it would be wiser to try waiting it out. If the bleeding does not stop of its own accord in that amount of time, *then* try the heroic measures.

Whether you apply pressure or wait the nosebleed out, the child should be in a sitting position, not lying down. If the child is lying on her back, the blood will run down her throat and may make her cough. She may then inhale some of it into her lungs, which will unnecessarily complicate the situation.

Recurrent nosebleeds may be due to an allergy, or, in the winter, lack of humidity in the air. Replacing the moisture in the air, either with a cool-mist humidifier or a vaporizer, will help to alleviate the problem.

SINUS INFECTIONS. If pressing on the sinuses causes the child pain, she may have a sinus infection. Most parents don't think of sinus infections in children, but they can and do get them. A baby with a sinus infection will be inexplicably cranky and feverish and, if breast-fed, will often refuse to nurse. An older child will complain of pain in the sinus area. My admittedly unorthodox treatment for sinus problems is drinking large quantities of water. I had chronic sinusitis for most of my life, and went through treatments that included having the openings to my sinuses enlarged and having my sinuses drained. Nothing helped until a friend suggested that I start drinking one and a half quarts of water first thing every morning. Since I've been doing so, I have not had a single sinus infection. If your child (or you, for that matter) develops chronic sinus problems, I highly recommend this treatment. You will, of course, have to adjust the amount of water according to your child's size (approximately one pint of water for every fifty pounds of body weight.) If you choose not to use this method, the standard medical treatment is to use decongestants and antibiotics to clear up the infection.

FOREIGN OBJECT. Children will sometimes insert a foreign object into one of their nostrils for reasons unfathomable to adults. A foul-smelling discharge from the affected nostril will signal this problem. If you know that the object is something porous, such as a bean or raisin, you will have to take the child to the doctor to have it removed, preferably within a day, if it has been in place long enough to have swollen.

If the object is something that will not swell (or if you catch it immediately), you may be able to dislodge it yourself. Place a pinch of pepper in your hand and blow it into the child's face while holding the unaffected nostril closed. (Make sure you cover the child's eyes as you do this.) The child will often sneeze the object out.

RESPIRATIONS/DIFFICULTY IN BREATHING. If at some time the child seems to be exhaling a smaller amount of air than usual, she may be in respiratory distress. Check to see if she is flaring her nostrils (moving the outer portions of the nostrils in and out in an attempt to open up the airway so she can take in more air), so that you can actually see the size of the nostril changing from small to large and back again. (For more on respiratory distress, see chapter 4.)

The Ears

This section covers a basic examination of the ear. In chapter 13, I deal with infections of the middle ear.

GENERAL EXAM

Check behind the ears. The skin should be smooth and healthy (not red and scaly) and there should not be any infections or growths. Check for drainage from the ear.

EAR CANAL AND EARDRUM. To examine the ear canal and eardrum of an infant or child, fit your otoscope with the medium-sized speculum. (The large speculum is for adults. The small one is used in special

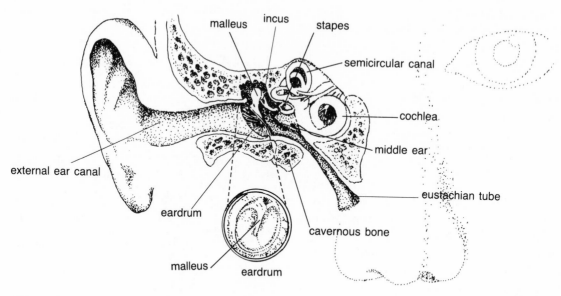

Fig. 5

situations, such as to see around excessive earwax, or on a newborn who may have a lot of cells in the ear from amniotic fluid.) Because there is a small crook in the ear canal, you must pull a child's ear down and out (for an adult's ear, pull up and out), to see all the way to the eardrum. Insert the speculum about one-half to three-quarters of the way into the ear. You don't have to worry about damaging the ear drum with the speculum, since it is impossible to insert it that far into the ear, but you should be careful not to scrape the inside of the ear canal. Should you slip up, don't panic. A scrape inside the ear canal may bleed, but there will not be any permanent damage.

If your child protests against having her ears examined, you may be able to make a game out of the procedure by asking her to try to open her ears as wide as she can open her mouth so that you can see all the way in. You might also have her put her finger in the ear you are not examining and shut her mouth tight so that "the light can't get out."

The eardrum should appear as a round, opaque, whitish membrane. (If it is red or you can see blood vessels on the surface, it is infected—see chapter 13). The eardrum will have a vertical white line on it, which is the bone called the malleus. The malleus normally occurs in the position shown in figure 5, but it may also occur in other positions without significance. You may also see dark spots, which are caused by cavernous bone behind the eardrum, and are nothing to be concerned about.

The first time you use your otoscope, you may be uncertain about what you're looking at. Don't give up, though. If you educate yourself by putting your otoscope to use on everyone you can get your hands on, you'll soon be able to distinguish between a healthy eardrum and one that is infected. Examine the middle ears of ten children, and you'll probably find at least one that is inflamed. My only word of caution is that you make a point of inspecting a lot of ears before your child is ill; if you wait until she wakes up crying at three A.M., you won't know what you're looking at, and diagnosis will be difficult at best.

HEARING.   Check the child's hearing. If you are examining a newborn, this can be done by lying the baby on her back and ringing a bell near one ear. She should turn her head slightly in the direction of the sound. This is not an infallible test, however, since ringing the bell will also create a tiny breeze near the baby's face, and she may turn her head in response to the movement of the air as much to the sound. In an older child, hold a ticking wristwatch or clock about a foot away from one ear as the child looks straight ahead. Ask her to tell you when she hears the ticking as you bring the watch closer to the ear. Repeat this procedure with the other ear. The child should hear the ticking at roughly the same distance from each ear. A marked discrepancy may be a sign of a blocked ear canal, a middle ear infection, or a problem with the hearing itself. This test is not infallible, either, however, since your child may figure out what you expect her to do and then react accordingly, in a misguided attempt to please you. You can also check the hearing in an older child by judging the child's re-

sponse to your voice. Be careful what you say when you're testing, however. Your child won't hear you ask her to clean up her room even if you yell, but an offer of ice cream or candy will probably be heard if spoken in the quietest whisper. If your child seems to have trouble hearing you or, for that matter, the television or her playmates, she should be tested by an audiologist even if she was able to pass the watch test above. The audiologist will be able to eliminate any of the clues that tell your child how she is expected to respond, and give you a more accurate evaluation of your child's hearing.

CHARACTERISTICS/PROBLEMS/DISEASES OF THE EAR

EARWAX.   Contrary to popular belief, earwax was not created so that cotton swabs would have a purpose in life. The ear canal should have wax in it. Among its beneficial properties are its oiliness, which helps to lubricate the ear, its slight odor, which repels bugs, and an antibioticlike substance that prevents the outer ear from becoming easily infected. For the most part, you should leave earwax alone. This does not mean, however, that you have to let it drip from the child's ear lobe. Anything that you can get at with your finger is fair game—just don't insert cotton swabs or any pointed objects into the ear in an attempt to clean out the wax. It is possible to have earwax so excessive that it fills up the ear canal and interferes with the hearing. In these cases, it is permissible to remove the excess wax. You still don't want to go after it with a cotton swab, however, because you will just push the wax down against the eardrum, further decreasing the hearing. Instead, flush the ears out with warm water. Use your ear syringe and water that feels warm to the ear. Test the temperature of the water by putting some in your own ear before you put it into your child's ear. It will probably feel cool even though it felt warm to your hands. You may have to repeat the process of flushing the ear out over several days before the wax is sufficiently loosened to fall out. If this doesn't work, you can loosen the wax with Cerumenex (available in many pharmacies).

Most people build up earwax on a fairly regular schedule so that for some individuals removal will need to be done every six months, and for others, only every few years. Once you become aware of your child's tendencies in this area, you can watch the earwax and only remove it when absolutely necessary.

RED, SCALY SKIN BEHIND THE EAR. If the skin behind the ear is red and scaly (and in some cases, itchy and slightly bloody from being scratched), the cause may be eczema. In my opinion, eczema usually is due to a food allergy (see chapter 12) and should be treated accordingly. In younger children particularly, the same symptoms may be due to a yeast infection, in which case the ear will have a yeastlike odor. This can be treated in the same manner as a yeast infection elsewhere on the skin (see page 41). Soaps, shampoos or other hair preparations can also cause a rash in this area.

DRAINAGE. If the child has drainage from the ear, it is important that you ascertain the cause. There are primarily three causes of drainage from the ear: a ruptured eardrum, external otitis (infection of the ear canal, commonly known as swimmer's ear), or a foreign object lodged in the ear canal.

Drainage/Ruptured Eardrum. A ruptured eardrum occurs when an infection of the middle ear has resulted in the buildup of so much fluid behind the eardrum that it perforates to relieve the pressure. Once this happens and the drainage begins, the pain the child has been experiencing disappears. (For more information on middle ear infections, see chapter 13.)

Drainage/Swimmer's Ear. With swimmer's ear, the drainage is coming from the infected ear canal itself, not the middle ear. The pain is greater as the drainage begins and progresses, because the infected auditory canal becomes increasingly more swollen and tender. Gently wiggling the child's outer ear will cause significant pain, which the child will let you know about in no uncertain terms. However, since a child with a middle ear infection may also protest loudly when you touch her ear, the strongest indicator that the infection is in the outer ear rather than the middle ear is the presence of drainage *and* pain.

Swimmer's ear is caused by getting water in the ears on a daily, or near-daily, basis. Pool water is the most harmful, but any water will change the pH of the ear and break down the defense mechanisms that normally prevent infection. It is easy to prevent swimmer's ear by using "dive drops," which are available at stores that sell scuba equipment. You can also make your own dive drops by mixing four parts rubbing alcohol to one part vinegar. The alcohol helps to evaporate the water trapped in the ear, and the vinegar restores the acid pH of the ear canal, making it inhospitable to bacteria. After your child swims, fill each ear canal about half full with the dive drops and then let them drain out. Once the ear canal has become infected, it may become so swollen that the drops are unable to penetrate deep enough to do any good. When this happens, you will have to take the child to her doctor, who will insert a piece of cotton in the ear canal and prescribe antibiotic and cortisone drops to apply to the cotton until the swelling has subsided and the cotton falls out. It is important to remember, however, that you should never place anything in the ear if the eardrum is ruptured. Not every doctor will agree with me on this point, but I feel that it is unwise to put chemicals into the ear if they are going to drain down to a ruptured eardrum, carrying along pus and bacteria.

Drainage/Foreign Object. If there is drainage from the ear but the child does not seem to have a middle ear infection or an infection of the ear canal, there may be a foreign object lodged in the canal. If you have an otoscope, you can look in the ear and try to identify the object. If it appears to be a porous object that has swollen, you will have to take the child to the doctor to have it removed. On the other hand, you may be able to flush out a nonporous object or one that has not yet had time to swell. Use your ear syringe and warm water, and apply a fair amount of pressure. You don't have to worry about damaging the eardrum with this procedure, since the syringe will not reach that far into the ear. If you are unable to loosen the object enough so that it will fall out, you will have to take the child to her doctor to have it removed.

The Mouth and Throat

GENERAL EXAM

The lips should be smooth and moist, not chapped or split, and should not have a bluish tinge (blue lips are an indication of cyanosis; see chapter 2). Shine your otoscope on the gums; they should look healthy and pink, and should be free of sores or swelling. The breath should smell sweet. Using the popsicle stick, butter knife or spoon, press the tongue down and shine your light into the mouth so that you can examine the uvula, the upper palate, the tonsils, and the back of the throat (see fig. 6). You may see small pinkish swellings on the back of the throat. This is lymphoid tissue, which swells in response to bacterial or viral infection, and sometimes to allergy. Often mucus will coat these elevated spots, causing them to appear white when you shine your light on them. This is not a cause for concern.

Next, have the child open her mouth as wide as she can, and press the tongue down with the popsicle stick, butter knife or spoon and look at the tonsils. You will be able to see one pair. There are six pairs in all, but the other four are above the soft

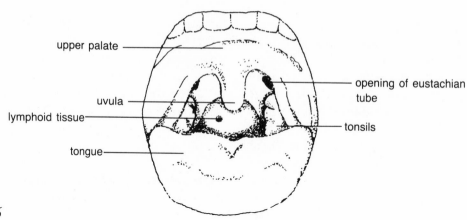

Fig. 6

palate and down the throat, so they are not readily visible. In young children, the tonsils should be enlarged. They will shrink in size sometime between the ages of six and eight years. Healthy tonsils will appear pink and moist. Any redness, swelling, or whitish exudate is an indication of infection. A single white spot is probably a piece of food that has gotten caught on the tonsil. It will disappear on its own, and need not concern you. Several white spots, however, can suggest viral lesions and should be reported to the doctor.

Feel the inside of the mouth. Place two fingers on the inside of the cheek and two fingers on the outside, feeling for any lumps. Repeat, running one finger along the inside of the lower lip, with two fingers on the outside. Finally, put one finger on the backside of the gum under the tongue and your other hand on the outside, underneath the lower jaw, and press the tissues between your fingers, again feeling for lumps. You will, in fact, be able to feel several kinds: the salivary glands on each side, the muscles, and other structures. If you examine your child when she is well,

you will become familiar with the normal lumps and bumps in this area, so that when she becomes ill, you will recognize any unusual swelling.

CHARACTERISTICS/PROBLEMS/DISEASES OF THE MOUTH

You may see a nursing blister at the midline of the upper lip in your nursing infant or toddler. This is perfectly normal, and may remain for several months, or, in some cases, until the child is weaned.

CHAPPING OR FISSURES. Fissures in the lips or a red ring around the entire mouth may be caused by chapping due to the sun, wind, or cold weather. Regular application of lip balm or petroleum jelly will help chapped lips heal.

Fissures may also be found in the corners of the mouth, and are commonly thought to be an indication of a deficiency of vitamin B, or riboflavin. We don't often see vitamin B deficiency in this country, however. More likely, the cracks are caused by a yeast infection that has spread to the corners of the mouth (see below) or even impetigo (see chapter 2).

COLD SORES. Herpetic stomatitis, amorphous ulcers, Vincent's stomatitis, herpes type I, fever blisters, and cold sores are all the same thing. They are usually caused by the herpes type I virus, which most people harbor in their mouths. As long as a normal level of lactobacillus (also known as acidophilus), a bacteria that resides in the mouth and intestines, is also present in the mouth, the virus does not usually cause any problems. However, when there is an upset to the system, the number of the bacteria may be limited, allowing the virus to grow. Replacing the lactobacillus in the mouth can prevent the ulcers from erupting if it is done before the skin has broken. Most people who are prone to the ulcers get a specific tingling sensation in the spot where an ulcer is about to erupt, usually about a day before. If lactobacillus capsules (available at health food stores) are used at this time, they may prevent the ulcers from appearing. Once the ulcers are actually present, the lactobacillus will help to alleviate the symptoms, although it will not shorten the duration of the outbreak. To replace the lactobacillus in the mouth, dump the contents of a lactobacillus capsule between the lower lip and the gum, so that they seep slowly into the mouth. Do this frequently during the day; you can't overdose on lactobacillus. (With a toddler or preschooler, you can just dump the contents of the capsule into the child's mouth. If you do this often, enough acidophilus will reach the site of the ulcer to do some good.) Recurrent ulcers may indicate a problem with the diet, such as too much red meat or a heavy concentration of dairy products. Taking lysine orally may also help to prevent recurrent outbreaks, although lysine is generally considered most effective for herpes type II virus. Figure the dosage at 500 mg per 50 pounds of body weight.

TEETHING. Teething can cause mild to high fever, diarrhea, earaches, crankiness, and diaper rash, although most child care manuals will claim it does not. When teething is at the root of any of these symptoms, the problem will clear up as soon as the tooth breaks through the gum. If your baby or toddler has any of these symptoms and her condition does not worsen over the course of several days, ruling out illness, teething may very well be the cause. I have found Hyland's Teething Tablets, a homeopathic medicine available at many health food stores, to be nearly a miracle drug for the symptoms of teething. The tablets are a mixture of camomilia, coffea, calcium calcifirate, and belladonna. Most people react negatively upon hearing that the pills contain belladonna, since they are aware that it is quite toxic. However, homeopathic solutions are highly diluted, so that massive doses—in the neighborhood of ten thousand tablets—would be required to pose any problem, even to an infant. The recommended dosage is two to three tablets four times per day. I have found, however, that slightly higher doses seem to be more effective, and generally recommend giving two tablets every twenty to thirty minutes until the symptoms are relieved, and then cutting back to two to three tablets three times a day until they have completely disappeared or the tooth has broken through. At this level, the tablets will substantially alleviate your child's discomfort, and yours, too.

BAD BREATH.   A foul odor to the breath can usually be attributed to food on the back of the tongue and can easily be eliminated by teaching the child to brush the tongue with a toothbrush. Bad breath can also be a clue to one of several conditions, including diabetic acidosis; severe dehydration; malnutrition; an infection of the tonsils, adenoids, or sinuses; gum disease; tooth abscesses; foreign bodies in the nostrils or sinuses; chronic kidney disease; or diphtheria, which produces a mouselike odor. If your child's bad breath persists in spite of a change in her oral hygiene habits, especially if her general health is not good, one of these conditions may be the cause, and she should be examined by your doctor.

BUMPS ON THE ROOF OF THE MOUTH.   Small cysts or white bumps in the mucous membranes and on the roof of the mouth are common. These will disappear spontaneously and are not a cause for concern. Small white bumps that appear shortly after birth are called Epstein's pearls and will also disappear without treatment.

GEOGRAPHIC TONGUE.   A tongue that looks as though it has a map drawn on it is called a "geographic tongue." This condition is perfectly normal, although some doctors attribute it to allergy or a vitamin deficiency.

I'm not convinced that either of these is the cause, and do not feel that it presents any problem.

FURRY-LOOKING TONGUE.   A furry appearance to the tongue is caused by elongated taste buds that have accumulated food. This condition appears in children who have been very sick, who have been severely dehydrated, who are chronically malnourished, or who have been on antibiotics for a long time.

RED TONGUE.   Scarlet fever will produce a strawberry-colored tongue in the early stages of the disease and a raspberry-colored tongue in its later stages. (For more on scarlet fever, see chapter 2).

TONGUE-TIED INFANT.   An infant may appear to be tongue-tied, but this is usually not a cause for concern. If the frenulum, the small piece of tissue that goes from the tongue to the floor of the mouth, extends all the way out to the end of the tongue and, especially, if the tongue is indented where the frenulum attaches to it, the frenulum may need to be clipped. (This is very rare.) Since there is no nerve tissue in the frenulum at birth, this procedure can be done then without using an anesthetic and without resulting in bleeding.

ORAL YEAST INFECTION.   Oral yeast infections (also called thrush) are relatively common in babies. Since thrush occurs most often in newborns, it is generally believed to be picked up in the birth canal, although it also occurs in babies born by cesarean section. (It is my theory that we all harbor some yeast on our bodies, and that the baby probably picks it up from the breast while nursing or even from sucking on someone's finger.) In an infant who has thrush, there appears to be milk hanging on the inside of the cheeks and coating the tongue. Milk does not hang on the cheek, however, so you can be sure that the cause is yeast. If the yeast travels through the digestive tract, the baby may also have coliclike symptoms from yeast growing in the intestines and a diaper rash from yeast in the stool.

Lactobacillus generally keeps the growth of yeast under control in older children and adults. (There are other bacteria that control the growth of yeast on the skin.) Newborns are particularly prone to thrush because they have insufficient quantities of lactobacillus in the mouth and the intestines. Thrush can be easily treated by placing the contents of a lactobacillus capsule in the mouth one to eight times a day. At this level, you do not have to worry about giving an overdose of acidophilus, which is virtually impossible anyway. Acidophilus is cultured in one of four mediums: cow's milk, goat's milk, soy, or pectin. In my own children, the goat's milk acidophilus has been the most effective. If your child is allergic to any of these four sources, you would, of course, want to avoid acidophilus from that source.

If a baby is also having coliclike symptoms from yeast in the intestinal tract, some of the acidophilus placed in the mouth will be swallowed and will end up in the intestines. It will begin to grow, and, aided by a substance in breast milk called the biciphidous factor, it will flourish and effectively eliminate the problem of excess yeast in the intestinal tract.

A rash caused by yeast is characterized by small red dots that seem to grow into one another. While most common in the diaper area, this type of rash can also occur in the folds under the baby's chin or arms, in the groin area, or in any area that is not exposed to the air, so that it tends to stay warm and moist. The rash appears very raw and looks painful but it generally does not cause any discomfort. In order for yeast to grow on the skin in quantities sufficient to cause a rash, it requires warmth, moisture, and an alkaline pH. To alter the pH so that the skin is no longer a hospitable medium to the yeast, wash the affected area with a vinegar solution of one-fourth to one-half cup of vinegar in one quart of water several times per day. If the rash is in the diaper area, leave the baby's diaper off as much as possible to try to keep the skin cool and dry as well.

A baby with thrush can leave yeast on the mother's breasts when she nurses, causing the nipples to become sore and cracked. Most nursing mothers experience some nipple soreness in the initial weeks following birth as the breasts adjust to the baby's frequent sucking. After the newborn period, however, the most common cause of sore nipples is thrush. To treat the breasts, expose them to air as much as possible to keep them cool and dry, and wash them frequently with a vinegar solution (be sure to rinse it off before nursing). If a nursing infant has thrush, it is wise to treat the mother's breasts even if she has no symptoms of the infection, since it is possible for the mother and baby to pass the yeast back and forth.

STREP THROAT.   Infections of the throat, particularly strep throat, are quite common in children. The symptoms that accompany a strep infection can range from very mild to quite severe. The child may have a high fever or none at all, a terrible sore throat complete with swollen tonsils dripping pus, or just a mildly red, scratchy throat. Because of this, there is no way to diagnose the disease accurately except with a throat culture to determine the presence of the streptococcal bacteria. Strep will generally clear up on its own in a child who is in reasonably good health.

Why, then, is there so much concern over strep throat? Strep infections have been related to two serious diseases that were relatively common in the earlier part of this century: rheumatic fever, which can permanently damage the heart, and chronic glomerulonephritis (Bright's disease), a kidney disorder. Because of the connection between these diseases and strep throat, doctors assumed that treating strep with a three-day course of penicillin would not only wipe out the infection but also eradicate the other diseases. As it turned out, three days of penicillin did clear up most cases of strep, but the incidence of rheumatic fever and Bright's disease did not decline as expected. Doctors then began prescribing penicillin for one to two weeks, a practice that continues to this day. They did

finally begin to see fewer cases of the diseases, and penicillin was given the credit for their decline. However, studies done in several countries have noted a significant decline in rheumatic fever and glomerulonephritis even before the advent of antibiotics, a trend that can also be seen in areas where strep is not routinely treated with antibiotics.[3]

Antibiotics are used not only to treat strep, but also to prevent complications of infections of the heart valve once a child has rheumatic fever. The usual recommendation is that the child be kept on a prophylactic dose for the rest of her life. This, too, is unwarranted. One study done in England showed a decline in recurrence rates of rheumatic fever in almost every age-group between 1921 and 1956 despite the fact that antibiotics were not routinely used as a prophylaxis. It is also interesting to note that the general decline in rheumatic fever began before antibiotics were used, and that the downward trend did not appear sharper during 1952–56, when the majority of children received penicillin either during a strep infection or to prevent recurrences of rheumatic fever.[4]

While no one knows for certain what caused the decline in both rheumatic fever and glomerulonephritis, and while there is continued debate over the use of antibiotics and the decline of rheumatic fever and nephritis, the relationship between the diseases and living conditions has been noted. An evaluation of socioeconomic status during the period 1936–45 showed that about one-half of the patients were in the poorest group. The socioeconomic status of less than one half was considered to be fair, and for only eight percent was it considered to be good.[5] This study supports my own theory, which is that the decline of the diseases is probably related to improved nutrition.

Whatever the reason for the decline, the important point is that the incidence of these two diseases would have declined no matter what those who conducted the studies with penicillin attempted to relate it to. If they had, for instance, treated each case of strep throat by giving a placebo to those infected, there would still have been a decline in the diseases. The fact that they related the decrease to the administration of penicillin made the conclusions of the studies plausible, but the diseases would have declined regardless.

For this reason, my approach to strep infections has been to emphasize good nutrition and overall good health, rather than to treat them with antibiotics. Admittedly, this is not common practice, but I believe more doctors are beginning to question—and change—their methods of treatment.

DISEASES OF THE GUMS. Gum diseases are often related to vitamin deficiencies, erupting teeth, or poor dental hygiene. Gums that bleed easily may be a manifestation of scurvy (vitamin C deficiency), poor dental hygiene, or rarely, leukemia. A black line at the edge of the gums may be an indication of heavy-metal poisoning, but it also occurs normally in black children. Thickening of the gums is seen in children who take the medication Dilantin for epilepsy, who habitually breathe through their mouths, or who have a vitamin deficiency.

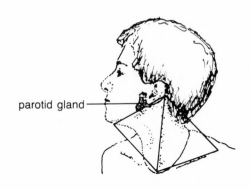

parotid gland

Fig. 7

The Neck

GENERAL EXAM

First, examine the neck for enlarged lymph nodes. To do this, picture each side of the neck as divided into two triangles: an anterior triangle and a posterior triangle. If you turn your head to the left and feel the right side of the neck, you will feel the muscle that goes diagonally from just behind the angle of the jaw down to the breastbone. Picture this muscle as the dividing line of the triangles on the right side. The anterior triangle is formed by this line, the jawline itself, and a center line from the notch of the breastbone to the tip of the chin (see fig. 7). The posterior triangle is formed by the line of the muscle, the midline of the back of the neck, and a line at the base of the neck. To examine the right side of your child's neck, gently tilt her head to the right (this will loosen the muscle so that you are able to feel it better) and feel the muscle on the right. You should be able to probe almost completely around it with your fingers.

Feel for enlarged lymph nodes or other swellings, and then repeat on the muscle on the left side. Next, run your fingers underneath the jaw, and down the front of the neck, and feel in the soft area between the muscle at the shoulder level and the clavicle in the front portion of the chest. You may also be able to feel lymph nodes here. Any lymph nodes you can feel are enlarged. This happens in response to any kind of infection, or sometimes as a reaction to a foreign substance. Most people, including children, have one or two lymph nodes that are permanently enlarged; this is perfectly normal.

The neck should not be stiff. Your child should be able to move her head in all directions without experiencing pain.

CHARACTERISTICS/PROBLEMS/DISEASES OF THE NECK

SWOLLEN LYMPH NODES. If one lymph node begins to enlarge and continues to do so, or if the swelling travels from the lymph nodes in one area of the body to those in another area, the child should be checked by a physician. Swollen lymph nodes throughout the body may be caused by mononucleosis or, infrequently, leukemia. Oddly enough, they can also be caused by black fly bites, which are common in some parts of the country during May and June. When the black fly bites, it injects an anti-coagulant into the blood, causing the lymph nodes to swell. Effective insect repellents for black flies include Shaklee Basic H (used full strength), Avon Skin-So-Soft (one part to eight parts water), Shoo (a flower and herb mixture), and Muskol (pure deet, a potent chemical).

STIFF NECK. There are two most common causes of stiffness in the neck, one quite harmless and the other potentially life-threatening. The first is simply a spasm of one of the muscles that run from the angle of the jaw to the breastbone (the same muscles you just located). When one of these muscles is in spasm, the child will be able to move her head down to her chest, all the way back, and all the way to one side. When the child attempts to move her head to the other side, however, it will be too painful, and she will turn her entire body around. A muscle spasm may be from having slept in an awkward position or from a fall or other minor injury while playing. A heating pad placed on the muscle will help to relieve the pain. If you know that the cause of the spasm was some sort of injury, apply ice to the muscle intermittently for the first twenty-four hours, and then use the heating pad.

Stiff Neck/Meningitis. The second cause of a stiff neck is meningitis. In this case, the child will be able to move her head to either side and to the back but will be unable to touch her chin to her chest. You can also check for this type of stiff neck by having the child lie on her back as you attempt to

46

lift her head with your hand and bring it toward her chest. If this is extremely painful, or if the entire torso lifts because the neck will not bend, the child may have meningitis. Meningitis is usually seen following another illness, either bacterial or viral in origin. The illness that precedes meningitis may be anything from a cold or ear infection to an intestinal virus. Typically, the child will be ill with the original infection for several days, and then begin to grow worse instead of better. In addition to the stiff neck, which is the most common indication of meningitis, she will probably have a headache (usually frontal, but sometimes on another part of the head) and a fever. In a baby with meningitis, the fontanel on the top of the head will bulge, raising up above the skull. Other symptoms, such as irritability, loss of appetite,

nausea, and vomiting, may also be present. The older child won't want to do anything except lie still, and a baby will usually want to be left alone in her crib. Somewhere between twenty-five to thirty-five percent of children with meningitis have seizures. As the disease progresses, a child with meningitis will slip into a coma if left untreated. If you have even the slightest suspicion that your child has meningitis, get immediate medical attention, as early treatment is crucial to a full recovery. It has been my experience that mothers whose children do have meningitis usually have an intuitive sense that their children are very sick even if the symptoms are mild. If you experience this sort of intuitive reaction when your child is ill, I recommend that you trust it and follow through by taking your child to a doctor as quickly as possible.

The Well-Child Quick Checklist

THE HEAD

1. Check the scalp for lumps, bumps, or tender areas, the hair for cleanliness, shininess, bounce, and texture, and the scalp for bald spots, flakiness or dandruff, and head lice or other insects.

2. Infants only: The fontanel should appear flat, not sunken in or bulging.

3. Infants only: Measure the head to be sure that it is growing properly.

THE EYES

1. Make sure that the eyes look normal for your child and that the whites are clear.

2. Check to see that the pupils react to light and that they are the same size.

3. Check for visual acuity.

4. Check for lazy eye.

NOSE

1. The child should be breathing through both nostrils and exhaling a normal amount of air.

2. Examine any discharge and note its color and consistency.

3. The turbinates should be healthy and pink.

4. The nasal passages should be of equal size.

EARS

1. The skin behind the ears should be smooth and healthy.

2. The eardrum should be white and opaque.

3. Check the hearing.

MOUTH

1. The lips should be smooth and moist, and the gums should be healthy and pink.

2. The breath should be sweet.

3. Examine the back of the throat; the tonsils should appear pink and moist.

4. Feel the inside of the mouth for lumps.

THE NECK

1. Feel the neck for enlarged lymph nodes.

2. The child should be able to move her head in all directions without experiencing pain.

Notes

1.   Richard E. Behrman, M.D., and Victor C. Vaughn III, M.D., eds., *Nelson Textbook of Pediatrics*, 13th ed. (Philadelphia: W. B. Saunders, 1987): p. 11.

2.   Meharban Singh, M.B.B.S., M.D., et al., "Human Colostrum for Pro-phylaxis Against Sticky Eyes and Conjunctivitis in the Newborn," *Journal of Tropical Pediatrics*, Vol. 28, No. 6 (Feb. 1982): p. 35.

3.   May G. Wilson, M.D., *Advances in Rheumatic Fever 1940–1961* (New York: Harper & Row, 1962): p. 13.

4.   Wilson, p. 20.

5.   Wilson, p. 31.

The Chest, Lungs, and Heart

The Chest and Lungs

Examination of the chest consists of inspection (looking), palpation (feeling), and auscultation (listening).

GENERAL EXAM

INSPECTION. First, look at the breasts. They should be symmetrical, and usually will not normally be swollen. Then watch the chest as the child breathes to determine whether or not the lungs expand well on both sides. The intercostal muscles, which are the muscles between the ribs, should normally be flat in appearance, not sucked in as the child breathes.

PALPATION. To palpate the chest, feel the entire chest cage—front, back, and sides—with your hands. You should not feel any-thing but the ribs and the intercostal muscles, which you will feel as soft spaces between the ribs. Next, place your hands on the rib cage and feel the motion of the child's breathing. You should not be able to feel a vibration as he breathes.

Next, check the "vocal phremitus," a type of vibration transmitted when the child speaks through the bronchial tubes and lung tissue to the chest wall, where it is palpable. Use the heel of your hand, or make a question mark with the fingers and palm of one hand, and place it against the back at the top of the lung, then in the middle of the shoulder blade, and then below the shoulder blade. For each of these positions, have the child say "ninety-nine" (if he is old enough to talk), which will transmit the vibrations well. The louder the child speaks, the better you will feel the vibrations. The intensity of the vibration should be the same on both sides.

AUSCULTATION. For auscultation, first listen to the child's breathing. Count the number of breaths per minute, with each breath consisting of one inhalation and one exhalation. The usual respiratory rate for children is from twenty to thirty breaths per minute, but this will vary somewhat with the age of the child. It will be much higher in the newborn period, and gradually decrease over the first eight to ten years of life. Since excitement, anger, joy, crying, anxiety, exercise, fever, pain, and hunger all tend to accelerate the rate of breathing, you will get the most accurate count when the child is resting or sleeping. The chart below indicates the normal ranges in breath rates for children between birth and ten years of age.

AGE	BREATHS PER MINUTE
Newborn	15–45
0–2 years	20–35
2–4 years	20–30
4–6 years	17–28
6–8 years	15–25
8–10 years	13–23

The next step in auscultation is to listen to your child's chest to evaluate the quality of his breath sounds. *Once again, I cannot emphasize enough how important it is for you to do this first when your child is well.* If you don't bother listening to his chest until he is sick, you won't be able to recognize abnormalities even if they are present. While it is virtually impossible to learn all of the different variations of breath sounds and their

meanings from a book, you can learn what your child's breathing sounds like when he is healthy. Then, when he becomes ill, you will be able to recognize any noises that are out of the ordinary.

A stethoscope will allow you to listen to the chest with both ears rather than one, but it is not essential. You will be able to hear enough simply by using one of your ears as you would the head of the stethoscope, placing it first against the child's back and then on the front of the chest. (Make sure you listen with your stethoscope or ear directly on the child's skin. Doctors do sometimes listen to the lungs through clothing, but doing so will result in your hearing unrelated noises.) Picture the child's back as divided in figure 1, and listen to each section sequentially, beginning with section one. For all six portions of the back and the four on the front, listen as the child breathes both in and out. The second section should sound approximately the same as the first, the fourth section the same as the third, and the sixth section the same as the fifth.

A final few words on healthy lungs: Cigarettes are not only bad for adults, but for children who live with smokers. Children who live in a household where someone smokes have a higher incidence of asthma, bronchitis, pneumonia, and upper respiratory infections.

Another threat to your child's lungs is baby powder, which contains talc. (Cornstarch-based baby products are not harmful.) Talc, which is related to asbestos, stays in the lungs indefinitely if it is inhaled, and can cause a variety of problems.

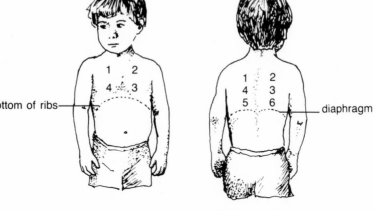

Fig. 1

CHARACTERISTICS/PROBLEMS/DISEASES OF THE CHEST AND LUNGS

BREAST SWELLING/NEWBORNS. Breast swelling is not uncommon in newborns, and it occurs in boy babies as well as girls. (Occasionally the breasts may even produce small droplets of milk, sometimes called "witch's milk.") This swelling usually disappears within the first few weeks of life, but it can last as long as the child is breast-fed and still be perfectly normal. It is *not* an indication that the child should be weaned or that a biopsy should be done, as is sometimes recommended. If a biopsy is suggested for your baby, one thing you should consider is that that little nubbin of tissue we call a baby's "breast" will normally grow and develop as the child does, and in a girl will eventually become a fully mature female breast. However, if twenty-five to fifty percent of the tissue is removed during infancy for a biopsy, there will not be sufficient tissue left for the breast to grow normally. For this reason, a biopsy should not be un-

dertaken unless there are other indications of a problem in addition to the breast swelling.

BREAST SWELLING/OLDER MALES. Breast swelling can occur in males as well as females at puberty. This is a normal, temporary stage of development that lasts from a few weeks to more than a year and a half. Some doctors also recommend surgical removal of this breast tissue, but there is no justification for this operation. However, breast swelling can be very difficult for even the most well-adjusted boy to deal with. A visit to the doctor just for reassurance is sometimes helpful. I have, on occasion, even written excuses for this condition, since there is no mercy in the locker room.

ACCESSORY BREASTS. Some children have accessory breasts, which appear as tiny nipples that occur in the "milk line," which runs up and down the chest, just as in other mammals (see fig. 2). A child may have one, two, or more of these, and a girl may even

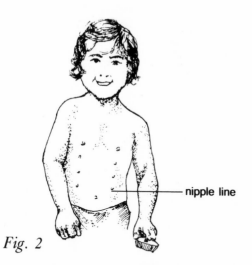

Fig. 2

have some breast tissue associated with them, so that they will swell slightly at puberty. Accessory breasts are seen frequently and, from a medical viewpoint, are nothing to be concerned about. However, a child with accessory breasts may require extra reassurance, especially at puberty.

PROTRUDING BONE. At the bottom of the breastbone is a small triangular bone called the xiphoid process, which may protrude and/or be somewhat mobile. Again, this is not a cause for concern. As the child grows and gains weight, the xiphoid process will no longer be apparent. Occasionally an older child or adult will lose enough weight for the xiphoid process to become noticeable once again, causing an unnecessary rush to the doctor to have this new "growth" examined.

FUNNEL CHEST. Some children have a deformity of the chest known as funnel chest, or pectus excavatum. While a slight depression of the chest will present no problems, a

severe malformation could interfere with the internal organs and must be examined by a physician to determine whether or not surgical correction is indicated. Funnel chest may be apparent from birth or, in some cases, may not be noticeable until the child is older.

CHEST PAIN. If a child complains of chest pain, it is more than likely caused by costochondritis. At the point where each rib meets the breastbone (see fig. 3) there is a small piece of cartilage, and between the cartilage and the bony rib, a joint. If one of these joints is somehow disrupted—perhaps because the child has been hit in the chest, sat upon, or even hugged hard—it can become tender. This condition is called costochondritis. You can diagnose it by pressing outward along each rib until you feel a ridge (about one-half to three-quarters of an inch from the edge of the breastbone), which is the joint. If the joint is tender, it is

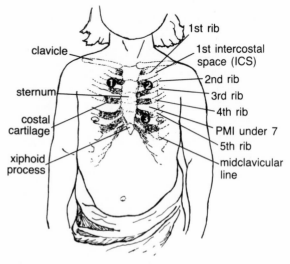

Fig. 3

undoubtedly the source of the child's chest pain. Costochondritis is probably the most commonly overlooked cause of chest pain in children, young adults, and women.

RAPID BREATHING. A respiratory or breath rate that is higher than normal may be an indication of a problem. An increased breathing rate is seen with respiratory distress, which has several possible causes (see below), or may be due to hyperventilation brought on by one of several diseases, including Reye's syndrome (see chapter 11) and encephalitis (see chapter 11), aspirin poisoning, or shock. To determine the normal respiratory rate for your child, see the chart on page 52.

PULLING IN OF INTERCOSTAL MUSCLES WITH EACH BREATH. If the intercostal muscles sink in with each breath the child takes, they are retracted and the child is experiencing respiratory distress. Retractions are especially striking when the cause of the distress is outside the lungs, such as a foreign object in the throat or the pharynx that is partially obstructing the breathing. In these cases, there is a large negative pressure below the site of the obstruction that causes the area to collapse dramatically with each intake of breath. (This effect is also seen in some cases of pneumonia.) If the retraction occurs only in the upper part of the chest, the obstruction may be somewhere between the nose and the mouth or voice box. If the retraction occurs only in the lower portion of the chest, the obstruction may be in the lungs themselves. Retraction is often accompanied by an increased rate of respiration and an accelerated heart rate. A child who is experiencing these symptoms should be evaluated for other signs of respiratory distress (see page 60).

COUGHING. Coughing, the most frequently observed sign of respiratory illness, is usually caused by postnasal drip. A child will usually develop this type of cough after a few days of an upper respiratory infection. Often parents will assume the child is growing sicker when the cough begins, but he is actually just entering into the final stage of the illness. The body is probably attempting to flush out the remains of the infection by producing mucus, which then drains into the back of the throat. A cough that is caused by postnasal drip will be worse when the child is lying down than when he is up and about. Some parents worry that the mucus is actually draining into the lungs, but this is not the case. In fact, just about the only way the mucus could get from the back of the throat into the lungs is if the child somehow managed to aspirate some of it. If mucus *could* drain into the lungs, so could water and applesauce, or just about anything a child eats or drinks. Children under the age of two months rarely develop coughs. When they do, the cause is usually quite serious, such as pneumonia or pertussis (also known as whooping cough; see chapter 14).

VIRAL CROUP/EPIGLOTTITIS. Another cause of coughing is viral croup, technically called laryngotracheobronchitis, which is a fairly common infection in children, particularly during the winter months. The term "croup" is also sometimes used in reference to epiglottitis, a bacterial infection, which is not as common. Both of these diseases cause an inflammation of the upper airway, producing difficulty in drawing air into the lungs, and sometimes resulting in respiratory distress. Most cases of laryngotracheobronchitis can be successfully handled in the home, but epiglottitis is far more serious and much more likely to require emergency care.

Viral croup. Laryngotracheobronchitis is usually seen in children between the ages of five months and three years, and it occurs more frequently in boys than girls.[1] The child has generally had an upper respiratory infection for a few days. The infection gradually develops into a cough that sounds like a seal's bark, and the child will begin to have difficulty in breathing. He will develop a stridor, which is a harsh medium-pitched sound that is usually heard with each inhaled breath. In this case, the stridor is caused by a narrowing of the upper airway due to swelling of the larynx. (Stridor is also heard in other cases of an obstruction outside the lungs, such as with epiglottitis, with a foreign body in the trachea that partially obstructs the breathing, or after a trauma or blow to the throat.) The child may have a fever, but otherwise will not appear particularly sick. A child with laryngotracheobronchitis is most comfortable lying down.

There is no effective drug treatment for viral croup, but you can significantly aid the child's breathing by sitting with him in a steam-filled room, such as a closed bathroom with the hot water in the shower turned on, until he is able to inhale more comfortably. The child's symptoms are caused by the drying out of the throat and the swelling of the larynx. If you get plenty of steam into the air, the dryness will be lessened and the child will breathe more easily. In addition to sitting in a steamy bathroom, a vaporizer in the child's room will help, as will a cool-mist humidifier, although the humidifier is the less effective of the two. Some pediatricians recommend taking a child with croup out into the night air, but I have never been comfortable with this advice. In my experience, the condition usually improves spontaneously around three-thirty A.M., regardless of whether or not the child has been taken outside. Since most emergency room visits seem to occur shortly after this time, doctors have probably erroneously attributed the improvement to some magical powers of the night air.

About ten percent of children with laryngotracheobronchitis do require hospitalization. If there is significant respiratory obstruction, evidenced by more than forty breaths per minute, fatigue, or cyanosis (see chapter 2) the child should be taken to the emergency room immediately.

A child with what appears to be frequently recurring viral croup, or croup that lasts for more than five days (most cases will clear up in three to four days), may be suffering from another disease that produces the same symptoms. These cases are extremely rare, however.

Epiglottitis. Epiglottitis is generally seen in children from ages three to six years. It occurs just as frequently in girls as in boys, and is not necessarily preceded by an upper respiratory infection. The onset of the dis-

	LARYNGOTRACHEO-BRONCHITIS	EPIGLOTTITIS
Personal Data		
Age	5 mo–3 yr	3–6 yr
Sex	males > females	males = females
History		
Preceding upper respiratory inf.	yes	no
Onset	gradual	abrupt
Progression	slow	rapid
Physical Findings		
Fever	maybe	no
Position	lying	sitting
Stridor	yes	yes
Drooling	no	yes
Cough	yes	no
Toxic appearance	yes	yes
Studies (This information may be helpful if your child is hospitalized.)		
White blood cell count	normal or slightly elevated	elevated
Blood culture	negative	positive (H. influenzae)
Soft tissue X ray of neck	subglottic narrowing	swollen epiglottis

ease is very abrupt and its progress rapid. With epiglottitis, the child will usually have a fever, a sore throat, and a muffled voice, and he will look very sick. He may or may not have a cough, but it will be difficult for him to swallow, so that he will almost certainly drool. (Drooling, in fact, is one of the key symptoms that distinguishes epiglottitis from viral croup.) The child will find it easier to breathe in a sitting position than lying down, and he will tend to lean forward. Children with epiglottitis often require hospitalization, and in some cases, a tracheotomy (an incision in the trachea made through the neck, to create an airway). Because the disease is potentially life-threatening and its progress is rapid, *epiglottitis requires immediate medical attention.* If your child is having trouble breathing and his condition is rapidly growing worse, get to an emergency room quickly.

ABNORMAL VIBRATIONS AND BREATH SOUNDS. Problems with the lungs generally result in a vibration that can be felt or heard when examining the chest, such as an increase or decrease in vocal phremitus, abnormal breath sounds, or a difference between the breath sounds heard in one portion of a lung and its mate on the other side. A vibration that is heard or felt usually indicates a lung infection, although it may also be due to nasal congestion (see below). The infection might be bronchitis, an inflammation of the large airways leading to the lungs; bronchiolitis, an inflammation and narrowing of the small airways; or pneumonia, an inflammation of the air sacs (the alveoli). If the vibration momentarily disappears when the child coughs, then returns, the child probably has bronchitis.

If the vocal phremitus is markedly stronger than is normal for your child, or if it is stronger on one side of the chest than the other, the infection may have resulted in fluid in one or both of the lungs, and the child should be seen by a doctor. Increased vocal phremitus may also be due to overly large bronchi or a consolidated lung, conditions that require a doctor's attention. A marked decrease in or absence of vocal phremitus may be due to fluid, air, or solid tissue around the lungs, more conditions that should be treated by your doctor. However, bronchial tubes that are blocked from bronchitis may also cause a decrease in vocal phremitus.

There are a variety of breath sounds you may hear in examining your child. Wheezing, a whistling sound due to a narrowing of the bronchial tubes, is most commonly associated with asthma, but may also be caused by a foreign body lodged in the throat or large bronchial tubes. In these cases, the wheezing will be heard only in the area of the blockage, not generalized throughout the lungs. Grunting, which is heard when exhaling against a partially closed glottis (voice box), is usually associated with an infection of the small bronchial tubes or pneumonia.

Crackling and rattling may be signs of infection either in the lungs or the bronchial tubes. However, because the distance between the lungs and the nose is very short in children, these sounds may actually be due to nasal congestion, even though they sound as if they originate in the lungs. This is the one time when I feel the use of chemical nose drops is justified, so that you can clear out the nasal passages enough to hear what is actually going on in the lungs. (If the child is old enough to be able to effectively blow his nose, you won't need the nose drops, and some young children may be motivated enough to learn to do so on the spot.) To use the drops, place the child on his back on a bed, with his head hanging off the edge. Suck out the nose with your ear syringe (see page 34 for the proper procedure), and then place one-half to three-quarters of an inch of ¼ percent Neo-Synephrine in each nostril. Turn the head back and forth, so that the nose traces an arc all the way from one side to the other and back again, rotating one hundred and eighty degrees, distributing the drops to loosen the mucus and open the nasal passages. Sit the child up slowly and let the drops run down the back of the throat, and then repeat the entire procedure, beginning with sucking out the nose. As you can well imagine, no child is going to take kindly to this process. By the time you have finished, your child will probably be quite upset. Hold him, comfort him, and get him calmed down; then you will be able to listen to the lungs again. If the noises have disappeared, you can be sure that they were caused by the nasal congestion. If the sounds are still present, there is an infection somewhere in the lungs or the bronchial tubes.

BRONCHITIS, BRONCHIOLITIS, PNEUMONIA. I realize that while bronchitis and even bronchiolitis will probably not cause you alarm, the very mention of pneumonia might make you want to hustle your child right to the doctor. Doctors are quite aware of this reaction, and will sometimes interchange the terms bronchiolitis and pneumonia. If a doctor wants to reassure you, he'll tell you your child has bronchiolitis, but if he wants to alarm you into doing things his way, he'll tell you the child has (or might have) pneumonia.

As terrible as pneumonia sounds, however, a visit to the doctor may not be necessary. Pneumonia has several causes, including viruses, bacteria, and, less commonly, an inhaled object (such as a peanut fragment). Since antibiotics are not effective against viruses, including viral pneumonia, a doctor has little to offer in the way of treatment if a virus is the cause. Viral pneumonia is generally quite mild, anyway, and even bacterial pneumonia can be mild enough for a healthy immune system to overcome without antibiotics, although they will certainly be necessary for some cases. When the pneumonia is caused by something the child has inhaled, the object will have to be removed before the inflammation can clear up.

As you can see, then, there's a range of different illnesses we label "pneumonia," and they do vary in severity. For that reason, I'm not going to tell you to rush right to the doctor should you happen to detect an infection in your child's lungs. This is one of those times when you need to consider the child's other symptoms and evaluate him as a whole person: How is his breathing? Is he lethargic or uninterested in playing? How is his color? If he does not seem particularly sick, there is no reason to become unduly alarmed at a sound in the lungs. Nevertheless, in the case of any type of lung infection, I think it's wise to do something to help the healing process along. What that "something" is will depend on your own biases and beliefs. While many pediatricians disdain herbal medicines, I have found the herb echinacea to be very helpful in treating lung infections. Echinacea is available in capsule form at health food stores (it can also be purchased as a tea, but most people dislike the flavor). An herbal preparation such as Immuno-klenz (which contains echinacea) is another alternative. If you have a home remedy you want to try, fine; this is the time to use it. In any event, you should also provide supportive measures such as using a vaporizer in the child's room to humidify the air and making sure he drinks plenty of water. Water is especially important for the person who has any kind of lung infection, since it is essential to help thin out the secretions and make them easier to cough up. You can also use gravity to help bring up these secretions and clear out the lungs. Have the child lie with his upper torso hanging off the side of a bed, or elevate one end of the child's bed and then have him lie so that his chest is higher than his head. You can even put him on a slant board, if you happen to have one or can safely rig one up. Have him lie on his back, front and each side for several minutes to clear out each portion of the lungs. (For this to be most effective, you should first have the child sit in a steamy room several minutes to help loosen up the mucus.) If his condition worsens in spite of your efforts, *then* you know it's time to call the doctor.

RESPIRATORY DISTRESS. A child with pneumonia, epiglottitis, laryngotracheo-bronchitis, severe asthma, or a foreign body lodged in the throat may begin to experience respiratory distress. This is, understandably, one of the most difficult conditions for a parent to deal with calmly. Not every case of labored breathing is a case of respiratory distress, however, nor,

for that matter, does every case of respiratory distress require emergency medical care. For example, as I've noted, most of the time viral croup can be handled in the home, in spite of the fact that a child with this disease will almost inevitably have some trouble breathing. The signs of respiratory distress are as follows:

Wheezing

Grunting

Stridor: a harsh, medium-pitched sound usually heard with each inhaled breath

Tension of the muscles in the neck and abdomen

Flaring of the nostrils (see chapter 3)

Retraction of the intercostal muscles

Irregular breathing: breathing very slowly at first, progressing to rapid breathing, then failing to breathe at all for a few seconds, then beginning to breath slowly again

Inability to respond to breathing commands (breathing in time with another person, or being asked to hold his breath for a count of five)

Difficulty thinking clearly or irritability due to having to concentrate on breathing

Insistence on sitting up, since lying down will increase his breathing difficulties

Pulse rate over 120 beats per minute

Cyanosis: A blue tinge to the skin, especially around the nail beds and lips, caused by an insufficient intake of oxygen. Cyanosis is a sign of serious respiratory distress, and indicates that the child urgently needs to be given oxygen. (For more on cyanosis, see chapter 2.)

It would be very handy if I could give you absolute guidelines for dealing with a child in respiratory distress, if I could say, for example, that if your child has two or more of the above symptoms, you should seek medical help immediately. It's not that simple, however. Once again, this is a situation in which you must evaluate the whole child in order to determine whether or not his problem is one that can be handled at home. The two most important considerations are the cause of the problem and whether or not the child's condition is stable. If your child has symptoms of epiglottitis and his condition is rapidly growing worse, you have no time to waste in seeking emergency medical care. If, on the other hand, he develops signs of respiratory distress because of pneumonia or viral croup, and his condition seems stable, you may be able to handle the problem in the home by calming the child down and sitting with him in a steamy bathroom until he's breathing more easily. If his condition grows worse instead of better, so that he is experiencing more of the signs of respiratory distress, you should seek immediate medical attention. If at any time your child's respiratory rate goes above forty breaths per minute, he has cyanosis, or he exhibits signs of fatigue from the effort of breathing, his condition should also be considered an emergency.

The Heart

GENERAL EXAM

HEART RATE. Determine your child's heart rate per minute by finding his pulse, counting it for thirty seconds and then doubling that number. The easiest places to find a child's pulse are at the carotid artery and at the brachial artery. To locate the carotid artery, place one finger on the Adam's apple and then slide it into the depression on either side (you should feel a strong pulse). The brachial artery is at the inside of the upper arm and can be felt in the space between the bicep and the tricep muscles.

The normal heart rate will vary with age. In utero, it is between 120 and 160 beats per minute. After birth, it gradually decreases to about 150 beats per minute during infancy, and then down to about 120 beats per minute throughout childhood. This rate will vary with the child's health and emotional state, with fever, excitement, and anxiety all accelerating the heart rate.

PMI. Now locate the point of maximal impulse, or PMI, of the heart. Have the child lie on his back and place your hand on the left side of the chest. Find the spot where you can best feel the heartbeat, then narrow your hand down to three fingers and then to one finger, leaving that one finger on the point where the heartbeat feels the strongest. Mark this point with a marker or a ballpoint pen. This is the PMI.

Next, determine where the PMI should be. Place your index finger at the top of the breastbone, at the notch. Run your fingers down the center of the breastbone until you feel a ridge that runs across the breastbone, about one to two inches down from the notch. Follow that ridge to the left until you reach the second rib. (You will probably be unable to identify the first rib, since most of it is behind the clavicle.) Below the second rib is the second intercostal space. The space below the third rib is the third intercostal space, and so on (see fig. 3). Keeping this in mind, locate the clavicle or collarbone, which runs from the edge of the breastbone to the shoulder. Mentally divide the clavicle in half, and then imagine a line that runs from that point, through the nipple, and on down the chest. This is the midclavicular line. The spot you marked for the PMI should, in a child between birth and four years of age, be at the fourth intercostal space outside the midclavicular line. In a child between the ages of four and six, the PMI should be in the fourth intercostal space on the midclavicular line, and in a child of seven or older, in the fifth intercostal space inside the midclavicular line.

Next, with the child still on his back, listen to his heart with the bell side of your stethoscope, making sure you press only lightly on the chest. (If you press too heavily, particularly on a chubby baby, the fat will creep in and block the opening so that you can't hear the heartbeat at all.) You want to listen in three locations: just to the right and left of the sternum in the second intercostal space, and over the PMI. The normal heart makes a quick, concise "lub-dub, lub-dub" sound. To get a feeling for the sound, try repeating "lub-dub" aloud to yourself at a rate of about twenty times

per fifteen seconds; you'll feel pretty silly, but it'll give you the right idea.

CHARACTERISTICS/PROBLEMS/DISEASES OF THE HEART

ABNORMAL LOCATION OF PMI. If the PMI does not seem to be in the proper location, your child may have an enlarged heart and should be checked by a doctor.

RAPID OR SLOW PULSE. A rapid pulse that can be attributed to fever, excitement, increased activity or other factor is not a cause for concern. However, if it rises above two hundred beats per minute without apparent cause, the child needs to be seen by a doctor. A heart rate that is below sixty is always considered abnormal, and also should be evaluated by a doctor.

ABNORMAL HEART SOUND. If you hear a "shhh" sound in addition to the "lub-dub" when listening to your child's heart, so that the sound is a "shhh-lub-dub, shhh-lub-dub" or a "lub-shhh-dub, lub-shhh-dub," he may have a heart murmur. To better identify what you hear, coordinate the sound with the feel of the child's pulse. The pulse you feel is the "lub" sound; you won't feel the "dub" or a "shhh" sound. While you are feeling the pulse and listening to the heart, watch the chest as well (mothers, who are used to doing three things at once, are particularly good at this). If you hear a "shhh" sound every time the child's chest expands with an intake of air, you may actually be hearing the child breathing, not his heart. If he is old enough, ask him to hold his breath, both after an inhalation and after an exhalation. If the "shhh" sound disappears when the child is holding his breath, it is not caused by a heart murmur.

Should you suspect a heart murmur, it must be evaluated by a doctor to determine the type and whether or not any treatment is in order. Approximately fifty percent of children are born with heart murmurs, although they are often undetected until about three weeks of age, when the heart rate has slowed somewhat. The majority disappear as the child matures. A normal, "innocent" heart murmur is usually heard most clearly between the ages of about three and seven. Often, it is heard best when the child is lying down, either fading considerably or disappearing completely when he sits or stands. If this is the case with your child, the heart murmur is most likely innocent, but it should still be checked by a doctor at least once.

To have a heart murmur evaluated, I recommend that you consult with a pediatric cardiologist rather than your pediatrician or family physician, who would probably recommend that your child have a chest X ray and an electrocardiogram (EKG). Since the EKG is a noninvasive procedure, it does not present a problem, but the X ray is a different matter. Five X rays in a lifetime is now considered the safe level of radiation, so avoidance of any that aren't absolutely necessary is essential. A pediatric cardiologist will instead do an echocardiogram, or ultrasound of the heart, which will provide him with more information and be safer for the child. After the cardiologist has completed his examination, he may tell you that it is an innocent heart murmur that should not present problems in the future and that no restrictions need be placed on the child. If this is the case, the doctor will probably recommend that the child return for a follow-up evaluation in six months to a year. There is no reason to return to the cardiologist, however, since your family physician or pediatrician is perfectly capable of handling a subsequent evaluation.

On the other hand, the cardiologist may inform you that the heart murmur is a fairly serious condition that needs to be monitored and could eventually require surgery. He may then recommend that you return in three months so that the child can be monitored for signs of a worsening of the condition that could lead to heart failure. Children don't just develop heart failure or other complications at three-month intervals, however, so it would be much wiser for you to find out from the cardiologist how to monitor the condition yourself. This way, if your child does begin to develop a problem, you can detect it as early as possible and seek medical help before the situation worsens. The monitoring may involve listening to the heart and lungs, taking the blood pressure, and counting the pulse, all of which you should be able to do at home. You will still need to have the child checked at the intervals the doctor recommends, but by accepting this responsibility you will be better able to recognize any changes and seek treatment at the first sign of difficulty.

The Well-Child Quick Checklist

. . . .

THE CHEST AND LUNGS

1. Inspect the breasts (look and feel).

2. Watch the chest as the child breathes. The lungs should expand well on each side, and the intercostal muscles should be flat, not depressed or concave.

3. Feel the chest cage with your hands. You should not feel anything but the ribs and the soft spaces between them.

4. Feel the motion of the child's breathing. You should not feel any vibration as he breathes.

5. Listen to the child's breathing and count the number of breaths per minute.

6. Listen to the child's chest (preferably with a stethoscope) and evaluate the quality of the breath sounds.

THE HEART

1. Check the child's heart rate.

2. Locate the PMI, find the spot where the PMI should be, and compare.

3. Listen to the heart.

Note

1. W. D. Clark, "Epiglottitis and Laryngotracheobronchitis," *American Family Physician*, Vol. 28, No. 4 (Oct. 1983): p. 804.

The Abdomen, Genitalia, and Rectum

The Abdomen

···

GENERAL EXAM

As with the examination of the chest, examination of the abdomen consists of inspection, auscultation, and palpation. When doing this portion of the exam, have the child lie on his back, undressed, with pillows under the head and knees. His hands should rest on his chest, and the knees should be slightly bent. Make sure the room is comfortably warm, and that your hands feel warm to the touch.

INSPECTION. Mentally divide the abdomen into four sections, with the navel at the center: right upper quadrant, left upper quadrant, right lower quadrant, and left lower quadrant (named according to child's right and left, not your own; see fig. 1).

Note the shape of the abdomen. Normally, babies have little pot bellies. As they grow, their abdomens gradually become flatter until, around five years of age, they no longer protrude. (The pot has a way of returning around the age of forty, however.)

BOWEL SOUNDS. For auscultation, use your stethoscope to listen in all four abdominal quadrants as described above. The noises you hear are bowel sounds, and they will vary according to the child's physical state. For this reason, you need to make a point of listening to the child's abdomen when she is well under a variety of conditions: when she is hungry, when she needs to have a bowel movement, immediately following activity, and when she is resting or sleeping. Monitoring the bowel sounds under different circumstances will give you the background you need to know what is normal for your child.

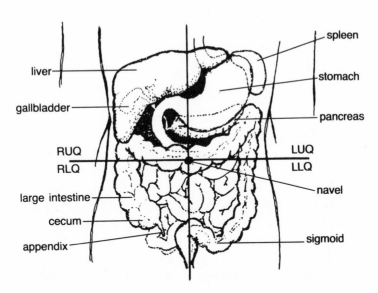

liver

gallbladder

spleen

stomach

pancreas

RUQ

RLQ

LUQ

LLQ

large intestine

cecum

appendix

navel

sigmoid

Fig. 1

PALPATION. Next, move on to palpation of the abdomen, working again in each of the four quadrants as the child lies on his back with his hands on his chest. When examining a well child, start in any of the four quadrants and work your way around the abdomen. If the child is in pain, start in a location away from where it hurts, and gradually work your way around to the sensitive area, since the child will not be very cooperative once you have caused her pain. If she's very ticklish, place your fingers between hers, and move your hands around the abdomen together as you do this part of the exam. Since a person cannot tickle herself, having your fingers between hers will serve to "disconnect" the tickling mechanism. Distraction can also be very effective when you're trying to examine a ticklish child: Talk about something the child is interested in, sing a silly song, or tell a joke, and she may forget all about what you're doing.

To palpate the abdomen, gradually press in as the child inhales, then press further in as she exhales. With each breath the child takes, press in a little further on the exhalation, making sure you don't let up as she inhales. If the child is cooperative, you will probably be able to press all the way to the spine. Just above the navel you will be able to feel the aorta pulsing, but you will not normally feel anything else.

The liver and gall bladder are in the right upper quadrant of the abdomen, the stomach is in the middle of the upper abdomen, and the spleen is in the left upper quadrant (see fig. 1). *You should not feel any of these organs.* If you do, the organ is enlarged and must be examined by your doctor.

In the lower portion of the abdomen, you will find the small and large intestines. To the left is the sigmoid colon, where fecal matter finally makes its way to the rectum. To the right is the cecum, the beginning of the large intestine, on which the appendix is located.

You will not normally be able to feel anything in the intestines, although in a child who is old enough to be on solid foods, you may feel tumor-like masses in the lower left quadrant. This is fecal matter, which should disappear once the child has had a bowel movement. If it does not, the child should be examined by a physician.

CHARACTERISTICS/PROBLEMS/DISEASES OF THE ABDOMEN

ROUNDED ABDOMEN. If your normally flat-bellied child suddenly develops a rounded abdomen, the cause may be an intestinal obstruction or tumor, or an enlargement of the organs. Swelling in the lower abdomen (groin area) may be caused by a hernia, hydrocele, or undescended testicles in boys (see below), or swollen lymph nodes in children of either sex.

UMBILICAL HERNIA. A navel that pops out is called an umbilical hernia. This occurs when the umbilical opening under the skin does not close completely, so that portions of the small intestine protrude. Umbilical hernias are most common in blacks and people of Mediterranean descent, and they vary in size from that of a peanut to four or five inches long. An umbilical hernia should disappear when the child is lying down, unless he is crying or straining to move his bowels. If it does not and you cannot easily push it back in, and especially if the child also seems to be in pain, the hernia may be strangulated and should be examined by a doctor immediately. It used to be thought that taping an umbilical hernia or using a belly band to hold it in would accelerate the healing process, but these measures are of no value. Ninety-nine percent of these hernias heal on their own before the child is six years old. If the hernia does not disappear on its own or becomes embarrassing for the child in social situations (e.g., when wearing a swimsuit), you may want to have it surgically repaired. Inguinal hernias are different and are discussed on page 77.

NEWBORN UMBILICUS. In a newborn there is usually some discharge, occasionally bloody, from the umbilicus. The area may look slightly infected and still be quite normal. This is, after all, a piece of tissue that the body is discarding—not a neat process. Parents are generally advised to keep the umbilicus dry by dabbing it with alcohol several times a day, but some studies have shown this procedure does not affect how quickly or well the navel heals. If the discharge contains a lot of pus, or if the area around the navel is very red, or if it seems to be causing the child discomfort, I would certainly recommend using the alcohol to keep the navel dry and sterile. Hygiene of the umbilicus shouldn't be taken *too* lightly, since very unsanitary conditions could lead to serious complications, but you needn't become overly concerned about it, either. Keep the area clean and dry and it will heal nicely on its own.

CONSTIPATION. Constipation is a common problem for children as well as adults. It is easy to tell if your child is constipated: When the food a person eats passes through his system, the indigestible matter (fiber) combines with water, the air he swallows, and the gases his body produces and becomes stool. If the stool contains the right amount of water, fiber, and gas, it will float in the toilet. If your child's stools sink, she is not getting enough water and/or fiber in her diet, or she may have a food allergy that is causing her to be constipated. So remember, floaters are good, sinkers are bad. (For more on food allergies, see chapter 12.)

Some people feel that a child who has a daily bowel movement cannot possibly be constipated. As important as the frequency of movements, however, is the length of time it takes food to pass through the system. You can judge this by feeding your child a small amount of corn, raisins, or other food that will pass through the body undigested. It should show up in the stool about eighteen hours later. If it takes longer to pass through the body, your child is constipated.

You may wonder why you should care about constipation, especially if your child is not uncomfortable. In countries where constipation is rare, there is a much lower incidence of appendicitis, hernia, hiatal hernia, diverticulitis, diverticulosis, irritable bowel syndrome, diabetes, varicose veins, gallstones, cancer of the bowel, hemorrhoids, and gas. If your child has a problem with constipation, it is important for her future health that you pinpoint the source of the problem. Consider the diet (is she getting sufficient fiber and water, or might she be allergic to certain foods?) as well as less common emotional causes (did it begin around the time you started toilet training, right after the arrival of a new baby, or some other upset?). If the child also has occasional diarrhea, it is possible that she is so constipated that some stool is leaking out around harder stools that she is unable to pass, making it difficult for her to control her bowels.

INCREASE OR DECREASE IN BOWEL SOUNDS. A significant increase in bowel sounds (called hyperactive bowel sounds) with lots of rumbling and gurgling, are heard with diarrhea and intestinal upset. A decrease in bowel sounds (hypoactive bowel sounds) occur with appendicitis and other conditions that affect the intestines' ability to function properly, and are usually a sign of serious illness. An absence of bowel sounds means that whatever infection or irritation is present has caused the bowels to completely cease functioning (as with, for example, a ruptured appendix) and indicates a need for immediate medical attention.

GASTROENTERITIS. The most common cause of vomiting and diarrhea is gastroenteritis, or intestinal virus. These symptoms are usually accompanied by loss of appetite, abdominal cramps, and, in some cases, a fever. With gastroenteritis, many children will have little or no vomiting, just a persistent, watery diarrhea as the main symptom. Symptoms usually begin within forty-eight hours of exposure to the virus and may last for up to five days, although a duration of three to four days is more common. Once the virus has run its course, the child needs another two to three days to recover fully his energy and appetite. Interestingly, the same virus in an adult will be milder and shorter in duration.

While it is not really possible to prevent your child from coming down with gastroenteritis, do keep in mind that doctor's offices and hospitals are excellent places to pick up these viruses. Some studies have shown that as many as thirty percent of children who are admitted to the hospital will contract a gastroenteritis-type infection during their stay.

DIARRHEA.   Diarrhea can also be caused by teething, allergy, or bacteria. One rarely considered source of diarrhea in children is animals: Puppies (not adult dogs), hamsters, and ferrets can harbor a bacteria that causes diarrhea in children (it does not affect adults, or the animals themselves). Generally speaking, diarrhea due to a bacterial infection tends to be more severe and persistent than that due to other causes, sometimes lasting as long as ten to twelve days. The child will almost always have a fever and in most cases will seem sicker than a child with gastroenteritis. The diarrhea caused by a bacterial infection may even be severe enough to result in bloody stools. When this happens, you will actually see blood in the toilet, not just a smear on the toilet paper due to irritation caused by frequent wiping. If your child has bloody diarrhea and is running a fever, you should have the stool cultured for bacteria immediately. You should also have a culture done if he has diarrhea that persists beyond five days, if his symptoms are particularly severe, or if he shows signs of dehydration (see below).

Loss of Appetite.   Most children will lose their appetite during a bout of gastroenteritis or a bacterial infection that affects the intestinal tract. This is probably the body's way of giving the bowels a rest. This is important, since the intestines are greatly affected by the infection and need a chance to rebuild their lining. Trust your child's body: If she does not want to eat, don't try

to force food on her. If she wants to eat, feed her bland, easily digested foods, or try to satisfy her hunger with a fluid- and electrolyte-replacement formula such as Pedialyte or the homemade formula later in this chapter. In some parts of the country a rice powder is available that, when dissolved in water (thirty to fifty grams to one liter of water), seems not only to help replace fluids and electrolytes but also to help cut down on the amount of diarrhea. The rice powder may be a better option, since the sugar in the formulas can sometimes exacerbate the diarrhea. If the child is breast-fed, she should certainly continue to nurse as often as she likes.

DEHYDRATION.   The major concern with both diarrhea and vomiting, whatever their cause, is dehydration. In this country diarrhea alone will rarely be severe enough to dehydrate a child, but it can happen. If your child has diarrhea, you need to take into consideration three factors in regard to the possibility of dehydration: the amount of liquid the child is taking in, the volume of the stools, and the frequency of the bowel movements. If she has a bowel movement every twenty minutes but only passes a tablespoon or so of stool and is drinking a normal amount of liquid, it's unlikely the diarrhea alone will cause her to become dehydrated. If her stools are both frequent and large in volume and she is drinking little, the chances of dehydration are greater. (You may find it difficult to judge how much liquid your nursing baby is actually ingesting, but this need not be of great concern. It is very rare for a breast-fed baby or toddler to become dehydrated from diarrhea alone. As long as the child is willing to nurse, she will take in enough liquid to compensate for what is lost.)

In addition to considering these three factors, you need to watch for any signs of dehydration. The early signs are decreased frequency of urination, lack of tears when the child cries, and dryness of the mouth, which will appear as parched lips. As dehydration progresses, the inside of the lips will become parched, followed by the tongue and the gums. If you pinch the skin on the back of the hand or on the abdomen of a child who is seriously dehydrated, it will momentarily stay in position, then sink slowly back to normal, rather than popping back quickly. In an infant, the fontanel will also appear sunken. If your child begins to show early signs of dehydration, begin giving the child a fluid- and electrolyte-replacement formula such as Pedialyte or the homemade formula below. (For a bottle-fed newborn, supplement the formula with plain water.) If her condition does not improve or grows worse, contact your doctor.

VOMITING. Vomiting is a much more serious problem than diarrhea, although most people have come to associate the two and consider them as more or less equal threats. The danger of dehydration is much greater with vomiting than with diarrhea, and the smaller the child, the faster her condition can become serious. You must be extremely vigilant when dealing with an infant who is vomiting. If the baby is breast-fed, the vomiting will generally occur shortly after a feeding. (Spitting up a small amount of milk after nursing is perfectly normal and not a cause for concern; if the baby is really vomiting, most of a feeding will come back up again, and the milk will smell sour, as it is partially digested.) In this case, put the baby back on the nearly empty breast and let her nurse again. If she vomits again, you'll have to cut down the amount of milk she is receiving. You may assume that this means that you should cut back to, say, fifteen minutes of nursing, since you normally nurse for half an hour. However, since a baby can empty ninety percent of the milk in a breast in seven minutes, this will not significantly change the amount she receives. Instead, you must cut back to *fifteen seconds* of nursing *by the clock*. You should then wait fifteen minutes, and nurse for another fifteen seconds. Continue in this manner, according to the following schedule:

Nurse thirty seconds, wait fourteen minutes.

Nurse thirty seconds, wait thirteen minutes.

Nurse forty-five seconds, wait twelve minutes.

Gradually increase the nursing time and decrease the waiting time. You will reach a point where the baby will vomit again. Move two steps back in your nursing and waiting schedule, stay at that point until the baby seems to be feeling better and then move forward again.

I realize that your baby is not going to be happy to be removed from the breast after fifteen seconds. Following this schedule is going to frustrate her, especially since she's not feeling well and you keep offering and then denying her the single most comforting thing she knows. You must understand, however, that the stakes are high here: If your baby becomes dehydrated, you will have little choice but to put her in the hospital, where she'll be hooked up to an IV and taken off the breast completely, possibly for several days. While difficult, following this schedule of nursing and waiting will prevent dehydration in the vast majority of cases, so it is well worth enduring your baby's discomfort. I have taught this technique to many parents over the past ten years, and do not know of any cases where it has failed to work.

A nursing baby or child who is on table food may return to the breast exclusively when she is feeling ill, particularly if she has an upset stomach. When this happens, the child's stools will also become watery, since her diet is now liquid. Because they don't revert completely to the yellow, seedy stools of a breast-fed infant, the parents may not realize the cause of the change, and will assume the child has now developed diarrhea in addition to her other symptoms. When the other symptoms include vomiting, this can cause alarm, since the chances of dehydration will seem that much greater. However, as long as the child has only two or three of these watery bowel movements a day, they should be considered a result of the change in diet and not diarrhea. When she begins to eat solid foods again, the stools will gradually return to normal.

To treat vomiting in a nonnursing baby or child under four, you can use Pedialyte, or, if you prefer, your own homemade fluid-replacement formula. The formula that follows, which is comparable to Pedialyte, was developed by the World Health Organization. It has been used extensively in third-world countries, where babies commonly die of dehydration due to diarrhea from bacterial infections. The WHO has credited it with saving hundreds of thousands of babies' lives around the world. Though the formula was developed primarily for use in treating dehydration from diarrhea, it is also suitable for preventing dehydration in a child who is vomiting.

••

ORAL REHYDRATION FORMULA

Sodium chloride (table salt)	1 teaspoon
Sodium bicarbonate, or baking soda	½ teaspoon
Potassium chloride (salt substitute)	4 teaspoons
Sugar	1 tablespoon
Water	1 quart

(When making the formula, be sure to use *measuring spoons*, not eating utensils, for accuracy.)

••

Just as with the nursing baby, you're going to need to give the formula or Pedialyte on a feeding/waiting schedule. Have the child take one tablespoon, then wait fifteen minutes. Give her two more tablespoons and wait another fifteen minutes, then three tablespoons followed by a fourteen-minute wait. Continue to increase the amount of the formula and decrease the waiting time until the child vomits again. At this point take two steps back in your schedule and stay there until she seems to be feeling better.

You can then begin giving the child small amounts of fruit juice, homemade vegetable juice or broth, or homemade chicken broth. If they are well tolerated, move on to rice, barley, or oats, and then gradually bring the child back to a normal diet over the next three to four days. In some cases, the child will rapidly recover her appetite and will not be satisfied with a limited diet. If she seems truly well, there is probably no harm in allowing her to eat whatever nutritious foods appeal to her, although you may still want to stick to the limited diet just to play it safe.

One assumption parents make when using the rehydration formula is that you can't possibly give your child too much of it, which is not true. The *maximum* amount that should be given each day is 150 milliliters (cc) per kilogram, or about 2.1 liquid ounces per pound of body weight. If the child consumes this much and is still thirsty, give her water.

For a nonnursing child of four years or older who is vomiting, I suggest you try Wootan's method of fasting for vomiting: Fast the child for one hour for each year of the child's age, up to eighteen years of age. By fasting, I mean nothing by mouth—no food, no juice, not even water. At the end of the fasting period, start giving the child "switzel," which is one tablespoon of honey and one tablespoon of apple cider vinegar diluted in one cup of lukewarm water. Give the switzel on the same schedule used for the oral rehydration formula. In fact, you can substitute the formula above, one of the juice and electrolyte preparations available at health food stores, such as Rebound or Third Wind, or even Pedialyte, if you prefer.

For severe cases of vomiting that do not respond to treatment, you should have on hand Phenergan suppositories. Phenergan is a fairly toxic drug, and as such is available by prescription only. Your doctor should be willing to give you a prescription of one or two for emergencies. If she refuses, I suggest you ask if she'll be willing to make a delivery in the middle of the night, if need be. Most doctors, I have found, will comply with a request for a small prescription, provided you promise to call if you need to use the suppositories (an entirely reasonable stipulation).

ABDOMINAL PAIN. I have found that parents tend to feel incapable of dealing adequately with acute abdominal pain in their children. Abdominal pain brings about such problems because its causes are varied, and, in younger children especially, parents may find it difficult (if not impossible) to determine the location and intensity of the pain. The best advice I can give for this situation is to remain calm and try to gather as much information as you can, from talking to the child, if she is old enough, and through the examination. If, after evaluating the child, you decide you need to consult your doctor, this information will be very valuable to him. The better the history you give him, the fewer tests he will need to do in order to pinpoint the problem.

In most cases of abdominal pain, you will be dealing with a common, non-life-threatening problem, such as colic, gastroenteritis, allergic gastritis, or constipation. I would guess that as much as ninety-eight percent of all abdominal pain seen by parents is due to one of these causes.

Appendicitis. Of the other possible causes, parents probably worry most about appendicitis. This concern is not without justification. Diagnosing appendicitis correctly can be very tricky, even for the experienced physician. In fact, most reports I have found in the medical literature on the subject estimate that approximately twenty to thirty percent of appendixes that are removed are actually healthy. It's no wonder, then, that it is the disease that most often trips up parents. When this happens, it is not because the parents have failed, but rather because the disease is one that presents problems even for the experts. When the appendix is in the normal position on the cecum, the classical symptoms are present and the diagnosis is easy. Occasionally, however, the appendix is tucked up behind a portion of the large intestine or is otherwise shielded by the abdominal contents, so that the classical symptoms are not present. In addition, since children respond differently to disease, two children with appendicitis will not necessarily have the same symptoms. Appendicitis can be so difficult to diagnose that entire books have been written on the subject, and there is now a computer program that has actually

proven slightly more successful than doctors in arriving at the correct diagnosis.

APPENDICITIS/SYMPTOMS. With this in mind, let's move on to the classical symptoms of appendicitis. *If your child develops these symptoms, contact your doctor immediately.* Don't rule out the possibility of appendicitis even if these symptoms are not present, however. If your child has abdominal pain and vomiting and, after your examination, you are not fairly confident that her symptoms can be attributed to gastroenteritis or another nonserious condition, call your doctor.

Appendicitis causes acute abdominal pain, vomiting, and sometimes fever. During an attack of appendicitis, the child will also usually pass one very loose stool, which is sometimes mistaken for diarrhea. Rather than true diarrhea, however, this is simply the result of the intestines emptying out their contents, after which the cecum will effectively shut down. The child will then seem to become constipated. (Vomiting, abdominal pain, fever, and diarrhea are also, of course, symptoms of gastroenteritis. To help in distinguishing the two diseases, I have made comparisons between the symptoms throughout the section below.)

With appendicitis, the pain generally starts in the area of the navel and gradually moves around to the right lower quadrant. It settles at "McBurney's point," the normal position of the appendix, which lies one-third of the way up on a line drawn between the right hip bone and the navel. (If the appendix is not located in the normal position, however, the pain may be elsewhere in the abdominal cavity.) In contrast, the child who has gastroenteritis will usually feel pain throughout the abdominal region, including the right lower quadrant, although the pain may be somewhat localized. A child's reaction to the two types of pain will usually be different, too. The child with gastroenteritis will tend to flop around and change positions in an attempt to get comfortable, while a child with appendicitis will move gingerly and as little as possible in order to avoid causing herself pain. The child with appendicitis may be most comfortable lying down with the knees drawn up and, when she walks, may lean to the right or limp on that side.

Because the bowels are reluctant to move much when there is an infection, bowel sounds are hypoactive or absent in the right lower quadrant, although you may hear some sounds in the other portions of the abdomen. In contrast, gastroenteritis causes hyperactive bowel sounds, so that you will hear lots of rumbling and gurgling, even without a stethoscope.

Appendicitis usually causes an inflammation of the lining of the abdominal cavity, or peritoneal lining. This inflammation results in "guarding" and "rebound pain." With guarding, the muscles that lie over the peritoneal lining in the area of the appendix become inflamed and rigid, so that the abdomen will feel rock-hard to your touch. A child who has gastroenteritis may tense up the abdominal muscles when examined, but the entire abdomen will become hard, and she will be able to relax the muscles voluntarily afterwards. With guarding, however, the rigidity is localized, and the

child has no control over it. Guarding occurs in approximately ninety-seven percent of children with acute appendicitis.

Rebound pain occurs when you press far into the abdomen in the right lower quadrant and then suddenly release the pressure. To determine whether or not the child has rebound pain, palpate the abdomen as previously discussed, beginning with the left lower quadrant. When you have worked your way around to the right lower quadrant, gradually press in as far as you are able as the child exhales. With the next breath, maintain even pressure on the inhalation, and then push in a little farther on the exhalation. Repeat this process for the next few breaths, until you have pressed very far into the child's abdomen. Then have her inhale, and on the next exhalation, pull your hand straight up as suddenly as you can, as if you were yanking it away from the surface of a hot iron. To visualize the effect you are trying to create within the body, imagine pushing down on a thin piece of rubber that has been stretched over a hoop. If you suddenly yanked your hand away, the rubber would snap back and actually stretch upwards slightly before settling down to its normal position. If the peritoneal lining is inflamed, that upward stretching is extremely painful, and your child will let you know about it. Appendicitis is by far the most common cause of rebound pain, and as such is the most significant finding in distinguishing appendicitis from gastroenteritis. However, if the appendix is positioned so that it is somehow shielded, it can be infected without causing an inflammation of the abdominal cavity. For this reason not every child with appendicitis experiences rebound pain.

A child with appendicitis may also experience pain when lying on his back and attempting to raise his right leg, although this is less common than rebound pain.

A rectal exam can be very helpful in diagnosing appendicitis. It is probably best, however, to let your doctor perform such an exam if appendicitis is suspected.

While appendicitis is not generally considered to be a preventable disease, it has been linked to constipation. In fact, appendicitis is one of the first diseases that appears when primitive cultures become more Westernized. This connection is probably due to a decrease in the amount of fiber in the diet. A diet that is rich in fiber will help to prevent constipation, and, possibly, appendicitis and other diseases as well.

APPENDICITIS/TREATMENT. There is some controversy over how appendicitis should be treated once it is diagnosed. Most commonly, of course, the appendix is removed immediately. However, some doctors are now treating appendicitis by placing patients in a hospital and putting them on intravenous fluids, antibiotics, and bed rest. In some cases where this type of therapy is used, surgery may be avoided altogether, assuming the appendicitis was caught early on and does not recur. If the appendicitis does recur, surgery may have to be performed at a later date. Some doctors who are using this treatment feel that the appendix should come out a few weeks later even if there is no recurrence, to ensure that there will not be one. When this is

done, the advantage of delaying surgery is that the antibiotic treatment markedly reduces the incidence of peritonitis (inflammation of the lining of the abdominal cavity), making the surgery a safer procedure with fewer complications.

Some doctors are also using the nonsurgical treatment in cases where the appendix has already ruptured or a mass (abscess) has formed around it. After the infection has been reduced, surgery must be performed. The traditional approach in these cases has been to operate immediately, but the surgery is simpler if antibiotic treatment is done first.

There is, however, a distinct disadvantage to choosing antibiotic therapy prior to (or even instead of) surgery: The average hospital stay is twelve to sixteen days, considerably longer than the average stay for an appendectomy. Two doctors who recommend immediate appendectomy found that of 133 patients, the hospital stay for those with acute appendicitis with no complications was 3.37 days. Those who had gangrenous appendicitis stayed an average of 4.75 days, while patients with perforated appendicitis with complications stayed the longest, an average of 9.45 days. (Of this group of patients, 11 [8.3 percent] had perfectly normal appendixes removed. Their average hospital stay was 3.27 days.)[1]

While none of the studies addressed this possibility, I see no reason a child who has been in the hospital on intravenous antibiotics for several days and whose condition has improved could not switch to oral antibiotics and finish out her course of treatment at home. Bed rest and blood tests done on an outpatient basis would still be necessary, but the child could then be spared both an operation and a long hospital stay. For parents facing a decision on which course of treatment is best for their child, this approach may be worth discussing with the child's doctor.

Abdominal Pain/Other Causes. There are several other conditions that can cause abdominal pain in children, including upper respiratory tract infection, urinary tract infection (see below), a twisted testicle (see below), infectious hepatitis (see chapter 2), and the following:

PNEUMONIA IN THE RIGHT LUNG. This condition may refer pain, tenderness, and muscle spasm to the right lower quadrant. In these cases the abdominal symptoms will be more apparent than symptoms in the lungs. Listening carefully to the lungs may uncover signs of pneumonia, such as rapid breathing or symptoms of respiratory distress. (See chapter 4 for more on pneumonia.)

TRAUMA TO THE ABDOMEN. If a child begins to experience abdominal pain within a few days of some sort of trauma to that area of the body (e.g., after a blow to the stomach while playing), the trauma should be considered the probable cause of the pain. The child should be seen by a doctor to determine whether or not any internal organs have been affected.

INGUINAL HERNIA. This will cause pain if it becomes strangulated. In most cases, you would already be aware of the presence of the hernia, and would be able to locate a painful mass in the groin area. (For more on hernias, see page 68.)

INTUSSUSCEPTION. Intussusception is a rare condition, usually occurring in the first two years of life, in which one portion of the bowel attempts to pass through another, causing an obstruction and severe pain. With intussusception, a normally healthy baby will suddenly have intermittent bouts of screaming (almost like colic, but more severe), may vomit and will pass "currant jelly" stools, which contain mucus and blood. This condition requires immediate medical attention and, in some cases, surgery.

MECKEL'S DIVERTICULITIS. Meckel's diverticulum is a pouch that forms near the lower end of the small intestine in about two percent of the population. If this pouch becomes infected, inflammation of the peritoneal lining may occur, and the symptoms of appendicitis will be present. In these cases, doctors diagnose the condition as appendicitis and then, during surgery, discover that it is, in fact, Meckel's diverticulum that is infected. The treatment is removal of the pouch.

ACUTE MESENTERIC LYMPHADENITIS. The mesentery is a fine membrane that holds the intestines in place and carries the blood vessels, lymphatic channels, and nerves to the intestinal tract. Acute mesenteric lymphadenitis occurs when lymph glands in the mesentery become infected, causing abdominal pain and, in some cases, inflammation of the peritoneal lining. This condition has a sudden onset and may result in symptoms of appendicitis, although usually the pain will not be localized in the right lower quadrant.

VOLVULUS. Volvulus is a twisting of the intestine that results in a blockage, causing severe pain and vomiting. This condition requires surgical correction.

Abdominal Pain/Doctor's Exam. If you suspect that your child has appendicitis or another serious condition, or have doubts as to what is causing his abdominal pain, your doctor will probably want to do a blood test to determine how many white blood cells are present and what type they are. If the child has appendicitis or other infection, the white blood cell count will probably be elevated.

A child who is in pain is not going to be cooperative during a doctor's physical exam, especially if she's at an age when she's wary of strangers or if she's previously had a bad experience in a doctor's office. This is perfectly understandable. After all, she was pretty uncomfortable at home, cuddled up on your lap, and now you want her to lie quietly on a big table while some stranger with cold hands pokes around in her sore tummy. No way. She's going to cry, scream, huddle in your arms, or do whatever she has to to avoid such torture. This makes it very difficult for the doctor to gather any helpful information. To make things easier for the doctor, hold the child on your lap so she will feel more secure. If she's still nursing, let her nurse, or give her a bottle if she takes one, or try to find something that will distract her from what the doctor is doing. If it's feasible, you may want to wait in the doctor's office, holding your child, until she falls asleep, and then have the doctor examine her. As a last resort, try examining the child yourself, letting the doctor observe where and how deeply you are pressing on the abdomen, and your child's reaction. This is less than ideal from the doctor's point of view, but it will give her more information than examining a screaming, squirming child will. In addition, if you have examined the child yourself at home, your observations can be extremely useful.

Giardiasis. Giardiasis is a parasitic infection of the small intestine that is characterized by diarrhea, gas, abdominal discomfort and loss of appetite. One of the identifying characteristics of giardiasis is foul-smelling, greasy feces that tend to float in the toilet. Other symptoms may include a low-grade fever, nausea, and vomiting.

Approximately twenty to sixty percent of children who become infected with the giardia parasite will have no symptoms. When symptoms do occur, they appear one to three weeks after exposure, and in most cases will disappear spontaneously in one to four weeks. However, the infection may become chronic, in which case it is characterized by intermittent bouts of excessive gas, a recurrent pain in the pit of the stomach, and mushy stools. It is not unusual for a child to develop chronic giardiasis without ever having experienced an acute phase of the disease. Preschool children who develop chronic giardiasis tend to grow poorly.

The giardia parasite is transmitted through contaminated water or food or through personal contact. In recent years, the disease has been on the rise among preschool children, with the incidence much higher in children who attend day-care centers than in those who do not.

Giardiasis can be diagnosed by microscopic examination of the stool, and if necessary, can be treated with prescription drugs.

Recurrent Abdominal Pain. Various studies have estimated that ten to fifteen percent of school-age children experience recurrent abdominal pain at some point in their lives. This can be a difficult and frustrating situation for both parent and child, who may be told that since no underlying organic cause for the pain can be found, it is psychological in nature. In my experience, most cases are related to problems with the diet and can be significantly alleviated through dietary changes. However, some cases may be related to emotional factors (for example, a child may experience very real stomachaches because she is having difficulty in school). In these cases, understanding the child's feelings and the stresses she feels may be the key to solving her problem. If you are unable to make any headway in discussing the situation with her, she may need to talk with another sympathetic adult.

In any event, keeping a diary that includes the foods your child eats, her symptoms, and any other factors that seem pertinent should help you get to the root of the problem. In this situation you—not your doctor—are in the best position to evaluate the situation and arrive at a solution.

If your child's recurrent abdominal pain has you really stumped, a consultation with your child's doctor may be useful, if for no other reason than to assure both you and your child that there is no serious underlying problem. The following list of guidelines was compiled by two doctors for other physicians to use when treating children with this problem. The points discussed below should be of value to you in working with your doctor and in dealing with your child.[2]

1. Assure the parents and the child that no major illnesses appear to be present. In particular, rule out and focus upon the precise diagnoses about which the family expresses most concern.

2. Identify the "red flags" for which there should be vigilance and which will suggest the need for further "organic" evaluation.

3. Avoid making emotional or psychogenic diagnoses strictly by process of elimination.

4. Do not communicate to the parents or the child that the youngster is malingering or that the problem is "only psychological"—unless there is very compelling evidence for this.

5. Develop a system of regular return visits to monitor the symptom.

6. Have the parents and the child keep a diary of pain episodes, diet, bowel habits, and stressful events to be reviewed during return visits.

7. Do not feel pressured to make any diagnosis on the first or second visits; allow for a denouement or gradual clarification of the clinical situation.

8. Avoid the temptation to apply pseudo-diagnosis or facile labels (e.g., "an allergy," "prolonged virus," a "nervous stomach"). Parents usually are willing to accept ongoing monitoring instead of a glib name.

9. Do not diagnose by therapeutic response. Potent placebo effects are especially the rule in the gastrointestinal tract.

10. During return visits, allow time with the child alone and also with the parents alone to uncover subtle stresses and/or maladaptive responses to pain.

11. Be willing and able to seek a "second opinion" when the parents and/or the child become disillusioned. Make it clear that after the consultation you would like to continue your involvement.

12. Make every effort to normalize the life of the child, encouraging him or her to attend school, to participate in regular activities, etc.

Getting to the root of recurring abdominal pain can be a long and difficult process, but I urge you to stay with it. If your doctor is unable to find anything wrong with your child, you may be tempted to brush it off as inconsequential or something that is all in your child's head. Just because your doctor can't find a cause doesn't mean there isn't one, however. Remember, you (not your child's doctor) are the person who is most capable of doing the necessary legwork to find the cause of an unusual problem. Play detective by reading the medical literature on the subject (and there is a wealth of information about abdominal pain, with many cases having obscure causes) and keeping a good diary. When you do discover the cause, both you and your child will be well rewarded for your efforts.

The Male Genitalia

GENERAL EXAM

If you are uncomfortable performing the examination of the genitals, or if your child objects because of modesty, you may choose to forgo this section of the exam. If so, you should have your doctor perform an examination of your child's genitals.

Check the tip of the foreskin if your son is uncircumcised. It will occasionally be slightly reddened, but this is not a cause for concern (in a circumcised boy, the tip of the penis may also become red, but this is less common). If the child is circumcised, you can also check the head of the penis. The urethra, the opening at the tip of the penis, should be large enough to allow a normal flow of urine.

Check to see if the foreskin has retracted. In an uncircumcised male, the foreskin will usually retract between two and three years of age, although it may not retract until later. When the foreskin retracts depends largely on the size of the fat pad in front of the pubic bone. If the fat pad is thick, it will push more skin down around the penis, so that when the boy gets an erection, the head

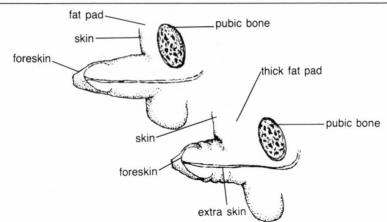

Fig. 2

of the penis will not be forced through the foreskin (see fig. 2). The foreskin usually will not retract until the fat pad is out-grown.

Check the scrotum for sores, redness, or tenderness. If you are examining an infant, also check to make sure the testicles have descended; you should be able to feel them in the scrotum. The testicles are usually in the scrotum at birth, or will descend within a few days, although this may take longer in a premature infant.

To make sure your son does not have a hernia or hydrocele, shine a small flashlight or a penlight behind the scrotum as the child lies on his back. You should be able to identify each testicle. They will appear as small, round dark spots that do not transmit the light well. In addition, check to make sure there are no tender bulges above the scrotum or on either side of the pubic bone.

CHARACTERISTICS/PROBLEMS/DISEASES OF THE MALE GENITALIA

SMALL URETHRAL OPENING. If the urethral opening seems too small, so that the urine isn't leaving the body in a stream, have your doctor check the opening during your next visit. Only rarely will it actually be so small that it requires correction.

UNRETRACTED FORESKIN. In most cases the foreskin will retract on its own in good time. If, however, your son reaches the age of about six and the foreskin still has not retracted, you should have it checked by your doctor. It may still be perfectly normal, but this is a good time to make sure. Your son will probably become more modest around this age, so that from this point on you may have few opportunities to observe whether or not the foreskin has retracted.

Many doctors recommend that parents push an infant's foreskin back, or will even attempt to force it back themselves, so that it will retract as soon after birth as possible. This is *not* a good idea, however, since the lining of the foreskin will tear if it is retracted too suddenly or aggressively. Once this happens, the foreskin will scar and may attach itself to the head of the penis, possibly resulting in the need for a circumcision later on. It is best to just leave the foreskin alone. It would also be wise, anytime a doctor is about to examine your child, to tell him *before he takes the child's diaper off* that you do not want him to push back the foreskin. If you wait until he is already examining the child, it may be too late.

Once the foreskin has retracted, uncircumcised boys should be taught to retract the foreskin and clean under it daily. Failure to do so can lead to an infection that causes scarring and phimosis, a narrowing of the opening of the foreskin. Once phimosis has occurred, the boy must be circumcised. Adolescent boys, in particular, may need to be reminded of the importance of cleaning under the foreskin, since the physical changes of puberty may make them slightly more susceptible to infection if they're a little lax about personal hygiene. Since adolescence can be a particularly difficult time to undergo a circumcision, I recommend a blunt reminder as preventative medicine. You can't follow your son into the shower, but you can make sure he understands how to take care of his body.

WHITE MASS UNDER THE FORESKIN. In an uncircumcised male, an oily substance called smegma is produced in the area where the head and the shaft of the penis come together. Smegma will sometimes accumulate under an unretracted foreskin, appearing as a white, tumorlike mass. If this happens, you should not push back the foreskin to try to remove the smegma, or attempt to work it out. It will clear up on its own.

CIRCUMCISION. In recent years the subject of circumcision has become very controversial. Much has been written on the subject, and I see no point in covering material here that is readily available elsewhere. If you are facing the decision of whether or not to have your son circumcised, I suggest you read up on the pros and cons of circumcision so that your decision will be an informed one. A helpful source of information is the article "Circumcision: The Uniquely American Medical Enigma," by Edward Wallerstein, which appeared in the medical journal *The Urologic Clinics of North America*, February 1985, Vol. 12, No. 1, page 123. There are several additional references listed at the end of the article.

I do have a few points to make on the subject, however. First, while there is no medical reason a male infant needs to be circumcised, in countries where boy babies are not routinely circumcised, twenty-five to thirty percent do require the operation in adolescence or adulthood. When performed after infancy, the operation involves the use of general anesthesia and a two-week recovery period. I'm not sure that these statistics justify circumcising all males at birth, but they should be considered.

At the present time, there is a controversy brewing over a recent study that concluded that the incidence of urinary-tract infections is significantly higher in uncircumcised males than in those who are circumcised. Critics of the study consider its conclusions invalid, and I tend to agree with them. At this writing, however, the issue remains unresolved, and may warrant further investigation on your part if you are considering circumcision for your child.

If you decide to circumcise your child, I believe it should be done according to the traditions of Judaism, most of which make sense for medical or psychological reasons. The operation should be performed on the eighth day, with the parents present, one of them holding the baby. Immediately after the circumcision, the baby should be nursed for comfort. I've done several circumcisions for which the parents brought in a sugar ball dipped in brandy that the babies sucked as the circumcision was performed, and the babies did not cry.

There is no doubt in my mind that babies do feel pain during circumcision. However, I don't agree with those who argue that the pain permanently damages the male psyche. If this were the case, we ought to be able to develop a psychological test that could separate circumcised from uncircumcised men, but so far this has not been done.

UNDESCENDED TESTICLE. If one or both of your son's testicles have not descended, he should be examined by your doctor. Testicles that do not descend before puberty will not produce sperm, although they will produce male hormones, so that the boy will develop normally. In addition, there is a higher incidence of testicular cancer in men who have a testicle that has not descended. Your doctor will probably want to give your son three injections of APL, a hormone found in the placenta, to get the testicle to descend. This works about a third of the time. When it does not, surgery is necessary.

PAINFUL TESTICLE. The testicles are always tender if too much pressure is applied, but a light touch will not be painful unless there

is an infection or the testicle is twisted. In either case, the testicle should be examined by a physician. If it is twisted, early detection may make it possible for the doctor to untwist the testicle and stitch it down so that it cannot twist again. If left untreated, the blood supply will be cut off, and the testicle will eventually cease to function, with respect to both sperm and hormone production.

HERNIAS/HYDROCELES. When the male fetus is in utero, the testicles are located in the abdomen. Before birth, the body secretes a hormone that causes the testicles to migrate from the abdomen through the inguinal canal and into the scrotum. If the opening through which the testicles migrate does not close properly, a hernia or hydrocele may result. A hydrocele occurs when a small opening is left, allowing fluid to accumulate in the scrotum. In the case of a hernia, a portion of the intestine squeezes through the opening that the testicle migrated through, and is either in the canal leading to the scrotum or in the scrotum itself. Hernias are more common in premature males and in males who cry frequently, who are often constipated, or who tend to strain a lot.

If, when you shine your penlight through the scrotum, the light diffuses through the tissue around the testicle, so that the tissue almost seems to fluoresce, your child has a hydrocele. The effect is similar to shining a strong flashlight through the palm of your hand, but greater. If you see a large dark mass when you shine the penlight behind the scrotum, there is a hernia that protrudes into the scrotum. It may or may not obscure the testicle, and there will be no fluorescent effect. A hernia in which the intestine protrudes into the groin area will appear as a tender bulge above the scrotum, or on one side of the pubic bone. The bulge may only appear when the child strains, cries, coughs, or laughs, or it may be apparent at all times and appear larger under these circumstances.

Hydrocele/Treatment. If you discover that your child has a hydrocele, there is no need to have it corrected. Hydroceles will usually correct themselves, and do not present a risk to the child. My son Jared had a hydrocele that did not clear up until he was seven, although it varied in size (getting larger at times). It did finally close spontaneously. If a hydrocele becomes large enough to interfere with daily activities or to cause emotional distress, you may want to consider surgery to repair it.

Hernia/Treatment. If you think your child has a hernia, he should be examined by your doctor. Surgery is advisable, even for an infant. Though you do not have to have the operation performed immediately, it is generally better to have it done sooner rather than later. In making this recommendation, I am assuming that the child is in reasonably good health and there are no pressing reasons for putting it off. I recently received a phone call from the parents of a premature baby boy, one of a set of twins, who had a hernia. The child's doctors wanted to operate immediately, even though the baby weighed only three pounds. In a case such as this, I see no reason for not waiting and allowing the child to gain weight, since the hernia is not placing him in any danger.

The reason it is usually best to operate on an uncorrected hernia relatively soon is that it can lead to serious problems if the protruding section of intestine becomes twisted or strangulated. If it does, the blood supply to the intestine will be cut off and gangrene can set in. A child with a strangulated hernia will become quite irritable and nauseated and will vomit. As the condition progresses, he will become feverish, and the abdomen may become hard, with a bulge in the location of the hernia. A strangulated hernia requires emergency surgery to cut out the section of dead bowel and rejoin the ends of the intestine.

Repairing the hernia before complications result is much safer and simpler, and will also allow you to choose the hospital, surgeon, and anesthesiologist you prefer. You may even be able to request that the operation be done in the morning, in which case the child should have recovered enough to go home by the afternoon, making the experience less traumatic for both of you. (The new "surgicare" centers that are cropping up in some parts of the country also generally send hernia patients home in a matter of hours, and are a good alternative to a hospital stay.) If you delay the operation, you could face an emergency situation when you've taken the child out of town, perhaps to visit his grandparents or take a vacation. In this situation, you'll have to settle for whatever hospital you can get to and the doctor and anesthesiologist who happen to be on call.

While surgery to correct a hernia is certainly preferable to the risks involved if the hernia becomes strangulated, it is still major surgery and not to be taken lightly. One study followed approximately nine thousand repairs per year over a four-year period, all on children under the age of fifteen. There were eleven deaths, most occurring in children who were not properly diagnosed and who were not operated on until complications had developed. Of the eleven children who died, eight were less than one year old, and one was a severely handicapped adolescent.[3]

While unlikely, it is possible for a hernia to recur after it has been surgically corrected, and to become strangulated. For this reason, it is important to watch the child carefully for any signs that the hernia has recurred.

As many as thirty to forty percent of children who have a hernia on one side later develop one on the opposite side, which can mean a second operation in the future. Doctors can perform a simple and highly reliable test (the Goldstein test) at the time of the first operation to determine whether or not a second hernia is likely to develop. If a weakness is detected on the second side, it can be repaired at that time, eliminating the need for a second operation at a later date.

The Female Genitalia

GENERAL EXAM

If you are uncomfortable performing the examination of the genitals, or if your child objects because of modesty, you may choose to forgo this section of the exam. If

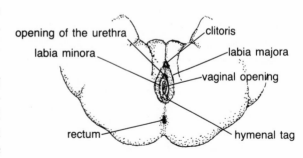

Fig. 3

so, you should have your doctor perform an examination of your child's genitals.

The female genitalia include two sets of vaginal lips: the inner lips, or labia minora, and outer lips, or labia majora. These lips form around the openings of the vagina and the urethra. The clitoris is at the top of the fold, covered by a hood of tissue (see fig. 3). The labia of newborn girls are swollen, and there is usually a clear mucous discharge from the vagina. There may even be a bit of blood in the mucus, due to the withdrawal of placental hormones. The discharge will clear up in two to three days, after which it should not reappear.

The area inside the labia should be pink and moist, and there may be an oily substance similar to smegma between the labia majora and the labia minora. If you spread the vaginal lips you should be able to see an opening in the hymen.

CHARACTERISTICS/PROBLEMS/DISEASES OF THE FEMALE GENITALIA

FUSED LABIA (NEWBORNS). The labia majora may be fused together at birth and may

85

need to be gently eased apart. If they do not separate easily, petroleum jelly can be applied to the lips to help in this process. Some doctors may prescribe female hormone cream for this purpose, but this isn't necessary.

LACK OF OPENING IN THE HYMEN. If you can't see an opening in the hymen, the girl has an imperforate hymen. This may pose a problem even in childhood and will definitely need to be corrected by puberty, when menstrual flow begins. An imperforate hymen can't correct itself, so your doctor will have to open it surgically to allow vaginal secretions and menstrual flow to pass through.

HYMENAL TAG. The hymen sometimes has a tag of tissue, from one-quarter to three-quarters of an inch long, that hangs down onto the buttocks and is quite obvious. There is no need to do anything about such a tag; it will usually shrink as the girl grows and eventually disappear. If it doesn't, it can be removed when the child is older.

VAGINAL DISCHARGE. After the newborn period, you need to evaluate any vaginal discharge in a child. A chronic vaginal discharge in a female of any age can be an indication of a food allergy, and may be eliminated by tracking down and removing the offending food from the diet (see chapter 12). A foul-smelling discharge is a sign of infection or of a foreign object in the vagina, which a little girl may think is a dandy hiding place (after all, no one ever looks *there*). If you can see an object in the vagina, you may be able to remove it your-

self. If you can't see one but suspect that an object is present, you should have your doctor perform a rectal exam. If there is an object, he will feel a hard lump, probably irregular in shape.

HERNIA. Hernias occur only infrequently in females, and when they do, often go unrecognized. A hernia in a female will appear as a painful swelling in the groin area or the top of the inner thigh. The symptoms of a strangulated hernia and the treatment are the same as for boys (see page 68).

Genitalia/Both Sexes

URINARY TRACT INFECTIONS

Urinary tract infections are the second most common infection seen in children (upper respiratory infections are the first), and are probably overlooked by both parents and doctors more than any other infection. They occur more frequently in girls than in boys, except during the first three months of life, when the incidence is higher in boys. Approximately three to five percent of school-age girls experience urinary tract infections, but the figure is less than 0.1 percent for school-age boys. About a third of the boys and forty percent of the girls who have been diagnosed as having one urinary tract infection will have another, and each subsequent infection increases the likelihood of additional recurrences.[4]

URINARY TRACT INFECTION/SYMPTOMS. The reason urinary tract infections are easily missed is that in children the symptoms are often vague and may come and go over several days. Typically, a child with a urinary tract infection will have an intermittent, low-grade fever (in fact, an unexplained fever may be the most significant symptom the child has) and will complain of feeling ill and of pain in her legs, back, and/or abdomen. She may also have a headache. Unlike an adult, she will probably not feel any pain or burning upon urination. She may or may not have to void more frequently, and there's a good chance she'll be constipated. Her discomfort will be mild enough so that she is easily distracted from it, but you will probably notice that her behavior and appetite are both slightly "off." She may complain of being sick in the morning, but once busy with school or play, forget about her symptoms until bedtime. In infants, the most common signs of urinary tract infection are irritability, poor weight gain, vomiting, diarrhea, and, in the newborn, early jaundice.[5]

A child who has an infection in the kidneys will often have pain in the costovertebral angle, or flank area—just below the ribs down to the top of the pelvis. If you pound lightly on the child's back in the flank area, using the little finger side of your hand (as if you were pounding on a desk), the child will feel pain if there is an infection in the kidneys. Older children who have a kidney infection also commonly have chills.

URINE CULTURE. If you suspect that your child has a urinary tract infection, a small amount of the urine should be examined under a microscope by your doctor for bacteria and white blood cells. The presence of bacteria may or may not indicate a problem, depending on how much time has passed between obtaining the specimen and examining it, since bacteria will normally grow in urine. If the urine is not examined until several hours after it is collected, the bacteria may have multiplied enough so that there appears to be an infection when, in fact, there is none. The presence of white blood cells indicates that there is a problem, either an infection or an allergy, and should be followed up with a urine culture.

URINE SPECIMEN/CLEAN CATCH. In order for your doctor to be able to gain any helpful information from the urine specimen, it must not be contaminated by bacteria from the skin. There are several methods of collecting a urine specimen. The bag method, which is used only on infants, is done by placing a small plastic bag either around the penis of a boy or over the urethral opening of a girl. This method is the least reliable, and yields a high rate of false positives due to bacteria picked up from the skin. The clean-catch method involves washing and drying the genitalia and then letting the child urinate a small amount into the toilet before you collect urine for the specimen. (Obviously, it is nearly impossible to get a clean catch on a child who does not yet have control of her bladder.) If the urine is only to be examined under a microscope, it may be collected in a clean jar. If it is to be cultured, however, the jar must be sterile. The disadvantage of the clean-catch method is that parents often do not sufficiently clean the genital area, so that, again, bacteria from the skin get into the urine. Also, with either this method or the bag method, the urine may be collected hours before it is examined. When this happens, any bacteria that have gotten into the urine will have multiplied enough to indicate the presence of an infection even if there is none. For this reason it is best to collect the specimen in the doctor's office, although it may be less convenient to clean the genital area there than at home. If the specimen must be obtained at home, it should be refrigerated until it is taken to the lab or doctor's office.

CATHETERIZATION. Another method is catheterization, in which a tube is inserted up through the urethra into the bladder to withdraw the urine. Catheterization can be particularly difficult to do in small children, and if done incorrectly, carries the risk of damaging the urethra or introducing infection into the bladder. It is also possible for the catheter to become contaminated by bacteria from the skin if proper technique is not used.

SUPRAPUBIC ASPIRATION. Finally, there is suprapubic aspiration, which is less common than it used to be. This involves inserting a needle through the skin just above the pubic bone, into the bladder, to draw the urine out. With suprapubic aspiration there is a small risk of hitting another organ with the needle or of hitting a blood vessel and causing bleeding into the bladder.

Assuming that the child is old enough to cooperate and the proper procedure is used, I feel that the clean-catch method is the best option, since it carries the least risk to the child. If a clean catch cannot be done,

however, catheterization or suprapubic aspiration may be indicated.

URINE CULTURE RESULTS. If your doctor finds bacteria or blood cells in the urine, he will want to do a bacterial culture, a colony count, and a bacterial sensitivity test on the specimen. The culture will confirm the presence of bacteria and identify their type, the count will tell him how many bacteria are present, and the sensitivity test will identify which antibiotic should be most effective (although, for various reasons, bacterial sensitivities are not always accurate). There is some controversy as to what level of bacteria indicates an infection, but the traditional criterion has been a count of more than ten to the fifth power (one hundred thousand) per milliliter of urine. This criterion is not an absolute rule, but several studies have found it to be appropriate approximately eighty percent of the time. Identifying the particular strain of bacteria can also be helpful in determining whether or not there is an infection. If the bacteria are a type commonly found in the intestines or on the skin, you and your doctor will have to take into account how the specimen was obtained and consider whether or not the bacteria might have gotten into the urine during collection.

Urinary Tract Infection/Treatment. It will take from three to five days to obtain the results of the culture. If your child is very uncomfortable, you and your doctor may decide to start her on an antibiotic immediately. If, on the other hand, the discomfort is mild, you may wish to treat her with large doses of vitamin C in the form of ascorbic acid, at least until the test results are available. The vitamin C that the body is unable to use will acidify the urine as it is excreted. Since bacteria grow best in an alkaline environment, lowering the pH factor of the urine in this manner will help to discourage its growth.

To determine how much ascorbic acid will be effective in acidifying the urine, you will need nitrazine paper, which is available in most drugstores. To use the nitrazine paper, dip one piece into a small amount of the urine. The paper will change color, becoming blue or green according to the acid level of the urine. You can then compare the color of the paper to the chart that is included to determine the pH. To treat the infection effectively, you want to bring the pH balance down to between 4.5 and 5, which is lower than normal. (A pH factor of below 7 is acidic, above 7 is alkaline.) Once you have brought the pH down to this level, you will have to recheck the urine every few hours and give the child enough vitamin C to keep it low for at least two weeks, after which you should have the urine reexamined by your doctor for bacteria and blood cells. In addition, have the child drink large quantities of water.

You may be tempted to substitute fruit juice for vitamin C, knowing that most juices contain a lot of ascorbic acid. While this is true, most also contain citric acid, which the body acts on in such a way that it actually raises the pH of the urine. The only fruit juice that will lower the pH is pure cranberry juice—*not* cranberry juice cocktail—and most children find it too sour to drink in sufficient quantities to have any effect.

You may find that your child responds so well to the above treatment that her symptoms significantly improve by the time the urinary culture results are available. In fact, some studies have shown that as many as eighty percent of first-time infections will clear up without antibiotic treatment. If your child has improved, it would be wise to have your doctor recheck the child's urine for white blood cells. If none are present, it is not necessary to follow up with antibiotic treatment. You should, however, have the urine rechecked for white blood cells about once a month for three to four months to make sure the infection does not recur. If her symptoms have not improved by the time the urine culture results are available, there are still blood cells in the urine, and the bacterial culture is positive, you will need to go ahead with antibiotic treatment to clear up the infection. In most cases the infection will respond quite well to one of the lesser antibiotics, such as sulfa, although your doctor may want to start out with one of the newer, more potent ones. Pharmaceutical companies often push newer products as the drug of choice for a specific disorder, such as a urinary tract infection, and doctors are swayed by this. However, unless your child has been very ill, it's not really necessary to use one of the stronger (and usually more toxic) drugs.

UROLOGIC WORKUP.   If a bacterial infection is present, your doctor may recommend a complete urologic workup to determine whether or not the cause is a congenital abnormality of the urinary tract, which occurs in a certain percentage of children with these infections. Such an abnormality must be corrected surgically, or it can lead to permanent damage to the bladder, urethra, or kidneys. The danger of damage is greater in a child under the age of six. For this reason doctors are usually particularly anxious to do the complete workup in a child under six, in order to detect any abnormality before damage occurs.

Making the decision to do a complete urologic workup is not simple, however. The workup consists of a blood test, additional urine tests, ultrasound of the kidneys, an intravenous pyelogram (IVP), and a voiding cystourethrogram (VCU). While the blood tests, urine test, and ultrasound of the kidneys are noninvasive and presumably safe, the IVP and VCU involve certain risks. The IVP is done by injecting a contrast medium or dye into the bloodstream. The dye is removed from the blood by the kidneys and then excreted in the urine. While this process takes place, a series of five to seven X rays are taken so that the progress of the dye through the kidneys, ureters, and bladder can be evaluated. As I've already noted, an individual should have only five X rays in a lifetime, so you would not want to subject your child to this many at one time unless absolutely necessary. In addition, a few children do have an allergic reaction to the dye, experiencing hives, nausea, vomiting, or even shock. The risk of death is approximately one in thirty thousand.

The purpose of the VCU is to determine whether or not "reflux" is taking place. Reflux is an abnormal backflow of urine from the bladder up the ureters as the bladder is emptied. The VCU, which is often done under general anesthesia, involves placing a catheter up through the urethra into the bladder and instilling a dye directly into the bladder. X rays are then taken while the child urinates, making it possible to determine whether or not reflux is taking place. If the child has an infection at the time the VCU is done, it is likely that there will be some reflux. For this reason it is best to wait until the child has been infection-free for four to six weeks before doing the test, unless the doctor detects a mass around the kidneys, in which case the test should be done immediately. Waiting for several weeks will ensure that the bladder has had adequate time to heal and that any reflux that may be detected is not due to the infection, but an abnormality in the urinary tract. The main risk involved in the VCU is the possibility of the introduction of bacteria into the bladder from the catheter, or damage to the urethra or bladder through improper technique during the catheterization.

Other tests that some doctors are now using include those in which radioisotopes or radioactive tracer elements are introduced into the bladder. These have the advantage of exposing the child to much less radiation than do X rays. However, the tests are generally considered to yield less information than the IVP or VCU. Computed tomography (CT or CAT scan) and magnetic resonance imaging (MRI) are also being used by some physicians. Both of these require that the patient lie still, which may be difficult for a young child unless she is sedated. CAT does use X rays, but MRI does not involve the use of any radiation and presents no known risks to the child. Both CAT and MRI are very expensive.

Many doctors now recommend doing a urologic workup after the first bacterial infection, while some prefer to wait until the child has a second infection. The decision of whether or not to submit your child to these tests is a difficult one that you will have to make in consultation with your doctor and a urologist, taking into account your child's medical history. There are some factors that indicate that a complete urologic workup is absolutely necessary: elevated blood pressure; signs of malformation of the kidneys, such as low-set ears (see chapter 3); abnormalities of the external genitalia or any other congenital defects that are commonly associated with abnormalities of the urinary tract; or an abnormal growth pattern. In the absence of any of these factors, I would hope, however, that you would not be pushed into a workup without first weighing the potential risks against the potential benefits for your child. This is not an easy task, nor is it a decision anyone else can make for you. I can tell you, though, the procedure I would follow if I were faced with this decision regarding one of my own children. I would first want to be absolutely certain that the bacteria found in the child's urine were actually growing there and were not a result of improper collection or handling of the specimen. In a child over one year of age, I'd treat a first infection as outlined above, with vitamin C and fluids. If that didn't work, I would also give her antibiotics. In this case I would not do the workup unless the infection recurred, but if it did, I would feel that at least some tests

were justified. For a child under a year, I'd do the workup after the initial infection. I feel this would be necessary because there are few reasons a baby would have a urinary tract infection, and I would want to determine whether or not a congenital abnormality was the cause. However, before any other tests I'd do a suprapubic aspiration and a culture on that urine, since in an infant that is the only way to be certain the bacteria did not come from the skin.

RECURRENT UTI. Recurrent urinary tract infections do become a problem for a significant number of children. If this is the case for your child, you should learn how to use one of the quick screening methods to test your child's urine at home so that you can detect an infection and begin treatment as early as possible. One study has shown that home screening would detect at least eighty-three percent of asymptomatic urinary tract infections.[6]

If your child's urine culture is negative and yet there are white blood cells present and the child is experiencing symptoms of a bladder infection, the problem is probably a viral infection of the bladder. Most physicians do not recognize such infections, but as viruses can affect every other organ in the body, including the brain, heart, and liver, it is my belief that they can also affect the bladder. A viral infection will cause acute symptoms that clear up and then do not recur.

If, on the other hand, there are white blood cells present but the culture is negative and the symptoms become chronic, a food allergy is at the root of the problem.

But don't be surprised if your doctor disputes this idea, too, since it is also not a view that is commonly held. Food allergy has been linked to kidney disease,[7] however, and it seems logical to conclude that if food allergies can affect the kidneys, they can certainly affect the bladder as well. (For more information on tracking down and eliminating food allergies, see chapter 12.)

The Rectum

GENERAL EXAM

No routine examination of the rectum is necessary, unless your child complains of discomfort or seems to have a chronic itch in the area. If he does, the problem will probably be one of the two below.

CHARACTERISTICS/PROBLEMS/DISEASES OF THE RECTUM

PINWORMS. Pinworms are tiny worms, usually smaller than a half-inch in length and less than half a millimeter in diameter (about the thickness of heavy-duty thread), that live in the human intestine and lay their eggs around the rectal opening. Pinworms are not a serious infection. The worst symptom is the itching. Occasionally the worms will lay their eggs in or around a girl's vagina, causing intense itching and, in some cases, a vaginal discharge.

Pinworms are very easily transmitted, and anyone can get them, regardless of race, religion, or socioeconomic status, and in spite of good personal hygiene. The substance the pinworm uses to attach the eggs to the skin is mildly irritating, causing the skin to itch. Once they have been scratched off the skin the eggs can end up on (and then be picked up from) any object the hand makes contact with, and they can also become airborne in dust particles and then inhaled. One study has shown that, in households with several members infected with pinworms, ninety-two percent of 241 dust samples collected from the floors, baseboards, tables, chairs, davenports, dressers, shelves, picture frames, windowsills, toilet seats, washbasins, bathtubs, bed sheets, and mattresses contained pinworm eggs, with the majority of the eggs found in the bedroom.[8] When one member of the family has pinworms, at least one other member is usually infected.

Once the eggs are ingested, they travel through the digestive system, hatching in the small intestine and then migrating down to the area around the cecum and appendix. Upon reaching maturity, the female pinworms crawl out of the rectal opening and lay their eggs—approximately eleven thousand per female. (It is not clear how long it takes for the pinworm to cycle through the digestive system and reach maturity, but estimates in medical literature range from two weeks to two months.) Many people believe that pinworms crawl back into the intestines after laying their eggs, but parasitologists seem to agree that they then die instead. The eggs can remain alive outside of the body for up to thirteen days under cool, moist conditions, although one study found that fewer than ten percent of the eggs survived two days even with favorable conditions, and that in hot, dry weather, the survival rate was below ten percent after just three hours.[9]

Pinworms/Diagnosis. Pinworms are diagnosed by placing a piece of clear tape (such as Scotch brand tape, but not the "invisible" type) around a tongue blade and then dabbing it around the rectal area. In order to be reliable, this test must be done early in the day, before the child has bathed or had a bowel movement. The tape is then placed on a slide and examined under a microscope for eggs. A single test of this nature reveals about fifty percent of infections, and three tests, about ninety percent. Seven consecutive days of negative tests are required before a patient is considered free from infection. Some doctors may also wish to have a stool specimen examined, but eggs are found in the stool only about five percent of the time. Another common recommendation is to examine the rectal area early in the morning hours (e.g., three or four A.M.), when the females are most likely to lay their eggs.

Pinworms/Treatment. The medical treatment for pinworms is Vermox (mebendazole), which is given in a one-dose, chewable tablet to children over the age of two and adults. The drug is usually taken again, approximately two weeks later. Vermox is known to cause birth defects and should not be taken by pregnant women. The medical alternative to Vermox is Povan, a dye that is taken internally. It is not absorbed into the body, but it does turn the stools bright red, and if vomited (as occasionally happens) can permanently stain clothing. Povan is also usually given a second time, two weeks after the initial treatment.

If your children are old enough to comply, you can also just be extremely careful that nothing that might be contaminated with pinworm eggs is placed in the mouth and that hands are kept away from the face. Since the eggs must cycle through the intestinal tract to hatch, this will prevent new pinworms from hatching, and eventually those living in the intestinal tract will die out.

In addition to taking care of the pinworms in the body, it is important to thoroughly clean your house to eliminate as many of the eggs as possible. Bedclothes and linens should be washed and dried on high heat. Stuffed animals can be treated by tumbling them in the dryer, again on high heat, and other nonwashables can be placed in the oven on a low setting to kill the eggs. Most chemicals, including insecticides and chlorine, are not effective against the eggs.

ANAL FISSURES. Anal fissures occur for two reasons. In an older child, they are usually the result of a large, hard stool that stretches the skin excessively when it is passed, causing a small tear. Once this has happened, having a bowel movement will cause intense burning and itching. The child will go to great lengths to avoid moving her bowels, dancing and hopping around to hold the stool as long as possible. This will make her even more constipated, so that when she finally does have a movement, the stool will be hard and difficult to pass, aggravating the problem. You can easily treat this problem by giving the child a mild laxative to keep the stools loose for a few days, allowing the fissure to heal.

A baby or toddler may develop an anal fissure because of a yeast infection. It will usually be accompanied by a yeast diaper rash (see chapter 3). In addition to treating the yeast infection by placing acidophilus in the mouth, you can also make a paste from the contents of the capsule and a small amount of water and apply it to the area around the rectal opening and just inside the rectum.

The Well-Child Quick Checklist

THE ABDOMEN

1. Note the shape of the child's abdomen.

2. Listen to the bowel sounds. They should sound normal for your child.

3. Feel the abdomen. You should not be able to feel any organs, although you may feel fecal matter in the intestines.

MALE GENITALIA

1. Check the tip of the foreskin if the child is uncircumcised.

2. Check to see if the foreskin has retracted.

3. Check the head of the penis if the child is circumcised or if the foreskin has retracted.

4. Check the scrotum. There should be no sores or redness.

5. Use a flashlight to check for a hernia or hydrocele.

6. Check the groin and the areas on either side of the pubic bone for tender bulges.

FEMALE GENITALIA

1. Check the labia; they should be pink and moist, and there should be no mucous discharge except in a newborn.

2. Check for an opening in the hymen.

Notes

1. Robert S. Bennion, M.D., and Jesse E. Thompson, Jr., M.D., F.A.S.C., "Early Appendectomy for Perforated Appendicitis in Children Should Not Be Abandoned," *Surgery, Gynecology and Obstetrics*, Vol. 165, No. 2 (Aug. 1987): p. 95.

2. M. D. Levine, M.D., and L. A. Rappaport, M.D., "Recurrent Pain in Children: The Loneliness of the Long-Distance Physician," *Pediatric Clinics of North America*, Vol. 31, No. 5 (Oct. 1984): p. 969.

3. S. J. Harper, M.D., and G. H. Bush, M.D., "Deaths in Children With Inguinal Hernia" (letter), *British Medical Journal*, Vol. 296 (Jan. 16, 1983): p. 210.

4. Ellen Kravis Hamburger, M.D., "Urinary Tract Infections in Infants and Children: Guidelines for Averting Permanent Damage," *Postgraduate Medicine*, Vol. 80, No. 6 (Nov. 1986): p. 235.

5. Ibid.

6. H. R. Powell, M.D., D. A. McCredie, M.D., and M. A. Richie, M.D., "Urinary Nitrate in Symptomatic and Asymptomatic Urinary Infection," *Archives of Disease in Childhood*, Vol. 62, No. 2 (Feb. 1987): p. 138.

7. R. Genova, M.D., et al., "Food Allergy in Steroid-Resistant Nephrotic Syndrome" (letter), *The Lancet* (June 1987): p. 1315.

8. Harold W. Brown, M.D., and Franklin A. Niva, M.D., *Basic Clinical Paracyntology*, 5th ed. (Norwalk, Ct.: Appleton-Century-Crofts, 1983): p. 128.

9. Ibid.

Chapter 6

The Spine and Extremities

The Spine
....

GENERAL EXAM

Have your child stand, either completely undressed or just in underpants, as is appropriate for his age, hands at his sides. Check to see that the shoulder blades protrude equally on each side and are level. Check to see that the pelvic bones are also level.

In a child age eight or older, check for scoliosis, or curvature of the spine. (Children are routinely checked in school for scoliosis, but you may want to do these simple tests anyway. If your child is among the increasing number who are taught at home, it is especially important to test him yourself.) To determine whether or not there is an abnormal curvature of your child's spine, have him bend at the waist and touch his toes. If you feel the spine while the child is in this position, you will notice that on each vertebra there is one point that is higher than the rest. This point is called the spinus process. With the child still bent over, use a felt-tip pen to mark each spinus process with a dot, and then have him stand up straight. The dots should be in a straight line.

You can also do the Forward Bending Test, which is used in some schools. For this test, have the child stand, feet together, and bend from the waist, holding the palms together. Look down the back for any asymmetry of the rib cage or lumbar area, which will appear as a hump on one side of the spine or as a noticeable lateral curve to the spine. If two or more of the three signs—rib hump, lumbar hump, or lateral curvature—are present but are minor, or if one sign is present to a major degree, the child probably has scoliosis.[1]

CHARACTERISTICS/PROBLEMS/DISEASES OF THE SPINE

PROTRUDING SHOULDER BLADE, UNEVEN SHOULDERS OR HIPS. If one of your child's shoulder blades protrudes excessively, in much the same way as it does when reaching one arm behind the back as if to grab the hair, she may have scoliosis, although this also occurs in some children with a deformity of the spine. Uneven shoulders or hips in a child of any age are also an indication of scoliosis, although this condition is uncommon in children under the age of eight.

CURVATURE OF THE SPINE. If your child "fails" either of the tests above, there is some degree of curvature in the spine. Scoliosis occurs with about equal frequency in girls and boys, but in boys the curvatures are usually of a lesser degree and they tend not to progress. Some studies have shown that approximately twenty times as many girls as boys develop scoliosis that progresses and/or requires treatment. Scoliosis does run in families, but seventy percent of cases are seen in children with no family history of the disease. Scoliosis is generally detected during puberty, around age twelve for girls and age fourteen for boys, when children are growing at a rapid rate. It tends to get worse through puberty, although in some cases it will progress only to a certain point and then stabilize. Scoliosis is seen in two to four percent of the general population and in two to sixteen percent of school children.

Scoliosis/Diagnosis. If your child seems to have scoliosis, she should be seen by your doctor, who will use a scoliometer to measure the degree of the curvature. A curve of less than ten degrees is considered normal and generally does not require treatment. The degree of the curve will help you and your doctor decide whether or not your child should be seen by a specialist. Your doctor may want to do X rays at this point, but I suggest holding off until you see the specialist to make sure that you do not end up having the X rays taken twice.

Scoliosis/Tests. If a visit to a specialist seems to be in order, I recommend that you take her to an orthopedic surgeon whose practice consists almost entirely of patients with this condition. (Ask him specifically what percentage of his patients are being treated for scoliosis.) Someone who deals with scoliosis on a daily basis will be more confident in assessing your child's progress without taking frequent X rays. Some doctors want to X-ray a patient with scoliosis every three to six months, but this is not justified unless there is evidence that the curvature is rapidly getting worse. The FDA has recently expressed concern over the X rays involved in scoliosis treatment. As many as twenty X rays may be done over a three- to five-year period, with the radiation affecting both the breast tissue and the thyroid. (On lateral X rays of the spine, the breast tissue can and should be shielded.) You will probably have to consent to an initial set of X rays to establish the extent of the problem, but after these are done the doctor should be able to use clinical means to determine whether or not the curvature is becoming more pronounced.

Some specialists are now using magnetic

resonance imaging (MRI) to evaluate patients with scoliosis. The advantages of MRI are a good, clear picture of the spine and no known risks (MRI does not involve radiation), but it does have the disadvantage of being very expensive. For this reason, most doctors will probably want to do X rays first to confirm the diagnosis, and then use the MRI to obtain further information. However, if you have a particular reason to want to skip the X rays altogether—such as your child's excessive exposure to radiation in the past or an abnormally high risk of cancer—you may be able to persuade your doctor to just go with the MRI. Some physicians are now recommending that MRI be done routinely on all patients with scoliosis in order to detect any correctable causes of the curvature (tumor, infection, herniated disc, or other disease), conditions that should be treated before the scoliosis is treated, or conditions that may actually be worsened by scoliosis correction.[2]

There are some factors that can be taken into consideration in predicting whether or not the curvature will grow worse. As noted, girls are more apt to have progression. The younger the child is when the scoliosis is detected, the more likely the curve is to progress.[3] As important as the child's chronological age, however, is her physiologic age. A mature twelve-year-old who is diagnosed as having scoliosis may have less progression than a late-blooming fourteen-year-old. In addition, curvatures in the upper spine tend to progress more than those in the lower spine, and the more severe the curve is, the greater the chances of progression. There are also some calculations your doctor can make,

involving measuring the rotation of the vertebral bodies, that may help to predict progression of the curvature.

Scoliosis/Treatment. If the curve is bad enough, the doctor may want to put the child in a brace, and, in severe cases, he may recommend surgery, which involves placing metal rods in the spine. This is major surgery and best avoided if at all possible.

You may be able to avoid using a brace and/or having surgery by taking your child to a chiropractor and a physiatrist (a physician who specializes in physical therapy) or physical therapist. Even though there is controversy regarding these practitioners, they do offer an alternative to surgery. The chiropractor will attempt to correct or arrest the curve through spinal manipulation and possibly through the use of a type of electrical stimulation called transcutaneous neuromuscular stimulation (TNS). I recently read of a case study in which a fourteen-year-old girl with a severe curvature was able to avoid surgery through chiropractic treatment involving both manipulation and TNS.[4] (The article also lists forty-four studies having to do with scoliosis; if you're looking for an alternative therapy, this list would be a good starting point.)

A physiatrist or physical therapist will provide exercises to help strengthen the muscles involved. Some physical therapists and physiatrists are now also using lateral electrical surface stimulation (LESS) to treat scoliosis. This therapy involves placing electrodes on the patient's back as they sleep at night. The electrodes are connected to a small battery-powered transmitter, so that the muscles are stimulated—and, it is hoped, strengthened—by electrical impulses. LESS is not appropriate in all cases, however.

While a chiropractor and a physiatrist or physical therapist may be able to help arrest or correct the curve, I suggest you also continue to see the orthopedic surgeon, as he will be the best able to monitor it for changes. While there is no guarantee that either therapy will work, they are worth trying, particularly if the alternative is surgery. However, if the curvature is severe and surgery seems to be the only way of correcting or arresting the problem, you should give it serious consideration. Scoliosis should not be ignored, as it can lead to crippling later in life if left untreated.

The Extremities

GENERAL EXAM

Examine the extremities to see if they are symmetrical. There may be some normal differences, such as hands or feet of unequal sizes or legs of different lengths. To check the size of the hands, place the palms together and compare the length of both the hands and the fingers. For the legs, lay the child on his back or stomach and hold the feet together. The ankle bones and the heels should line up. If they do not, or if you are still not sure that the legs are the same length, you can measure each leg from the pubic arch down to the ankle bone on the inside of the leg and compare the measurements, which should be about equal.

Look for swollen joints and check to see that the arms, hands, fingers, legs, and feet all move in a full range of motion. Test them for flexibility, making note of any stiffness or pain during movement. Watch the child walk. She should walk normally, with no limping, shuffling or staggering, and the feet should be straight, with no toeing in or out.

Examine the hands for calluses, warts, and sores, and check the nails for brittleness or peeling.

NEWBORNS' HIPS. If you are examining a newborn, it is important to check for congenital dislocation of the hips, which occurs in approximately one of every two thousand to three thousand babies. It is more common in breech babies and girls, and the condition tends to run in families. Dislocation is easiest to detect before a baby is six weeks old and is best treated in the first four months of life.

To check for dislocation, place the baby, undressed, on his back on a table, with his legs pointed toward you and his buttocks near the edge of the table. Hold the knees, bending them so that they are at right angles to the abdomen (see fig. 1). Place the knees at the midline of the body, almost touching each other. With both hands on the knees so that your thumbs are touching the inner thighs and your fingers are touching the outer thighs, gently turn both thighs outward and down. You should be able to turn the thighs out to a ninety-degree angle, or until they almost touch the table, without any resistance. If you are unable to get the thighs out to at least a seventy-degree angle, one hip is probably dislocated. A

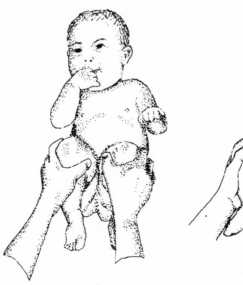

Fig. 1

click that you feel or hear in one of the thighs as you turn them out is also a sign that that hip is dislocated. As you bring the legs back up and extend them out toward you, you may also hear the click of the ball slipping back into the socket. If one hip is dislocated, you may also notice that the folds in the skin on the fronts of the thighs and/or the backs of the thighs are dissimilar.

Another sign of a dislocated hip is extra folds in the skin on the front or back of one thigh. A leg that has extra folds may be shorter than the other, and that hip is probably the one that is dislocated.

BABIES' FEET. Check the feet. All newborns have feet that appear to be flat, but in fact they are just fat. As this baby fat disappears, the normal arch of the foot becomes apparent. Even if your child does have flat feet, there is nothing you can do to change them. No shoe can alter the arch of your child's foot, or strengthen his ankles, or make any other structural changes in the

foot. Shoes are strictly for the protection of the foot from the environment. Babies don't need hard-soled shoes the minute they begin to walk; bare feet are great indoors, and socks and sneakers are perfectly adequate for providing protection from the heat or cold outdoors.

CHARACTERISTICS/PROBLEMS/DISEASES OF THE EXTREMITIES

LEGS OF DIFFERENT LENGTHS. It is not uncommon for the legs to be different lengths. A difference of more than half an inch will probably cause the child some back problems, and even a difference of a quarter inch may result in backaches. This problem can be treated by a chiropractor or by an orthopedist, who may suggest placing a lift in the shoe of the shorter leg.

LIMPING. A sudden limp, particularly on the right side, may be a sign of appendicitis, and a limp that appears soon after a child begins to walk may indicate a congenitally dislocated hip. Limping without a history of injury may indicate disease of the hip bone.

TOEING IN OR OUT. A child who is just beginning to walk may turn his toes in or out because the leg muscles are not yet fully developed. Over the next eighteen months these muscles should become strong enough to correct this turning in or out. If your child has been walking for more than a year and a half and the problem persists, you have three options for treatment. The first of these is to see an M.D., who will prescribe quarter-inch wedges to be placed on the outside of the soles of the child's shoes. If the child's feet turn in, the wedges will be placed on the outer edges of the soles, causing the feet to turn in even further. This signals the body to strengthen the muscles that pull the feet out, so that when the wedges are removed, the feet will be straight. If the toes turn out, the wedges will be placed on the inner edges of the soles, so that the body will try to correct the exaggeration by strengthening the muscles that pull the feet in. It is not necessary to see an M.D. to have these wedges made for your child's shoes; you can have the same wedges put on just by taking the shoes to a shoemaker.

Chiropractors often feel they can correct these problems with adjustments. If you choose this course of treatment, you should be able to see a change after a few visits.

The third option is to take the child to a physical therapist or physiatrist, who can prescribe a set of exercises that will strengthen the weak muscles. If you do the exercises with your child, there is no need to make repeated visits to the therapist.

BRITTLE/PEELING NAILS. Nails that are always brittle and tend to peel may indicate a problem with the child's diet or a disease condition. They should be brought to your doctor's attention.

DISLOCATED HIP. Should you suspect that your infant has a dislocated hip, have him examined by a doctor to confirm the diagnosis. If she feels the click but feels that it is too slight to present a problem, have the baby examined by someone else. One study found that of several newborns with minor clicking of the hips, a significant number were found to have serious hip pathology about four months later, even though the clicking was considered "normal" at birth.

If your baby is found to have a dislocated hip, your doctor will recommend that she be dressed in two or three diapers to hold the legs in a froglike position, probably for a period of about six weeks. This will keep the ball of the femur in the socket. The socket will then be stimulated to grow and form around the ball, so that the hip cannot dislocate. If an older child is discovered to have a dislocation of the hips, treatment may consist of traction to relocate the muscles, after which the child may need to wear a cast for as long as six months.

SPRAINS/STRAINS. Traumas to the extremities, such as bruises (see chapter 2), fractures (see chapter 18), and strains are common in children. Much less common are sprains, although they do occur in teenagers, particularly those who are active in sports. A strain is an injury to a muscle, usually caused by overuse, and is characterized by pain, swelling, and, sometimes, discoloration of the skin. A sprain, which is an injury to a joint involving damage to the ligaments, is also characterized by pain, swelling, and bruising. A strain or a mild sprain will heal without treatment, but you should apply ice or a cold pack to reduce the swelling, and try to rest the affected muscle as much as possible to speed healing.

A child with a strained limb might stop using that limb, leading you to suspect that it is broken when it is not. Even if the limb is broken, it is not an emergency situation (see chapter 18 for important exceptions); you can actually wait overnight before making arrangements to have it set. If you suspect that a limb is strained, and it is not obviously broken, I recommend that you do just that: Wait until the next day. If the condition has improved, the limb isn't broken, and it will heal nicely on its own. If it hasn't, follow the procedures for a fracture outlined in chapter 18.

If an injury to a joint, particularly the knee or ankle, is very painful or does not improve after two to three days, the problem may be a severe sprain involving torn ligaments, or even a fracture. Torn ligaments can be difficult to diagnose, and are often undertreated, which can result in poor healing and a permanently weakened joint. If the joint quickly puffs up and gets very large, and then over the next couple of days develops a bluish coloration, suspect a torn ligament. The bluish coloration is due to a broken blood vessel in the ligament. Over the next few days, the colored area will grow larger as the blood is spread out to be reabsorbed, and if the injury is to the knee or ankle, it may spread all the way to the toes. Proper treatment for torn ligaments usually involves putting the injured limb in a device that immobilizes the joint, much like using a cast on a fracture. Be careful about any treatment for a torn ligament or severe sprain, particularly if your child is athletically inclined. The injury should be treated by a doctor who specializes in sports medicine to help ensure that the ligaments are set so they will heal as completely as possible and the joint will not be weakened.

Neurological Exam

I do not feel that the physician's neurological exam of the newborn is helpful in the majority of cases. Certainly, if you have reason to suspect a neurological disease (I'll have more to say on this later), it can be invaluable, but the vast majority of the time the best "neurological exam" is simply to be aware of how your baby or child functions throughout the various stages of his growth. Nevertheless, I've found that when I start talking to parents about relying on their own neurological evaluation of their child, they get nervous. I suppose part of this is simply due to the connotations of the term "neurological," which conjures up visions of neurosurgeons and a sophisticated understanding of the complex workings of the brain. You should realize, however, that most of the problems that parents and even doctors label as "neurological" are really developmental in nature: developmental delays or peculiarities that really aren't within the neurologists' realm of expertise. The pediatric neurologist has more knowledge on the subject of neurological disease than on variance of development.

There is, in fact, a very wide range in what is considered normal development. For example, some children walk when they're seven months old and some not until twenty months. In any study of human development there results an inevitable bell-shaped curve, with most of the children right in the center, all reaching the same milestones at about the same time, and a much smaller number of children at each end of the curve, either faster or slower than the majority. Now, you will undoubtedly compare your child to others you know: your own older children when they were infants and toddlers, your friends' children, your nieces and nephews. Most of them will probably be in that large majority of kids at the center of the curve. If your child is one of those whose development is progressing at a slower but still normal pace—and your best friend's baby just happens to be one of those who does everything early—you may end up unnecessarily worried about your child. Feeding into your anxieties will be comments from well-meaning friends and relatives who can't understand why your little Tommy still isn't walking at eighteen months, when their little Susie toddled her first steps at nine. The result may be that you enter into a seemingly endless cycle of medical evaluations, trying to determine what is "wrong" with your child.

So you take your child to the pediatrician for a consultation, telling her you think there might be a neurological problem. This puts enormous pressure on the doctor. If you, who know the child better than anyone else, suspects that something is wrong, the doctor has to do everything she can to rule out even the most rare neurological problem before she can in clear conscience label your child "normal." The result may be numerous visits to specialists until a consensus can be reached that your child is just developmentally delayed, not abnormal. If just one of these specialists raises the possibility of some rare condition that your child might have, the result will probably be a whole new batch of tests to rule it out.

You may also find yourself caught up in a round of neurological evaluations because of concerns your doctor raises, even if you have been relatively certain your child is fine. This sometimes happens because the doctor is focusing too much on numbers on a chart and not enough on your individual child's development. The doctor may also be expecting your child to "perform" at a time when he's feeling shy or anxious. He may be perfectly capable of walking across a room unassisted at home but end up falling down several times when asked to do the same thing in the doctor's office. If your doctor's assessment seems to be based on your child's failure to pass little "tests" you know he could easily do at home, you should feel perfectly comfortable in deciding that the problem lies with the circumstances under which the judgment is being made, and not with your child.

You might also take into consideration the doctor's experiences with child development and his or her own biases. If you're seeing a young doctor with no children of his own and relatively little experience in practice, he may be relying too heavily on those charts. Or your doctor may be biased toward a certain subspeciality. For example, I've known some doctors who were particularly interested in learning disabilities and who seemed to pick them up in a disproportionately high percentage of the children in their practice. Or your doctor may even be comparing your children to his own. If they happened to be early in developing, he may expect the same from your kids. This type of expectation on your doctor's part may be hard for you to assess, but it is worth consideration when you're evaluating the doctor who is evaluating your child.

If you feel that your child is not developing normally, you'll want to speak with someone about your concerns. For all of the reasons stated above, your doctor may not be the best person to speak to first. If, for example, your one-and-a-half-year-old is still not walking, it may be more helpful to talk to various family members. The child's grandparents and great-grandparents may be able to assure you that all of the boys in their family walked late. If this is the case and your child seems normal in other respects, you can simply chalk up his late development to a family trait. If you are unable to get reassurance from a family member about your child's development, you may then want to see your doctor for a further evaluation.

NEUROLOGICAL EXAM/NEWBORNS

Now let's get back to the reasons you might suspect there are problems in a newborn that would justify a neurological workup. When you a hold a normal newborn in your arms she seems to respond to you; she has an awareness of your presence. If the baby just lies still, does not interact with you at all, and has poor muscle tone, there may be a problem. A baby who has trouble sucking and nursing may also have a neurological problem, although this is certainly not an absolute indication. Seizures, jerky movements, and physical abnormalities are also red flags that would indicate the need for a neurological evaluation. Other considerations are difficulties during labor and delivery, such as the baby not getting enough oxygen at times, or the presence of meconium (an infant's first stool) in the amniotic fluid.

In addition, there are three simple tests for the newborn that will give you an indication of whether or not there may be some neurological problems. To do the first of these, lay the infant on his back, and ring a bell near one ear. He should turn slightly in the direction of the sound. Next, take a bright red disc, about six inches in diameter, and hold it twelve to eighteen inches above the baby's nose. Move it slowly to one side. The baby should follow the movement of the disc somewhat, although he will probably be unable to track it very far. Finally, take a piece of cheesecloth or gauze and drop it over the baby's face. He should attempt to bring his hands to his face to push it away. He does not need to succeed in removing the cloth from his face, but just to attempt to do so. If the newborn passes these three tests, it is unlikely that there are any neurological problems.

However, if there are indications that your newborn may have a neurological problem and you and your doctor feel that a complete neurological exam is in order, you should be aware that the tests are far from infallible. It is entirely possible for a child who tests abnormal on the exam to grow up perfectly normal, or vice versa. If the results are abnormal, however, this is an indication that the child's progress should be carefully followed for further signs of neurological problems. You should also note that the tests are indirect measurements of brain function, not direct evidence of brain damage. The only way you get direct evidence of brain damage is through examining a piece of brain tissue, which is a far cry from the type of tests being performed. Even if limited progress in some area of development is predicted for your child, he may far surpass the expectations, depending on the underlying cause of his problem, which will not be determined by the doctor's neurological exam.

Congratulations! You have completed the physical exam.

The Well-Child Quick Checklist

. . . .

THE SPINE

1. Check to see that the shoulders and hips are level and that the shoulder blades protrude equally on each side.

2. In a child of eight years or older, check for scoliosis.

THE EXTREMITIES

1. Examine the extremities to see if they are symmetrical.

2. Look for swollen joints and check the flexibility of the arms, hands, fingers, legs, and feet.

3. Watch the child walk.

4. If examining a newborn, check for congenital dislocation of the hip.

5. Examine the hands for calluses, warts, and sores, and check the nails for brittleness or peeling.

NEUROLOGICAL EXAM

1. If examining a newborn, conduct the three neurological tests.

Notes

1. Annabel Chan et al., "The Case for Scoliosis Screening in Australian Adolescents," *The Medical Journal of Australia*, Vol. 145, No. 8 (Oct. 20, 1986): p. 380.

2. Steven R. Nokes, et al., "Childhood Scoliosis: MR Imaging," *Radiology*, Vol. 164, No. 3 (Sept. 1987): p. 791.

3. John E. Lonstein, M.D., "Natural History and School Screening for Scoliosis," *Orthopedic Clinics of North America*, Vol. 19, No. 2 (Apr. 1988): p. 227.

4. Donald D. Aspegren, D.C., and James M. Cox, D.C., "Correction of Progressive Idiopathic Scoliosis Utilizing Neuro-Muscular Stimulation and Manipulation: A Case Report," *Journal of Manipulative and Physiological Therapeutics*, Vol. 10, No. 4 (Aug. 1987): p. 147.

Part Two

The Well Child

Breast-Feeding, Weaning, and Nurturing

A lot has been written about breast-feeding in recent years, and if you are the parent of an infant or small child, you have undoubtedly read at least a little on the subject already. You may, in fact, have read so much that you wonder what more could possibly be said on the subject that would be news to you. A great deal, surprisingly. Although medical literature is full of reports of studies concerning breast milk and breast-feeding, very little of the information is actually available to the general reading public. One of my goals in this chapter is to make some of that material more accessible to parents. In addition, I hope to clear up a few of the common misconceptions about nursing and to present my views on the more controversial topics surrounding the subject of breast-feeding.

What I will *not* do in this chapter is rehash in detail information that is readily available from other sources. If you need help with the basics of breast-feeding or one of the day-to-day problems that nursing mothers sometimes encounter, pick up a copy of *The Womanly Art of Breast Feeding* by La Leche League,[1] the definitive handbook on the subject. You'll find it extremely helpful. Support and information are also available in abundance from local La Leche League leaders. (Your family doctor, obstetrician, or pediatrician should be able to supply you with a local telephone number or you can call 1-800 LA LECHE for a free catalogue and information about local groups.)

It is my belief that virtually all women with at least one breast are physically capable of nursing a baby. Contrary to popular wisdom, the amount of breast tissue a woman has has no bearing on how much milk she is able to produce. When women do run into problems, the cause is almost always a lack of knowledge, support, or both. I do not mean to suggest that all women can easily breast-feed, however. For some, significant changes in life-style or diet may be required. However, I found that all the women in my practice who were willing to follow the advice provided by La Leche League were able to nurse their babies successfully.

The system of supply and demand of breast milk is really quite remarkable. It is so perfectly balanced that even a woman who has twins will produce enough milk to support them both without the need for supplements. It is also feasible for a woman to have three children of different ages who all nurse, or for a woman to resume nursing months or even years after her baby has been weaned. Simply having a baby or child sucking at the breast will signal the body to begin producing milk again. In fact, the mother of an adopted baby may also be able to stimulate her breasts to produce milk, even if she has never been pregnant. In many of these situations, if the demand is there, the breasts will supply enough milk to meet it.

It is also possible to nurse while pregnant. A woman must realize that her nutritional needs will increase substantially during this time, however. A pregnant woman's metabolism is up twenty-five percent, and a nursing mother's metabolism is up sixty percent. A woman who is both pregnant and nursing must watch her diet carefully to be sure she is getting enough calories and nutrients to support her own body and those she is nurturing. Even if she is careful about meeting her nutritional needs, however, a woman in this situation will probably experience a significant decrease in her milk supply. If the baby is only two or three months old, she may not produce enough to provide adequate nourishment. (If this happens to you, I suggest you consult with a La Leche League leader regarding your concerns. But if the baby seems to be continually hungry, or is not gaining weight, then consult your family doctor about choosing a supplement.) Another difficulty the pregnant nursing mother may encounter is her own sudden resistance to the idea of breast-feeding her infant. Women I've talked with have described this as an "antsy" feeling that comes over them whenever they sit down to nurse, so that they feel that they just can't stand to do it. If the nipples are tender during the early stages of pregnancy, nursing may actually be painful, too. (For some mothers, this restless feeling and nipple soreness are often the first indications that they are pregnant again.) Whether or not a woman chooses to wean at this stage will usually depend on the age of her baby and her commitment to breast-feeding, although I recommend sticking with it if at all possible.

The pregnant mother of a nursing toddler may find that he chooses to "wean" around the third or fourth month of her pregnancy, when her milk turns to colostrum. Often, however, the toddler will return to the breast after the baby is born. Even the toddler who truly weans during the pregnancy—or the older child who has not nursed in years—may ask to nurse after the baby comes as a way of checking that his place is still secure. If the mother refuses him, he'll feel that he has been replaced by the baby. For this reason, I think it's important to let the child know that he can nurse if he wants to. He may very well change his mind once he finds out that the breast is still available to him. In my own family, my son Jared was about eight before he stopped asking to nurse after each of our subsequent children came along. Once reassured that the option was still open to him, he would change his mind.

Some women are discouraged from nursing their babies because they must take medication, but this is usually unnecessary. I know of only three medical conditions that should prevent a woman from nursing her baby: tuberculosis, cancer, and AIDS. The medications necessary to treat tuberculosis and cancer are passed on through the breast milk and are unsafe for a baby, and AIDS itself may be communicated through breast milk. Many doctors also recommend against nursing if the mother contracts infectious hepatitis, but I do not feel that this is necessary. Remember, hepatitis is transmitted through fecal content (see chapter 2). If the mother is absolutely scrupulous about hygiene, she should be able to continue to care for her baby and even nurse without passing on the disease.

For almost every other medical condition of which I am aware, there are drugs available that either will not be passed along through the breast milk or will not adversely affect the baby. People often make the mistake of associating the breast with the placenta and assume that everything a woman ingests will find its way into her milk, in much the same way as everything (or just about everything) passes through the placenta. However, the placenta is an organ whose specific purpose is to transfer nutrients to the fetus, while the breast is a gland whose purpose is to secrete milk. You would not assume that any medication you take would affect the secretions of your adrenal glands or your pituitary gland, and yet many people assume that any drug will affect the breast milk. This does not mean, of course, that a nursing mother can be careless about what she ingests, since some drugs will be transferred through the breast milk. But for every illness except cancer and tuberculosis, there are safe drugs. You may find, however, that your doctor categorically rejects the idea of nursing while taking medication. This happens because doctors rely on the *Physicians' Desk Reference* (PDR) to determine whether or not a particular drug is safe for the nursing mother. The information in the PDR is supplied by pharmaceutical companies. In most cases, the companies recommend against the use of the drugs in nursing mothers because it is too expensive for them to do all the testing required to meet the Food and Drug Administration's criteria to be approved for such use. Often, however, studies have been done, usually by independent researchers. Should you have specific questions regarding drugs and breast-feeding, the La Leche League recommends consulting the American Association of Pediatrics' Drug List.[2] You may also call your La Leche leader, who will check the list for you.

For many drugs, you can also just use a commonsense approach. For example, if your doctor prescribes an antibiotic that is considered safe for a baby to take directly in small quantities, it is logical to assume that the same drug will not be dangerous to the baby in the levels it reaches in breast milk.

Some doctors may also recommend against breast-feeding if the mother is diabetic. However, one study has shown that the only difference between the milk of diabetic women and that of others is a slight elevation in sodium and glucose levels, which would not affect the baby.[3] While there are special health considerations that the diabetic mother must take into account, it is possible for her to nurse, just as it was possible for her to bear a child in spite of her diabetes.

Breast-Feeding and Healthier Babies

From their experiences in practice, doctors have long known that breast-fed babies are much healthier than bottle-fed babies, and the medical literature on the subject bears this out. In 1977, one study found that 88.4 percent of babies who were exclusively bottle-fed after the age of three weeks had a significant illness during the first year. The numbers dropped to 76.2 percent for babies who were nursed up to four and a half months of age, and down to 42 percent for those who were nursed longer.[4] Several different studies have shown that the incidence of middle ear infection is much lower in breast-fed babies, as is that of gastroenteritis. One study done in 1978 in a middle-class American community found that of thirty-five infants hospitalized for gastroenteritis, all but one were bottle-fed.[5] In addition, several studies have also found breast milk to be protective against eczema and food and upper respiratory allergies.

So the health advantages of breast-feeding are well documented and have been for many years. It is only recently, however, that we have begun to understand *why* breast milk makes babies healthier. In the past several years, scientists have been able to identify thirty-seven different immune mechanisms in breast milk. One of the most interesting of these is white blood cells, which are present in abundance. For years their purpose was misunderstood, and some doctors and scientists actually went so far as to consider their presence in breast milk a "mistake." We now realize, however, that these white blood cells serve a very specific and important function. When a nursing mother contracts a viral or bacterial infection, she harbors the infectious agent in her body for a few days before she becomes ill—and contagious. She then passes the virus or bacteria on to those around her, including her baby. The infectious agent will begin to multiply in the baby's system, and around the second day, the baby would usually begin to get sick. Since the mother has had the same illness, however, the breast milk now contains a white blood cell called a phagocyte, whose sole function is to eat that particular virus or bacteria. This defense mechanism actually may prevent the illness or reduce its severity. Because of this mechanism, it is unwise for a mother who is ill to stop nursing her baby.

Some of the other immune properties of breast milk are the five immunoglobulins, which are antibodies normally produced in the lymph tissue in response to an invasion of foreign substances such as viruses, bacteria, or allergens. Each has a specific function within the immune system, and breast milk contains all five. In addition, breast milk contains interferon, which inhibits viral activity (see chapter 11); lysozyme, which breaks down the cell walls of certain bacteria; and lactoferrin, an iron-binding protein that inhibits the growth of a harmful bacteria in the intestines, to name just a few.[6]

Other components in breast milk, while not specifically involved in the prevention of disease, contribute to the better health of breast-fed babies. One of these elements is taurine, an amino acid that is present in large quantities in breast milk. Though taurine is not considered essential to life, it has many functions. These include maintaining the structural integrity of certain cellular layers of the eye, facilitating the formation of synaptic connections in the brain, and regulating cell growth, particularly in the brain and the eye, where the highest concentrations of taurine are found. Taurine deficiency has been found to result in growth retardation in monkeys,[7] and, if sufficiently prolonged, in retinal degeneration in humans.[8]

The role taurine plays in brain growth may be its most important, and it is certainly significant that the highest concentrations of taurine are found in developing tissues during periods of rapid growth, such as infancy. In fact, ninety-five percent of brain growth takes place by the age of five years. With this in mind, what do you think is the average age for infant-led weaning in countries where it is truly allowed to occur? Five years. I'm convinced that this is not a coincidence.

Since a baby is even less capable of syn-

thesizing taurine than an adult (who has only a poor ability to do so), a dietary source of taurine is extremely important. Cow's milk, which is rich in amino acids that promote large muscles and big bones (entirely appropriate for cows, but less than ideal for people), contains no taurine. Taurine *has* recently been added to some formulas, but it does not provide the same benefits as taurine from breast milk.[9]

Taurine is particularly important for premature babies, who need large amounts for proper development of the brain. An "outside" source (that is, other than breast milk) of taurine does not increase the amount found in the body. One researcher has suggested that "taurine should be considered an essential nutrient for premature infants."[10] Premature babies, then, have an even greater need for breast milk than full-term babies. (Interestingly, the breast milk of mothers of premature babies has been found to be different from that of full-term babies, and appears to be particularly suited to their special needs.[11])

In the adult diet, taurine is found in meat, poultry, and seafood. Vegetarians have been found to have somewhat lower quantities in the plasma and breast milk than omnivores. Whether or not this reduction in breast milk taurine is great enough to have any significance for a nursing infant is not yet clear.[12]

As important as they are, the physical properties of breast milk are only one aspect of what makes nursing so good for babies and small children. The emotional nurturing that takes place at the breast is also invaluable. If instinct alone were not enough to convince us that babies need an abundance of physical contact, science has convincingly demonstrated that touch is extremely important, and even plays a significant role in the development of the central nervous system. In one study, primate infants were denied all physical contact. Later examination of their brain tissue showed that they had sixty percent fewer dendrites—the tree-like parts of the cell that convey impulses to the body of the cell—than primates who were touched and held.[13] (I get very concerned when I hear parents say they're afraid of spoiling their baby by holding him when he cries, even though he doesn't "need" anything. Maybe he's trying to get a message across: "Hey, Ma, my dendrites need stimulating.") In addition, a study done at the University of Miami Medical School found that the nervous systems of premature babies who were gently massaged every day developed more quickly. (They also gained weight faster.)[14]

Bottle-fed babies, of course, are held and cuddled, too, and I don't mean to suggest otherwise. The baby who is breast-fed, however, is virtually assured of having his need for nurturing through touch fulfilled. An overworked, harried mother can hand over a bottle to her one-year-old or prop it for an infant, but there is no way to nurse without holding a baby close. That physical contact is just one more way that breast-feeding contributes to a baby's overall good health and well-being.

Although most doctors do concede that breast-fed babies are generally healthier, many still persist in thinking that they need iron and vitamin D supplements, considering breast milk to be a less than adequate source of these nutrients. Supplements are not necessary, however. The idea that breast-fed babies need supplementary iron stems mainly from two misconceptions. The first of these is based on the fact that many bottle-fed babies who receive cow's-milk-based formulas become anemic, usually around the age of six months. Since cow's milk actually contains slightly more iron than breast milk, doctors assume that breast-fed babies must also be iron-deficient. However, the reason a bottle-fed baby becomes anemic is that the child's body is able to absorb only about thirty percent of the iron in cow's milk. In contrast, the iron in breast milk is virtually one hundred percent absorbable, so that the breast-fed baby is actually less likely to become anemic.

A doctor may also conclude that a breast-fed baby is anemic after doing a hematocrit that shows a low ratio of red blood cells. If the child has just had a growth spurt, a low red blood count may simply indicate that his blood production is lagging slightly behind his weight gain. Given a little time, his blood production will catch up to his weight, and he will no longer show a deficiency of red blood cells.

I also believe that a baby may appear to be anemic simply because babies and toddlers do not need the same iron count as older children and adults. This may be because of the immune mechanism lactoferrin, which is dependent on a low level of iron in the baby. If the baby is saturated with iron, lactoferrin may be hampered.

Unless a breast-fed infant is severely anemic (and this is rare), I do not believe there is any reason to use iron supplements. However, if the baby's red blood cell count is unusually low, the mother's should also be checked. If she is anemic, her body may be unable to provide enough iron in her breast milk to keep her baby adequately supplied. In this situation, the mother should be given supplements, not the baby. Once she is receiving enough iron, there will be enough in her breast milk to provide for her baby.

Like the presence of white blood cells in human milk, the presumed lack of vitamin D in breast milk has sometimes been considered another of nature's little "mistakes." In reality, however, there is plenty of vitamin D in breast milk—if you know where to look for it. Because most sources of vitamin D are fat-based, researchers have separated the fat from the aqueous portion of breast milk, examined the fat, and found no vitamin D. Some scientists have looked for vitamin D in the aqueous portion of the milk—the part they had previously tossed into the sink—and found as much as a baby needs. One large study showed no deficiency of the vitamin in breast-fed infants who did not receive supplements.[15]

Breast Milk, Formula, and Solid Foods

There has been a tendency in the medical community to compare the composition of breast milk against that of formula as if formula were the model that must be lived up to as a baby's perfect food. Consider, for example, this quote from a medical journal:

"Although breast milk contains less protein and energy than formula, this does not constitute a problem because breast milk is so well suited to the infant."[16] It would make more sense to turn this statement around, to say that the composition of formula may present problems because it contains more protein and energy than breast milk. This same backward thinking is applied to expectations concerning infant growth patterns. At around the age of six months, bottle-fed infants tend to start getting larger than babies who are breast-fed. As a result, doctors will often conclude that breast-fed infants need supplemental feedings in order to take care of this "lag" in growth. However, they are comparing the growth of the breast-fed babies against reference standards for bottle-fed babies, who grow at a faster rate. To date, there has been no large study to chart the normal growth patterns for babies who are exclusively breast-fed. A doctor who tells you that your breast-fed baby "needs" solid food or formula is working under the faulty assumption that breast-fed and bottle-fed babies should have the same growth patterns. In fact, studies have been done in Japan of children who were highly allergic and so received nothing but breast milk for the first two years of life. These children showed no nutritional or growth problems whatsoever. As one researcher in the field has suggested, "as long as the infant is growing, there is no need to add supplemental foods."[17]

As you may have guessed by now, I am of the opinion that infants should *not* be started on solid foods between the ages of four and six months, as is often recommended by doctors. (Even La Leche League suggests beginning solids at six months.) There are some very good reasons to delay the introduction of solid foods into your child's diet. One important reason is that the introduction of either solid foods or supplemental formula seems to reduce the effectiveness of breast milk's immune properties. One study conducted in India observed three groups of children: one group was exclusively breast-fed, one was fed both breast milk and supplemental formula or solid foods, and one was fed only formula and/or solid foods. The breast-fed children had the lowest incidence of disease and mortality. The babies who had mixed feedings had slightly fewer gastrointestinal problems than those who were artificially fed, but their rates of respiratory diseases, middle ear infections, and skin diseases were essentially the same.[18] Two more interesting studies were done in Guatemala, where the children are typically breast-fed for the first two to three years, with solid foods being added to the diet around five to six months. While the purpose of these studies was to illustrate how disease and diet work together in causing malnutrition, one of the findings was that the incidence of overt disease increased substantially after complementary foods were started.[19]

Another good reason to keep your baby on a diet of breast milk alone is that a baby's intestinal tract is not fully developed until several months after birth, perhaps as late as eighteen to twenty-four months.[20] Digestion is a complicated breakdown process that begins in the mouth when food is mixed with saliva, and continues throughout the digestive tract, with the stomach, pancreas, liver, and intestines all playing a unique role. Various enzymes are involved in each stage of digestion, speeding up the breakdown of food and converting it into a form that can be utilized by the body. Some of these enzymes are present only in very low levels or are entirely missing from the infant digestive system.

One of these enzymes is amylase, which plays a key role in the digestion of carbohydrates. The common suggestion for a baby's first food is cereal or fruit, both carbohydrates. However, amylase is present at just ten percent of adult levels in an infant's small intestines, and is virtually nonexistent in the pancreas until at least six months of age.[21] Ptyalin, an enzyme in saliva that breaks down carbohydrates, does not appear until around twelve months of age. When carbohydrates are introduced into a baby's diet too early, he may be unable to digest them completely. The result can be poor nutrition due to failure to absorb the nutrients in the food, and possibly diarrhea.

This lack of enzymes presents no problem to the breast-fed baby, since human milk contains more than twenty enzymes that become active in the stomach so that the milk is easily digested. One of the most important enzymes contained in breast milk is lipase, which helps to break down fats, from which forty to fifty percent of the energy in both human milk and formula is derived. Not only is formula completely lacking in lipase, but at least one researcher has suggested that "these compensatory, or complementary, mechanisms for fat utilization . . . are less effective when cow's milk fat or other fats are introduced into [the] diet,"[22] so that the baby who is fed supplementary formula may have more trouble digesting even breast milk than if he were on a diet of breast milk alone.

Some lipase is produced at the back of an infant's tongue as he nurses. You may have noticed the "milking" action that's made with the back of the tongue as an infant sucks. It seems probable that this action helps to stimulate lipase secretion and to mix the lipase with the milk to begin digestion. Since drawing milk from a bottle involves just sucking, this effect is eliminated if a baby is bottle-fed.

Because formula contains no enzymes, the bottle-fed baby is more prone to digestive problems. Protein molecules, which may cross the underdeveloped intestinal lining before they have been completely broken down, can be particularly troublesome. These molecules can then act as antigens, causing an allergic reaction.

Digestive problems are often compounded when modified food starch, a common ingredient in commercial baby foods, is added to the diet. Modified food starch, usually derived from corn or tapioca, has an even lower level of digestibility than other carbohydrates. In order for modified food starch to be effective, it must make up approximately five percent of the product. While this may not sound like much, at this level it contributes about thirty-two percent of the food's total calories.

My recommendation regarding solid foods before one year is to start with proteins rather than carbohydrates and to introduce them no earlier than eight months of age, but preferably not until one year. Hydrochloric acid, which helps digest protein, begins to appear in the stomach around the seventh or eighth month of life.

It would seem, therefore, that the body would first be ready to digest proteins (at eight months) and then carbohydrates (at one year). By holding off on introducing any solid foods (or formula) until the age of one year, you can be certain that the digestive tract is sufficiently developed to be able to handle the foods you put into it. Remember, too, that *breast milk contains everything your baby needs to thrive and be healthy for at least the first year of life, probably for the first two*. There's really no reason to feed him anything else, and there are several good reasons *not* to.

"Wait a minute," you may say, "my five-month-old is ready to eat. I know, because he practically grabs food out of my mouth, he wants it so desperately." It's true that babies do get intensely interested in food around this age, but not because they are dying to eat. They just want to imitate your rather strange custom of sitting around a table and putting something in your face three times a day. It doesn't matter to the baby whether that something is food or the dust balls from under your bed; he just wants to do what you're doing. The way we've solved this little problem at our house is to buy some small toys, which we call mouth toys, that we bring out only at mealtimes. This tactic won't work if you just give your baby one of the mouth toys when you sit down to dinner, however. Instead, put it on your plate, so that when she wants what you have, you can hand the toy over. If you take things one step further and actually put the toy in your own mouth a few times, the baby will be doubly convinced that this great mouth toy is really what mealtime is all about.

When you do introduce solid foods to a child older than one year, I suggest you do so by letting the child feed himself. Give him soft foods, such as cooked vegetables, that are easy to chew (if you wait until he's a year old, you don't have to strain and mash everything), and let him go at it. Allowed to discover food this way, your baby won't overeat, and will tend to stay away from the foods to which he is allergic, unless they are somehow made socially desirable. (If you, for example, down a bowl of ice cream in front of him every day, with obvious delight all over your face, your baby is going to want that ice cream whether or not he is allergic to dairy products.) Children are generally very good at picking out the foods they need and eating the right amounts. Offered only nutritious foods and allowed to eat as much or as little as they want, they will usually eat a balanced diet over the course of several days, although it may appear terrible on a day-to-day basis. If you insist on spooning the food into your baby's mouth, you will influence what and how much he will eat, and interfere with his own inherent good judgment. True, leaving a baby to have his way with a bowl of peas and carrots may result in an awful mess, but it will also give your child a strong start toward good eating habits. You can minimize the damage by putting some sort of drop cloth under the high chair—or, better yet, getting a cat or dog, who will soon become your baby's best friend, at least at mealtimes.

A toddler who is allowed free access to the breast will eat solid food sporadically until he is about eighteen months of age. One day he will consume almost nothing, and the next will put food away like a two-hundred-pound field hand. You needn't worry about your baby's fluctuating appetite while he is still nursing, however, since his nutritional needs will be met from breast-feeding.

You will also find that your toddler does not eat three meals a day, but instead prefers to pick and snack all day long. I suggest you work with this tendency rather than trying to fight it. Prepare a plate of food in the morning, then let the child choose whatever he wants from it as the day goes on. This will save you the trouble of dropping everything to prepare some tidbit every hour or so, while it will allow your child to graze to his heart's content.

Weaning

This topic is a difficult one, partly because people do not often discuss it openly, and partly because I am a man, and so have never nursed a baby (as I sometimes tell people, I'm still trying to get pregnant). However, I feel that the viewpoint that I am about to present is an important one, and one that is receiving more and more support from the studies that are currently being done in the field.

I firmly believe that the child should determine when he wants to wean. Unfortunately, this does not often happen in our culture. For a variety of reasons, we tend to wean our children before they are ready, and I fear we overlook the needs of the child in doing so. Wootan's theory on emotional needs (and this is, certainly, just Wootan's theory) states that we are each born with an empty jar inside that needs to be filled with love, tenderness, and kindness in order to develop a good self-image and become a kind and loving adult. I believe that we as parents have about eight years in which to stuff that jar as full as possible. After that, the jar seals over and it becomes difficult to get anything more inside. From my experience, nursing well into a child's early years is absolutely the best way to be sure his jar is filled to the brim.

From my work with couples in my practice, I have found that one of the most common reasons a woman decides to wean is that she has reached a point in her breast-feeding career when she feels that she just cannot stand to do it any longer. She feels like she's had her baby attached to her breast throughout her own entire life, not just the baby's. I think this feeling is a response to the unrelenting demands of motherhood in a society that does not particularly value the work mothers do. Mothers give, give, and then give some more, until their own resources are thoroughly depleted. Unfortunately, our culture does little to reward them or even acknowledge their efforts; there is no financial gain or prestige associated with the career of mother. Consequently, the nursing mother's emotional bank runs dry, so that she looks for ways of replenishing it. Often this means returning to a job, school, or some other activity that allows her to feel that she is getting back to her own life, *and* weaning her child so that she will have the freedom to do so. The job provides her with a paycheck that tells her in very tangible terms that she is appreciated and that her skills are valued; schooling or volunteer work brings her recognition and positive feedback—the very things she is not likely to get staying at home and nurturing her child.

Ultimately, however, I think both mother and baby would benefit if her need to feel valued and appreciated could be met in the home. Society's attitudes toward motherhood aren't going to change overnight, but husbands can meet these needs if they are sensitive to the problem. Too often, it seems, husbands are not very supportive of a woman's decision to breast-feed their baby beyond the first few months, and, more importantly, they don't understand that the woman who spends her days giving everything she's got to her child needs a little love and nurturing in return. Compounding this problem can be the fact that fathers (especially first-time fathers) very often feel neglected and left out after the baby is born. The nursing mother and baby make a new kind of couple, with seemingly little room for a third party. As a result, the father may withdraw his support and/or increase his demands in order to get a little more attention. It has been my experience that if a husband is able to provide enough emotional support and to let his wife know that her work is valued, she will feel happier in her role as a mother and more willing to continue giving to her child by nursing him; she will also have more energy left over for her relationship with her husband.

Let me add, too, that often emotional support is not enough, particularly for the mother of more than one child. Caring for small children *and* managing the cleaning, laundry, shopping, and cooking is a job and a half, and the woman who tries to do everything around the house will probably end up hassled and exhausted. She may feel that it's easier to prop a bottle for the baby rather than nurse him, so that she can get some work done while he's getting his nourishment. Husbands can make an immeasurable contribution here by taking on a fair share of the housework.

Before I get myself into too much trouble, let me point out that I certainly don't mean to imply that a woman's desire to do more with her life than care for her children is not legitimate. There is, after all, more to life than nursing and changing diapers. It is my belief, however, that nursing through the first year of life is crucial, and that every child should, ideally, nurse until ready to wean. From what I have seen, once a woman's needs are met and she begins to receive some nurturing as well as always giving it away, she is able to continue nursing without feeling that it is a strain.

For the woman who absolutely must return to work, a job and breast-feeding need not be considered mutually exclusive. If a woman's work situation enables her to pump milk during the day to save for feedings when she is away, her baby will benefit from receiving breast milk exclusively. While this might not seem practical, keep in mind that breast milk can be kept at room temperature up to eight hours; it can be stored in a cooler to take home; and it can be refrigerated for three to five days. In either case, the nursing mother who must spend the day away from her baby may find that he wants to latch onto the breast the minute she returns from work and stay there for most of the night. While this will un-

doubtedly be inconvenient, I think it's important for the mother to realize that her baby may need extra reassurance. She can provide this by letting the baby nurse as much as he wants and by sleeping with him (for more on sleeping with your child, see chapter 10).

Weaning may also come about as a result of a "nursing strike," which the mother will interpret as a true readiness to give up the breast. With a nursing strike, the baby will suddenly seem to lose interest in breast-feeding. The cause of a nursing strike may be physical discomfort, perhaps from teething or an ear or sinus infection, or it may be due to social conditions, such as when a baby is unable to nurse in peace because the mother is distracted by older children. If the problem behind the strike can be eliminated, the baby will happily return to nursing.

A nursing strike should not be confused with the normal declines in interest in nursing that every baby experiences. These tend to occur between the ages of about eight to eleven months and thirteen to sixteen months. This seeming lack of interest is a consequence of the socialization process. The baby between eight and eleven months of age has become so interested in everything around him that he can't concentrate on nursing. The slightest noise will distract him, and he'll turn his head in an attempt to discover its source (unfortunately for the mother, he often tries to take her nipple with him). Between about thirteen and sixteen months, the baby has become mobile and intensely interested in exploring. It's hard for him to settle down to nurse because he's got work to do: There are drawers to empty, newspapers to shred, and stairs to climb, and he wants to get on with it all. Typically a baby of this age will nurse for thirty seconds, climb down to do a little "work," only to return in five minutes, wanting to nurse for another thirty seconds. During these stages, the mother may feel that the baby isn't really interested in nursing, since he does not nurse the way he once did. If she waits the stage out, however, she'll find that he eventually passes through it and once again easily settles down at the breast.

Occasionally a mother assumes her child is weaning himself because she is able to distract him from his desire to nurse. She may never overtly reject the child when he wants the breast, but may instead offer an attractive alternative, such as cookies and milk. The child may be looking for the emotional satisfaction of being held and nursed, not something to fill his stomach. If he knows he'll have to work his way through milk and cookies before being allowed to nurse, he'll give up asking, because he doesn't really want that kind of nourishment. The mother may feel that the child has weaned himself, when in fact he has been reacting to her influence.

Even a woman who is reluctant to wean her child may end up doing so because of pressure from outside sources. It is hard enough to ignore critical comments from friends or acquaintances, let alone from one's own husband, parents, or in-laws. One of the worries I have often heard expressed about late nursing is that a child will become "addicted" to nursing. Fathers especially seem to worry that a son will grow up to be a "sissy," or be overly attached to his mother, if he is not weaned

soon enough. These fears are groundless. Nursing is not addictive; every child will wean eventually. And in some of the ethnic groups that we view as producing the most "manly" men, such as the American Indians and the Japanese Samurai warriors, children were commonly nursed throughout early childhood, often until as late as eight years of age. Children do not get hooked on breast milk, and there are no female hormones in it to compromise a boy's maleness.

Dealing with parents or in-laws who push for weaning can be a sticky situation. In my own family, my wife had a run-in with her mother over nursing our son Jared. The issue first arose when Pat visited her parents when Jared was eighteen months old. Her mother was surprised and unhappy to find him still nursing. Two years later, when Pat was contemplating another visit, she wrote and suggested that perhaps she had better wait until Jared was weaned—which might not be for a couple of years—since the issue seemed particularly upsetting for her mother. Once my mother-in-law realized how serious Pat was in her commitment to nursing Jared, she let the subject drop.

Should you have similar problems with your own parents or in-laws, I suggest you approach the issue by writing a letter rather than trying to discuss it face to face or over the phone. When you talk with someone about a touchy subject, the other person may be so busy preparing her rebuttal that she never really listens to what you have to say. In addition, if the problem is with your own mother, she may have trouble getting past seeing you, her daughter, as a child ("I raised you and now *you're* telling *me* how to be a good mother?"). A letter will give the person you are dealing with a chance to digest your point of view before reacting, and, in the case of your own mother, will allow her to get beyond feeling that you are still a child yourself. You may find the response to your letter more favorable than you had dreamed possible.

To a child, mother-initiated weaning is rejection. Beyond the age of about two years, it is certainly possible for a child's nutritional needs to be met through other foods (although I would argue that they are best met through breast milk, given its unique properties). However, the act of breast-feeding goes beyond physical sustenance to fill a very real emotional need. Your child will know when he is ready to wean. When the time comes, it will be a slow process, so that he will gradually want to nurse less and less, until he finally loses interest entirely. Weaning is perhaps the most significant way in which a child changes from a dependent being to an independent person, and he needs to be allowed to make this change at his own pace. Approached this way, weaning is a painless, healthy, and natural process that produces a happy child whose emotional jar is truly full.

Plugged Milk Ducts

I'm going to go back on the promise I made at the beginning of this chapter to spend a little time on plugged milk ducts, one of those day-to-day problems that may confront the nursing mother, because I feel that it is often misunderstood by patients and mis-

treated by doctors. Most physicians refer to a plugged milk duct as a breast infection, or mastitis. While I may be splitting hairs here, I feel the term "infection" is a little misleading. A plugged duct is characterized by fever, chills, body aches, and a localized tenderness in the affected breast, which will also appear red and feel hot. Left untreated, a plugged duct can become extremely painful and lead to an abscess, at which point I feel it truly becomes an infection.

A plugged duct is nature's way of telling you that you're trying to do too much. The treatment, accordingly, is two full days of bed rest. This does not mean two days of lying down except when making lunch or straightening up the house; it means two days *in bed*. You should also drink plenty of fluids (at least two quarts every eight hours), apply a heating pad to the affected breast, take vitamin C (eighty milligrams per pound of body weight per day), and nurse the baby frequently on the affected breast to loosen up the plug. Once the milk is able to flow freely again, the tenderness, fever, and chills will subside. The most common mistake doctors have made in the past in treating a plugged duct is to advise women to discontinue nursing on the tender side. This will almost inevitably lead to an abscess. Doctors will often also want to prescribe antibiotics for a plugged duct. In twenty years of practice—with almost all the mothers breast-feeding—I have had only two patients who needed antibiotics to clear up a plugged duct. In the rest of the cases, bed rest and frequent nursing, along with the other methods suggested, have quickly corrected the problem.

I hope that this information on breast-feeding has served to convey to you some of the enthusiasm and wonder I feel about the process. As I've gathered this material, my interest has been fueled by some of the remarkable research that is currently being done on the subject of breast-feeding. For example, scientists have found evidence that the areola tissue surrounding a woman's nipple may actually have a receptor quality to it, so that an infant's mouth on the tissue conveys information back to the woman's body regarding that baby's special nutritional needs.[23] Over the next ten years or so we may discover that breast milk and the act of nursing hold even greater benefits for babies than we now realize. It's truly a fascinating subject, and one that bears watching.

Nurturing Your Toddler

Toddlerhood—that period of time between about fourteen months and three years of age—is a unique time in your child's life. Suddenly he's walking, talking, and beginning to assert himself as a little person in his own right. His emerging sense of self can make him a handful and a half at times. On the flip side, he'll thrill you with his growing capabilities and warm you down to your toes with his love. He'll be your cuddly baby one minute and a royal terror the next, making each day a roller coaster ride of emotions.

The toddler's most important job is beginning the process of maternal-infant separation in earnest. Unlike his baby self, he has started to realize that he and his mother are not part of the same entity, but are two separate people. This realization is both thrilling and scary, and the toddler will attempt to explore it by physically and emotionally venturing away from his mother, a little more each day. He always returns to her, however, for she is his security. This is a highly individual process, so that two children of the same age can be at very different stages at any given time. Our son Jared was very slow to separate from his mother, while our daughter Nina became independent very quickly. Jared was four years old before he felt comfortable going off for a few hours with only me, and seven and a half before he spent a night away from home. Nina spent her first night away from home at the age of three. At times we worried that Jared was never going to separate from Pat, but, in his own time, he did. Now, at thirteen, he is as independent and resourceful as any child I've met. The same could be said for Nina also, for whom independence was easy at an early age.

As he works through this separation process, the toddler can be both determinedly independent and extremely dependent. He may venture far from his mother one minute, and then turn around and cling to her the next. This happens because those forays into independence are sometimes scary and he needs the reassurance that Mom provides. Some toddlers suddenly begin to exhibit a fear of strangers, or have a great deal of separation anxiety, both evidence that they are finding their new independence a little frightening. For some, a giant step forward may be preceded by two small steps backward, so that the parents fear their child is regressing when he is really just preparing himself to progress. Whatever a toddler's pattern or methods, he needs to be allowed to find his own pace. He should not be pushed toward independence too early or told "you're not ready" when he wants to make his move. One common way of pushing a toddler is to take his first signs of independence as an indication that he is ready to be left overnight with his grandparents or a babysitter. The parents may be surprised that he becomes very clingy when they return, a reaction to being forced to cope with a greater separation than he is ready for. Parents need to be flexible when dealing with the toddler's progress toward independence rather than expect the child to conform to a rigid schedule that suits their own needs.

Given the inevitable pendulum swings of the separation process, getting through toddlerhood with your sanity intact can be a struggle. While it is not within the scope of this book to describe the toddler's development in detail (though I do recommend that you read one of the many good books available on the subject), I would like to point out a few of the traits you can expect to see:

A toddler operates on what I call the pleasure principle. Whatever gives him pleasure right now is what he wants to do. He's a bundle of impulses, and he lacks both self-control and the ability to delay gratification cheerfully. This gets him into trouble sometimes, since what he wants to do will not necessarily meet with the approval of those around him.

Toddlers have boundless energy and curiosity. They love to climb and explore, and their rapidly developing motor skills allow them to get into things that were previously inaccessible. They are still not well-coordinated, however, and the imbalance between their abilities and their interests can lead to accidents. (For this reason, baby-proofing the toddler's environment and adequate adult supervision are essential.)

During toddlerhood, the aimless play of a baby starts to disappear, and play becomes more purposeful. Imagination begins to emerge, and the child will pretend to take on different roles and to use dolls or toy figures as characters in her own little dramas. Toddlers like to play next to other children, but they do not truly interact in their play, and they are vehemently opposed to sharing toys. To a toddler, what's mine is mine, and if I give it to you—even for a minute—it won't be mine anymore. This attitude can lead to aggression, jealousy, and that bugbear of the toddler years, temper tantrums.

Toddlers have a very strong need for attention. When your toddler has your complete attention—whether you're hugging him or yelling at him—he knows for certain that he's important to you. He'd prefer positive attention, of course, but negative attention will serve the purpose. This need directs many of his actions, and will be at the root of most of his "bad" behavior. After all, nothing gets your attention faster than doing something that's forbidden, like smacking the baby or dumping out the goldfish. All his behavior is purposeful, undertaken to fulfill a need. I remember one day, when Jared was a toddler, he was constantly getting into trouble and driving Pat crazy. By the afternoon she was ready to throttle him, when suddenly, inspiration struck. She put aside whatever she was doing and suggested that they have a tea party. They picked spearmint leaves from the garden, brewed a pot of tea and sat at Jared's little table to enjoy it. The rest of the day he was fine. His behavior was just his way of telling Pat that he needed a little one-on-one attention.

Given the inherent characteristics of this age, a toddler can be very hard to handle, a true challenge for even the most capable parent. For the first time in the child's life, discipline enters the picture. I can't emphasize enough the need to use methods of handling misbehavior that enhance rather than diminish your toddler's self-esteem. Your child is very actively developing her sense of self during this time, and she needs your help in making sure it's a positive one. If you can get her through the toddler years with a strong self-esteem, you will have come a long way toward raising a delightful individual.

Much of the material on communication and discipline in chapter 9 applies to toddlers as well as to older children, but there are a few additional points it's helpful to keep in mind when dealing with a toddler:

Don't neglect your child's need for quality attention. Find the time to play with him, read to him, and talk with him. You'll bolster his self-esteem and lay the groundwork for a loving relationship and good communication throughout his life. Remember, the success you have in disciplining your child is directly proportional to the quality of your relationship with him. Build a foundation of love, trust, and good communication by giving him lots of quali-

ty attention, and you'll have fewer behavior problems both now and in the future.

When you have something to tell your child, get down to her level and look her in the eye. Eye contact is extremely important to small children. Just think about playing peekaboo, a game your child probably still enjoys. As long as your eyes are covered your child thinks you've disappeared, even though the rest of you is right in front of her. Whether you want to tell her that she's one terrific kid or that you really hate it when she dumps her juice on your clean floor, get down on your knees, hold her hands, and look into her eyes. She'll be much more receptive to whatever it is you're trying to communicate.

Try to keep your expectations reasonable and your priorities in order. You can't expect to have your house in perfect condition and to live a reasonably peaceful existence with your toddler, too. Your child isn't yet capable of putting away toys as she finishes with them, nor does she have the ability to stay focused on a goal of yours long enough to accomplish it. If you want her to pick up her toys, you'll have to help, and you'll probably end up doing ninety-five percent of the work, too. This is the only way she'll learn, however, so let her know you appreciate her efforts. Try to remember what is really important, and don't expect your toddler to behave like a miniature adult, because she isn't one.

Don't force your toddler to share his toys. I think we make a mistake in pushing our children to share at this age, when they are not capable of understanding the concept. Our desire to make children share comes out of a strong Judeo-Christian ethic, and it is certainly important that our children learn these values. The way a toddler learns to share, however, is by watching his parents and seeing their loving, giving interactions with other people, not by being forced to share a doll or truck. So set a good example, and praise your child's early efforts to share of his own volition, but don't force him to give one of his precious toys to another child.

Be patient. Often parents try to teach a child a particular lesson (e.g., toilet training, sharing) too early. She may be a month or week away from being ready to retain the information, but the parents insist that she learn today. Give her plenty of time to grow.

In disciplining your toddler, keep in mind that while it is appropriate to let him know what kind of behavior is acceptable and what is not, this is not a time for actual punishment. A toddler's memory span is too short for punishment to be effective; he is barely able to remember the things that are important to him, let alone those that are important to you. Even if you've successfully drummed it into his head that walls are not the right place to use his crayons, he won't necessarily have the self-control to stop himself the next time that white wall seems to be crying out for some artwork. Exiling him to his room or—heaven forbid—spanking him is not going to keep him from repeating the behavior at a later date, because he's not capable of retaining the information or controlling his impulses.

When your toddler does something that you disapprove of, tell him how you feel about the behavior (more about this in chapter 9). If he is actively involved in the behavior—such as coloring on the walls—you can also institute a logical consequence, like taking away the crayons until he is ready to use them properly, allowing him to make the decision of when to have them back again. If you come upon the deed after it is done, just make your disapproval known and tell him what he should have done instead (color on paper). He will undoubtedly have to be reminded of this lesson several times before it sinks in, but eventually it will. If you really want to make sure he doesn't color on the walls, however, you have to be vigilant whenever the crayons are within his reach, because it will take him time to learn this rule.

As you attempt to shape your toddler's behavior, watch out for operant conditioning, a learning process described in detail in chapter 9. Here's an example of operant conditioning at work: Your child asks for a cookie, but you say no. Your refusal is met with tears, and when they continue for five minutes, you get exasperated and give in, feeling it's not worth making an issue over one little cookie. The next time he wants a cookie and you refuse him, your child will know that a five-minute cry will probably buy him that cookie. If you get tough and hold out for ten minutes and then give in, he'll be prepared to cry ten minutes the next time. You have, in effect, rewarded him for his tears.

Operant conditioning is also at work when your child uses negative behavior to get your attention. He knows that doing a tap dance on the coffee table is a surefire way to get you to focus one hundred percent on him. Since toddlers have a wealth of resources when it comes to doing things you absolutely can't ignore, you can end up with operant conditioning working against you before you even realize it. It just sort of sneaks up on you. Try to be aware of the kind of behavior you reward, and when you can't ignore something, try to redirect the child. Show him a better way to act and then reward him for the positive behavior. For example, when our daughter Nina was a toddler, she figured out that biting is a great way to get a lot of attention, fast. We had never had to deal with biting before, but decided to approach it by trying to redirect her. When she started to approach someone (usually her brother Jared), teeth bared, we'd grab her and say "Nina, you're going to kiss Jared, aren't you?" and then praise her lavishly when she did. The first few times she looked at us as if we were out of our minds, but eventually the thought took hold, and she changed her behavior without having to be constantly monitored. The times we didn't get to her quickly enough and she actually bit Jared, we used the same tactic, telling her we thought she meant to kiss him. We'd then turn our attention to the injured party, so she wouldn't get a payoff for her bad behavior. We reinforced the lesson by praising her when her behavior was good in order to use operant conditioning to our advantage rather than letting it work against us.

Your toddler wants desperately to please you. If you are generous and sincere in praising good behavior, he'll work hard to win that approval. There's really only one thing your child won't do to please you:

sacrifice his own ego or his own needs. When he whines and screams for candy in the grocery store, chances are he's doing it because his need for your attention is stronger than his need to win your approval by sitting quietly as you shop.

It is easy to get into power struggles with toddlers, who often seem to have whims of iron. A power struggle is like a tennis game, however, in that it takes two people to keep one going. No one wins in a power struggle with a toddler. If you come out on top, your child may lose face and suffer from a loss of self-esteem. If he's the victor, you'll come away frustrated, angry, and feeling manipulated. To avoid power struggles, let your child have his way in unimportant matters. He needs to make decisions in order to learn about himself. Remember, he is just beginning to realize he has some control over his environment, and he's going to try to exercise that control in the areas he knows something about. So let him decide to wear one red sock and one green sock with his purple pants, if that's what makes him happy. If you give him some control over little things, he will be easier to handle on the big issues. When you do run into resistance on something that's important to you, try to go around the problem rather than tackling it head on. Let your toddler's short attention span be your ally. Distract him by singing a silly song or pointing out something new and interesting, and he'll end up doing things your way without even realizing it.

Make sure your toddler has constructive outlets for his aggressions. Children of this age may sometimes feel overwhelmed by anger or frustration, and they need to learn ways to handle these feelings. Let him show you how angry he is by punching a pillow or stamping his foot hard. Acknowledge his anger and give him a chance to express it in a way that doesn't hurt anyone. Much of the time you may find that just being encouraged to demonstrate his anger will dissipate it and turn the whole process into a game. Remember, too, that children model adult behavior. If your means of coping with anger is to scream insults, throw things, or pound on the walls, you can expect your toddler to do the same.

Mother-Toddler Separation

I'm going to open up a big can of worms here, one that gets me into as much trouble as my opinions on weaning: mother-toddler separation. Imagine, for a moment, that you are at the grocery store with your six-month-old. She starts making hungry noises, and you look down and say reassuringly, "I'll feed you in half an hour, as soon as we get home." Will she smile and wait patiently for you to finish your shopping? Absolutely not! As far as your baby is concerned, either there is food now, or there is no food in the world. Right in the middle of the grocery store, famine has struck!

Babies and toddlers, up to about the age of three, have little concept of time. To them, there are only two times: *now* and *never*. Telling a toddler that Mommy will be back in an hour or at five o'clock is essentially the same thing as telling her that

Mommy is gone forever, because she has no idea what those times mean.

Let me submit to you that the need for mother is as strong in a toddler as the need for food, and that there is no substitute for mother. When he's tired, hurt, or upset, he needs his mother for comfort and security. True, he doesn't need Mommy all the time, but when he does, he needs her *now*. If he scrapes his knee or gets his feelings hurt, he can't put his need on hold for two hours until Mommy is home, and the babysitter—or even Daddy—just won't do.

So, yes, that's what I'm saying: A mother shouldn't leave her child until about the age of three, when he has developed some concept of time. You'll know this has begun to happen when he understands what "yesterday," "tomorrow," and "this afternoon" mean, and when your child voluntarily begins to spend more time away from you.

Of course, if you know that your child *always* sleeps during certain times, you can leave her briefly with someone while she naps. If you do this, however, the babysitter should be someone she knows, since there is no guarantee that she won't choose this day to alter her schedule and wake up when you're gone. This could be traumatic for her if the person is someone she knows, and doubly so if the babysitter is a stranger. It is important that you make every effort to be available to her when she is awake and may need you.

I realize that not separating a child from his mother for the first three years of life may be difficult. Living up to this ideal presupposes that the family is financially secure without the mother's paycheck, and, unfortunately, this is not a reality for many people. I would not argue that a mother who must work to support her family is doing less than her best for her children by working. However, I think that many women return to work not out of necessity but because they (and/or their husbands) want to maintain the two-income life-style to which they've become accustomed. I think these parents need to do a little soul-searching about what they really need. I feel they are sacrificing their child's best interests for the sake of a nicer car, bigger house, or more expensive vacations.

If you must leave your child for several hours a day, there are some things you can do to try to compensate for the separation. One of these, of course, is nursing until the child weans himself. Another is sleeping with your child until he decides he is ready for his own bed (for more on sleeping with your children, see chapter 10). If you have to spend eight hours away from your child, make an effort to spend the remaining sixteen in close contact. That extra effort will go a long way toward helping him feel secure.

In our family, we have found that many events that would require leaving our baby or toddler at home are ones that we don't particularly mind missing. We have also found that because our children have their needs attended to promptly they are happy and secure, and we are able to take them to most social gatherings. I don't mean to suggest that you'll never encounter any problems, but generally, I think, you'll find that if you take care of your child's immediate needs by holding him, nursing him, and loving him, he'll be a pleasure to have around.

Day Care and Nursery Schools

Many people feel that day-care centers are beneficial to a child's development, and early studies did show that children in day care were more independent and made friends more easily than children who spent their days home with a parent.[24] More recent studies have reached disturbing conclusions, however. Pennsylvania State University psychologist Jay Belsky has expressed concern over mounting evidence that babies in day care are more likely to develop insecure attachments to their mothers and are at an increased risk of emotional and behavioral problems later on.[25] Other studies of children who have been cared for by someone other than a parent have shown "more serious aggression, less cooperation, less tolerance of frustration, more misbehavior and, at times, social withdrawal."[26]

This doesn't surprise me. Even the best nonparental child care arrangement asks that a child deal with considerable anxiety and stress. I believe that childhood should be a carefree time that builds a child's sense of security and trust, not a time for learning to cope with difficult situations.

Aside from the possible detrimental effects of day care on a child's emotional well-being, there are serious disadvantages from a standpoint of physical health. Children who are in day care tend to contract infectious diseases more often and at younger ages than children who spend most of their time at home. According to the Centers for Disease Control in Atlanta, children in day-care centers are more likely to get both minor and major illnesses, including influenza, giardiasis, dysentery, hepatitis A, and ear and cytomegalovirus infections.[27] The problem of infection is so great that the American Academy of Pediatrics is considering passing a resolution recommending all children in day-care centers be kept on an antibiotic, a prospect I find alarming. The antibiotic under consideration, Rifampin, is highly toxic, but the association feels that the high incidence of hemophilus influenza in day-care centers may warrant its use.

I do not have a much higher opinion of nursery schools, although for different reasons. Many preschool programs are intended to advance early learning. While there is no question that you can teach young children and even infants phenomenal amounts of information, there is no benefit from pushing a child in this way. No system of early education shows detectable results beyond the third grade. Whether your child learns to write his letters and add simple figures at the age of three or at the age of six will not matter in the long run, and his ability to learn these things at an early age is not necessarily any indication of the level of his intelligence. During the preschool years children need to learn values, a positive outlook on life, and how to be loving, understanding people. These are things that children learn from their interaction with other people, particularly their mothers, not from schools. Nevertheless, some people feel that nursery school is necessary to teach children how to play well with other children. I feel that a child who learns to care for, respect, and communicate with the people in his home will have no problem transferring these skills when he has the opportunity to play with other children. These values and skills should be learned in the home, not at nursery school.

Summing Up: Breast-Feeding, Weaning, and Nurturing

••

1. Nearly all women can breast-feed, with the proper information and support.

2. It is possible to nurse twins without adding supplements, to nurse while pregnant, and to nurse children of different ages.

3. There are medications for nearly every condition that are safe to take while breast-feeding.

4. Breast-fed babies are healthier than bottle-fed babies, and don't need supplementary vitamins or iron.

5. The introduction of solid foods should be delayed until a baby is one year old.

6. A child should be allowed to wean himself when ready.

7. A toddler's most important job is separating from his mother, and he should be allowed to pursue it at his own pace. Let him decide when to separate from you.

8. A toddler's strong need for attention is at the root of much of his behavior, particularly "bad" behavior.

9. In dealing with your toddler, keep your priorities in order and your expectations reasonable.

10. Don't let operant conditioning work against you.

11. Avoid power struggles.

12. Give your toddler appropriate outlets for his aggressions.

Notes

1. La Leche League International, *The Womanly Art of Breast Feeding* (Franklin Park, Ill.: 1991).

2. "Transfer of Drugs and Other Chemicals into Human Milk," *Pediatrics*, Vol. 84. No 5 (Nov. 1989).

3. Nancy F. Butte et al., "Milk Composition of Insulin-Dependent Women," *Journal of Pediatric Gastroenterology and Nutrition*, Vol. 6, No. 6 (Nov.–Dec. 1987): p. 936.

4. Alan S. Cunningham, M.D., "Morbidity in Breast-Fed and Artificially-Fed Infants," *Journal of Pediatrics*, Vol, 90, No. 5 (May 1977): p. 726.

5. S. A. Larsen, Jr., M.D., and D. R. Homer, M.D., "Relation of Breast vs. Bottle Feeding to Hospitalization for Gastroenteritis in a Middle-Class U.S. Population," *Journal of Pediatrics*, Vol. 92, No. 3 (Mar. 1978): p. 417.

6. Fima Lifshitz, M.D., Nancy Moses, M.N.S., R.D., Eduvigis Carrera, M.D., Ph.D.; "Normal and Abnormal Nutrition in Children," *Textbook of Pediatric Gastroenterology*, Mervin Silverberg and Frederick Daum, eds. (Chicago: Yearbook Medical Publishers, 1988): p. 116.

7. J. Ghisolfi, "Taurine and the Premature," *Biology of the Neonate*, Vol. 52, Supplement 1 (1987): p. 78.

8. N.F. Sherard, S.C.D., R.D., and Alan Walker, M.D., "The Role of Breast Milk in Development of the Gastrointestinal Tract," *Nutrition Reviews*, Vol. 46, No. 1 (Jan. 1988): p. 1.

9. Russell W. Chesney, M.D., "Society for Pediatric Research Presidential Address: New Functions for an Old Molecule," *Pediatric Research*, Vol. 22, No. 6 (Dec. 1987): p. 755.

10. Ghisolfi, p. 78.

11. A. el M. Darwish et al., "Comparative Study on Breast Milk of Mothers Delivering Preterm and Term Infants—Protein, Fat, and Lactose," *Nahrung*, Vol. 33, No. 3 (1989): p. 249.

12. Russell W. Chesney, M.D., "Taurine: Is It Required for Infant Nutrition?" *Journal of Nutrition*, Vol. 118, No. 1 (Jan. 1988): p. 6.

13. "A Touch of Sensitivity," *Nova* episode 718, produced by WGBH-TV, Boston, Dec. 1980.

14. Tiffany M. Field, Ph.D., "Tactile/Kinesthetic Stimulation Effects on Preterm Neonates," *Pediatrics*, Vol. 77, No. 5 (May 1986): p. 654.

15. Gilberto R. Pereira, M.D., and Nilse M. Barbosa, M.D., "Controversies in Neonatal Nutrition," *Pediatric Clinics of North America*, Vol. 33, No. 1 (Feb. 1986): p. 73.

16. Patrick J. Fahey, M.D., John M. Boltri, and John S. Monk, Ph.D.; "Key Issues in Nutrition: From Conception Through Infancy," *Postgraduate Medicine*, Vol. 81, No. 1 (Jan. 1987): p. 301.

17. G. Harvey Anderson, Ph.D., "Human Milk Feeding," *Pediatric Clinics of North America*, Vol. 32, No. 2 (Apr. 1985): p. 335.

18. A. J. Chitkara and S. Gupta, "Infant Feeding Practices and Morbidity," *Indian Pediatrics*, Vol. 24, No. 10 (Oct. 1987): p. 865.

19. B. A. Underwood and Y. Hofvander, "Appropriate Timing for Complementary Feeding of the Breast-fed Infant," *Acta Paedieatrica Scandinavica*, Supplement 284 (1982): p. 1.

20. C. Jeffry Kessler, M.D., and Emanuel Lebenthal, M.D., "The Exocrine Pancreas," *Textbook of Pediatric Gastroenterology*, Mervin Silverberg and Frederic Daum, eds. (Chicago: Yearbook Medical Publishers, 1988): p. 365.

21. M. Behar, "Physiological Development of the Infant and Its Implications for Complementary Feeding," *Indian Pediatrics*, Vol. 24, No. 10 (Oct. 1987): p. 837.

22. Ibid.

23. Armond S. Goldman, et al., "Future Research in Human Milk," *Pediatric Research*, Vol. 22, No. 5 (Nov. 1987): p. 493.

24. Pat Wingert and Barbara Kantrowitz, "The Day Care Generation," *Newsweek*, Special Issue (Winter 1989–Spring 1990): p. 86.

25. Ibid.

26. Karl Zinsmeister, "Hard Truths About Day Care," *Reader's Digest*, (Oct. 1988): p. 88.

27. Ibid.

Chapter 8

Nutrition

Nutrition is a complicated subject, and one that has gotten a fair amount of attention in recent years. I think most Americans have wised up to the fact that a burger, shake, and fries are not a well-balanced meal and that what you eat does have some bearing on the state of your health. Unfortunately, our heightened awareness of the connection between sound nutrition and good health hasn't appreciably changed the way we eat. Moreover, although we are probably more nutrition-conscious now than ever, there is still a striking lack of information available about the quality and content of the foods we eat.

I grew up in a family that ate meat three times a day and considered Jell-O with canned fruit a healthy dessert. The more processed or refined something was, the better we liked it. After Pat and I married and had children of our own, our approach to food was about the same. Gradually, though, we both became aware of the need to change the way we ate, and we slowly tried to modify our eating habits. Since that time our interest in the subject has grown, so that over the years we have been involved in a continual process of learning and change. In this chapter I would like to raise your consciousness about the foods you eat and feed your children, and, I hope, spark an interest in nutrition that will lead to healthier eating habits for your whole family.

Wootan's Philosophy of Good Nutrition

As you read on, you will discover that I do not advocate any one type of diet (e.g., vegetarian, macrobiotic, yeast-free). There

136

are a lot of different philosophies of nutrition and, consequently, many different diets, each thought by some to be the ultimate healthy diet for everyone. I approach nutrition with the assumption that human beings are meant to enjoy the wide variety of foods that are available on this earth, all in moderation and with one major qualification: Foods should be eaten in a form that is as close as possible to their natural state. They should not be processed, refined, injected full of hormones, sprayed with insecticides, or shipped two thousand miles from the place they were grown. If your food could not make it onto your plate without the help of high technology, it almost certainly has undergone nutritionally detrimental changes. Adhering to this principle means eating the fruits and vegetables that are in season in your area at any given time, growing your own foods when possible, and preparing your food yourself. That, in a nutshell, sums up my approach to nutrition. Now let's take a look at some of the more interesting things I've discovered about the foods available to us today.

Vegetables and Fruits

One of the reasons I originally got interested in the nutritional value of our food was that I decided to start a garden. I thought that producing and canning our own vegetables would be a foolproof way to improve the quality of the food we ate. To that end, I spent an entire winter poring over seed catalogs and planning a huge garden. One of the things that caught my eye in the catalogs was square tomatoes, which

got me wondering about all the new hybrids that have been developed. Does a square tomato have square vitamin C in it? Could my old-fashioned body, built for round vitamin C, use the square kind? How could I be sure that whatever process had taken place to alter the shape of the tomatoes hadn't also altered their nutritional content or its availability to my body? I certainly wasn't finding the answers to my questions in the seed catalogs. All they promised me was big, beautiful tomatoes that would conform precisely to the shape of my Wonder bread. So I started my own investigation. I contacted my local county extension agent, who happened to be a good friend, and gave him a list of the vegetables I was considering for my garden. He promised to call me back with information on their nutritional value. Well, two months went by, and I still hadn't heard from him, so I called again. As it turned out, he hadn't been able to come up with any information, because there are no laws requiring the disclosure of nutritional information on seeds or foods that are sold fresh. When a new seed is marketed, the seller need only provide a general statement saying that the seed is an improvement over the one from which it was developed. The improvement doesn't have to be nutritional. It can be purely a matter of personal opinion, such as a change in the color of a tomato's skin—or its shape.

All of this occurred about eight years ago. Since then, I've been gathering bits of information on the nutritional content of vegetables and fruits from various sources, and the things I've learned are frightening. For example, one study compared four thousand hybrid varieties of corn with one old fashioned open-pollination variety. Fourteen different planting areas were used, and both the corn and the soil were analyzed. As it turned out, the open-pollination variety contained, on the average, 485 percent more nutrients than each of the hybrids. There was 65 percent more protein, including 35 percent more usable protein, in the open-pollination corn. Interestingly, in every area in which they were grown, the hybrids failed to pick up between five and seven minerals from the soil, even though the minerals were present. The mineral that was most often missing was cobalt, which is needed as the central nucleus for some enzymes and for vitamin B_{12}.[1] This would be particularly significant for vegetarians, who are unable to manufacture their own vitamin B_{12} if they are lacking in this trace mineral.

One year I happened to be in Sacramento at the time of the tomato harvest. As it turned out, it was the first year that all the tomatoes had been harvested by machine, because, after ten years of research, a hybrid had finally been developed that could survive such treatment. The criteria for the final product? It had to be red, round, and able to survive a drop from a height of three feet onto a concrete floor without having the skin break.

Some hybrid peas contain no vitamin C at all, while the vitamin C content of oranges varies as much as four hundred percent.

Many people feel that they are getting the best vegetables and fruits when they buy organically grown produce from their local health food stores. While I'm no fan of the pesticides and chemicals used on most of the produce found at the grocery store, I question the nutritional value of the organically grown varieties, which most likely are hybrids that have been developed to be disease- and pest-resistant. It's entirely possible that they have fewer vitamins and minerals than those that have been sprayed with pesticide.

Due to the miracles of modern technology, we are now able to buy a huge variety of fresh produce at any time of year. However, these seemingly nutritious foods may actually lose most of their value by the time they reach your dinner table. Spinach, for example, may travel two thousand miles to your grocery store, losing thirty-eight percent of its vitamins in the process. It will then lose another thirty-eight to forty percent when you cook it, so that your final product has only a small fraction of the nutrients you might expect it to contain. Frozen vegetables may fare even worse, losing much of their value in the shipping and freezing processes.

Meta

Meat—especially red meat—has been much maligned in the last decade or so, and not without cause. I think the problem with meat, though, is not that it is inherently bad for you, but that the quality of most of our meat is very poor and that people just eat too much of it. If you limit your meat consumption to a small portion one to four times a month, I think it is probably beneficial to your health, if (and this is a big if) the quality of the meat is good. The meat that is available in your local grocery store, regardless of its price tag, is not what I consider good meat. It is almost invariably loaded with hormones, antibiotics, and other chemicals. Several years ago I had a patient who worked in a meat processing plant, injecting tenderizers into the meat to make it palatable. After seeing the effect those tenderizers had on his hands, I swore off all meat from commercially raised and processed animals. We have been able to find a source for range-fed beef or organically raised beef, chicken, and pork, however, and I see no harm in eating this type of meat in moderation.

One of the biggest concerns about red meat is cholesterol, of course, and its effect on the heart. If the desire to lower your cholesterol provides the impetus you need to limit your intake of meat, that's all to the good. I don't think we understand all the ramifications of cholesterol, though, and I think we may be in for a few surprises as its role in the body becomes more clear to us. For example, you may remember the diet popularized by Dr. Robert Atkins, which was popular for weight loss many years ago. It excluded almost all carbohydrates, emphasizing protein and fats. Several of my patients went on this diet, and because I was apprehensive about it, I checked their cholesterol levels frequently. Almost invariably, they went down instead of up. I'm not sure why this happened, but I think it may have something to do with their having cut out all sugar in the diet. As research on the subject continues, we may discover that there are factors other than cholesterol in the diet, such as sugar consumption, that affect cholesterol levels in the body.

Women who are pregnant or nursing who eat no meat, eggs, or milk products may become deficient in vitamin B_{12}. The only reliable sources for B_{12} are animal products or supplements from animal sources. There are some supplements on the market that claim to contain vitamin B_{12} from vegetarian sources, but I have not seen any convincing evidence to substantiate their claims. However, in recent years I have seen several vegetarian mothers who were using these supplements whose babies became deficient in B_{12}. For this reason, I do not recommend them.

Milk

There is a general acceptance in this country of the idea that milk is the "perfect" food, and one that every child should consume in abundance. I agree entirely that cow's milk is the perfect food—for calves. However, I believe it has little or no place in the human diet. Whole milk is high in saturated fat and is thirty-seven percent sugar. Skim milk, of course, has had all the fat removed, but is sixty-seven percent sugar. The sugar found in milk is lactose, which most people are unable to digest fully. It has long been thought that the only people who do not have problems with lactose are those of Scandinavian descent, but an increase in lactose intolerance has recently been noted even in these people.

That's not the worst of it, however. Most of the nutritional value of raw milk is lost in the pasteurization process. All of the vitamins and enzymes are destroyed. The minerals are altered, as is the iron, which is now mostly unavailable to the body. Drinking milk can actually aggravate anemia, since it may cause microhemorrhages in the intestines, which leads to a loss of blood. The calcium in milk is also altered so that the body can't use it efficiently. However, the phosphorus remains unchanged, so that it is well absorbed, creating an imbalance in the calcium-phosphorus ratio in the body, which can actually lead to a calcium deficit. Pregnant women who drink a lot of milk and suffer from leg cramps may have this problem, and can eliminate it by cutting out the milk in their diets.

Most pasteurized milk contains BHA, BHT, and formaldehyde. I know those ingredients aren't listed on the carton, but they're there nevertheless. Dairies aren't required to list them because they are added to the vitamin D concentrate that is then added to milk. The law requires that the ingredients be listed on the boxes of vitamin D concentrate, but not on the milk. Among the ingredients in General Mills' vitamin A & D concentrate are corn oil, diacetyl tartaric acid, ester of monoglycerides and diglycerides, as well as vitamins A and D. General Mills' Arpo 250, another vitamin D concentrate, contains propylene glycol and polysorbate 80.

There are also several other chemicals that can be legally added to milk without appearing on the label. One of these is oat gum, a plant extract that frequently causes allergic reactions. It seems quite possible that many of the "milk allergies" we see are actually caused by the oat gum that's in the milk rather than the milk itself. Another additive is NDGA (nerdihydrogaiaretic acid), an antioxidant that was banned as a

food additive in Canada in 1967 after it was found to cause kidney cysts and other damage in rats. Milk may also contain hydrogen perozide, which, while it appears on the "Generally Recognized as Safe" list of the Food and Drug Administration (FDA), is also under consideration to be studied for mutagenic, teratogenic, subacute, and reproductive effects. (In other words, they think it's safe, but haven't tested it yet.) Even if the FDA decides to ban hydrogen perozide, though, they will have no control over its use in milk, since milk comes under the jurisdiction of the Department of Agriculture, not the FDA.

If there's any redeeming nutritional value left in the milk on your supermarket shelves (and I'm not convinced there is) it may be about to disappear completely. Ultrapasteurized milk, which has been available in Europe for years, may soon hit the stores. Most of our cream and half-and-half is already ultrapasteurized, which is why they last so long without spoiling. Consider Wootan's basic law of nutrition: If it won't rot, don't eat it. How many nutrients could be left in a product that cannot even sustain the life of bacteria?

Sugar

Sugar, which Americans consume at the rate of one-hundred twenty five pounds per person per year, is bad for you. Refined white sugar (sucrose) is one of the most chemically pure substances you can buy. A quart and a half of cane juice is required to produce one teaspoon of sugar. Drink that cane juice and you'll ingest not only sugar, but also sixty-four different food elements, many of which are needed to properly digest it. These include water, calcium, phosphorus, iron, potassium, copper, manganese, zinc, magnesium, sodium, vitamins A, D, E, and B-complexes, and some amino acids and fatty acids. Eat a teaspoon of sucrose, however, and all you'll get is sugar. In order to digest it, your body will have to rob its stores of these other nutrients.

The concentration factor of sugar is 300. At a factor of 100 you get molasses, which still retains some iron, calcium, and other minerals. At 200 you get brown sugar, which retains only a few trace minerals. These final "impurities" are then removed with lime or phosphoric acid, and refined white sugar is obtained.

Honey, while not highly refined, is no better for you than white sugar. It is 99.9 percent sugar, with 0.1 percent of trace nutrients—not enough to make it nutritionally sound. Fructose is also no great improvement. There are no vitamins or minerals in fructose, either, although it is absorbed more slowly by the body than sucrose. Aside from a slight benefit for hypoglycemics, however, this has no significance. It's still sugar, and it's still bad for you.

Sugar's reputation has spawned an explosion of new sweeteners on the market in recent years as people attempt to find healthier alternatives. A visit to your health food store will yield cookies, ice cream substitutes (made from rice or soybeans), and other goodies sweetened with fruit juice concentrates, barley malt, and other sweeteners derived from various carbohydrates, even rice. The problem with sugar,

though, is not its source, but its concentration factor. To get a comparable amount of sweetness from fruit or any other carbohydrate, you have to similarly process and refine it until it is highly concentrated, too. Once you do this, the sweetener that is left will not be much better for you than sucrose.

If you're really going to benefit from cutting sugar out of your diet, you have to eliminate it in all its forms. When I first gave up my two cups of sugar a day, I simply substituted two cups of honey, and considered myself very virtuous indeed. That doesn't work, however, because to your body, white sugar, honey, fructose, maple syrup, corn syrup, barley malt, and any other form of sugar are essentially the same thing.

Occasionally parents ask me about artificial sweeteners such as aspartame (NutraSweet) or saccharin. I recommend avoiding them, too. Aspartame has been linked to mood changes, sleep disorders, abnormal EEGs, seizure disorders, headaches, and irritability. When stored in water or heated, aspartame breaks down, losing its sweetness and forming a product that may combine with chemicals in the stomach to produce cancer-causing compounds. In addition, aspartame seems to block the appetite-controlling chemical in the body and to cause a craving for sweets. People with phenylketonuria (PKU), a genetic inability to break down the amino acid phenylalanine, and pregnant women who are carriers of PKU, should avoid aspartame entirely, as it can seriously damage their health or their baby's. As for saccharin, we have known for several years that it is a weak carcinogen, and recent studies have shown that it causes bladder tumors. I think the only reason saccharin has not been banned completely is that it is three-hundred times sweeter than sugar but only costs one-tenth as much to produce, making it extremely economical to use.

That's the bad news about sweets. I know no one likes to give up sugar, least of all children. We are naturally drawn to sweet-tasting foods; breast milk is sweet. Give a five-year-old who has never tasted sugar a lollipop and he'll fall instantly in love. This natural inclination toward sweet foods is probably a protective mechanism. If you were lost in the forest and didn't know what to eat, you'd be safe sticking to berries and plants that tasted sweet. Unfortunately, this mechanism is of absolutely no use when you're lost in the grocery store, trying to choose between a carrot and a chocolate-frosted donut for an afternoon snack.

The good news about sugar is that once you give it up, you begin to realize just how sweet other foods are. The person who consumes large quantities of ice cream, cookies, and sugar-coated breakfast cereals will find a fresh strawberry or peach "not sweet enough." A child whose definition of "sweet" is a candy bar is not going to be attuned to the delicate sweetness of broccoli or peas. Once you cut out sugar, however, you become more aware of the subtle sweetness in many other foods, possibly even your drinking water. There's a flip side to this effect, too: When your taste buds have readjusted, those sugary foods become less appealing and may even taste "too sweet."

I'm not going to promise that any child will ever have that reaction to a lollipop, but getting your child off sweets *will* eventually reduce his craving for more and more sugar.

Processed and Prepared Foods

Just as cane juice loses most of its nutrients when it is processed and refined, so do other foods. Wheat, for example, loses thirty-seven vitamins and minerals on the way to becoming white flour. (Seven are then added back in again, and the final product is labeled "enriched.") All of our oils are highly refined, too, so that olive oil and corn oil do not contain the nutrients found in olives or corn. When brown rice is turned into polished white rice, a large proportion of vitamins and minerals are removed along with the bran. If you apply this concept to many of the prepared and processed foods available today, you begin to see how deficient the average diet really is. The more refined and processed foods you eat, the more essential nutrients your body is going to lack, and the more nutrients it will have to rob itself of just to metabolize that food. The result can be malnutrition, even in people who are seemingly well-fed.

Contributing to the problem, of course, is the food industry's deceptions and misrepresentations. Consider, for example, the following facts:

Margarine that is labeled "100 percent vegetable oil" may still legally contain other types of oil. In order to find out what's really in that margarine, you have to know how to read the fine print. If the list of ingredients begins with the letter "L" (usually the word "liquid" or "liquefied,") the margarine does in fact contain only vegetable oil. These may be coconut or palm oil, which are both highly saturated fats (coconut oil, in fact, is even more highly saturated than butterfat). If the list begins with the letter "P" (usually in the word "partly" or "partially") the margarine contains some animal fat.

"One hundred percent all-beef frankfurters," by law, must contain ten percent beef. "Whole-wheat" bread, by law, must contain ten percent whole wheat. Some breads that are labeled "high fiber" contain alpha cellulose, which is wood fiber that has been treated with approximately thirty-five chemicals to make it soft and palatable.

One tablespoon of ketchup contains one teaspoon of sugar.

Low-fat milk (two percent fat) is actually eighteen percent fat on a dry-weight basis (that is, if measured with the water taken out). It contains five grams of fat per eight-ounce serving, compared to eight grams of fat in the same amount of whole milk.

Obviously it's not easy to feed your family a healthy diet, even if you have the best of intentions. If you want to improve your family's eating habits, however, I do have a few suggestions that should help you do so more effectively and less painfully. The first is to find a way to keep yourself informed on the practices of the food industry and on the latest developments in nutrition research. One excellent source for this type of information is the nutrition action newsletter published by The Center for Science in the Public Interest, 1501 Sixteenth St. N.W., Washington, D.C. 20036.

Next, change your diet gradually and quietly. The older your children are, the more resistance you are likely to encounter. Several years ago my wife and I decided to cut back on our consumption of red meat. The children didn't really notice the change until Pat announced that she had decided to become a vegetarian. Suddenly, every morsel of meat that appeared on our table was counted, because the kids feared it would be their last. Previously the emphasis had been on whether or not the food tasted good, but now, suddenly, what was important was how much meat was in it. Learn from our mistake: Don't announce a ban on anyone's favorite food, or you're likely to meet with mutiny at the dinner table.

Become an international cook, particularly if you're trying to cut back on meat and dairy products. Many cuisines, such as Chinese, Japanese, and Indian, have a greater emphasis on vegetables and carbohydrates than meat and dairy, but they contain enough spices and intriguing flavors to make you feel adventurous rather than deprived.

Plan meals for an entire week at one time, and do all your shopping ahead of time. It takes time to learn to cook new and different dishes. If your meals are planned and you have all the ingredients on hand, you'll be less likely to fall back on familiar, less healthy standbys. If you generally do not have much time to cook dinners, you can also make the task quicker by cooking large quantities of some foods, such as rice or beans, up to a week before you plan to use them, and then incorporating them in your meals as you need them.

Take good-quality nutritional supplements. If you're not getting all the right nutrients from your food (and chances are you're not), you need them. Unfortunately, there is no test that can tell you exactly which vitamins and minerals you are lacking from your diet. Studies in animals have shown that nutritional needs vary greatly even from one animal to another in the same species, and I suspect the same is true for human beings. In order to determine what supplements you should be taking, you need to read up on the roles the various vitamins play, and then experiment with different supplements to see what levels suit your particular body (or your child's). I don't believe that the recommended daily allowances (RDAs) set forth by the Food and Nutrition Board of the National Academy of Sciences are very helpful in this process. For example, the RDA for vitamin C is only sixty milligrams, the bare minimum needed to prevent scurvy. I am certain that more vitamin C is necessary for optimal health. It is possible to have too much of a good thing, though, so I do not recommend routine use of megadoses of vitamins for general health purposes. Megadoses may be beneficial when used as drugs for a brief period of time and for a specific condition. When taken regularly, however, they tend to stress the system and are counterproductive to good health.

Choosing nutritional supplements wisely can be a tricky business. There are approximately two thousand vitamin manufacturers in this country, and I've looked at about three hundred of them. The range in the quality of the products is astounding. Just as in the food industry, there are plenty of regulations and rules, but also numerous ways around them, and often you may end up getting less for your money than you expect. For example, there are two ways to determine the vitamin E content of a supplement. The most commonly used method allows the manufacturer to claim that the product contains "400 IUs," when in fact only 280 are available to the body.

Many supplements use vitamins that are man-made rather than natural, and some nutritionists and doctors will tell you that there is no difference between the two. However, the molecules of man-made vitamins spiral to the left, while those of natural vitamins spiral to the right. Similarly, researchers have actually developed a type of sugar in which the molecules spiral to the left rather than the right. It looks and tastes just like regular sugar, but it is not digested by the body. Knowing this, I can't help but wonder about how well left-handed vitamins are absorbed. There is no doubt that they have some effect on the body, but they may not do everything their natural counterparts do.

My family and I use Shaklee vitamins and supplements, which are among the most natural on the market. Shaklee also spends more on research and development (about $10 million a year) than other companies, which I find impressive. For the most part, their supplements are intended to be used for basic nutrition rather than for treatment of specific conditions, so they do not offer large doses or many isolated supplements. (Other companies that have some good products for basic nutrition are Nutridyne, Neolife, and Thompson.) For supplements to treat a specific disease, I have found Standard Process (usually sold through chiropractors and other health care practitioners) to be of good quality.

Just in case you feel it's not worth the effort required to change your family's diet, let me point out that there are two groups of people in this country who have a better outcome from many diseases and who live longer than the rest: Seventh-Day Adventists and Mormons.[2,3] They have in common health codes that prohibit the use of alcohol, tobacco, and caffeine-containing beverages. Seventh-Day Adventists also do not eat meat, and Mormons eat it only sparingly, usually just in the winter or in times of famine. On the average, Mormons live 1.2 years longer than Seventh-Day Adventists.[4,5] I often tell people that this is the reason I won't give up meat completely, but that's probably not the reason for the difference. More likely, it's due to the fact that Seventh-Day Adventists do eat meat by-products and imitation meats that are often full of chemicals.

One study examined the life spans of Mormons and non-Mormons in both rural and industrial areas.[6] I was particularly interested in this, since I live upwind of New York City, and have often wondered whether it was worth the effort to clean up my diet when I have to breathe air that's less than clean. As it turned out, the non-Mormons in rural areas lived longer than non-Mormons in industrial areas, but the Mormons in both areas had about the same life spans. I interpret this to mean that exerting control over one's diet can make a difference. If you're careful about what goes into your body (and your child's), you may be better able to handle the pollutants over which you have no control.

While improving your family's nutritional status may seem like a difficult undertaking, it is worth the effort. The foods you eat have a direct effect on your health; it's as simple as that. When I talk to people about nutrition, I am often confronted by someone who informs me that he feels just fine, is in good health, and doesn't see any reason to give up red meat or chocolate cake. That's a hard statement to argue against, but I do have a couple of thoughts on the subject. First of all, many of the diseases and conditions that doctors are seeing today are related to life-style: smoking, lack of exercise, stress, and most important, what you eat and drink. The effects of your life-style on your health are cumulative, so that the fact that you are healthy today does not necessarily mean that it won't all catch up with you in five years, or even next year or next month. Second, I think many people have come to consider small, nuisance-type health complaints—headaches, backaches, lack of energy, depression—as normal. They're not normal, and they may very well be related to diet. But because the symptoms creep up gradually over the years, people don't relate them to the foods they eat. I think you'll find, however, that if you make the effort to clean up your diet, you'll see a vast improvement in the way you feel. By changing your child's diet, too, you'll be ensuring that he is in the best possible health, both now and in the future.

Summing Up: Nutrition

•••

1. Foods should be eaten in a form that is as close as possible to their natural state.

2. For a variety of reasons, the fruits and vegetables you eat are probably not as nutritious as you think.

3. Good-quality meat, in moderation, can be a healthy part of your diet.

4. Sugar is bad for you and milk is overrated.

5. From a health standpoint, the time and effort you put into improving your family's nutritional status is very worthwhile.

Notes

1. Charles W. Allers, Jr., and C. J. Fenzare, *An Acres U.S.A. Primer* (Raytown, Mo: Acres U.S.A, 1979): p. 38.

2. J. L. Lyon, M.D.; J. W. Gardner, M.D.; and D. W. West, Ph.D., "Cancer in Utah: Risk by Religion and Place of Residence," *Journal of the National Cancer Institute*, Vol. 65, No. 5 (Nov. 1980): p. 1063.

3. D. W. West, Ph.D.; J. L. Lyon, M.D.; and J. W. Gardner, M.D., "Cancer Risk Factors: An Analysis of Utah Mormons and Non-Mormons," *Journal of the National Cancer Institute*, Vol. 65, No. 5 (Nov. 1980): p. 1083.

4. J. L. Lyon, M.D., et al., p. 1063.

5. D. W. West, Ph.D., et al., p. 1083.

6. Roland L. Phillips, M.D.; Lawrence Garfinkel, M.A., J.W.; W. Kuzma, Ph.D.; et al., "Mortality Among California Seventh-Day Adventists for Selected Cancer Sites," *Journal of the National Cancer Institute*, Vol. 65, No. 5 (Nov. 1980): p. 1097.

Chapter 9

Communication and Discipline

*I*don't doubt that as a parent you are as concerned with your child's emotional well-being as his physical health, and you are probably aware that there is a strong connection between the two. You may have found, however (as I did), that it is much harder to accomplish the goal of a well-adjusted, happy child than you had ever imagined. Before we have children, I think we are each convinced that we will know just how to handle difficulties, how to communicate effectively with our children, and, most important, how to discipline them. Once we actually become parents, however, we often find ourselves at a loss in dealing with the inevitable difficulties and misbehavior that arise. Not knowing what else to do, we tend to respond in much the way our own parents did, with results that are less than ideal.

The purpose of this chapter is to provide some very basic guidelines for raising children who are emotionally as well as physi-cally healthy. In reaching this goal, the importance of good communication between parent and child cannot be stressed too strongly; it is the essential key to any quality relationship. Effective, fair discipline—which is, in fact, one of the most potent forms of communication you have with your children—is extremely important, too. The way you correct a child's misbehavior can have a tremendous effect both on your relationship with her and on her self-esteem.

I was raised in a family in which there was very little communication and a great deal of harsh physical punishment. When I became a father, I vowed I would treat my children differently. You can imagine how surprised I was, then, when my automatic response to my oldest son's misbehavior was to spank him. I wasn't as severe as my own father had been, but nevertheless I felt compelled to resort to physical punishment to teach him how to behave. My wife strongly objected to physical punishment, though, and I was not entirely happy about it either, so we started looking for a better alternative. I have to admit that changing my methods of communicating with and disciplining my children involved a long internal struggle, so deeply ingrained were the attitudes with which I was raised. We persisted, though, and over the years Pat and I have compiled a lot of information on these subjects. The sources for that information have been various parenting courses, books, and personal experience. What you will find in this chapter is the cream of the crop: the most practical, effective and easy-to-implement suggestions that we have encountered. There is much more to be learned on the subject, however, and I have listed several good books that I found helpful in the "Suggested Reading" section. In addition to putting the suggestions here into practice, I hope you will be inspired to read some of these books and further develop your skills in this area.

Communication

A Short Course in Human Relations

The six most important words in the English language are:

I was wrong—please forgive me

The five most important words in the English language are:

You did a good job

The four most important words:

What is your opinion?

The three most important words:

Can I help?

The two most important words:

Thank you

The one most important word:

You

The least important word:

I

Anonymous

In order to build good communication with your children, you must take time for dialogue with them, right from the start. It can be tempting to put them off when they want to tell you something, especially when their most urgent need is to find out why there aren't any dinosaurs in the zoo. "Look, I'll talk to you as soon as I finish paying these bills," you say. Or, "Can't you see I'm right in the middle of cleaning up the kitchen?" Or "Don't talk now, this is my favorite TV show. Tell me later." When you're trying to get things done you may well want to postpone a discussion. Unfortunately, if this happens often enough, your child is going to get the idea that on a relative scale of importance, he comes after the dishes, the bills, and the TV show. And that's not the message you want to get across.

I can almost hear the storm of protests, especially from parents of small children. "I'll never get anything done if I drop what

I'm doing every time my kids open their mouths!" Now, I'm not saying you have to take a lot of time, or that you should always jump to attention at the sound of your child's voice. There are times when you just can't. But most of the time you can take a few minutes to find out what's on his mind. The subject matter might not be important, but the communication is. If you make it a habit to listen to your child, he will return the favor and listen to you.

The *way* you listen is important, too. When your child has something to say, she needs to know that she's got your full attention. Get down on her level, and make eye contact. Once she knows you're really listening, she'll be able to tell you what's on her mind and, knowing that she can get your attention when she needs it, go back to amusing herself. Then you can get on with what you were doing, too. This is especially true when you're on the telephone or have friends over. Have you ever noticed that your child can be off playing, happy as can be, until the moment you pick up the phone or become engaged in an adult conversation? Suddenly, she's wrapped around your legs, whining, or scaling the kitchen cabinet to get at the cookie jar. She senses that you have suddenly become emotionally removed from her, even though you are still physically present. This creates a great deal of anxiety in the child, so she's going to do something you can't possibly ignore. When you hang up the phone or turn away from your friend to deal with her, she'll have you back. You may be yelling at her, but to her that's better than having you focused somewhere else. If you take thirty seconds to kneel down, look her straight in the eye and

find out what she needs when she first starts bugging you, she'll probably go back to amusing herself, and you can finish your conversation. She just needs reassurance that you'll be there if she needs you.

Toddlers and preschoolers have short attention spans, which usually preclude the possibility of lengthy discussions. With older children, however, there will be times when you'll want to set a limit on a conversation. I remember one time when my son Brian wanted to tell me about a great movie he'd just seen. "Come tell me all about it," I said, unsuspecting. An hour later I knew every detail of *The Green Slime*—or some such horrible film. A month later, when he wanted to tell me all about *The Revenge of the Green Slime*, I was a little smarter. "I'd love to hear about it," I said, "but I've only got five minutes." He tailored his synopsis accordingly, so I got the abbreviated version. A time limit can keep you both happy: Your child gets to have his say, and you get to get on with whatever it was you were doing. It will also teach him that your work is important, too, without making him feel that it always comes first.

Of course, you don't always have to let your child take the lead. Sometimes you'll want to initiate a conversation, particularly when your children have reached that age when they never stop talking to their friends but barely have a moment to share their thoughts with you. To make those conversations fruitful, there are a few things you should keep in mind:

Don't interrogate. Your child comes in from school, pauses in the kitchen for a snack, and you pounce. "Do you like your new math teacher? Are you going to join the swim team? Was there any trouble on the school bus today?" Your child answers in monosyllables and grunts, and you're left frustrated. What went wrong? Well, you've done one of two things, or maybe both: You've asked about things that just aren't that important to him at the moment. He doesn't have an opinion about the math teacher and he isn't thinking about the swim team right now. Or you've put him on the defensive. There was trouble on the school bus—as you knew there had been in the past—and he was right in the middle of it. It's a sore subject between you, and now you're practically attacking him, at least from his point of view.

Try asking open-ended questions instead. "How did it go today? I'd really like to hear about it." Your questions should require more than a "yes" or "no" response. Keep open-ended words like "how," "why," and "what" in mind. Let him tell you what was interesting, or upsetting, or exciting about his day. Make yourself available and express your interest, but don't make him feel like he's the star witness at a murder trial.

Take timing into consideration. Seven-thirty in the morning may seem like a dandy time to you to discuss your daughter's choice of a college. But she's only been awake for half an hour, and her brain doesn't truly engage until her eyes have been open for forty-five minutes. Or you'd like to talk to your son about his argument with his best friend, so you approach him just before dinner. Unfortunately, he's so hungry he can only concentrate on his stomach at the moment. Look for a time

when you're both feeling receptive, and you'll be much more successful.

One way you can tell that you're making an error in your attempts to communicate is that your child will get defensive. Defense mechanisms usually take one of three forms: (1) denial: "I am not being grouchy today . . ."; (2) rationalization: "You'd be grouchy too, if . . ."; and (3) counterattack: "You're the one who's being grouchy." Real communication can't take place when your child is on the defensive. If you find that his responses fall into one of these categories, review your approach to see what's causing the reaction.

When your child comes to you with a specific problem, you've got a real challenge on your hands. You can quickly squash any possibility of communication by jumping in with criticism or by moralizing or judging the child. A child who is upset needs to be listened to, reassured, and encouraged, not preached at.

A communication technique that I have found highly effective in dealing with my own children is reflective listening. To use reflective listening, you let the child have her say and then summarize, in your own words, what she has told you, focusing on her feelings. For example:

Child: "Karen isn't going to be my friend anymore because she always cuts me down in front of Michael. She makes me feel like a jerk. She's such a creep. I hate her."

Parent: "It sounds like you're really mad at Karen for saying mean things about you in front of another friend. It must hurt you when she does that."

You've now let your child know that you understand what she's feeling, and she can go on to a deeper level of communication. Had you responded by moralizing about friends always being nice to each other, or put your daughter on the defensive by telling her she's too sensitive, you could count on the conversation—or at least the real communication—ending right there. By reflecting what she has said back to her instead, you're showing her that you're really listening to her and making an effort to empathize with her feelings. Now she'll feel free to continue to open up and explore the problem further.

In order for this technique to be effective, you have to make a sincere effort to understand how the child feels. If you simply parrot her feelings back to her without any true empathy, she'll sense that you're not trying to understand and may assume that you don't care. Of course, there may be times when you don't immediately understand what she is feeling. When this happens, you can still rephrase what you think she's saying and ask for further clarification. As long as you are truly listening and making an effort, you'll get positive results.

Once you have reached an understanding of the child's perception of the problem, you need to encourage her by giving support and genuine reassurance. If the problem is something that seems trivial to you, it might be tempting to brush her off with false reassurance: "Don't worry, I'm sure you and Karen will work it out." All this tells your child, however, is that her feelings are not important. Maybe the problem is a small one by adult standards, but to your child it matters, and therefore warrants your full attention.

Genuine reassurance can be given only after you have understood and acknowledged the child's feelings: "I know you're hurt by the way Karen is acting, and I can understand why you're angry. But you and Karen have been such good friends for so long that it seems like there must be a way to work things out between you. I know you're a wonderful friend to her." Responding in this way reaffirms your child's self-worth, which will help her get past her hurt feelings and on to a solution to her problem.

When it comes to actual problem-solving, your goal should be to guide your child through her feelings so that she can arrive at her own solution. Don't try to solve the problem for her. While her way of handling things may not seem like the best to you, the results may be perfectly satisfactory to her. In most cases that's all that matters. After all, you can't expect a ten-year-old to solve problems at an adult level. The only way she will become more sophisticated in her approach is through trying out her own ideas. She needs the chance to do this and needs to know that you believe in her ability to solve her own problems. This doesn't mean you can't encourage her with suggestions; you can, and the younger the child, the more you will have to help out. The ultimate decision on how to handle the problem should be her own, however. Allowing her to make that decision will teach her self-reliance, an essential part of the growing process.

Once you're convinced it's important, listening to and encouraging your child is not all that difficult when the child is the only one who's upset. When you're feeling angry, disappointed, or frustrated with your child's behavior, you may find it much harder to keep the lines of communication open. Suppose that your son, who has always been a good student, suddenly comes home with a D in math. He's upset about it, and you're furious. Until you get your own feelings under control, you're not going to be able to listen sympathetically and offer him the encouragement he needs. (This scenario assumes that your child agrees that he has a problem. When you're the only one who feels that his behavior needs correcting, you're moving more into the area of discipline, which I'll discuss shortly.) Reflective listening requires that you feel genuinely loving toward your child. If you are angry or upset, you'll be too busy with your own feelings to focus on his. In a situation like this, it's better to postpone the conversation until you have cooled off.

There are several common errors people make when attempting to use reflective listening. One is to use it to manipulate the child into feeling differently. Your purpose should be to understand what the child is going through, not to influence him. Another common mistake is to use the technique to gather information that you then hold against the child: "So you really did go to that party last night. You're grounded!" You must also be aware of when your child wants to talk about feelings and when he is simply asking for concrete information. The question "When will I be old enough to drive?" requires a straightforward answer, not a discussion of how your child feels about getting his license.

There may be times when you will be tempted to take what the child tells you and analyze it, trying to interpret motives and

diagnose problems. In the example of the girl who's angry with her friend, you might respond like this: "I know what the problem is. You and Karen both want Michael to like you best, so you're fighting with each other." Your focus should be on the child's feelings, not on the causes of the problem. Nor should you allow the focus to shift so that your child uses the opportunity to put the blame for her problems on others. If you were to echo your daughter's proclamation that her friend is a creep without trying to get at the feelings behind it, you'd probably get a tirade on the subject of Karen the Terrible, which is really beside the point. Only by exploring her own feelings—not externalizing the problem—will your daughter be able to work her way through to a solution.

A final note: Remember to reinforce the good efforts your child makes to communicate with you. Let him know that you feel good when he talks to you, and that what he tells you is important. If your child knows you are open to him and interested in what he has to say, he will seek you out more often.

Discipline

I feel there are only two approaches to discipline, and that every school of thought on this subject falls into one of these two categories. The first is based on the premise that you have faith in the power of love to bring out the basic good in children. The second is just the opposite: You have faith in the power of fear and pain to suppress the essential evil in children.

This classification is not my idea. I have lost track of its originator, but I first heard it back in the days when I was still struggling to overcome my inclination toward spanking, and it made more of an impression on me than anything else I had heard or read. I realized that I was using fear and pain to discipline my children, and that I didn't want our relationship to be based on that. It was still difficult to let go of the idea that physical punishment is necessary to get children to behave, mostly because I had trouble accepting the concept that love and respect for his parents could possibly be sufficient to motivate a child to behave well. While my wife's and my desire to find a better way to discipline our children was enough to persuade me to try putting my faith in the power of love, it took actual experience to convince me of its effectiveness. In retrospect, it doesn't surprise me that motivation through love works better than motivation through fear and pain. Just look at it from a child's point of view: Which way would you prefer to be handled, and to which method would you respond better?

My conversion has been so complete that I am now strongly and unequivocally opposed to spanking. As far as I can see, there is no justification for ever raising a hand to a child. In addition to being ineffective for making long-term changes in behavior, it damages a child's self-esteem and teaches him, by example, that it's all right to beat up on someone, as long as you're bigger and more powerful. Nevertheless, whenever I state this view in a group of parents, there is always at least one person who will quote the Scriptures to me: "Spare the rod and spoil the child." Aside from the fact that this quotation is inaccurate (see Proverbs 13:24), I believe people who use it to justify spanking their children misunderstand the proverb's meaning. The rod referred to is a shepherd's rod, which was used to guide sheep, not to beat them. It is true that we cannot spare guidance in raising our children, but physical violence does not constitute guidance.

Of course, fear and pain can be powerful motivators in the short term, which is why spanking may appear to be effective. The trouble is, they only work if the parent is there to carry out the punishment when the child misbehaves. Let's look at the internal reasoning of a child who is motivated by fear and pain: "I know that if I get caught with my hand in the cookie jar, I'm going to get spanked. I really don't want that to happen, but Mom's outside and Dad's not home so I'm sure I can get away with it. . . ." The child who is motivated by love, however, is going to approach the situation this way: "I want a cookie, but Mom said not to eat them because she's saving them for her meeting tonight. . . . I love my mom and I don't want to upset her. . . ." For the child motivated by love, it doesn't matter whether Mom or Dad is present, because the motivation to be good comes from within, out of a desire to please his parents rather than out of a fear of punishment. This child is developing *self*-discipline, which is really the parents' ultimate goal.

Another problem with motivation through fear and pain is that the child may sometimes decide that the payment for his misbehavior is worth whatever reward the behavior brings him. For example, if your teenager knows that staying out past his curfew will result in being grounded for two weeks, he may well decide that's not too high a price to pay for staying late at a party. If he is motivated by love, however, he will feel that hurting his parents' feelings and losing their trust in him *is* too high a price for what he gains.

Using the power of love to bring out the basic good in children involves building self-esteem through sincere, appropriate praise and the expression of your unconditional love. Fostering high self-esteem in your child is, in fact, key to shaping his behavior in a positive manner. A child who feels good about himself will not only have a happier outlook on life, he will be better able to overcome obstacles and to learn how to conduct himself appropriately.

Your expressions of love for your child increase her feelings of self-worth and help her to love herself. Your praise teaches her that you respect her and that her behavior can benefit others. When she receives this positive attention she will be less likely to look for negative ways of getting attention, so that there will be fewer incidents of misbehavior. It is important to note, however, that your assertions of love should not be linked with praise for her actions. Don't make her feel that you love her only when her room is clean or her grades are good. In order to feel good about herself, she needs to know that your love is unconditional— that you love her for who she is, not what she does.

When you praise your child, tell her how you feel about what she has done and how it benefits you. As a guideline, remember the words "I feel," "about," and "because." "I feel good about your clean room because we have more time to read together when I don't have to clean it for you." "I feel pleased when you come home on time because I don't have to worry about you." These key words will help you to express pleasure with your child's actions without making your love contingent on her good behavior. Consider, for example, the way you might react if your two-year-old, whom you are trying to toilet-train, comes to you with a dry diaper and tells you she wants to use the potty. You help her, then praise her for her success: "Good girl! You used the potty just like a big girl!" The next day she comes to you with a wet diaper, needing to be changed. You don't comment on it, but if she was a good girl yesterday for having a dry diaper, what is she, by inference, today? A bad girl, of course. If you use the words "I feel," "about" and "because" instead, ("I feel good when you use the potty because then we have more time to read together,") you are letting her know how her behavior benefits you without linking your praise to her worth as a person.

Keep in mind, too, that children learn anything faster, proper conduct included, when they are encouraged rather than discouraged. I am greatly disturbed by parents who verbally cut their children down in an attempt to change their behavior: "What's the matter with you?" "If you weren't so stupid . . ." "You idiot! Why did you . . ." "You're selfish and inconsiderate!" Aside from the fact that this kind of talk slaps a negative label on the child (I'll have more to say about that later), it damages his self-esteem. In the long run, this can only have a detrimental effect on his behavior. If you belittle or humiliate your child—even if you speak out of anger and don't really "mean it"—he will learn that he is worthless, and will not feel capable of living up to your high expectations. Cutting your child down will only make it that much harder for him to learn the lessons you want to teach him.

And now, about those labels. You are a powerful person in your child's eye, the all-knowing parent. He takes what you say to heart, and incorporates what he thinks is your view of him into his own self-image. If you continually tell your child that he is selfish, lazy, stupid, mean, or whatever, that is how he will come to see himself, and he'll act accordingly. Don't lock your child into a negative self-concept. Instead, when he misbehaves, criticize the behavior. Focus your negative reactions on the act: "Hitting your sister is a bad thing to do," not on the child: "Bad boy! You hit your sister." Your child isn't really bad anyway. He's still the same little boy you adore; it's the behavior you dislike. If you criticize the action rather than the child, he'll learn that doing something bad doesn't make him a bad person.

Even positive labels can be harmful to a child's self-concept. The child who is constantly told by his parents that he is a super athlete or a great artist or a real brain may come to feel that their love for him is contingent on living up to that label. That's a terrible pressure to put on a child, and it ultimately undermines rather than builds

self-esteem. So save labels for cans; don't paste them on your kids.

Guiding Your Child's Behavior

Whenever you ask your child to behave in a certain way, your goal is to get that child to be responsible for his actions so that you are not. This is true whether you are assigning a household chore, imposing a curfew, or disciplining your child for beating up on her little brother. As long as you are responsible for your child's behavior, you will be responsible, not your child. Though this may seem obvious, as parents we sometimes overlook it in practice. For example, several years ago Pat and I realized that we had taken on all the responsibility for putting each of our children (we had eight at the time) to bed. It occurred to us that except for the youngest ones, they were all perfectly capable of getting themselves to bed at a reasonable hour. Up until that time we'd started putting the youngest children to bed around seven o'clock, and finally finished with the oldest around ten. We spent so much time on bedtimes that our entire evening was gone by the time we were done. So we called them all together, and told them that each of them was to go to bed when he or she felt ready. They thought this was a grand idea, and stayed up until all hours of the night for the next few days. Eventually, though, they got tired, had trouble getting up for school, and felt generally lousy. One by one it dawned on them that they needed more sleep, and they started going to bed when they felt they needed to. One of our daughters, in fact, started retiring half an hour earlier than her previous bedtime. Suddenly, we had our evenings back, because we were no longer responsible for bedtimes.

One of our sons had a great deal of trouble getting up in the morning when he was in high school, so Pat and I would take turns dragging him out of bed to make sure he got the bus. If he missed it, we'd race off in the car and try to catch it, or we'd take him all the way to school if necessary. Finally, we decided that getting to school had to become his responsibility. He missed the next two and a half weeks of school and got a warning notice that he was about to fail. He did better for the next few weeks, but miscalculated the number of days he could afford to miss and still pass. As a result, he had to repeat several courses. It was very difficult for us to watch him sleep, knowing he was going to fail, but we knew getting to school had to become his responsibility, not ours. And it did; the next year he decided he had to make it to school on time because he wanted to go to college.

Children are surprisingly capable of handling responsibility for their actions, once you decide to let go of it. I once got a call from a mother who was at her wit's end because her eighteen-month-old son insisted on climbing up onto and then throwing himself off of every piece of furniture in the house. She spent practically her entire day catching him. I asked if he was ever still, and she answered that he took a nap in

her bed each day, and when he woke, would cry until she came in, at which point he'd start to fling himself off the bed. I suggested that she let him jump off the bed and get hurt once or twice. Once he knew she wouldn't always be there to catch him, I was pretty sure he wouldn't persist in trying to jump off the dining room table or the refrigerator. He just needed to know that he was responsible for his actions.

Another aspect of fostering responsibility in your children is assigning jobs or chores that they must do. This is an area that frustrates parents, because children are often unwilling to accept this kind of responsibility. In taking on any new responsibility, there are essentially five levels of initiative through which a child progresses. First, the child waits to be told to do the job. Second, he asks if he should do it and gets your recommendations. Third, he does the job without asking and reports to you immediately. Fourth, he does the job and reports routinely, or whenever the subject comes up. And fifth, he uses his own initiative entirely, so that the job is done without your getting involved at all.

Whenever you set up a job for your child, it may be helpful to keep in mind these guidelines: (1) Tell the child what he is required to do and what the criteria, or desired results, are. (2) Give the child guidelines to use in doing the job. (3) Tell him what resources he may use. Can he ask you or a sibling for help if he needs it? (4) Tell the child when he will be accountable for the job. Will you check on it whenever he is finished, or in half an hour, or every Thursday? (5) Inform him of the consequences of doing or not doing the job. Positive consequences are more effective than negative ones, so it is to your advantage to use them whenever possible. Using these guidelines will ensure that the child knows what is expected of him, how and when he is supposed to do the job, and what will happen if he does it well or doesn't do it at all.[1]

When you are trying to get your child to do what you want him to, there are several other ways to ensure that you accomplish your goal. Remember that how you speak to him is as important as what you say. Give instructions in a quiet voice and in a simple, direct fashion. If you turn down the volume, your children will have to listen harder. Screaming at children to get them to behave is like trying to drive a car by honking the horn. The more you yell, the more they will yell, and the less anyone will listen. If you start out screaming at your toddler, by the time he's a teenager, you'll need a power megaphone to get through.

Don't ask your child to do something when he really has no choice in the matter; tell him. Don't ask "Would you like to go home now?" when you really mean, "It's time to go home now." If you offer him an option, be prepared to let him take it.

Use common courtesy: If you say "please," "thank you," and "you're welcome," your child will not only learn from your example, she will know that she is afforded the same respect as you show adults. Also, remember to convert don'ts. "Don't sit that way," doesn't convey any positive information. "Please sit up straight and put both feet on the floor," tells your child unequivocally what you expect her to do.

If you find yourself saying the same things over and over again, try a new approach. Old strategies come with known boundaries and limits, but new ones have to be tested and proved. For example, if you are constantly telling your child not to run through the house during the baby's naptime, but he does it anyway, he has stopped hearing you. Set up a new rule, like "Everyone must tip-toe down the hall during the baby's nap" and he'll have to test that out. If you enforce it, he'll conclude that you're serious this time.

With younger children, you must also be careful not to give too many instructions at once. If you tell your four-year-old to put her toys away, get into her pj's, put her dirty clothes in the hamper, wash her hands, and brush her teeth, she'll probably end up just playing with her doll, because she can't retain all those instructions long enough to accomplish them. Limit your directions to one at a time. When your child is involved in something, it's also helpful to give him a five-minute warning. You wouldn't want your son to drop that imaginary 747 he's flying, killing all those people inside, just to rush to the dinner table, would you? It's important to him to finish what he's doing, so give him the chance.

While children are capable of accepting a surprising amount of responsibility for their behavior, they should not be required to take on more responsibility than they are ready for in other areas. For example, you shouldn't require your three-year-old to keep track of her "blanky" even if she insists on taking it grocery shopping. She's just not capable of being that single-minded or of holding onto two thoughts ("I want Mommy to buy me a cookie" and "I can't lose my blanket") at the same time. By the same token, a twelve-year-old should not be privy to the details of the family's financial problems or be expected to mediate in an argument between you and your spouse. Pushing too much responsibility onto children too early can make them anxious and depressed.

Too much freedom, like too much responsibility, can also be harmful to a child. In spite of the fact that they may forcefully resist your attempts to shape their behavior, children need limits placed on them in order to feel secure. At one progressive grade school, educators decided to remove the chain-link fence around the playground to give the children more freedom. Much to their surprise, the children reacted by huddling near the center of the playground. Without the limits imposed by the fence, they did not feel sufficiently secure to explore the outer edges of the playground. The same is true in life. In order to grow emotionally, children need to know what constitutes acceptable behavior—what the limits are—to feel safe enough to explore their own potential. (You can, however, count on them leaning on the fence just to make sure it really is a boundary.)

Handling Misbehavior

All behavior, including misbehavior, is purposeful. To illustrate this point, I often tell this story: Imagine that your eleven-year-old son, Johnny, goes out to empty the garbage one night. Three boys suddenly appear and start throwing iceballs at him. Johnny, quick thinker that he is, pulls off the lid of the garbage can and uses it to shield his head. As he ducks back into the house, one iceball hits the lid of the can with particular force. *Wow*, thinks Johnny, *it's a good thing I've got this garbage can lid. It saved my life.* From then on, no matter where he goes, Johnny's always got that garbage can lid with him. As his parent, you find this very frustrating, but you can't talk him out of it, because once that garbage can lid got Johnny what he wanted. His behavior may be inappropriate now, but there is a purpose behind it.

Now transfer this same kind of thinking to your child's misbehavior. Take whining, for example. Let's say you take your child to the store one day and you buy him a new toy. He's so thrilled that when you take him to the store the next day, he asks for another new toy, but you say no. He starts to whine and cry, and, not wanting a scene in the store, you give in. The next time you go to the store and he asks for a toy, you put your foot down. He whines and cries, but you've made up your mind: no toy. This doesn't mean he won't whine the next time you go shopping, however. After all, the behavior worked once, so it might work again. And sure enough, he's right. Maybe this time, or maybe the time after that, he starts whining, and because you're in a hurry, you buy the toy. What he has learned is that sometimes whining and crying works. It doesn't work every time—sometimes you might even have to whine through two or three trips to the store before you get results—but it works often enough to be worth a try. Like Johnny, your child has learned a behavior that might not be appropriate, but he's going to continue to carry it around with him because it worked once. (This learning process is called operant conditioning.) The only way Johnny is going to give up carrying that garbage can lid is to go outside so many times without getting hit by iceballs that he is finally convinced he doesn't need it anymore. The only way your child is going to stop whining for a toy is to be told no so consistently that he is convinced it will *never* work.

When your child misbehaves, then, you may be better able to handle him if you look at the purpose behind his actions. The only way to get him to give up the behavior is to be extremely consistent in your refusal to reward it. You should also consider whether the child who is acting up is just trying to get your attention. It may not seem to you that yelling at him is a reward, unless you look at the purpose behind the behavior. When your child's purpose is to get your attention, you need to change your tactics so that you reward good behavior, not bad.

I have found that the most effective, positive approach to correcting a child's behavior does not entail anything that even remotely resembles "punishment." It consists, primarily, of telling your child how you feel about his behavior. Once again, the key words are "I feel" "about" and "because." "I feel upset about your messy room because it embarrasses me when my friends come over." "I feel disappointed about your

poor grades because I know you're capable of doing better work." Note that the focus is still on the behavior, not on the child: "I feel upset about your messy room" or "your poor grades" not "I'm upset that you're such a slob" or "that you're a poor student." Often, just stating your feelings to your child, openly and honestly, is enough to cause him to reconsider his actions and change the behavior to please you.

If it isn't, you need to follow through with a corrective action. When doing this, it is important to keep in mind that the goal of discipline is to get the child to accept responsibility for his actions. Often when you impose a punishment on a child, it involves placing as many or more restrictions on yourself than on him. You decide what is right, prescribe the punishment, and police him to be sure it is enforced. The result is that you become more responsible, not the child.

In order to avoid this, you need to act calmly and according to a plan, rather than react out of anger or frustration. For example, let's say that you are eating chicken noodle soup for dinner, and your six-year-old decides it is great fun to toss the noodles across the table. When the first noodle hits you in the face, you calmly remove it and let him know his behavior is unacceptable, just in case he doesn't realize that. You state your feelings about the behavior: "I can't enjoy my dinner when you are throwing noodles. It ruins my appetite." A minute goes by, and then, *splat!* You get another noodle in the face. You now have two choices. You can take away the soup or quietly ask him to leave the table. Either way, you offer him the option of ending the punishment when he is ready to display better manners. In acting this way—rather than reacting with threats of "no dessert" or scolding—you accomplish several things. First, you've put the responsibility for his behavior on his shoulders, giving him the choice of eating in a civilized manner or not eating with you. Second, you've made it clear that you disapprove of his behavior without humiliating or belittling him, so that he will be up to the challenge of accepting that responsibility. And third—if you've kept your response brief and to the point—you've eliminated any payoff the child gets from his bad manners by ensuring that his actions are not getting him undue attention. In fact, if you actively encourage him to rejoin the family when he's ready, he'll realize that the only way to get your attention is through appropriate behavior.

In some cases, you might be surprised at how long it takes a child to decide he is ready to change his behavior. I once told my son Jared to sit on the stairs until he was ready to stop fighting with his sister. After about half an hour I asked if he was ready to leave the stairs yet. He shook his head no. He sat on those stairs for four hours. Another time, my daughter Nina was told to sit on the stairs for similar reasons. She sat there for less than a minute before she jumped up and returned to playing. A parent-imposed, fifteen-minute time limit would have been inappropriate for both these children. Jared would not yet have been ready to change his behavior, but for Nina the punishment would have been de-

pressingly severe. When the child is allowed to decide when he is ready to act in an appropriate manner, the steps taken to correct his behavior are automatically tailored to that child's particular need.

In order for a corrective action to be effective, you must adhere to the following principles:

1. The consequence must be closely related to the offensive behavior. Sometimes the natural consequence of a child's actions is all that is needed to change a behavior. Allowing our son to miss the school bus was ultimately more effective than dragging him out of bed each morning. When the natural consequence is something you can't allow to occur, you need to find a logical consequence, such as taking away a child's blocks because he insists on throwing them at his playmate's head. When you use a logical consequence, your child sees that connection between his behavior and the result, rather than seeing punishment as an arbitrary display of parental power.

2. The parent must understand the purpose behind the child's offensive behavior. You must be willing to talk to the child about why she's doing whatever it is you object to. (Remember your reflective listening.) If she's throwing blocks at her friend because she's angry about something, she needs you to understand and accept her feelings before she will be ready to act differently.

3. There must be freedom of choice. If you ban him from the dinner table, your child must decide when he wants to rejoin the family and eat in a civilized manner. You've set up the condition, but he is the one who has to decide when he is ready to change his behavior.

4. The child must be given support and encouragement while being asked to change her behavior. Again, children learn faster when they are encouraged rather than discouraged—and this is especially true when a mistake has been made. Your child's awareness that you believe in his ability to behave acceptably will make it easier for him to live up to your expectations.

5. The parent must have the advantage in implementing a logical consequence. If you are late for a function that you must attend and your daughter begins to act up, you can't very well tell her that you'll just stay home unless she behaves properly. On the other hand, if you're taking her to a movie that she wants to see, you can refuse to go until you're happy with her conduct. When you're in a situation in which you do not have the advantage, your best bet is to make sure your child's needs are met—that she is listened to and understood—before a full-blown conflict occurs. If sacrifices have to be made, try to make sure that you're both making some compromises, not just the child. For example, if you know you must drive a long distance with your children even though they hate car trips, try to involve them in the planning beforehand. You might agree to leave an hour early so that you can do something they want to do, like have a picnic at a park on the way. Another way you might anticipate their needs is to buy some small trinkets to dole out at regular intervals during the trip to alleviate their boredom, thereby heading off misbehavior before it begins.

6. There must be trust between the parent and child. The degree of success you have in disciplining your child is directly proportional to the quality of the relationship between you. If your relationship is based on mutual understanding, love and acceptance, your child will be much more responsive to your attempts to correct his behavior.

Resolving Major Conflicts

Good communication skills and effective disciplinary techniques combined with a relationship based on love and trust will help to keep major conflicts with your children to a minimum. No matter how skillful you become, however, problems will arise. Although it is not within the scope of this book to discuss these times in detail, it may be helpful to note that there are essentially nine steps to the problem solving/reconciliation process:

1. Talking: Sharing your feelings, values, and goals.
2. Listening: Hearing the other person's feelings, values, and goals.
3. Understanding the problem: Achieving empathy and insight, even if you are unable to reach agreement.
4. Planning solutions: Through brainstorming, study, prayer, or inspiration, generate as many solutions as possible to meet the needs of those involved.

5. Agreeing on a plan: Evaluating the worth of the solutions proposed (not of the persons proposing them) and agreeing on one to try.

6. Implementation: Putting the plan into action.

7. Assessment: Seeing how the plan is working and reporting results to each other. If it does not seem to be working at all, you may have to go all the way back to the beginning to reach a better understanding of the problem.

8. Refining the plan: Making any changes that seem necessary to improve progress.

9. Becoming one through cooperation and singleness of purpose. This will happen in due time if you have a strong relationship and have made a genuine effort to work through the first seven steps.

Whether you are dealing with small problems or large ones, don't be afraid to make mistakes. Children are amazingly resilient and will be both forgiving and willing to try again when things go wrong, as long as you are open about admitting your mistakes. Don't feel that you have to hide the techniques you are using, either; these aren't gimmicks or tricks, and they will work.

Summing Up: Communication and Discipline

1. Good communication is the essential key to a good relationship with your child.

2. Learn to really listen to your children and to use reflective listening.

3. In disciplining children, use love to bring out the basic good in them, not fear and pain to suppress the bad.

4. Don't put labels on your children, even "positive" ones.

5. Let your children be responsible for their own behavior.

6. Remember "I feel," "about," and "because" both in praising your children and in handling misbehavior.

7. Use logical consequences to correct misbehavior.

Note

1. Steven R. Covey, *Seven Habits of Highly Effective People* (New York: Simon & Schuster, 1989): p. 223.

Marriage, Sex, and Family

Y ou may well wonder what a chapter on marriage, sex, and family is doing in a book on children's health. In fact, when I first began teaching my seminars for parents, this topic was not included. It came about as a result of watching the marriages of some of the couples in my practice disintegrate into divorce. These were people I knew quite well; I'd delivered their babies and treated their families for years. I found it hard to believe that the same couples I'd seen happy together could drift so far apart. I realized then that couples are rarely counseled about the marital relationship and, especially, the effect that children have on it. Because they have few resources from which to draw advice and support, many are at a complete loss if things go a little sour.

Marriage is important. While very few people could claim to be more devoted to

raising children than I am, I feel that the relationship between husband and wife must take precedence over even that between parent and child. Someday my children will be grown and out of the house. When that day comes, if my wife and I haven't spent time on our relationship—if we, in effect, have no relationship—there will be no reason for us to stay together. Marriage exists apart from the children who are produced within it, and it needs to be nurtured so that it continues to grow even after those children have lives of their own. In "The Ripple Effect of a Satisfying Marital Relationship,"[1] Dr. Domeena Renshaw points out that there are many benefits of a good marriage, including continuity and security, the opportunity for personal growth and enhanced self-esteem, and a sense of belonging. Perhaps it goes without saying, but a fulfilling marriage is also a much better framework for raising children than a family that has been split apart by divorce.

Because of my strong feelings about marriage and divorce, and because I have been married for thirty-two mostly happy years myself, several years ago I decided that couples might benefit from hearing about some of the experiences Pat and I have had in our marriage. I made the marriage and family section a part of my seminars then, and while I can't say for certain that I have saved any troubled marriages, I do know that this has become the most popular segment of the course.

So if you'll bear with me for a minute, I'd like to take you through a brief chronicle of my own marriage. I met Pat over an open abdomen during a gallbladder operation. I was a college student working part-time as a scrub technician; she was a student nurse. In spite of the unromantic circumstances, it was love at first sight, and we were married shortly thereafter. I was twenty; she was eighteen.

Ours was a marriage made in heaven. Pat grew up in a family where her mother was the domineering force; I came from one where my father was in charge. We both took after our fathers, which worked out nicely. She needed someone to dominate her, and I needed someone to dominate. So for the first eight or nine years of our marriage, I did my best to take charge of everything she did. I taught her how to make the bed, how to line up the silverware properly in the silverware drawer, even which laundry detergent to use. I was pretty busy with medical school by then, but I put a lot of

time and effort into getting her shaped up. And although she had four children to care for by the time I finished medical school, she did her best to shape up, with, admittedly, some of the foot-dragging that is usually present in this type of relationship.

We continued in this mode through my internship and a brief stint in the Navy. Finally I went into private practice, and at last had a little extra money and a little free time. One day I read a magazine article about what happens to doctors' vast fortunes when they die. According to the article, if I died, Pat would either squander all my hard-earned money, or someone would come along, take advantage of her, and squander it for her. Either way, she and our children would end up penniless. This whole concept came as a shock to me, particularly since it hadn't occurred to me that doctors died just like everyone else. Not too surprisingly, I completely controlled the money in our family, doling out a little cash to Pat now and then as I saw fit. After reading this article, however, I began to worry about that arrangement, and felt that Pat should learn how to manage money. To that end, I opened a checking account for her, putting in our grocery allowance, enough money to pay the electric bill each month, and (quite generously, I thought) five dollars that she could spend however she chose. How do you think she did with that account? Well, in those days, when you bounced a check, the bank charged you two dollars. At the end of a year, Pat had racked up three hundred and fifty-four dollars in bounced check charges.

This little experiment was not a failure

because my wife was incapable of handling money. Several years later, Pat decided to go back to school and get a part-time job. She took twelve credits a semester, made a 4.0 average, and worked in my office, all in addition to running a household with eight children. She also began managing her own money with no problems whatsoever. She had made the decision to become more self-sufficient, whereas the first time I had decided to make her that way when she wasn't really interested.

Now, you might think that I would have been thrilled with the change in Pat, since I had attempted to engineer a similar change a few years earlier. To the contrary: In fact, this was probably one of the hardest times in our marriage. I was convinced that my wife, now obviously able to take care of herself, no longer needed me. I expected her to pack up and leave any day. Luckily for me (and our marriage), Pat realized that my emotional needs were not being met, and she made an extra effort to see that they were. (One of the things she did was to take me out and buy me some fancy new clothes. To this day, I still run into people who ask what's become of that plum jumpsuit.) She managed to convince me that I was still loved and appreciated, even though her needs had changed.

Things went pretty smoothly until a few years later, when Pat decided we should attend a Marriage Encounter weekend. This was in the seventies, when encounter groups were popular, and I had the erroneous impression that a marriage encounter would involve being screamed at, or that I would be required to bare my innermost thoughts and feelings to strangers. I resisted the whole idea, but then in one weak moment conceded that maybe I'd go. On the basis of that maybe, Pat paid the registration fee. Because I was too cheap to consider losing it, I ended up going along.

Much to my surprise, I had a wonderful time. I got in touch with my feelings, which had been so deeply buried that I hardly knew they existed. When we came home, I wanted to talk endlessly about my discoveries and I wanted to change my life. Suddenly I realized that my family was the most important thing to me and I wanted to see more of them. At that time I was seeing about a hundred patients a day in my office, and usually had another twenty to thirty to visit in the hospital. I was stomping out disease like crazy. Suddenly, I cut the number of patients I saw in half and also reduced my staff by about fifty percent. Fifty patients a day is still a healthy practice, but Pat was convinced that we were on our way to the poorhouse. To allay her fears, I brought her into the office and introduced her to the financial aspect of the practice so that she would have a more realistic view of our finances and some control over them.

My point is this: Eighteen years or so into our marriage, Pat and I were not the same people who had started out together. As we grew and changed as individuals, our needs grew and changed, and the relationship had to grow and change, too. If we had continued treating each other as we did when we were first married, our marriage would not have lasted. As with any marriage, there have been periods when things weren't great. In fact, there were even times when each of us was so disillusioned we considered calling the whole thing off. We've never separated, though, and through one means or another we have managed to adapt to each other's changing needs. As a result, our relationship has been a success.

I don't believe that divorce occurs because people choose the wrong partners, but because couples fail to grow and change together. Wootan's theory of marriage states that a person knows within hours of meeting someone whether or not he or she will make a suitable partner. In fact, one study has shown that we process some 180 bits of information per second, or 648,000 per hour. Another estimated that we assimilate approximately 425,000 bits of information about another person even during a brief encounter. Because it's not socially acceptable in our culture to propose marriage at a first meeting, we don't interpret those little bits of information as "He'd make a good husband," or "She'd make a good wife," but rather as "I like his (or her) eyes," or smile, or whatever. I know that when I first met Pat, I didn't give a thought to the kind of wife and mother she'd make, but I did fall in love with her immediately. I think my subconscious was taking care of the other details, and sending up signals that told me I was attracted to this woman.

Eighty-five percent of all divorces occur within one of three time periods: five to seven years, eleven to thirteen years, and twenty-two to twenty-seven years of marriage. Add in the periods of the birth of the first child, the youngest child's starting school, midlife crisis, the last child's leaving home, and the husband's retirement, and the figure rises to ninety-seven percent. Everyone, when they first get married, likes to think that their relationship is different. In many senses, of course, it is, just as each human being is different from all others. But like all human beings, all marriages are also alike in many ways—and one of these ways is that they tend to end during the same critical time periods.

You might figure that I have a theory about that. You're right: Wootan's theory of divorce states that a marriage, like any individual, goes through awkward growth stages and times of disequilibrium. When two people join together in marriage, they create a new entity, just as a sperm and ovum do when they join. Together, the sperm and ovum become an embryo, a fetus, and finally an infant. That infant continues through many different growth stages, and not all of them are enjoyable. The marriage, too, grows and changes, and some of its stages are awkward and unpleasant. You've heard of the terrible twos? How about the terrible five to sevens? The agonizing teens? How about the agonizing eleven to thirteens? The depressed young adult? How about the depressed twenty-two- to twenty-seven-year-old marriage? No one would throw out a child in the midst of the terrible twos (although the temptation might be great), but many people tend to be all too willing to toss out a marriage that's going through an awkward stage. If people could learn to approach their relationships with the same tolerance that they show their children, more marriages might survive.

Of course, not only does a marriage grow

as an entity, but each partner in the marriage also grows as an individual. Leo Buscaglia suggests that when we marry, we should look at our spouse in this way: "I select you, out of all the people in the world, to grow with."[2] Individual growth is desirable and more or less inevitable, but it can precipitate one of those awkward stages in the relationship. If, for example, the wife is in the process of changing in a way that her husband isn't, he can end up feeling like someone who has been invited to play checkers only to find the rules changed in the middle of the game. He may feel like giving up on the marriage because she's "not the woman I married anymore." For her part, the wife may begin to want out because "I've changed, and he doesn't meet my needs now." In this situation, both partners need a large measure of patience to carry them through until the second person changes and grows, too, and harmony is attained once again. When Pat first decided she no longer wanted to be dominated, I felt as though someone had pulled the rug out from under me. I *needed* someone to dominate, I expected that someone to be my wife, and now she was taking that away from me. She had to wait for me to change too, until I grew enough to realize that I didn't want to be a daddy to my wife, but a husband and lover. At other times in our marriage (as, for example, after our Marriage Encounter weekend), I was the one who was doing the growing, and had to wait for Pat to catch up.

In addition to having the patience to wait an awkward stage out, it is helpful if the partner who is doing the growing makes an extra effort to meet the other's needs in some other way. When Pat took me on that shopping spree, she let me know I was still important to her and that this new game had rewards for both of us.

At times, of course, you may want to actively change your partner. When this is the case, there are two things you should keep in mind: First, it is always easier to change yourself than someone else, and second, you will have more success in changing someone else if you discuss things reasonably and work out agreements rather than make demands. The only person who really likes to be changed is a baby with a wet diaper. If you complain, nag, or criticize, you will almost inevitably meet with resistance. Instead, try the soft, gentle approach.

Let me give you a couple of examples. Many years ago, when we had been married for about four years, Pat brought the children to me at bedtime and said, "George, kiss the kids good-night." "Where are they going?" I asked, and when I found out they weren't going anywhere, I protested a little. "Aren't I going to be here when they wake up?" "Just shut up and kiss your kids," I was told. Since it's difficult to argue with giving your kids a good-night kiss, I did. I was uncomfortable about it, though, because I came from one of those families where no one showed affection. In fact, the first time I ever hugged my father, I was thirty-five years old. Pat, on the other hand, came from a family where taking out the garbage warranted a good-bye kiss, and now she wanted to make me more like them.

Well, I resisted. Soon I decided that it was important that I read every night around seven o'clock, and I'd lock myself away in my study. That didn't stop Pat in her mission; she just knocked on the door and brought in the troops for their kisses. Next I decided that I needed a run every night before I settled down with my reading, so I was out getting my exercise when bedtime rolled around. Much to my surprise, the children were still up, waiting for a sweaty kiss, when I walked back in the door.

At the time I didn't think about trying to avoid the routine of good-night kisses; after all, no one wants to admit they don't want to kiss their children. With twenty-twenty hindsight, however, I realize that that was exactly what I was doing. I just wasn't comfortable with open displays of affection. Pat knew it was important, however, and she set about to change me. She didn't yell or criticize, which would have only made me defensive, but instead just gently guided me in the direction she wanted me to go. And it worked. I love being affectionate with my children now, and if any of them happens to forget to kiss me good-night, I feel slighted.

Another time, Pat decided that it was important that I make a point of being home for dinner with the children a few times a week. This was in the days when I was a champion disease-fighter, and my mission didn't leave much time for such niceties as family dinners. Looking back now, I also realize that I resisted this idea, too, partly because of my family history. My father was rarely home for dinner, and when he was, he used the occasion to criticize and belittle his children. Consequently, we weren't anxious to have him around, and he undoubtedly picked up on that. I'm sure I assumed that I'd have to act the same way,

and suffer the same consequences, if I did join my family for dinner. While this wasn't a conscious decision, on some level I must have realized it was easier not to show up at the dinner table at all.

Nevertheless, Pat brought up the subject of family dinners in casual conversation one night, and I agreed that it was a good idea, expecting to let the subject drop. Instead, Pat persisted by asking which nights would be best for me to join the family, and together we pinned it down to Tuesday and Thursday. I still didn't look at this as a firm commitment, however. I think we all have a list of things we've promised to do (the "honey, do" list) for our spouse. Some of these we really do intend to get accomplished, and others we vaguely realize will never get done, but we feel better knowing they're on the list. For me, the promise to join the family for dinner fell into the latter category. I didn't expect to have to follow through.

However, the next Tuesday night, Pat called at about five o'clock and reminded me that I'd agreed to have dinner with the family. I protested a little, because I had a patient to see at the hospital. There was another doctor who was on call after hours, but I wasn't one to give up an opportunity to work, and I insisted on seeing her myself. I promised Pat I'd be twenty minutes late at the most. Now, I knew full well that I wouldn't make it home until after dinner, but at this point I still wasn't convinced I'd made a commitment I couldn't get out of.

When I finally rolled in around eight-thirty, I knew I was facing a confrontation, so I had worked up an airtight excuse for being late. Much to my surprise, though, I was met not with anger and accusations, but with dinner, still on the table. Pat had given the kids a snack so they weren't starving, but dinner was still waiting, cold and congealed and about as unappetizing as it could get. Pat calmly suggested that we eat, and we all sat down and did our best to consume this terrible meal. I never got the chance to use my perfect excuse. Believe it or not, this happened a few more times before I finally got the message that this would not blow over. When I saw how important it was to Pat, I gradually changed my behavior. The change was accomplished quietly and calmly, because that was the way Pat approached it. If she had nagged or screamed at me, I'd have resisted with equal force, which is just human nature.

"Great," you may say, "but you don't know my husband. He is positively cast in granite. He'll never change, no matter what I do." (I'm sure this complaint could apply to someone's wife, too, but in talking with couples I've most often heard it about the husbands.) I don't think anyone could be more stubborn than I was, however. My father used to take pride in saying that he was the captain of the ship and that he would never waver from the course he steered, in spite of the storms in his path. I come by my stubbornness honestly, through both genetics and his excellent training. Still, with patience and ingenuity, my wife was able to change me, and I'm grateful she went to the trouble to do so.

The two factors that most often cause marriages to fail are selfishness and a lack of communication. Being unselfish in a marriage requires that each partner be willing to give one hundred percent to the relationship.

Couples often tell me that they have a fifty-fifty relationship. I can't help but think that this means they are each giving only fifty percent. If one of them backs off even one percent, there's suddenly a gap between them. When each person gives one hundred percent, one of them has to back off a long way to create this same gap. I know it isn't easy to be unselfish, especially in a society that emphasizes always looking out for number one. However, if you give your partner's needs priority, he or she will feel special and truly loved. That feeling is not easy to come by, nor is it one from which most people would willingly walk away.

Communication is essential to intimacy. Traditionally in our culture, women are brought up to be communicators and men are not. Men are taught that expressing their feelings is unmanly, and many of them, like me, grow up out of touch with their emotions. Partly as a result of their training, partly because of the unique viewpoint women acquire when they become mothers and must share themselves completely with another person, and partly because of other factors, women tend to become the ones who are responsible for the emotional well-being of a marriage. They're the ones who are in charge of keeping the lines of communication open and making sure each partner's needs are met. Not too surprisingly, this system often fails. Since the man doesn't express his feelings, he ends up with needs and desires that his wife can't possibly meet, because she doesn't even know about them. The wife, in turn, may resent the burden she's carrying and begin to feel that it's not worth the effort. In order for a relationship to really work, both partners must be able to talk about their feelings and feel that they are understood. The emotional health of a relationship has to be a mutual responsibility.

Most men aren't going to take on their share without a little prodding, however. In some ways, men remind me of a bird that during the mating season puts on a spectacular show for his mate. He struts around in his colorful plumage, puffs out the brilliant red air bladder beneath his beak, and generally goes all out to convince his love that he's really something spectacular. They mate, and he *never* does it for her again. When he's courting, a man is sweet, considerate, and affectionate. He listens to the woman he loves, and even ventures to talk about some of those emotions he feels pretty safe expressing. As soon as the words "I do" are out of his mouth, however, boom!—all the colorful plumage falls off, and that beautiful bird is never seen again.

Now, the man might be to blame for not realizing that he's stopped communicating and has shifted all responsibility for the health of his marriage onto his wife. Too often, though, I think a woman reacts by becoming disgruntled and dissatisfied but never trying to get her husband to change or even letting him know that his behavior leaves something to be desired. I think most men fail to carry the emotional weight in a marriage because they're afraid to, not because they don't want to. If women would take on the task of helping their husbands to be more emotionally responsible and to express their feelings, and if men would make a little effort to change, more people would find fulfillment in their marriages.

As part of any couple's effort to com-municate more fully with each other, I recommend a Marriage Encounter weekend. These were begun by the Catholic church, but are now often sponsored by Protestant denominations and even some nonreligious organizations. No matter how strong your marriage is, I believe you will find a Marriage Encounter weekend a positive experience that immeasurably strengthens your ability to communicate with and understand each other.

Even those couples who find talking about their feelings the most natural thing in the world discover that having children can be a major impediment to communication, if for no other reason than that they place enormous demands on both parents' time. In our house, with eleven children, the demands of childrearing have been great enough to try the skills of even the best communicators. Largely through trial and error, Pat and I have devised some strategies that help us to keep the lines of communication open at all times. I think these suggestions should be an enormous help even to those couples who have only one or two children:

1. We have a "closed door" policy. When we close our bedroom door, *no one* is allowed to disturb us. (Babies and toddlers are exempt from this rule, of course.) This does not always sit well with our older children. One of our daughters, as a teenager, could hear the click of our bedroom door closing even if she was a mile away wearing stereo headphones cranked up to full volume. She'd come home and stomp up and down the hall, knowing it would do no good to knock, until we came out again. We

don't open the door for anything short of a life-or-death crisis. What do we do behind our closed door? Sometimes we talk, sometimes we make love, and sometimes we simply hide. Having a closed-door policy gives us a chance to be alone together, even in a household full of children.

2. We control the television; it doesn't control us. TV is the most invasive, disruptive thing that people allow into their homes. If you leave it on constantly, no one will communicate with anyone, because they will all be too busy with the television. In our house, we have worked out a schedule: The TV can be turned on only from Friday night through Saturday night, although we do make exceptions for special programs and those that have redeeming social value. (It's interesting to watch our children attempt to convince us that "Laverne and Shirley" reruns fit into this category. They've gotten so good at it that sometimes they almost succeed.) Our schedule may not be appropriate for you, but you do need to work out a system whereby the TV is not allowed to take on a life of its own in your home. This ban on TV includes sports programs, by the way. I love football, but came to the conclusion a long time ago that my marriage and my family had to take precedence over sports. The disappointment of missing a few good games has been far outweighed by the improvement in my relationships with my wife and children. Men who tend to get glued to the set for every sports event need to reconsider their priorities. (Erma Bombeck has suggested we pass a new law that states that any man who watches 168,000 football games in a season be declared legally dead. All in favor say "aye.")

3. We go out once a week. Because we believe that a child should not be separated from his mother until about the age of three, we have often taken a baby or toddler out with us. We've been able to manage this by finding places that interest the child as well as us. For a while, we frequented an Italian restaurant where our two-year-old could visit with the mother of the proprietor while we ate and talked. She got a dose of grandmotherly love and we got to enjoy each other's company. We have also made numerous trips to the shopping mall, where a toddler can walk up and down while we follow along behind, holding hands and talking. Our "dates" don't always involve spending a lot of money, but they do give us the chance to talk to each other away from the demands of children and other responsibilities at home. There have been times when we had no money to spend, but still we would go for a drive or a walk, just to get out together.

If you have only one child under the age of three, you may wonder why you should bother to go out at all. The answer is simple: When you're home, the phone rings, the laundry calls out to be folded and put away, the leaky bathroom faucet suddenly has to be fixed *right now*. In order to concentrate on each other, you and your spouse need time away from your day-to-day chores, even if only for a couple of hours.

At one point in our lives, when our younger children were old enough to be left with their older siblings, Pat and I would go check into a motel for a few hours. We'd get

174

takeout food, eat, talk, make love, and just enjoy each other's company. On one of these occasions we happened to arrive home before the kids, who had all gone out to a movie. It was obvious they knew what we'd been up to; they were very careful to announce their presence loudly when they came in. I think the message this sort of situation sends to children is a healthy one, in that it gives children a glimpse of the joy and satisfaction that results from a good marriage.

4. We write letters. Even when Pat and I are together every day, we write each other love letters from time to time. Remember how good it felt to get a love letter, back when you and your spouse were dating? You don't have to give up this romantic gesture just because you live under the same roof and sleep in the same bed; it's still a great way to make you feel good about yourself and each other.

5. We have learned to speak the same language. People don't always express love in the same way. Back in my workaholic days, I equated love with being a good provider. One summer, during my years in medical school, I was working sixteen hours a day at two jobs. I got another job, bringing me up to twenty-two working hours a day. I couldn't wait to tell Pat about it, because now we'd be able to afford new clothes for the kids and other things we needed. I expected her to be as excited as I was. Instead, she was furious. She had this crazy (I thought) idea that if I really loved her and the children, I'd want to spend more time with them. To me, love was money, but to her, it was time. Obviously, we weren't

speaking the same language. It took us quite a while to work this one out, but eventually we came to understand each other (and, in my case, to change my perspective).

Occasionally people tell me that they are convinced their marriage was doomed from the start because they have "nothing in common." It's not surprising for married couples to be very different from each other. Having nothing in common can actually be a positive trait in a relationship. Your strengths may be your husband's or wife's weaknesses, and vice versa, so that the two of you fit together perfectly. Your partner's temperament, if different from your own, is probably complementary to yours. When giving this part of my lecture, I am often reminded of those medallions some couples wear. The two halves—one worn by the husband, one by the wife—fit together to make a circle. The two people who make up any couple are rather like that medallion. Their opposite strengths and weaknesses inevitably lead to some discord, but they also fit together in perfect union. This analogy reduces a relationship to simple terms, of course, but I think there's an element of truth in it for almost every marriage. If you can learn to look at your spouse's "faults" as complements to elements of your own personality, you might begin to understand better how the two of you can work well together. Happiness in a marriage comes not from always being alike or always being in agreement, but from understanding and accepting each other as you are.

Generally, I think most relationships start out strong. In the beginning of a marriage, we tend to focus on the good feelings and see only the things about our spouse that we like. As little problems begin to creep into a relationship, it becomes easier to tune into all the things that are "wrong" with one's partner and to overlook the attributes that attracted you in the first place. The more you accentuate the negative, the bigger the faults seem to get, until you've almost completely forgotten why you married that person. If you can train yourself to accentuate the positive instead, those traits will loom larger in your mind. One good way to emphasize the positive is to make a point of complimenting your spouse every day. Sometimes just taking the time to remember how you used to feel—and why—can also help rekindle the positive feelings.

No matter how faithfully you follow my suggestions, it is inevitable that there will be some conflict in your marriage. If we learn to look at conflict as a challenge to be met and a test of our skills, it can ultimately be a positive experience for both partners in a marriage. In her book *Conflict: Friend or Foe?*[3] Joyce Huggett has these suggestions for making conflict productive: "Firstly, face the conflict with a positive attitude. A problem or conflict is not a sign of failure but a reason for good energy and motivation. We need to examine the sources of conflict and look at our options. Secondly, we need to accept our share of the responsibility for the creation of the difficulties and for finding their solutions. Thirdly, we must use positive communication skills . . . and always look for what is right, not who is right." Morton Hunt, in an article in *Parade* magazine,[4] suggested four very helpful steps in resolving a conflict: (1) Establish a working relationship based on mutual respect for the other person's viewpoint (one way to do this is to switch roles temporarily, so that, for example, the sloppy person becomes neat and the neat person becomes sloppy). (2) Identify the problem. Make sure that what you think is the problem really is. (Sometimes you may need an outside observer to help with this). (3) Brainstorm solutions. (4) Negotiate and put mutually agreed upon solutions on paper. Writing it down is important to ensure that the solutions are clearly understood by both parties.

In spite of your best efforts at building a strong marriage, you may decide you need help in getting through a difficult time. If you do, by all means seek it, and don't wait until the marriage is so sick that radical surgery—divorce—is the only solution. You may get the best help from within your own family: from your parents or in-laws, (if they've had a successful marriage and you get along well with them), or from a favorite aunt or uncle. The reason I suggest seeking help within the family first is that certain traits run in families. If your husband is "just like his father," your mother-in-law may have a few hints on how best to get along with him. Or your own mother may, if you happen to have married a man who is a lot like your father.

If seeking help within your family isn't a good idea, turn to a friend who has had marital problems that have been successfully worked out. Don't consult the friend who has been divorced three times, because that person obviously has not figured out how to have a successful marriage. If there is no one among your friends you feel you can turn to, consult a marriage counselor. But, again, choose someone who has had a successful marriage, and who has been married at least as long as you have, and so has some idea of the problems you are facing.

Is There Sex After Children?

For the couple who has just had a baby, the discouraging answer might seem to be no. Pregnancy, birth, and childrearing all have profound effects on a couple's sex life, and, unfortunately, not all of them are good. Keeping both partners sexually satisfied—perhaps an effortless endeavor before children—suddenly requires thought and loving consideration on the part of both husband and wife.

Pregnancy may affect both of the prospective parents' levels of sexual desire. A woman may be more interested or less interested in sex, depending on how the complex mix of psychological and physical factors associated with pregnancy affect her as an individual. In the beginning, she may feel too tired or nauseous even to think about sex. Or if she had always feared getting pregnant, her sex drive may go up because she no longer has to worry about birth control. Still another possibility is that she may resent being pregnant (if she had not wanted to be) and that resentment might be reflected in her feelings toward her husband and sex. As the pregnancy progresses, both hormonal fluctuations and her feelings about the changes in her body may also affect her level of desire. While his own body is not changing, the father-to-be, too, may find that the pregnancy alters his sex drive. His wife's new body may turn him on or off, and his impending fatherhood may bring on feelings that diminish or increase his need for sex. Furthermore, if a couple had trouble getting pregnant, they may both have grown accustomed to looking at intercourse as a job that had to be done. Now that their goal has been accomplished, it may take time to readjust their thinking about sex.

And that's just the beginning. Once the child is born, there's a whole new set of circumstances to cope with. Typically, the nursing mother is almost completely uninterested in sex. There may be several reasons for her lack of desire, but one of the most significant is that her body secretes a hormone called prolactin as long as she is lactating. In some respects, prolactin resembles a miracle drug. It acts as a natural tranquilizer, which is why nursing mothers are so calm, and it effectively suppresses ovulation, usually for at least three months and sometimes for as long as three years. Unfortunately, prolactin also tends to dry up vaginal secretions, sometimes making intercourse painful for a woman, and it also lowers her sex drive to a few micromillimeters above zero. Constantly nursing and holding her baby may also leave a woman feeling "touched out." All day long she holds this little body and has his tiny hands and mouth making demands on her. Finally she crawls into bed, and then, in the dark, comes another pair of hands with another set of demands. Rather than feeling turned on, she may have an overwhelming urge to scream and push them away. Add to this the fact that she's probably tired from nighttime feedings and the work involved in caring for a baby, and it's not hard to see why her libido may go into a deep freeze.

Unfortunately, the father of the nursing baby is unaffected by prolactin, and he's not touched out. He's going to feel as amorous as ever, and may be disturbed to discover, when he comes bounding up the stairs after "Monday Night Football," that his playful sex kitten is not bouncing around the bed waiting for him. More than likely, she's sound asleep. The only thing that's going to wake her is her baby's cry—certainly not her husband's sexy body. To make matters worse, the husband may begin to resent the baby for monopolizing all of his wife's time and energy—a common feeling among first-time fathers, especially.

Needless to say, all this can put some stress on marital relations. In an ideal world, the process of pregnancy, birth, and childrearing would all serve to bring a couple closer together. It's easy to see, however, how it might very well drive them apart, especially in bed. Before you decide to kiss your sex life good-bye, though, let me add that there is hope. With a lot of communication and a little creativity, this marriage *can* be saved.

When discussing sex in marriage, I always work on the assumption that each person has a right to have his or her sexual needs met within the marriage. This doesn't mean that either partner should be at the other's beck and call for sex, but that each must show consideration and understanding of the other's sexual needs and make an effort to meet them.

In order to do this you must communicate those needs. All those strange new feelings, sexual or not, need to be shared and examined from the time they first start cropping up, not pushed aside as "unimportant." Neither spouse can be expected to understand his or her partner's reactions to parenthood (or even impending parenthood) without a generous dose of communication. I know of one father who, about five weeks after his second baby was born, finally admitted to his wife that he felt neglected, emotionally and sexually. Both of his sons were receiving all this love and tenderness from his wife, and he felt left out. His wife was amazed to discover that he had no idea how she felt: exhausted and drained, as if she could not possibly meet another need. She'd been coping so quietly that he didn't realize how depleted her resources were. She, in turn, was unaware of how he felt. By talking about and understanding each other's feelings, they were able to work things out so that she got more of the help and support she needed, enabling her to have some energy left over for him at the end of the day.

Good communication can also help you over the rough spots that may crop up in the actual mechanics of lovemaking. When a couple has been physically intimate for some time, they generally establish a routine that is mutually satisfying. When she is pregnant or nursing, however, a woman's responses may suddenly change. For example, often a nursing mother will feel that her breasts are for her baby alone, and would rather not have them touched by her husband, even if she had once enjoyed this sort of stimulation. If she doesn't talk to her husband about her feelings, he'll have no way of knowing that the game plan has been changed. She may end up annoyed that he's touching her *there* again, while he's patiently waiting for her to get aroused by his touch. Not talking about the situation can lead to frustration, anger, and dishonesty (if the woman feels compelled to fake a response), all of which are detrimental to good sex.

A woman may also want to communicate to her husband that she needs a little time to change gears from being a mother to being his sexy wife. He may need to be told that she can't just stop nursing the baby and instantly start making love to him without a little break in which to change roles mentally. Again, honest communication is necessary to avoid misunderstandings and hurt feelings.

One way to make sure that both partners' needs are met is to make a distinction between "having sex" and "making love." As I define these terms, making love involves both partners feeling interested, getting aroused, and reaching a climax. By contrast, having sex is more one-sided: One partner does not feel as interested, but agrees to satisfy the other's needs. If a nursing mother isn't up to making love but is willing to have sex, she should let her husband know up front that that's how she feels, so he can adjust his expectations accordingly. Of course, sometimes a couple can start out having sex and end up making love, but I highly doubt that anyone will complain about *that* change in plan.

It should be noted that while a woman is nursing, she and her husband are going to be having sex most of the time, not making love. This is not an abnormal situation, and should not be viewed as a "problem." When a couple first marries, they usually have essentially one "plan" (plan A) for making love. This generally entails arousal and climax for both partners. After a baby arrives, however, you may also have plan B, which may be quickie sex that allows the man to feel satisfied and the women to get to sleep as quickly as possible. You may even have a plan C, for when the woman enjoys being touched and stimulated but doesn't feel the need or desire to reach a climax. There's nothing wrong with having different levels of sex, as long as both partners communicate and understand each other. Plans B and C may not be as earth-shakingly satisfying as plan A, but they have their merits.

While a woman is pregnant and/or nursing the scales of sexual desire will usually be tipped so that it is the man who wants sex and the woman who must meet his need even though she feels none herself. To put things into perspective, it's helpful to realize that in just about every relationship there will be times when the situation is reversed. When that's the case, the woman has just as much right as the man to communicate her needs and expect them to be met. The scales tipped in our marriage when Pat was at a comfortable stage in her pregnancy with Nina and Jared was almost completely weaned. The first night she approached me, I thought, "Wow. This is great." The second and third nights I was still pretty enthusiastic, but by the fourth, sleep seemed like a nice alternative, and on the fifth, I couldn't help but protest. "Look," she said, "as a man who's facing the desert, you'd better take a drink while you can." Undoubtedly, at some point in time, the tables will be turned in your marriage, too. Make sure you're both willing to consider and meet each other's sexual needs, for that is, after all, one of the things that marriage is about.

In addition to communicating your needs to each other, you must also accept the fact that, as far as your sex life is concerned, spontaneity flew the coop the day the stork arrived. If you and your spouse were married for a while before having a child, you have probably been accustomed to enjoying a little lovemaking on a moment's notice, whenever the time seemed right. You could come home from work, give each other a knowing look, and tumble into bed before dinner, or even during dinner. Those days are over. If the baby is awake, he demands your attention, and if he's asleep, Mom is probably napping, too. Even if, by some stroke of luck, the baby is asleep and you both are willing and able, all you have to do is touch each other, and invariably the air will be filled with baby's cries. (This happens with such amazing consistency that I am convinced there is some psychic connection between mother and infant, so that he knows when someone else is touching her.) Rather than get frustrated by the limitations, try to work within them. Make a date to make love. The baby's nap time on weekend afternoons is a wonderful time for a little passion. Forget the dishes that need to be done, the bills that should be paid, the grass that's crying out to be cut, and devote an hour to enjoying each other. If you have older children, send them over to their grandparents' or a friend's for a couple of hours so that you won't be disturbed. Granted, making a date to make love takes planning, and some people—particularly men, I've found—object that planning takes

the fun out of sex. However, consider the man (or woman, for that matter) who is having an affair. He may only get to see his paramour on Tuesdays at three-thirty, but he doesn't trudge to her house, dragging his feet because it's that time again. Instead, he's got a spring in his step and a smile on his face. You can have the same kind of enthusiasm for making love to your spouse if you let go of the idea that the only good sex is spontaneous sex.

There are other ways in which you can be creative about when you make love. The nursing mother who is tired all the time may find that she has more energy for sex after a two A.M. feeding than she did at ten o'clock, or she may even find that the urge to make love strikes in the middle of the afternoon. What should she do? Call her husband at work: "Hello, John. Would you like to come home and make love?" I guarantee you that he'll get home as fast as is humanly possible. (If you try this little trick, be sure to time your husband, because then you will know exactly how long it *really* takes him to get home.) I can well remember the day Pat called me to suggest I come home to make love. I somberly told my secretary that there was an emergency at home and then walked out past thirty people in the waiting room. An hour later, I returned, a big smile on my face, and relayed the news that everything at home was just fine. And, truly, it was.

With all this discussion of sexual needs, I feel compelled to devote a little time to nonsexual touch, a subject that is often neglected in our culture. I mentioned earlier that a nursing mother may feel "touched out" by the end of the day. When this happens, she may think that she doesn't want anyone touching her in any way. I think, however, that one of the reasons this happens is that the woman is not getting enough affectionate, nonsexual touching from her husband. In our society, we all—and men in particular—tend to use touch with our mates mainly as a means of communicating a desire to have sex. A man may feel that his sexual feelings for his wife are an adequate expression of his love for her. In order to feel truly loved, however, the woman may need affection and romance, to be told in actions as well as words, "I love you" in addition to "I want you." I've sometimes found that men have trouble understanding or accepting this distinction, so I ask them to think back on all the jokes or comments they've heard about how it doesn't matter who you're having sex with as long as the lights are out. In our culture, sex and love are not inextricably linked, especially not for men. The fact that a man wants to have sex with his wife may only convey to her that he has strong sexual needs, not that he is madly in love with her. I think this holds true at just about any time in a couple's marriage, but it is especially true in the postpartum period, when a woman may feel less sexually desirable than she ever has in her life. To feel that her husband wants her for herself and not just because she's readily available, a woman needs affection and tenderness that are not connected to sexual demands or expectations.

While men often seem to have trouble understanding why their wives need all that affection to feel loved, women frequently fail to comprehend how intense their husbands' need for sex is. I think part of the reason this happens is that generally speaking, men are easily aroused through visual stimuli, while women need to feel a strong emotional bond before they want to make love to someone. Because they are not so easily turned on, women may not understand how frequent or intense a man's desire for sex is. If the woman is not getting enough affection, she may stop responding sexually to her husband, with the inevitable result of unhappy people on both sides of the bed. However, if men make a point of cultivating affection and romance in their marriages and women make an attempt to understand their husbands' sexual needs, they will both benefit. The woman whose need for affection is met is much more likely to feel like making love to her husband. The ultimate result, of course, will be emotional and sexual satisfaction for husband *and* wife.

The Family Bed

Before I end the topic of sexuality in marriage, I'd like to discuss a subject that is only peripherally related: having your children sleep in your bed. I know that the current view of this practice is that it is emotionally unhealthy, but I don't subscribe to it. Many other mammals sleep with their babies, and it seems perfectly natural that humans should do the same. In fact, about eighty-five percent of the children of the world sleep in their parents' bedroom, and, in many places, it is not uncommon for them to continue doing so until they marry and leave home. Sharing your bed with your children has many advantages, such as fostering emotional security and eliminating some of the bedtime hassles. (If you're unconvinced, *The Family Bed*, by Tine Thevenin [Avery, 1987] goes into the subject in detail.)

One of the concerns people have about children sleeping in their parents' bed is that the practice will cause sexual deviation. In societies where a family bed is the norm, however, deviant behavior is not seen unless sex itself is treated as unnatural or bad. I think our attitude toward sex greatly influences whether or not our children grow up to be sexually healthy, and this holds true regardless of where they sleep. Nevertheless, you may be uncomfortable making love if there's a small child in bed with you. This is why we need nurseries. The nursery shouldn't be the place a baby sleeps, but the place the parents go to make more babies. If your children are small, you can use any room in the house for making love, but the nursery is a fine choice if you happen to have older children who are likely to be in and out of those other rooms. Another good option is to keep a small mattress on the floor next to your own bed. You can move the children off onto it while you make love, and then move them back again later.

Should you choose to stay in your own bed, you don't have to worry about your child waking up and seeing you in the act, or even about an older child walking in on you. The younger child isn't going to be concerned about what you're doing. I can guarantee you that your two-year-old is not lying in bed, half-awake, waiting to catch you making love. He doesn't have any idea what you're doing, and unless you act as if something terrible has happened, he's going to remain unaware and unconcerned in the unlikely event that he wakes up. The older child won't be traumatized either, unless you act as though you've been caught doing something wrong. If you jump up, cover up, and scream at him to get out, he might get the wrong idea about sex. Instead, just calmly suggest he go downstairs and have a bowl of ice cream, and tell him you'll join him later. He'll undoubtedly take you up on the invitation (this is the only good reason I can think of to keep ice cream in your freezer at all times). There's no reason to be overly concerned about a child accidentally witnessing sex, which is, after all, perfectly natural behavior. As a matter of fact, if you have more than two children and none of them has ever caught you making love, you're probably not doing it often enough.

If it works for you—and for many people it's the easiest way to make sure everyone gets some sleep—by all means, make your bed a family bed. (If you need an authoritative source to tell you it's okay to sleep with your children, I suggest you look up Luke 11:7 in the New Testament.) Don't go out of your way to tell people about it, however, especially not your child's teachers, the school nurse, or your doctor. Sharing a bed with one's children is not considered normal behavior in our culture (although I'm sure it's more common than most people realize). Once you tell people you advocate this practice, they'll start looking at your children in a different light, and this "abnormality" in their lives will be all that is focused on. Your children don't need that, and neither do you.

Family

••

A strong, close-knit family, like a good marriage, doesn't just happen; it takes work and commitment. The fact that you and your spouse have children together doesn't automatically turn you into a family. Both Pat and I come from what are often termed "dysfunctional families," that is, families that don't act like families for one reason or another (e.g., emotional problems, alcoholism). Because of our backgrounds we had very little foundation on which to build a strong family of our own. Gradually, though, we learned to act like a family—to talk like family and treat each other like family—until we became a real family. I often compare the process of becoming a family to that of becoming a plumber: If you wore a plumber's uniform and carried around plumbing tools, talked plumber talk, and learned the work of a plumber, pretty soon people would begin inviting you over to do a little plumbing, and you really would be a plumber. If you act like a family and do the things that families do, you'll become a family. Some of those things might not feel natural at first, just as carrying around those plumbing tools would not. As you get accustomed to them, however, they become second nature. A good example of this in my own life is learning to be physically affectionate with my children. Kissing and hugging them felt strange at first, but the more I practiced being affectionate, the more natural it

seemed, and now I wouldn't dream of being any other way.

In practicing to be a real family, it helps to know what qualities characterize strong, happy families. Several studies have been done in an attempt to identify these qualities, and the following tend to surface over and over again:

1. Family members care for each other and show their love and concern often. Consideration for other family members is not just trotted out on special occasions and holidays, but is made a part of daily life.

2. They truly respect each other. This is a two-way street: The parents respect the children, and the children respect the parents.

3. They empathize with each other.

4. They do things together.

5. They have a spiritual view or a religious orientation. It doesn't matter what religion they practice, but a belief in an almighty power that can be relied on for guidance seems to be important.

6. There is a dedication or commitment to the family as a whole and to each individual member that outside influences are not permitted to usurp.

7. There is good communication. They are good talkers and good listeners, and even the youngest members are listened to.

I think families, particularly in our society, encounter difficulties in spending time together and in making the family a priority. From a very young age our children become involved in all kinds of activities outside the home: Scouts, gymnastics, music lessons, and Little League, to name just a few. While the activities in and of themselves may be worthwhile, often they make it difficult for the whole family to be together at one time, especially if both parents work and have *their* outside interests as well. As a result, family time—and the family itself—may slip down on the list of priorities, or even fall right off. If you want your family to count for something in your children's lives, however, you have to put it right back at the top, where it belongs. Your home has to be more than a place to eat and sleep, or your children will feel no more loyalty to it and your family than to the local diner or motel.

One way to do this is by scheduling time that is strictly reserved for the family. As you can imagine, a family as large as mine would never manage to have all the members in one place at one time if we did not go out of our way to be together. We have made Sundays our family day and Monday nights our "family home evening." On Sundays work is forbidden—you couldn't mow the lawn on a Sunday at our house if you *begged* to—and we spend the day talking, playing games, going on outings, or just being together. Sunday nights are reserved for our family meeting, which, in a household as large as ours, is absolutely essential to plan the week, air grievances, and solve problems. If you have only one or two children, you might not see any reason to have a family meeting. I think you'll find, however, that your week goes more smoothly if you do plan it together. The

family meeting also helps to get children involved in running the household and to see that their contributions are valued.

Monday nights are also exclusively family time. Sometimes we work together on collective projects, like gardening, canning vegetables, or cleaning, or go to a movie or shopping, but whatever we do, we do it together. Nothing is allowed to interfere with family home evening, not even schoolwork. In the past, I occasionally had to call a teacher to explain that one of the children would not be able to study for a test the next day because of family home evening. Without exception, the teachers respected our tradition and seemed impressed with our priorities.

Occasionally, each of us has to give up other activities for family home evening, but the sacrifices are worth what we gain in family unity. The older children sometimes complain about giving up time with their friends or being forced to sit through a kiddie movie they've already seen twice, but we do not make exceptions on family night. If we choose an activity that is geared to the younger children one week, we'll do something for the older children the next. (Not only does this teach the children to put family first, it also helps them learn to be unselfish.) We have found, too, that although we may have to endure occasional complaints, our grown children have carried on the tradition with their own family home evenings.

If you want to set aside one night a week for family activities, keep in mind that you must respect the obligation as much as you expect your children to. You can't decide suddenly to skip it one week because you need to go shopping or want to go out with an old friend. Even if you can get away with this when they're small, by the time your kids are teenagers they'll feel that they shouldn't have to be committed to the tradition if you're not. And they'll be right: After all, their activities are just as important to them as yours are to you. If something tempting comes along that makes you want to skip your family night just this once, you might find it helpful to remind yourself that "there is no success that will make up for a failure at home" (David O. McKay, the former President of the Church of Jesus Christ of Latter-Day Saints). The effort you put into strengthening your family bonds will pay off immeasurably.

Another way to build loyalty to the family is to create and maintain enjoyable traditions. These can be small, day-to-day things, like who sits where at mealtimes, or bigger traditions, like letting the birthday child choose the dinner menu on her special day, or always leaving a special snack out for Santa on Christmas Eve. Family traditions create happy memories, and these in turn produce loyalty to the family.

There are two other topics related to the family that I like to discuss in my lectures. The first of these is why we have children, and the second is the development of parenting skills, particularly as it relates to family size.

People often don't stop to think about why they have children, aside from the obvious reason of wanting to carry on one's family or see oneself in the child. I think there are other, very good reasons for having children, however, and they deserve some thought. One thing that has impressed me throughout my children's lives is how much I have learned from each one of them. In many ways, I feel they have influenced my growing up more than I have affected theirs. Pat and I have had the special privilege of having children in almost every decade of our lives so far. (She was nineteen when our first child was born; I was twenty-one. Our last child was born more than twenty years later.) The lessons I have learned have been different in each decade of my life, but they have all been invaluable to my growth as an individual.

Children also remind us of our own mortality. When we bring a child into the world, we begin to realize that someday we will be leaving it. For many people, this is the catalyst that brings them back to the religion they had abandoned or leads them to seek out God in some other way. I think this is a good thing and an inclination you shouldn't try to resist.

Finally, children sometimes provide us with an excuse to do something that fulfills our own needs. Returning to one's religion is a good example of this. You may say you're joining a church or synagogue for your child's sake, while in reality you are doing it to fulfill a need within yourself that the child has awakened.

Each child brings to us something unique, and with each child our skills as parents increase. The first child is always a bit of a guinea pig, as we try out our ideas and theories about childrearing, and inevitably make a lot of mistakes. With the second child, we attempt to correct those mistakes by swinging to the other extreme, but by the third child we have worked out the difficulties and learned to take a moderate course. Among all the couples I have talked with, almost invariably those with three or more children say that the third child was the first one with whom they felt comfortable and confident in their parenting abilities. Parenting is like any other skill: You learn by doing, and the more you do it, the better you get at it. It once occurred to me that between us, Pat and I have 452 years of parenting experience, if you credit us with one year for each year of each of our children's lives. Parenting is a skill that you learn through practice, so that the more you practice, the better you become at it. By the third child you're becoming semiproficient. By the fourth child and fifth, an expert. By the sixth, a semipro, and after that, a true pro. Professional parents, like professional ballplayers, do things differently from the amateurs. They can play a reasonably good game on any day, in any field, in any town. People often exclaim over the number of children we have and comment that they have enough difficulty handling their own two or three. What they're not taking into account is that we did all the groundwork—learned most of the tricks of the trade—with the first two or three children. By the time we had four children, we had the herd headed in the right direction. The others, influenced by

our own custom-designed "peer group," which exerts our brand of "peer pressure," just fell into line. So if you want to be an exceptionally good parent, having a large family is a good way to start.

Aside from creating great parents, large families have other advantages. In a large family, the parent-child relationship is not as intense as in a small family. The kids can sometimes get away with things they couldn't otherwise—and everyone needs to get away with something occasionally. Also, in a large family, everyone has to pitch in to keep the household running smoothly. As a result, the children learn to be responsible and self-reliant at an earlier age, and they learn that their contributions are valued, which builds their self-esteem. For example, we heat our house with wood, and our children have always shared the job of chopping the wood we use. They know that without their help we'd have to find another, more expensive means of heating our home, and they take their responsibility seriously. It's not impossible to foster this kind of responsibility and the resulting self-esteem in a small family, but it takes more of a conscious effort. Parents of one or two children tend to do most of the work themselves, just because it's easier than watching their children learn new tasks. It's not feasible to do this in a large family, so children learn to do their part from an early age.

Summing Up: Marriage, Sex, and Family

MARRIAGE AND SEX

1. Learn to be unselfish and to communicate your needs—including sexual needs—to each other.

2. Accentuate the positive in your marriage.

3. If your marriage is in trouble, seek help early.

4. Distinguish between "having sex" and "making love."

5. Make dates to make love.

6. Don't neglect nonsexual touch.

FAMILY

1. Spend time together as a family.

2. Establish and maintain traditions that build happy memories.

3. Maintain discipline with fair rules and regulations.

4. Express unconditional love to one another in actions as well as words.

5. Develop within each child self-esteem and self-respect by believing in the child and having him belong.

6. Provide the security that children need.

Notes

1. Domeena Renshaw, M.D., "The Ripple Effect of a Satisfying Relationship," *Physician and Patient*, Vol. 3, No. 6 (June 1984): p. 13.

2. Leo Buscaglia, *Loving Each Other* (cassette tape), published by Nightingale, Conant (Chicago).

3. Joyce Huggett, *Conflict: Friend or Foe?* (Downers Grove, Ill.: Inter Varsity Press, 1984): p. 136.

4. Morton Hunt, "Opposites Attract: But Can They Live Together?" *Parade* (Mar. 20, 1988): p. 16.

The Unsick Child

Fever

Call your mother, your spouse, or your best friend to report that your child is ill, and undoubtedly one of the first questions you'll be asked is: "What's his temperature?" In spite of the fact that it is just one symptom of disease, we pay a great deal of attention to fever, usually more than is warranted. When you stop to think about it, this isn't really surprising. Fever is often the first symptom to appear, and, when it begins to fall, the first sign that a child is getting better. It is quickly detected and verified, and, unlike fatigue, weakness, or pain, easily quantified.[1] Add to this the fact that a high or rapidly rising fever is commonly (though erroneously) believed to cause convulsions and even brain damage, and it's pretty clear why we invest this one symptom with so much importance, and why parents often suffer from "fever phobia."[2]

For their part, doctors do little to discourage fever phobia, and may even encourage it. When your child is ill and you call your doctor, his first question will also be, "What's his temperature?" He doesn't ask this to assess the severity of your child's illness, as you might expect, but to determine your level of anxiety. If you tell him the child has a fever of 105°, he knows that you're a nervous wreck, so he's not going to tell you just to watch the situation for the next twelve hours while he goes off to play golf. If he did that, you'd find yourself another doctor immediately. Instead, you'll get the 105°-temperature-treatment to alleviate your anxiety.

I think we're wrong to invest fever with so much importance, and there's a great deal of evidence to support my point of view. *Fever is one symptom.* The severity of the fever does not necessarily have any correlation with the severity of the disease that's causing it. A child can have a fever of 104° to 105° for several days and have nothing more than roseola, a very common, mild childhood illness. Or he can have a fever of only 101° or 102°, but be very sick with meningitis, a potentially life-threatening disease. Not every serious illness causes a high temperature, and not every mild illness results in a low one. True, there are some very serious diseases, such as encephalitis, in which a high temperature is typical, but even with that disease, you can't correlate the height of the fever with the severity of the illness. A child with encephalitis and a fever of 105° is not necessarily in greater danger than a child with encephalitis and a temperature of 104°. By the same token, someone with a ruptured appendix will not necessarily have a higher temperature than someone with a badly inflamed appendix, even though the first condition is more dangerous. In order to determine how sick a child is, you have to look at fever in the context of the whole child and in conjunction with any other symptoms he has.

In and of itself, a fever—even a high one—is not dangerous, and may, in fact, be beneficial. Recent research has begun to find a correlation between fever and enhanced immune functions. During a fever there is an increase in the number of leukocytes, a type of white blood cell that engulfs and digests bacteria, and in the production of antibodies that fight viral and bacterial infections and allergens.[3] Perhaps most significant is the increase in interferon, a potent antiviral, antibacterial agent that is normally found in small quantities in the blood. In one study, researchers subjected certain types of blood cells to heat shock and found that, depending on which type of cell was involved, interferon was increased

by anywhere from 1,600 percent to 12,800 percent. This same study found that increased interferon production did not occur below temperatures of 102.2°, and that maximum output was reached at 104°. The increased production of interferon occurred within an hour of the temperature increase and reached a peak after one and a half to four hours. If the heat shock was continued for as long as six hours, interferon activity dropped to below the level at which it started.[4] Other studies have verified that this increase takes place in the body during a fever[5] as well as in cells subjected to heat shock in the laboratory.

The drop in interferon activity is particularly interesting if you think about the normal course of a fever: It will rise, level off for a period of time, and then drop as the person breaks into a sweat (the body's own "evaporative air conditioner") and then rise again later, repeating the cycle until it finally breaks for good. It may be that after a period of intense interferon production the body needs a respite, so the temperature falls for a time, then rises again to restimulate production.

Apparently, then, fever plays an important role in enhancing the response of the immune system to disease. If you look at the immune system as an army with disease as its enemy, then fever is the general responsible for mobilizing the reserves when disease attacks. This role really isn't surprising, either, when you consider that fever is a universal biologic response to infection; logic dictates that it have some survival benefit. When you artificially lower the fever, either with medicines or by physically cooling the body, you're telling the army's reserves that it's okay to go off duty, even though the infection is still present. I think it's much wiser to take the opposite approach. When I feel an illness coming on, I try to raise my body temperature by taking a hot bath and climbing under the electric blanket. I drink lots of water and try to "sweat it out" for awhile. I've never been able to get my temperature above 101.5°, but that seems to be enough to help me recover quickly. A similar though more extreme approach is even being tested in a hospital in Illinois, where some cancer patients are treated by raising body temperatures to 108° for short periods of time.

"But what about convulsions?" you say. "What about brain damage?" Every parent has heard that high fevers, particularly those that rise rapidly, can cause convulsions and even brain damage. Let's take a look at where these ideas come from.

Back in 1939 a prominent pediatrician, Dr. Myron E. Wegman, conducted a study of body temperatures in kittens and cats. He subjected kittens, young cats, and fully mature cats to rapidly rising temperatures and found that, at elevations of 5.2°C (the equivalent of bringing a person's temperature up to 108°F), nearly half of the kittens had convulsions. Only one quarter of the young cats and less than twenty percent of the adult cats had seizures. Because he was able to induce convulsions in a greater percentage of the kittens than the older cats, Wegman concluded that they were less able to withstand a rapid rise in body temperature and that the rise caused seizures. He then expanded this theory to include children, concluding that a rapid rise in body temperatures was also responsible for febrile seizures in children.[6] Although several researchers have since determined that the rate of the rise does not have any connection to febrile seizures in children, acceptance of Wegman's theory persists to this day.

After reading his study, my conclusion is that Wegman proved definitively that high temperatures are bad for kittens. However, I can't see that this has much to do with fevers in children. One of the more obvious problems with this study is the height to which he raised the cat's temperatures. In people, a fever infrequently exceeds 104°, rarely exceeds 106°, and never exceeds 108°, so that Wegman was working with the equivalent (for cats) of temperatures that would be extraordinarily high in a child.

Another reason the idea of a high fever causes alarm is that many people tend to equate it with heatstroke. Heatstroke occurs in very hot weather, often after vigorous exercise, when the body's cooling mechanism is unable to compensate for the high temperatures. Fever, on the other hand, is heat created within the body and regulated by the body, so that it never rises too high. With heat stroke, body temperatures can go up to 114°F, and you begin to see serious damage to the internal organs, even death (but interestingly, not brain damage), because external temperatures are so high the body can't adequately cool itself. With fever, the high temperature comes from within and is controlled from within. This points up another flaw in Wegman's study: The temperatures to which he subjected the cats was externally, not internally, controlled.

The idea that high fevers cause brain damage probably stems from the fact that severe encephalitis, which is characterized by a high fever and convulsions, sometimes results in brain damage. Encephalitis is an inflammation of the brain, usually caused by a virus, although it may occasionally be a complication of an infectious disease such as measles or chicken pox. Most cases are so mild as to pass unnoticed, and severe cases are quite rare. (Other symptoms of severe encephalitis include drowsiness so pronounced that it is difficult to wake the child, headache, sensitivity to bright lights, and, less frequently, unconsciousness or paralysis of the limbs. If your child has these symptoms, seek immediate medical attention.) When encephalitis results in brain damage, it is the disease—the inflammation of brain tissue—that causes damage. The fever, and even the convulsions, are just symptoms of the underlying illness.

Febrile Seizures

There is such a thing as a febrile seizure, however. Any seizure associated with fever and without evidence of intracranial infection or a defined cause is considered a febrile seizure. According to one study, approximately three to five percent of all children will experience at least one such seizure before starting school.[7] A child who is having a febrile convulsion will arch her neck so that the head goes back, roll her eyes back in her head, and arch her back. Her extremities will become stiff and her body will shake. If she's standing, she'll lose control of her muscles to the extent that she will fall.

More than eighty percent of these convulsions will be characterized as "simple" febrile seizures, that is, an isolated seizure occurring in a febrile child who is between approximately three months and five years of age, usually occurring within twenty-four hours of the onset of the fever. A simple febrile seizure lasts for less than ten minutes and has no "focal" features[8] (no disturbance in motor or sensory function, such as profuse salivation, lip smacking, or a tingling feeling in part of the body). The rest will be considered "complex" seizures: occurring in a younger or older child, lasting more than ten minutes, and/or having focal features. Better than ninety percent of all convulsions with fever occur between the ages of six months and three years, with approximately two percent presenting in younger, and six percent in older, children. They affect boys more often than girls, but girls tend to have them younger than boys. A family history of febrile seizures may increase the likelihood that a child will experience them, but this seems to be more of a factor for boys than for girls.[9]

No one really knows what causes febrile seizures, and there is a great deal of controversy on the subject. My theory, which is supported by the work of at least one researcher in the field, is that there are two or possibly three subgroups of children who have febrile seizures. The first consists of children who have a febrile convulsion as the result of "an unrecognized brain insult caused by the febrile illness."[10] These children will have one seizure, caused by a particular illness (in all likelihood, a mild encephalitis), and no recurrences with subsequent fevers, because it is that one illness that caused the convulsion, not their own physical susceptibility or the fever per se.

Another subgroup is made up of children who have an individual, probably genetically determined, susceptibility to febrile convulsions. Up to a certain point in their development, these children will have a convulsion any time they have a fever above about 101° or 102°. For the child who falls into this group, it is not the height of the fever that causes the convulsion, but his predisposition to febrile seizures.

It has also been suggested that a third, extremely small subgroup might exist, this one consisting of children in whom the fever acts as a trigger, unmasking chronic epilepsy. In these cases the seizures will eventually occur even without a fever.[11]

The majority of children who have a febrile convulsion appear to fall into the first group. Only about thirty percent will have a recurrence, and less than two percent will eventually develop epilepsy. The children most likely to have subsequent febrile seizures are those who have their first occurrence before they're a year old or who have parents or siblings affected by seizures.[12] Children at the highest risk of developing epilepsy are (1) those in whom febrile convulsions occur before the age of thirteen months (especially in girls); (2) those who have febrile seizures between the ages of thirteen and forty-eight months who have a family history of epilepsy (especially in boys); (3) those with a history of significant complications during the mother's pregnancy and during birth; (4) those with neurological abnormalities prior to the first

febrile convulsion; (5) those who have a prolonged (longer than fifteen minutes) or unilateral (affecting only one side of the body) first seizure, or repeated convulsions at the time of the first attack; and (6) those in whom there are persistent neurological abnormalities, either temporary or permanent, after the first attack.[13]

Febrile seizures are virtually always benign, and the risk of death from one is zero. When neurological abnormalities become evident after a febrile seizure, they are a result of either the illness that caused the seizure or a previous condition.[14] Having said this, however, I still don't expect that you will sit back in your rocking chair, quietly sipping your tea, if your child happens to have one. It's a scary experience, no doubt about it. While the seizure is happening, you can do little more than let it run its course. This will probably take from two to five minutes, but it will seem like an eternity. You can loosen the child's clothing to ensure that she can breathe without difficulty, and turn her on her side so that any vomit or secretions in the mouth will drain out rather than into her lungs, but there's nothing more you can or should do. (*Don't* try to put your finger in her mouth, as you will only get bitten. She won't swallow her tongue or choke.)

When the seizure is over, call your doctor and arrange to have your child examined. Since the seizures are benign, you may wonder why this is necessary (although it's probably what you're inclined to do anyway). Your child needs to be examined not because the fever or the seizure itself is dangerous, but because certain serious illnesses may be present with a fever and convulsion. Meningitis, a potentially life-threatening infection of the lining of the brain (the meninges) is the most common of these, and as such the one that concerns doctors the most. Encephalitis, Reye's syndrome, a brain abscess, intracranial hemorrhage, and acute hemoplegia (paralysis of one side of the body) of infancy are other possible causes, although they are quite rare.

Your doctor's main concern will be to determine whether or not your child has meningitis. It is very common for a child with a first febrile seizure to be subjected to a lumbar puncture (also called a spinal tap) and various other lab tests to determine whether or not she has meningitis. A lumbar puncture, which is done under local anesthesia, involves inserting a needle between the vertebrae at the base of the spine to tap cerebrospinal fluid, which is then examined and cultured to determine the presence of bacteria. The side effects of a lumbar puncture include a severe headache, nausea, and possibly infection. If it is done by an inept technician, there is also a danger of damage to the spinal cord.

The risks and side effects of a lumbar puncture might be beside the point if it were the only way to diagnose meningitis. However, in the vast majority of cases there are other signs of the intracranial pressure caused by meningitis: an altered mental state, vomiting, strabismus (one or both eyes turned inward or outward), a "setting sun" appearance to the eyes, and/or changing vital signs, such as increased blood pressure, increased or decreased pulse rate, and

a decreased rate of respiration. In an infant, the fontanel may bulge and no longer pulse.

If, after examining your child, your doctor tells you that he thinks the child does have meningitis and that he wants to do a lumbar puncture, by all means consent, unless you have reason to distrust his clinical judgment. An examination of the cerebrospinal fluid will make it possible to identify whether the infection is caused by a virus or bacteria, and if it is a bacteria (which is most likely), which antibiotic will be most effective. Since the treatments for viral and bacterial meningitis are entirely different, the lumbar puncture will yield important information if your child does have meningitis.

On the other hand, your doctor may tell you that based on his clinical evaluation, he does not think your child has meningitis, but he wants to do a lumbar puncture just to "rule it out." In this case, your doctor is practicing what is known in some circles as CYA (cover your hindquarters) medicine, and I suggest you refuse the procedure. (If the doctor later feels that there is clinical evidence that the child has meningitis, you'll want to reverse your decision, of course.)

That said, let me now add a few qualifiers. Like many other things in medicine, the decision on whether or not to do a lumbar puncture is not black and white. In fact, this is a question that causes a lot of controversy. Many doctors feel that the dangers of meningitis justify routine use of lumbar punctures in children with febrile seizures. However, judging from several articles that reviewed numerous cases of children on whom lumbar punctures were performed following a febrile seizure, it seems clear that this test is overused, to say the least. Several different reviews, each dealing with 80 to 300 cases of lumbar puncture done after a first febrile seizure, found no cases of meningitis. One review, this one of 314 cases, found 3 instances of meningitis, each in a child under eighteen months of age.[15]

I am by no means the only doctor to question the wisdom of doing so many lumbar punctures. Some experts recommend that lumbar punctures be done on a child with a febrile seizure only if a child is younger than eighteen months, when meningitis is more likely to occur with febrile convulsion as the only symptom, or if there is clinical evidence of meningitis.[16] One researcher also recommends lumbar puncture if the seizure was complex, since meningitis is more likely to present with a complex seizure, or in a child older than three, when first febrile convulsions are unusual.[17] Most thorough, however, are the suggestions of a group of physicians who reviewed the histories of 241 children, ages six months to six years, who were brought to the emergency room with a first febrile seizure and who had a lumber puncture. They found that there were five history and examination items that when considered together, were as accurate as lumbar puncture in differentiating between the children who had meningitis and those who did not: (1) a visit to the doctor within forty-eight hours before the seizure; (2) the occurrence of convulsions on arrival at the emergency room; (3) a focal seizure; (4) suspicious find-

ings on the physical exam; and/or (5) suspicious findings on the neurological exam. Suspicious findings on the physical exam included a rash or petechia (tiny reddish or purplish flat spots on the skin caused by tiny hemorrhages within the skin), cyanosis, hypotension, and grunting respirations. On the neurological exam, abnormalities included a stiff neck, an unusual position of the eyes, "doll's eyes" (sit the child up and the eyes open, lay her down and they close), ataxia (a lack of coordination of muscle action, e.g. staggering or unsteady movements), a lack of response to a voice, an inability to fix on and follow an object with the eyes, lack of response to painful stimuli, floppy muscle tone, nystagmus (an involuntary, rhythmic eyeball movement), and a bulging or tense fontanel. The most sensitive factor for predicting meningitis was abnormal findings on the neurological exam. The absence of any single item did not exclude the diagnosis with certainty; however, when all five risk factors were present, they served to identify all children with meningitis. Just as important, they had a negative predictive value (that is, they predicted who did not have meningitis) of one hundred percent. If these risk factors had been considered, they would have saved sixty-two percent of the children the need for a lumbar puncture. The doctors concluded that when these risk factors are lacking there is no need for a lumbar puncture, assuming that a careful history and physical exam are performed, and that immediate follow-up is available.[18]

Your doctor may also want to do various other tests, possibly including but not limited to a blood culture, urinalysis, and CAT scan. In the vast majority of cases, not much is learned when these are done as a matter of routine rather than because the doctor has found something suspicious in his physical exam. While it is not practical for me to describe all the possibilities and the pros and cons of each, I do want to caution you not to agree indiscriminately to a battery of tests. I suggest you question the doctor in depth about each one to find out just what he expects to learn from it and how it will change the treatment. (See chapter 16, "Your Child's Physician," for a list of questions you should ask regarding any medical test.)

In all likelihood, your doctor will rule out meningitis, encephalitis, and any other serious illness as the cause of your child's febrile seizure. At this point he may suggest putting the child on medication to prevent recurrences of the seizure. If he wants to put the child on dilantin and phenobarbital for two years, find yourself another doctor fast—this one is so far out of touch with current practice he'll never catch up. If he suggests phenobarbital alone for two years, he's still pretty far behind, since this hasn't been the recommended practice for some time. Phenobarbital, when taken on a continuous basis, is effective in preventing febrile seizures, but it has negative long-term effects on a child's ability to learn. Another suggestion he may have is to give the child phenobarbital and acetominophen (Tylenol) any time she has a fever, but this isn't a great idea, either, since phenobarbital isn't effective against seizures when taken at the onset of fever. There are several other anticonvulsion medications that may be sug-gested, all of which have serious side effects. Children should not, however, be categorically denied medication. Again, this is a matter to discuss with your doctor.

The usual justifications for anticonvulsant treatment are that it may prevent the future development of epilepsy, and/or that witnessing a convulsion causes considerable parental anxiety. However, there is no evidence that preventing febrile seizures will also prevent the onset of epilepsy in a child who is predisposed to it.[19] As for parental anxiety, I see no justification for putting a child on a medication in order to treat the parent's nerves. If you take into consideration the fact that there's a good chance your child will never have another febrile seizure, putting him on medication for two years seems all the more undesirable, in my opinion.

In 1980 a panel of experts got together to consider the question of when anticonvulsant medication may be warranted. Their conclusions were as follows: (1) when there is abnormal neurological development, cerebral palsy, mental retardation, or microcephaly; (2) when the febrile seizure is longer than fifteen minutes, is focal, or is followed by transient or persistent neurological abnormalities; and (3) when there is a history of nonfebrile seizures of genetic origin in a sibling or parent. The panel also felt that anticonvulsant therapy is occasionally warranted for infants under twelve months of age who have had multiple febrile seizures, in cases where the parents are highly anxious about the seizures in spite of counseling, or when the family lives far from a medical facility.[20]

One author has noted that since these

recommendations were published, concern about the long-term effects of anticonvulsant medication has increased. He does not recommend medication for children with suspect or abnormal neurological status after their first seizure, since they are at risk for a single rather than multiple recurrence, for children with a positive family history who have had only one seizure, nor for those who had an initial complex seizure, since they are not at an increased risk for a recurrence.[21]

Treating a Fever

All things considered, I strongly believe that in the normal child, fever should be allowed to run its course. Just in case you still feel that it's a good idea to lower a fever with acetaminophen or aspirin, let's take a look at the possible side effects of those drugs. Aspirin is known to cause gastrointestinal bleeding, vomiting, nausea, heartburn, liver problems, fluid in the lungs, skin rashes, and asthmatic attacks, among other things. It has also been associated with Reye's syndrome, a life-threatening illness that usually occurs following a viral infection (most commonly chicken pox or influenza). Reye's syndrome, which occurs in adults as well as children, is characterized by sudden vomiting, violent headaches, and unusual behavior. It requires immediate diagnosis and admission to a hospital; the death rate is close to fifty percent. A breastfeeding mother can pass aspirin along to her baby, which may build up to toxic levels and can even cause Reye's syndrome in the child if he has been ill. Acetaminophen in large doses can cause mild to severe liver damage (deaths have been reported among both adults and children), can adversely affect the heart, kidneys, and pancreas, and can cause hypoglycemia. I do not feel that there is any reason to give either of these drugs to a normal child who has a fever.

There are some conditions that can be complicated or worsened by a fever, such as heart-lung, kidney, or metabolic impairment; shock; sickle-cell disease; and fluid/electrolyte problems. In these instances there may be excellent reasons to bring the fever down. Fever in the newborn, which is unusual and may indicate a serious problem, should *never* be treated as normal.

Aside from these possible exceptions, fever is generally best left to run its course. Sometimes when I present these views to parents they point out that a child with a fever can be cranky and miserable and that bringing the temperature down eases his discomfort. This may be true in the short run, but everything I have been able to learn about fever leads me to believe that doing so will actually prolong the illness or even make it more severe.

Nevertheless, I don't really expect that the next time your child has a fever you will calmly watch it shoot up, reassuring your irritable one-year-old that it's all for her own good. It takes time to reorient your thinking about fever. You may even start out with good intentions, but then find that after an hour you feel you've got to do something. Before you do anything else, make sure you're not increasing her discomfort by having her overdressed. In the summer, a diaper and undershirt is all she needs. In the winter, lightweight pajamas or indoor clothing should be sufficient, unless your house is very cold. Believe it or not, just fanning your child's face will make her much more comfortable (a study has even been done that shows this is effective[22]), since thirty percent of body heat is lost through the head.

When I ran a fever as a child, my mother would put me in a warm bath while she put clean sheets on my bed and warmed up a towel in the oven. Then she'd take me out of the bath, wrap me up in that warm towel, rub my chest with Vicks VapoRub, and put me in clean pajamas. (To this day, when I smell Vicks, waves of love ripple through my body.) While I'm sure none of these actions in and of itself could cure anyone of anything, the love and attention I received from this routine made me feel immensely better. When your child has a fever, the TLC you give will go a long way to making her feel better without needing to lower her fever. Your routine, whatever it may be, may be all your child needs to help her through the discomfort of a fever.

If, after all, you reach a point where you feel you must lower your child's fever, *do something nontoxic*. Don't reach for that bottle of Tylenol. Instead, use a homeopathic remedy or an herbal one, or put the child in a tepid bath. Tepid, in this case, means two degrees below her body temperature, which will still feel quite warm to you. Put your thermometer in the bath water to make sure it isn't too cool, since a colder bath will make the child very uncomfortable and crankier than ever. Sponge off her head, under her arms, and between her legs for forty-five minutes, and you will have lowered her temperature approximately two degrees. Never use cold-water sponging, ice blankets, or an ice-water enema to lower a fever. They are only appropriate in treating some cases of heatstroke, and in my opinion constitute cruelty when used on a child with a fever.

Keep in mind, though, that you are treating only a symptom, not the actual disease, and maybe your own anxiety. And perhaps the next time your child runs a fever, you'll be able to hold out for several hours, and the time after that, until the fever breaks of its own accord. Eventually you'll be free of fever phobia, and ready to trust the body's own good sense.

Summing Up: Fever

....

1. Fever is only one symptom, and must be considered within the context of the total child.

2. A fever, even a high one, is not dangerous in and of itself, and is helpful in fighting disease.

3. Febrile convulsions do not cause brain damage and in the vast majority of cases should not be treated with prophylactic medication.

4. The best "treatment" for fever is to let it run its course.

Notes

1. Martin I. Lorin, M.D., *The Febrile Child: Clinical Management of Fever and Other Types of Pyrexia* (New York: John Wiley & Sons, 1982): p. 6.

2. B. D. Schmitt, ed., "Fever Phobia: Misconceptions of Parents About Fever," *American Journal of Diseases of Children*, Vol. 134, No. 2 (Feb. 1980): p. 134.

3. J. F. Downing et al., "In Vivo Hyperthermia Enhances Plasma Antiviral Activity and Stimulates Peripheral Lymphocytes for Increased Synthesis of Interferon Gamma," *The Journal of Interferon Research*, Vol. 7, No. 2 (Apr. 1987): p. 185.

4. M. W. Taylor et al., "Induction of Gamma Interferon Activity by Elevated Temperatures in Human B-Lymphoblastoid Cell Lines," *The Proceedings of the National Academy of Sciences*, Vol. 81, No. 13 (July 1984): p. 4033.

5. J. F. Downing and M. W. Taylor, "The Effect of In Vivo Hyperthermia on Selected Lymphokines in Man," *Lymphokine Research*, Vol. 6, No. 2 (Spring 1987): p. 103.

6. Myron E. Wegman, M.D., "Factors Influencing the Relation of Convulsions in Hyperthermia," *Journal of Pediatrics*, Vol. 14 (Feb. 1939): p. 190.

7. M. A. Gerber, M.D., and B. C. Berliner, M. D. "The Child With 'Simple' Febrile Seizure: Appropriate Diagnostic Evaluation," *American Journal of Diseases of Children*, Vol. 135, No. 5 (May 1981): p. 431.

8. R. Anandam, "Febrile Seizures: Controversies and Current Concepts," *Indian Pediatrics*, Vol. 23, No. 11 (Nov. 1986): p. 899.

9. Ibid.

10. Jean Aicardi, *Epilepsy in Children* (New York: Raven Press, 1986): p. 212.

11. Ibid.

12. Robert E. Kaplan, M.D., "Febrile Seizures: When Is Treatment Justified?" *Postgraduate Medicine*, Vol. 82, No. 5 (Oct. 1987): p. 63.

13. Anandam, p. 899.

14. Seth W. Wright, M.D., "The Child With Febrile Seizures," *The American Family Physician*, Vol. 36, No. 5 (Nov. 1987): p. 163.

15. N. Rutter and O. R. Smales, "Role of Routine Investigations in Children Presenting with Their First Febrile Convulsion," *Archives of Disease in Childhood*, Vol. 52, No. 3 (Mar. 1977): p. 188.

16. Gerber and Berliner, p. 431.

17. N. P. Rosman, "Febrile Seizures," *Emergency Medicine Clinics of North America*, Vol. 5, No. 4 (Nov. 1987): p. 719.

18. A. Jofee, M. McCormick, and C. DeAngelis, "Which Children with Febrile Seizures Need Lumbar Puncture: A Decision Analysis Approach," *American Journal of Diseases of Children*, Vol. 137, No. 12 (Dec. 1983): pp. 1153.

19. Kaplan, p. 63.

20. Wright, p. 163.

21. Kaplan, p. 63.

22. H. Brinnel et al., "Enhanced Brain Protection During Passive Hyperthermia in Humans," *European Journal of Applied Physiology*, Vol. 56, No. 5, (1987): p. 540.

Allergies

*One only sees what one looks for; one only looks for
what one knows.*

GOETHE

This chapter deals primarily with food allergies, since I feel that adequate information on other types of allergies is available from other sources. Don't stop reading right here, though, if your child suffers from hay fever, asthma, or any other type of allergy. The allergic person tends to suffer from more than one type of allergy and usually has an "allergy threshold," a minimal level of exposure to allergens that must be reached before a reaction sets in. Exposure to any combination of allergic triggers might put the person over that threshold, so that, for example, someone who is allergic to pollen may find that his hay fever improves if he keeps certain foods out of his diet. By bringing down the total level of allergic stresses in his life, he will have fewer reactions to those allergens that can't be avoided. This chapter will help you to determine whether or not food allergies are a factor in your child's case and, if so, how to deal with them.

The subject of food allergy has stirred up a great deal of heated controversy in the medical community in the past several years, to the point that some leaders in the field no longer even speak to each other. This is perhaps unsurprising when you realize that twenty years ago the very term "food allergy" was widely despised within the medical community. There are many doctors who still feel this way and who recognize only the most obvious food allergies. At the other extreme, there are those who attribute just about every symptom imaginable to the diet. I fall somewhere between these two camps. I feel that food allergies very often go unrecognized and that many of the complaints that doctors see, particularly those that are mild but chronic or that tend to come and go, can be attributed to problems with the diet.

Technically speaking, an allergy is a misdirected response by the immune system to a normally innocuous substance. The immune system protects the body against invading organisms (i.e., bacteria and viruses) primarily through the production of antibodies. In an allergic response, these antibodies are produced against harmless substances that are inhaled, ingested, or injected into the body or that come into contact with the skin. The battle between antibody and allergen creates the reaction we label allergy: sneezing, wheezing, hives, headache, etc. Modern medicine has been fairly successful in defining the causes and effects of inhalant allergies (e.g., pollen, animal dander, dust, mold), allergies suffered from injected substances (e.g., penicillin), and contact allergies (e.g., detergents or wool). Food allergies, on the other hand, have proven to be much more difficult to understand.

One of the problems behind the food allergy debate is agreeing on a definition of the term. Some doctors feel that only those cases in which the antibody response described above can be demonstrated should be considered true allergies.[1] Others note that in some people certain foods can produce various symptoms without a demonstrable antibody response. Wootan's theory of allergy states that allergy is a wastebasket diagnosis. Things that we don't understand are routinely tossed into this basket simply because we don't know what else to do with them. In some cases, we may be dealing with a true allergy involving an identifiable antibody response. In others, there is a clearly a food-related reaction but no measurable antibody response. Let's say your daughter gets diarrhea every time she eats wheat, for example. Her reaction may actually be due to an antibody response, or,

possibly, she may react to the wheat because it has been genetically altered to make it drought- and disease-resistant, and this hybridization has affected the digestibility of the wheat. In this case, the problem isn't really that your daughter is allergic to wheat, but that she's eating wheat that is hard to digest. On the other hand, the wheat might affect her because her diet lacks some micronutrient that is needed in order to produce a certain enzyme that is essential to the digestion of wheat. If it were somehow possible to discover which micronutrient she is lacking and then add it to her diet, she would be able to eat wheat without problems. Or she may simply have been born without the ability to produce the enzyme she needs.

Any of these factors—or perhaps others that we haven't even begun to understand—might cause an "allergic" reaction. If our knowledge of the mechanism behind the reaction were more complete, we might be able to identify each of these causes and sort out the true allergies from what some doctors consider food "sensitivities," and tailor our treatments accordingly. Until our knowledge increases, however, we must work with our current imperfect understanding. This presents obvious problems both in diagnosis and in treatment, and, I think, gives rise to much of the controversy surrounding food allergies. (For the sake of simplicity, in this chapter the term "food allergy" will apply to any kind of diet-related reaction.)

Another reason that some doctors tend to resist the idea of food allergies is that there seems to be a very wide range of ways in which the allergies are manifested. Allergic reactions to food are very individual, so that one person who is allergic to wheat may not have the same symptoms as the next person who is allergic to wheat (perhaps because the mechanisms behind the reactions are different). One person may find that he gets diarrhea any time he eats wheat. Another may find that eating wheat gives him a headache, but only if he has it more than two days in a row. The individual nature of these reactions makes it very difficult, if not impossible, to set up well-defined, controlled studies that show precisely how a person with a food allergy will react. Much of the medical literature on food allergy is case studies, not controlled experiments that draw definite conclusions from the experiences of many people. They are considered by some doctors to be biased and subjective and, as such, insufficient proof that food allergies constitute a significant medical problem.

Nevertheless, I think some of the case studies provide important evidence that food allergies do cause medical problems, both minor and major. Though uncommon, there have been various reports in the medical literature that link food allergy to acute diseases. In a study of twelve children with kidney disease (nephrotic syndrome), six experienced a remission when their diets were changed. Three of these children had the offending foods later reintroduced, and all three suffered immediate recurrences.[2] Another article reports the case of a two-month-old boy who was admitted to a pediatric intensive care unit after a sudden onset of fever, vomiting, abdominal distension, and acidosis (too much acid in the system). After X rays and numerous tests,

including exploratory surgery, he was found to have an excessive outpouring of fluid into his small intestine, causing an intestinal obstruction. This was eventually determined to be a reaction to milk and soy formulas.[3] Another doctor has found that uveitis (infection of the eyeball) may be related to food allergy in some cases.[4]

The response of many doctors to these types of cases is that they are extremely rare and so have very little bearing on general medical practice. I see them a little differently. If food allergy can cause these extreme reactions in some people, it seems reasonable that it may also be responsible for milder symptoms that have no other apparent cause. We in the medical profession—and the public in general—have long resisted the idea that what we put into our bodies has any bearing on how we feel. The more we learn about how the body works, however, the more clear it becomes that what we eat directly affects how well the body functions. Looking at food allergy as a possible cause for physical symptoms is just carrying this idea one step further, taking into consideration not only the quality of the food but also how any particular food affects an individual.

Allergy Symptoms

Below are two lists. The first is a general list of allergy symptoms that occur in children and adults of all ages, and the second is a list of symptoms that may be seen in babies. The first list consists of the symptoms commonly recognized by specialists in food allergies as related to the diet, including those I have seen most often. (For a more complete list, see *Detecting Your Hidden Allergies*, by William Crook, M.D.,[5] or *Dr. Mandell's 5-Day Allergy Relief System*, by Marshall Mandell, M.D., and Lynne Waller Scanlon.[6]) The second list is one I have compiled through my own observations, and includes symptoms that are not commonly considered to be related to food allergy.

GENERAL ALLERGY SYMPTOMS IN CHILDREN AND ADULTS

Eczema, hives, adult acne, rashes

Anemia

Headache: migraine, tension-type, sinus

Eye pain, occasional blurring of vision, tearing, conjunctivitis, dark circles under the eyes

Ear infections, ringing of the ears, Ménière's disease, hearing loss, vertigo

Runny nose, sinusitis, pale and swollen nasal turbinates, asthma, shortness of breath, wheezing

Abnormally rapid heart beat, palpitations, flushing, chilling

Nausea, vomiting, heartburn, gassiness, cramps, diarrhea, other gastrointestinal problems

Infections of the bladder or urethra, bedwetting, painful urination, frequent urination

Muscle spasms, cramps or weakness, stiff neck

Fatigue, depression, learning disorders, episodic dullness or dreaminess

Restlessness, insomnia, hyperactivity, behavior problems

ALLERGY SYMPTOMS IN BABIES

ECZEMA. Eczema is a red, scaly, dry, often itchy rash that appears primarily in the flexion creases but may occur anywhere on the body. It is usually, although not always, related to allergy.

DIARRHEA. If a breast-fed baby has bowel movements both during and between feedings and they are greenish in color, he has diarrhea. The frequency may not be that much greater than normal—perhaps up from eight to ten—but the green color is a tip-off. It is caused by milk passing through the baby's system so quickly that the bile that is excreted in the intestines is not reabsorbed by the body as it should be but is instead passed in the stool.

In a bottle-fed baby, an increase from the normal number of daily bowel movements and watery, greenish stool are signs of diarrhea. Diarrhea may, of course, be an indication of illness. If the onset is sudden and the baby has other symptoms such as a fever, allergy is not indicated. However, if the baby seems well aside from the diarrhea, allergy is most likely the cause.

EAR INFECTIONS. More than one ear infection per year almost always indicates an allergy until proven otherwise.

DARK CIRCLES UNDER THE EYES. Sometimes called allergic shiners, these are not caused by lack of sleep, as commonly assumed. The baby may, in fact, sleep poorly, but it is the allergy that prevents him from sleeping well.

RESTLESS SLEEPER. Virtually all breast-fed babies wake during the night to nurse, but any baby who also tosses, turns, and kicks while he sleeps is probably allergic. Some restless sleepers may have a calcium deficiency and may be helped by supplements, while others may sleep better if given L-Tryptophan, an amino acid that is available in health food stores. The vast majority, however, are allergic.

SKIN RASH. Red, rosy cheeks, often misinterpreted as a sign of a healthy baby, may indicate allergy (unless the cheeks are chapped due to exposure to cold, dry air). Rashes on other parts of the body should lead one to suspect food allergy, although they may be due to another cause.

RED RING AROUND THE ANAL OPENING. Approximately the size of a dime or a nickel, this ring will come and go depending on what the babt eats or, if he's being nursed exclusively, depending on what his mother eats.

PASSING GAS. Sometimes a breast-fed newborn will be gassy because the mother has an overabundance of milk, and the baby gets more than she can handle when she first latches onto the breast, causing her to gulp air with the milk. Once the milk supply has evened out and the baby has stopped gulping down air—usually within two to three weeks—the baby should not produce a lot of gas. If she does, allergy may be the cause.

SPITTING UP. Bringing up a teaspoonful of milk just after a feeding is perfectly normal, but spitting up an ounce or so of curdled milk, usually about an hour later, is not.

SWEATING WHILE NURSING. If it's ninety-eight degrees out and everyone else is sweating, it's certainly normal for your baby to sweat as he nurses. There's something more at work than the heat, however, if the temperature is at a comfortable level and only your baby is perspiring.

COLIC. Doctors have different ideas about what constitutes colic. To me, a colicky baby is one who is irritable and cranky, who seems to be in pain, and who draws his knees up to his chest when moving his bowels. A colicky baby will have periods of acute discomfort no matter what you do to try to relieve them. Colic usually starts around the second week after birth, and often disappears, for no apparent reason, between three and six months of age. I have found that colicky babies usually have other symptoms of allergy.

FUSSY BABY. This is a normally cheerful, happy baby who turns suddenly cranky and irritable for a period of time and then just as suddenly returns to his sunny self. (For some unknown reason, this usually occurs between 4:30 and 11:00 P.M.) When he's cranky, he's inconsolable: He doesn't want to be nursed, he doesn't want to be not nursed, he doesn't want to be walked, he doesn't want to be not walked. No matter what you do, he is just plain miserable.

CONSTIPATION.   A breast-fed baby should have between four and eight bowel movements per day. The stool should be watery, so that the majority of it soaks into the diaper. It should be the color of yellow mustard, and contain little yellow curds, about the size of poppy seeds. If the stool is less frequent, the color of brown mustard, and thick like Cream of Wheat, the infant is constipated.

La Leche League feels that in some cases it is normal for a breast-fed baby to go for several days without a bowel movement. Though I agree that these babies are not pathologically ill, they usually have other symptoms that are also allergy-related and that will clear up along with the constipation when the allergy is treated.

A bottle-fed baby will have less frequent bowel movements, perhaps one or two a day. They will be more formed than those of the breast-fed baby, but should still be soft. If they are less frequent than once a day or are hard, the baby is constipated.

ON-AGAIN, OFF-AGAIN NURSING. The baby wants to nurse, but will have trouble settling down to the breast. Instead he will suck briefly, then pull himself back off the breast and cry, then nuzzle up to the breast and begin to suck, then pull back and cry again, repeating this process several times before finally settling down to nurse.

Colic, fussiness, and on-again, off-again nursing are all probably related to constipa-tion. One way you can test this is by using glycerin suppositories to temporarily clear up the constipation. A few words of caution, first, though: Do *not* use suppositories to treat the problem. I suggest them only as a means of convincing yourself that constipation is causing the symptoms. If your baby's behavior changes after his bowel movements are back to normal, you will have to follow through with dietary changes to eliminate the problem. Also, don't use the suppositories if your baby seems ill. This test is only appropriate for a baby who has a history of infrequent bowel movements, who has one or more of the symptoms discussed above, and who seems generally healthy.

To do this test, insert one-half of an infant glycerin suppository in the baby's rectum when the symptoms occur. The baby will probably have a bowel movement within ten to fifteen minutes. If he doesn't, or if he produces a "constipated" looking stool, you can use two, three, or even four suppositories—whatever it takes to get him cleaned out. You want to get him to the point where the stools are watery and yellow if the baby is breast-fed, or soft but formed if he is formula-fed. When he's reached that point, his symptoms should suddenly clear up. Your colicky baby will become calm, your fussy baby will be cheerful and happy, or your on-again, off-again nurser will settle down to the breast in peace. If this happens, you will have dramatic evidence that constipation—and hence food allergy—is at the root of these symptoms.

In my experience, there are two reasons a breast-fed baby has an allergic reaction to his mother's milk. The most common one is that the baby is allergic to a food the mother has eaten and is reacting to some element of it that is passed along in her milk. I have found, however, that in some cases it is the mother who is allergic to a food, and I suspect that the baby reacts to a chemical change that may occur in the milk because of her allergy. The difference between these two reactions is that in the latter case, the baby will be able to eat the food without a reaction when he is old enough to consume it directly. A nursing toddler, for example, may react any time the mother eats peanut butter, but not if he eats it himself. I have not yet found an allergist who agrees with me on this, but I have seen it happen often enough to know it does occur.

Allergy Tests

Doctors offer many different types of allergy tests, including prick skin tests with food extracts, RAST (radioallergosorbent), ELISA (enzyme-linked immunosorbent assay), cytological tests, kinesiology, and sublingual tests. In "failure to thrive" babies, an intestinal biopsy may even be used to look for changes in the intestinal mucosa which indicate a food allergy. For all of these tests, even the intestinal biopsy, the best that can be said is that they work some of the time for some people. However, most of the tests generally miss between ten and thirty percent of the allergens in children who have demonstrated allergies, and even the intestinal biopsy sometimes yields a negative result in a child with an obvious allergy. Each allergist generally has certain tests that he believes in and uses frequently, while condemning the other tests as unreliable. At the same time, however, most allergists will admit that even their favorite tests are not all that accurate. For this reason, it is almost always recommended that the results of any of the tests be confirmed through the use of food challenges. What this means, essentially, is that the most you'll get out of the tests is a list of foods to avoid to see if this produces a change in symptoms. Considering that these procedures are expensive and in some cases cause considerable discomfort, they are rarely worthwhile.

The "double-blind" food challenge is the only allergy test that is considered reliable. In a lab or hospital setting, the double-blind food challenge involves giving the patient capsules containing eight to ten grams of a dehydrated food after he has been on a diet that eliminates that food for several days. (In a small child who is unable to swallow capsules, the food is hidden in something else he will eat.) Neither the patient nor the person observing the reaction knows the contents of the capsule to ensure that the conclusions will not be influenced by psychological factors. The contents of the capsule are revealed after observations have been made as to its effect on the child.

While it may not be possible to re-create these conditions exactly in the home, an elimination diet/food challenge can be conducted there, and may ultimately be more accurate than even the double-blind challenge. To do this test at home, you eliminate the suspected allergen from the diet and watch for a change in symptoms. If a change is perceived, you set up the challenge by reintroducing the food to see if it causes the symptoms to return. (In the extremely rare cases when a food has actually resulted in anaphylactic shock, a challenge should never be attempted.) Granted, a food challenge conducted at home is not "double-blind," but it does have the advantage of allowing you to repeat the test as often as is necessary to validate your results and to control the circumstances. You may find, for example, that after eliminating dairy products for two weeks and then reintroducing them, you do see an allergic reaction, but only after milk has been ingested for two successive days. Or you may find that there is no reaction from two ounces of milk, but that six will produce one. (In this respect, you have a distinct advantage over using capsules in a laboratory setting, where the amount of a food that can be given is limited.) These are the kinds of variations that are impossible to duplicate when testing hundreds of people in a laboratory setting, but that may be highly relevant when dealing with food allergies. When testing a child, you may even be able to make the challenge somewhat blind by having one parent feed the child, and the other, who remains ignorant of what food has been eaten, make the observations concerning symptoms. This could be particularly effective in convincing a doubtful parent about the effect a suspected allergen has on the child.

When you abstain from a food to which you are allergic and then reintroduce it into your diet, the reaction you have to the food may be much stronger than if you had continued to eat it on a daily basis. To understand the reason for this, let's go back to the analogy of your immune system as an army, this time with a particular food such as milk as the enemy. If you send in the enemy every day, your army is continually assaulted, so that it is unable to fight back with any great show of strength. When you eliminate the enemy for a period of two weeks, you give your body a chance to build up that army again. The next time you drink a glass of milk, your army is going to march to battle in full force with your body as the battleground. Your symptoms, whatever they may be, will be greatly exaggerated. This will hold true even for the baby who reacts to his mother's milk because she's eaten something she's allergic to. If you think about it, this reaction is actually helpful, since it makes the connection between what you eat and how you feel so clear.

Signs of a reaction may be noted within minutes or may be delayed for as long as a few days. In the case of delayed reactions, repeated exposure to the food is usually required, with the reaction eventually occurring within minutes to hours of the last time the food was eaten.[7] In other words, if you reintroduce milk into the diet on Monday and have no immediate reaction to it, go off it again on Tuesday and Wednesday, and then experience what seems to be a reaction on Wednesday night, it was probably not caused by the milk you drank on Monday. On the other hand, if you've been drinking milk every day, the reaction you experience on Wednesday probably is attributable to the milk (unless you've also added another new food into your diet, in which case that may be the culprit). The reason for this delayed reaction is that it may take a few days of eating the food to lower your threshold of tolerance to it. In all likelihood, there have already been some physical changes due to the milk on Monday and Tuesday, but they have not yet resulted in noticeable symptoms.[8] In your nursing baby, allergy symptoms will usually appear about four hours after you have eaten the food, although you may notice them as soon as half an hour later, or as late as twenty-four hours later. The reaction will vary with the type of food, how often you eat it, and the amount you have eaten.

There are essentially three ways of going about an elimination diet/food challenge in the home, but for the nursing mother and for children, only one is truly workable. This method, described in detail in *Detecting Your Hidden Allergies*,[9] involves eliminating a food group (such as all dairy products or any food containing wheat) from the diet for a period of time, then reintroducing it and watching for a reaction. Although most authorities on allergies suggest that you stay away from the food for five to seven days, I favor a two-week period of abstinence. I arrived at this length of time after observing the experience of one mother in my practice. Her breast-fed baby had terrible colic, was always constipated, and spit up frequently. This mother's favorite food was milk, which she consumed at the rate of about a half-gallon a day. When I suggested that her baby might be allergic to the milk she was drinking, she vehemently denied the possibility. There was no way she was going to give up milk, she said. A colicky baby can drive a person to desperate measures, however, and she finally agreed to try cutting out all dairy products. Over

the next two weeks, her baby's symptoms gradually disappeared. Still unconvinced, the woman suggested that perhaps the baby had just outgrown his symptoms, so I proposed that she challenge the test by trying a small amount of milk. She drank one glass, and her baby was sick for eleven days. Granted, this was an extreme case; most people will stop feeling the effects of an offending food in less time than this particular baby. However, a few may be affected for an even longer period. By staying away from the food you are testing for two full weeks, I think you can feel reasonably confident that it is no longer producing a reaction in your child.

Another, more effective means of testing foods is to fast for five days, taking nothing by mouth except bottled spring water, and then introduce foods one at a time, again watching for reactions. This method is described in detail in *Dr. Mandell's 5-Day Allergy Relief System*.[10] Because it involves a fast, I do not recommend it for nursing mothers or young children. An older child or teenager, if sufficiently motivated, could do such a fast, but under no circumstances should a parent try to force one on a child of any age. Another option that Dr. Mandell discusses is a rotation diet, in which you plan out all meals for a certain period, making sure that you do not eat the same food twice during that time. Dr. Mandell suggests a five-day rotation, but I have found a fourteen-day rotation to be much more effective. A rotation diet may not be as helpful as an elimination diet for discovering the foods to which you are allergic. Depending on the nature of your allergies, however, it may be enough in itself to control your symptoms, since you will not be eating any one food on a regular basis.

A final method that is often recommended is to eat nothing but five foods—usually lamb, rice, pears, water, and salt—for a period of two weeks. These five foods are usually chosen because they generally do not cause allergic reactions, although they can. If you happen to eat lamb, rice, or pears frequently, the chances are greater that you may be allergic to one of them. In this case, you should substitute another food that you do not consume on a regular basis. At the end of the two weeks, you begin introducing other foods one at a time, as with the first two methods. Because this diet is so unbalanced, I feel it, too, is unwise for nursing mothers and children. However, if for some reason it seems appropriate for you, it may be worth consideration.

I've said that the most you will get from expensive allergy tests is a list of foods to try eliminating from your diet. If you forgo the tests, how do you know which foods to eliminate? The five most common offenders are eggs, dairy products, wheat, corn, and soy, but a person can be allergic to absolutely anything she eats or drinks, including her drinking water (although this is rare). If you are a nursing mother trying to track down whatever food is causing an allergic reaction in your baby, you have to be suspicious of everything that goes into your mouth.

If that sounds overwhelming—and I realize it might, considering that you *do* have to eat—take heart. I have found that the best place to start is with sugar and any caffeine-containing beverages, since these are relatively easy to eliminate and do frequently cause problems. (Some people may experi-ence caffeine withdrawal headaches. These will subside within a few days.) At the same time, cut out your (or your child's) favorite food, the one you crave or sneak, or one that you eat every day. People are often allergic to the food they like best, and/or to foods they eat frequently. If eliminating these foods does not yield results, try cutting out your intuitive choice: the food you think you might be allergic to, for whatever reason or for no real reason at all. If that doesn't work, test yourself for eggs/dairy, then wheat/corn, and then soy. If you happen to eat a lot of soy, move it to just before eggs/dairy in your testing, since soy is actually more allergenic than these other foods. The reason it is relegated to the end of the list is that most Americans rarely eat soy—except occasionally in Chinese food—so it does not cause many problems. (Soy oil, which people do consume frequently in mayonnaise, salad dressings, and many baked goods, has had the protein portion of the bean removed, and is not as likely to cause an allergic reaction.) When you are testing these five foods, I suggest you continue to stay off sugar and caffeine, but you can add your favorite food back in before cutting out something else, provided it is nutritious. If eliminating eggs and dairy does not clear up the symptoms by the end of two weeks, add them back in before moving on to wheat and corn, and then add *them* back in before testing soy, if there is still no change in symptoms, otherwise, you'll soon find yourself with nothing for dinner but a glass of water and a toothpick.

By the time you have tested yourself or your child for these foods, you will in all likelihood have tracked down the cause (or causes) of your allergy. If you have not, and have run out of ideas as to which food is causing the problem, you may need some help. If you refer to any of the books on food allergies or look at the medical literature on the subject, you'll find that nearly every author has a different list of the "most common allergens." These lists, which usually have a number of foods in common, may be useful in giving you ideas about which foods to test next. Don't rule out a food just because it doesn't appear on someone's list, however—that doesn't mean it's not at the root of your problem. One reason the lists are rarely identical is that any food can cause a problem, so don't assume otherwise. Another useful source is a biologic classification of foods: a list that divides foods into families. In some cases the relationships are unsurprising—such as that between cheese and milk—but in others they may be unexpected. For example, onions and asparagus both belong to the lili family, and tomatoes, eggplant, and green peppers are members of the potato family. A person who is allergic to one food in a family will not necessarily react to related foods, but they are a good place to start in tracking down additional offenders. (A biologic classification of foods is included in *Dr. Mandell's 5-Day Allergy Relief System*.)

You should also consider the possibility that your child reacts not to the food itself but to an additive such as a coloring, stabilizer, preservative, or artificial flavoring. The following is a list of some additives and other substances that commonly cause problems. More information on food additives can be obtained from FAUS (Feingold Association of the U.S.), P.O. Box 6550, Alexandria, VA 22306.

FOOD ADDITIVES AND OTHER SUBSTANCES THAT MAY CAUSE ADVERSE REACTIONS

ADDITIVES AND CONTAMINANTS

Dyes (tartrazine yellow)
Nitrates and nitrites
Monosodium glutamate
Aspartame
Sulfiting agents
Antibiotics
Pesticides
Insect parts
Molds

PHARMACOLOGIC SUBSTANCES

Caffeine
Theobromine (chocolate, tea)
Histamine (fish, beer, wine, chocolate)
Histamine-releasing foods (strawberries, shellfish, tomatoes)
Tyramine (cheeses, pickled herring, avocados, oranges, bananas, tomatoes)
Tryptamine (tomatoes, blue plums)
Serotonin (bananas, tomatoes, plums, avocados, pineapples)
Phenylethylamine (chocolate)
Hallucinogens (certain mushrooms, nutmeg, morning glory seeds)
Alcohol

Adapted from "Food Allergy," by Erik C. Walker, M.D., *American Family Physician*,

Vol. 38, No. 1, July 1988, p. 209, and from "An Overview of the Controversy Concerning Questionable Manifestations of Food Allergy," by Brett V. Kettelhut, M.D., and Dean D. Metcalfe, M.D., *Annals of Allergy*, Vol. 59, (Part II, Nov. 1987).

Another avenue of help is to consult a health practitioner who has some knowledge about food allergies. It may be that you simply need the chance to talk through the problems you are having, and that another mind may be able to see something you keep missing. If you reach the point where you are ready to resort to allergy testing, I suggest you try Applied Kinesiology, a type of muscle testing done by some chiropractors. Though, like the other tests, it is not very accurate,[11] it is both inexpensive and noninvasive, and does yield good results in some cases. You can even learn to do Applied Kinesiology yourself by reading *A Touch for Health* by Thies, which can be ordered by mail. Write to T.H. Enterprises, 1200 N. Lake Ave., Pasadena, CA 91104, for information.

Testing a toddler for food allergies can be particularly difficult. Many toddlers are picky eaters, and the extremely fussy eater who likes only five or six different foods is very likely allergic to all of them. To get around this without starving your child, you must use a little ingenuity and a lot of patience. If, for example, four of the five things your two-year-old will eat contain wheat, you may have to find substitutes gradually for each of them: wheat-free bread for white or whole wheat bread, homemade chicken nuggets with a cornmeal coating instead of those from your local fast-food restaurant, even wheat-free crackers and pasta. Your local health food store can provide a surprising variety of substitutes for whatever foods you are trying to cut out, and you will probably find something there that's acceptable to your fussy eater. Once you have gotten him completely off the food you want to eliminate, you can start your testing in earnest. A word of caution, however: You'll probably have to give up that food also, since you can't reasonably expect him to understand that Mommy or Daddy can eat his beloved spaghetti and meatballs, while he's stuck with soy pasta.

While you are conducting your food trials, it is absolutely essential that you keep a food diary. This diary should contain a list of everything that you eat and notes on how you feel at various times during the day, plus any allergy-related symptoms in your nursing baby. If you are keeping it for a young child, it should include notes on the foods he eats, his moods and, again, any allergy-related symptoms.

I realize that keeping such a diary is difficult, especially if you are trying to meet the demands of a new baby. There you are, overwhelmed with new responsibilities, functioning on very little sleep, and possibly coping with a colicky, miserable baby to boot, and I'm suggesting you take time out to write in a diary several times a day. However, you really must find a way to manage it. A diary will provide you with invaluable information: Not only will it make clear any connections between diet and your baby's health, but it will also make it possible for you to detect any food combination allergies. For example, you may find that you are able to eat bananas or peanut butter, but that eating the two together causes you to have an allergic reaction.

Once you have determined which food or foods causes you or your baby problems, you will have to experiment with the food to discover the exact nature of your reaction to it. You may find, for example, that you cannot drink milk but that you can eat cheese or yogurt, since they are partially digested. Or you may discover that you can tolerate a teaspoon of milk each day but that more brings on allergic symptoms, or that you can have milk once a week but not more often. Remember, the severity and nature of an allergy varies from one person to the next and from one food to the next, and the only way to pin down the extent of your particular sensitivities is through trial and error.

Breast-Feeding and Allergies

As I've already noted, it is possible for a breast-fed baby to have a reaction to some component of his mother's milk. Generally speaking, though, it is much less common for the breast-fed baby to have allergy symptoms than the bottle-fed baby, probably because breast milk itself contains protective factors against allergies. As you may remember from chapter 7, an infant's immature intestinal tract may allow large food molecules to pass through the intestinal wall, setting off an allergic reaction. IgA, one of the five immunoglobulins present in breast milk, coats the intestinal wall, making it difficult for these molecules to get through. In addition, breast milk facilitates the maturation of the cells lining the intestinal wall and enhances the absorption of digested foods.[12] While these mechanisms may not serve to eliminate allergic reactions completely in the breast-fed baby, it is virtually certain that the allergic baby will fare much better on breast milk than on a substitute. (Because of the immaturity of the digestive tract, I feel that it is especially important to delay introducing solid foods to the allergic child until one year of age. For more on solid foods, see chapter 7.)

The other advantage of breast-feeding the allergic child is that it allows the mother to have control over what goes into the milk. There's no way to tailor a formula to a particular baby's needs, but a mother *can* do this with her breast milk, although it sometimes places severe restrictions on her diet. Most mothers I have talked to are perfectly willing to go along with diet modifications up to a certain point, and have little trouble eliminating two or three foods, such as dairy products, eggs, and tomatoes, for example. In some extreme cases, however, this isn't enough. One of the most memorable cases I know was presented at a La Leche League convention by Tatsuo Matsumura, M.D., of Gunma University School of Medicine in Japan. He spoke of the case of a Japanese baby, exclusively breast-fed, who had severe eczema. Each time the child was hospitalized, taken off the breast and put on an IV, the eczema improved. An elimination diet finally proved that the only foods his mother could eat without provoking the eczema were five vegetables and snake meat. Luckily, most cases are not this extreme, but the breast-feeding mother may find that she has to alter her diet significantly if her baby is allergic. Whether the changes that must be made are minor or drastic, the inconvenience is greatly rewarded by the child's improved health.

Living with the Allergic Child

Many parents of allergic children feel that they must police the child's diet every minute of every day. In my own family and among my patients, however, I've found that it is much more effective to shift this responsibility onto the child's shoulders fairly early. Most four-year-olds are capable of understanding cause-and-effect relationships, so that around this age the allergic child can begin to make the connection between what he eats and how he feels. Instead of trying to control everything that goes into the child's mouth, help him to understand the consequences of his choice of food. If he complains of a stomachache or a headache, don't offer immediate relief in the form of a pill. There's nothing wrong with letting your child endure a little discomfort in order to learn that his actions have consequences. Instead, explain to him that the food he has eaten has caused his symptoms. He might resist seeing the connection, but eventually it will sink in. I recently went on a Boy Scout camping trip with my son Jared, who has some food allergies. He made the decision to eat whatever he wanted during the trip. After three days he began having abdominal pains, and by the third night he felt bad enough so that he chose to stay in my tent. The next morning he told me that he had decided to go back to his usual diet for the rest of the trip. Had I offered Jared something that made him feel better, I don't think the lesson would have had any impact.

Once your child has made the connection between food and her health, it's up to her to decide what to do about it. After all, it's her body. My daughter Margo is allergic to dairy products, including cheese. Unfortunately, Margo's favorite food is pizza. She plans her pizza binges around a schedule: When she's got the time to take it easy for two days, Margo will go out for pizza and have a great time. She knows from experience that she'll feel sick afterward, but sometimes the pizza is worth that price. Jared is particularly sensitive to sweets. When he overindulges he becomes difficult to deal with and out of control. When this happens, he knows it's his responsibility to remove himself from the family until he can get himself back under control and then rejoin us as his normal civil self. These kids are aware of their allergies, and we leave it up to them to handle them as they see fit.

When dealing with a child with allergies, you should also keep in mind that total compliance with a diet is unrealistic. After all, if you think back on the times you've been on a restricted diet for some reason, I'm sure you'll also recall times you cheated. You had your reasons, and children have their reasons too. If you take the attitude that it is more important that your child learn to take responsibility for his body than that he never eats the wrong food, you'll have greater success—*and* you'll retain your sanity. Your role is to help your child understand the connection between his health and his diet, not to be a policeman.

Prevention and Treatment of Allergies

....

Unfortunately, you can't prevent an allergy from developing in someone who is already allergic. However, if you have a child who is allergic and are contemplating having another, it is worth noting that limiting your diet during pregnancy is considered by some to reduce the chances of later allergic reactions in the unborn child. (Interestingly, the woman who had to limit her diet to five vegetables and snake meat resumed eating normally after her first child was weaned and went back to the restricted diet during her second pregnancy. Her second child did not have severe allergy problems.) As a general guideline, during pregnancy you should eliminate any foods to which you or any of your children is allergic. In this way you may be able to avoid "sensitizing" your unborn baby to those foods. This is not an idea that is widely accepted, and some studies have been done that refute its effectiveness. From what I've seen, however, these studies generally rely on the mother limiting her exposure to the offending foods or eliminating them only in the last trimester of pregnancy.[13] When the offending foods are eliminated from the diet for the entire pregnancy, results are much better.

If you choose to limit your diet during pregnancy, you must be sure that you do not sacrifice calories or nutritional content, otherwise, a restricted diet could prove harmful to the baby. For example, if you give up dairy products, make sure you are getting adequate calcium and protein from other sources.

The only truly effective treatment for food allergy is to avoid the allergen. However, there are some doctors who use sublingual drops to treat food allergies. These work in much the same way as desensitization shots do for inhalant allergies. In both treatments, the child is repeatedly exposed to small amounts of the allergen, until the body is no longer able to react to it. I do not feel that sublingual drops are very effective, nor do I feel that it is wise to assault the body continually with the very substance to which it is allergic. (For more on allergy shots, see "Allergy Shots" on page 219.)

Also, some doctors are beginning to use the drug cromolyn sodium, which is sold under various trade names, to block allergic reactions to foods. Cromolyn sodium has been shown to be effective when used as a nasal spray to provide symptomatic relief for upper respiratory allergies. (Cromolyn is a derivative of bioflavonoids, one of the ingredients of the allergy remedy in chapter 17). Studies of its efficacy when taken orally to treat food allergies have produced conflicting results. Until more is known about it, I would not recommend using it to treat food allergies.

In addition, several mothers have told me that they have been able to treat allergies in their breast-fed babies by giving them a series of diluted solutions of breast milk. The principle behind this is essentially the same as that of homeopathic medicine: "like cures like." In homeopathy, the medicine for a particular symptom is formulated by taking a substance that in its purest form would normally cause that same symptom. The substance is then diluted by several hundred or thousand times to produce a medicine that is believed to stimulate the body's own defense mechanisms. To make an allergy remedy from breast milk, add one teaspoon (5 ml.) of breast milk to four teaspoons (20 ml.) of spring or distilled water. Make a second solution by adding one teaspoon of the first solution to another four teaspoons of water. Repeat this process with a teaspoon of the second solution and four teaspoons of water to make a third solution, and then again with the third solution and water to make a fourth solution. To use the solutions, place three drops of the first one under the baby's tongue. If the baby's symptoms seem to be relieved (e.g., the colic, gassiness, or crying improve) in the next few minutes, continue to repeat that dose every five to ten minutes. If the first dilution is not effective, try the second, and work your way through the third and fourth solutions as necessary. (You might expect to start with the weakest solution, but in homeopathy this is considered the most potent.) If one of the solutions works, you'll probably find that it is consistently effective for your child, so that you can just go to that dosage the next time you need it. While this remedy is not really a solution to an allergy problem, it may help you cope with a miserable infant while you're trying to determine which food or foods are causing the reaction.

Since there really is no treatment for allergies, parents hope their children will outgrow them, and many doctors do feel this happens often. One report from a medical journal states that sixty to seventy-three percent of infants will lose their food sensitivity in the first year, while twenty-six to fifty-three percent of older children will eventually lose theirs.[14] However, Dr. William Crook, speaking at a La Leche League conference, has said that he does not think children outgrow their food allergies,[15] and I think this is true for most cases. What may be happening in cases in which the allergy seems to disappear is that the food is cautiously added back into the diet in small amounts over a long period of time, so that the immediate effects are minor and may go largely unperceived. Rather than acute symptoms, the person gradually develops chronic problems (headaches, fatigue, restless sleep) which he may not associate with the food but that are actually allergy-related. I think the only way to be certain a food allergy has been "outgrown" is to eat a large quantity of the food after abstaining from it completely for at least two weeks. Even then, the food may cause a problem when eaten repeatedly over the course of several days, but a reaction does not seem as likely if this sort of challenge has not resulted in acute symptoms.

Allergy Shots

While my intention in writing this chapter has been to discuss food allergies, I do want to discuss one treatment that may be suggested for children with inhalant allergies: desensitization shots. These are done by repeatedly injecting the child with the substance to which he is allergic, such as dust or pollen. I have strong objections to the indiscriminate use of allergy shots for several reasons. As I've noted, it makes little sense to me to assault the body continually with an allergen. I know there are seemingly reasonable theories as to why the shots work, but I have never been comfortable with them. This type of perpetual exposure has to lower the body's natural defenses. Second, it has not been adequately proven that such shots are effective, and finally, I have not been able to find any studies that show whether or not there are any harmful side effects ten or twenty years after the shots have been received. I will not go so far as to say that allergy shots are *never* justified, however. If your child has, for example, severe asthma for which he must take cortisone and that often lands him in the hospital, shots are really the only reasonable treatment available. But they are, at best, an imperfect solution, and should never be undertaken without weighing the potential risks against the potential benefits.

Summing Up: Allergies

··

1. While the subject of food allergies is controversial within the medical community, there is evidence that they can cause significant health problems. In my opinion, they are also at the root of many minor complaints.

2. With the exception of the double-blind food challenge, the allergy tests offered by doctors are very inaccurate and tend to be expensive.

3. The only way to determine which foods affect your child (or you) and the extent of his particular sensitivities is through an elimination diet and trial and error.

4. When trying to track down food allergies, it is essential to keep a food diary.

5. Babies who have food allergies will particularly benefit from breast milk if the mother is careful about what she eats.

6. The allergic child should be allowed to take responsibility for what he eats from an early age, so that the parent does not have to be a policeman.

7. Allergy shots should be avoided except in extreme cases.

Notes

1. Carlo Zanussi, M.D., "Concluding Remarks, VI International Food Allergy Symposium," *Annals of Allergy*, Vol. 59, Part III (Nov. 1987): p. 200.

2. R. Genova et al., "Food Allergy in Steroid-Resistant Nephrotic Syndrome" (letter), *The Lancet* (June 6, 1987): p. 1315.

3. Joan McIlhenny et al., "Food Allergy Presenting an Obstruction in an Infant," *American Journal of Roetgenology*, Vol. 150 (Feb. 1988): p. 373.

4. Lawrence S. Loesel, M.D., "Allergy and Enlarged Adenoids" (letter), *Journal of the American Medical Association*, Vol. 260, No. 12 (Sept. 23, 1988): p. 1716.

5. William Crook, M.D., *Detecting Your Hidden Allergies*, (Jackson, Tenn.: Professional Books, 1988): p. 30.

6. Marshall Mandell, M.D., and Lynn Waller Scanlon, *Dr. Mandell's 5-Day Allergy Relief System*, (New York: Thomas Y. Crowell, 1979): p. 15.

7. Robert J. Dockhorn, M.D., "Clinical Studies of Food Allergy in Infants and Children," *Annals of Allergy*, Vol. 59, Part II (Nov. 1987): p. 139.

8. S. Allan Bock, M.D., "A Critical Evaluation of Clinical Trials in Adverse Reactions to Foods in Children," *Journal of Allergy and Clinical Immunology*, Vol. 78, No. 1, Part 2 (July 1986): p. 165.

9. Crook, p. 40.

10. Mandell and Scanlon, p. 226.

11. J. S. Garrow, F.R.C.P., "Kinesiology and Food Allergy," *British Medical Journal*, Vol. 296, No. 663 (June 4, 1988): p. 1573.

12. Richard A. Schrieber, M.D.C.M., F.R.C.P., and W. Allan Walker, M.D., "The Gastrointestinal Barrier: Antigen Uptake and Perinatal Immunity," *Annals of Allergy*, Vol. 61, Part II (Dec. 1988): p. 9.

13. N.-I. Max Kjellman, M.D., "Food Allergy—Treatment and Prevention," *Annals of Allergy*, Vol. 59, Part II (Nov. 1987): p. 171.

14. Peyton A. Eggleston, M.D., "Prospective Studies in the Natural History of Food Allergy," *Annals of Allergy*, Vol. 59, Part II (Nov. 1987): p. 179.

15. William Crook, M.D., "The Effect of Food and Food Additives on Children" (lecture), La Leche League International Conference (Chicago, July 24, 1981).

Middle Ear Infections

Infection of the middle ear (otitis media) is one of the most common illnesses of childhood and is the one disease that most often prompts parents to take their children to the doctor. One study that followed 2,565 children from birth found that by the age of three years, seventy-one percent had had one or more episodes of otitis media and thirty-three percent had had three or more episodes.[1] Frequently recurring or chronic otitis media is quite common in children under the age of six years, affecting about ten percent of this age-group.[2] In fact, we spend about two billion dollars a year on medical and surgical treatment of middle ear infections.[3] Nevertheless, our knowledge about this condition is admittedly incomplete, and the treatments doctors routinely offer are considered far from ideal, even by those who wholeheartedly subscribe to them.

My approach to otitis media is different from most medical doctors', although it is becoming more common. Before I get into the way I treat ear infections and why, let's look at how an infection develops and the standard treatments:

The outer ear is made up of both the ear that we see (the skin and cartilage technically known as the pinna) and the outer canal, the short passage that leads from the external ear to the eardrum. The middle ear consists of the eardrum; three small, connected bones (the malleus, incus, and stapes); and the eustachian tube, which produces a lubricating fluid that normally drains into the back of the throat. The eustachian tube also serves to equalize pressure in the inner ear. The inner ear is made up of the cochlea, which has to do with hearing; the semicircular canals, which affect balance; and the nerves that carry impulses from the middle ear and inner ear to the brain (see fig. 1).

The opening of the eustachian tube into the back of the throat is surrounded by lym-

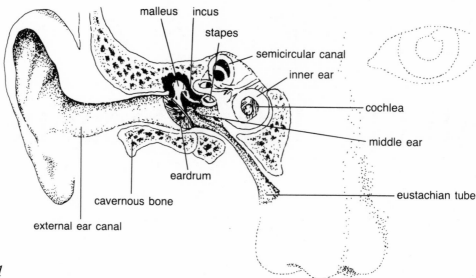

Fig. 1

phoid tissue. Although not all of the causative factors that contribute to otitis media are fully understood, we do know that one important element is the swelling of this lymphoid tissue, which may result from a virus, an allergy, or bacteria. When this happens, the swollen tissue closes off the opening of the tube, so that the lubricating fluid is unable to drain. This fluid collects in the tube and, when the tube is full, pushes up into the middle ear cavity, where it puts pressure on the eardrum. This stagnant fluid provides the perfect medium for the growth of bacteria. It's like a pond that's fed by an adjacent stream. If you dammed the stream, your pond would soon be the home of countless little organisms that would turn it green and slimy. In much the same way, the blocked eustachian tube leads to an overgrowth of bacteria and then infection.

Interestingly, one study has found that the bacteria present in the middle ear dur-ing an infection may be opportunistic. That is, they are always there, but not at high enough levels to create a problem.[4] When the body's immune system is somehow hampered—perhaps by another illness or allergy—the bacteria will proliferate. There is also evidence that this growth may take up to four weeks to reach significant levels. In a study in which the eustachian tubes of monkeys were surgically closed, infections did not develop until between one and four weeks had passed.[5] This may explain why, after a course of antibiotics, some children seem to remain well for several weeks and then develop another infection. In these cases the "new" infection may not be new at all, but simply a delayed continuation of the previous condition.

Technically, there are several different types of middle ear infections. The most commonly used differentiation is between OME, or otitis media with effusion (fluid accumulation) and OM, otitis media without effusion, which is just an inflammation of the middle ear. The two categories I find most useful in distinguishing ear infections are otitis media that recurs frequently and that which does not. Otitis media that occurs once every year or two does not pose a significant problem, and treatment is accordingly simple. Recurrent or chronic otitis media is a significant problem, and warrants an investment of time and effort to discover its cause.

There are certain children who are at an increased risk of developing recurrent or chronic otitis media. These include children with a cleft palate, Down's syndrome, native Americans (Indians and Eskimos), and those with Kartagener's syndrome. At a lower but still increased risk are children who have a family history of chronic or recurrent otitis media, those who have an early first bout (before eighteen months of age), premature and allergic infants, and those who are malnourished, neglected, or abused.[6]

The standard medical approach to otitis media is to treat it with antibiotics for ten days. In the nonrecurring cases, the infection will clear up and that will be the end of the problem for a year or longer. In other children the infection will return every few months in spite of the antibiotics, and in the most difficult cases, it will recur within a few days to a couple of weeks after the antibiotics are finished. These subsequent infections are usually treated with still more antibiotics, and the child may end up in a yo-yo syndrome, continually going on and off the drugs. (This process is a bit like keeping your stagnant pond clear by dumping chlorine into it every day.) Since you're

not doing anything to allow the fluid to drain, the bacteria will start to proliferate again as soon as the antibiotics are stopped. Some doctors even use antibiotics prophylactically, putting a child on them for months on end to keep the infection at bay.

However the antibiotics are used, they present significant hazards. Like all drugs, they are toxic to the body as well as to the organism they are intended to kill, and so have undesirable side effects. Most of these are relatively mild, such as vomiting, diarrhea, and skin rashes, but they may be severe and even life-threatening, though only rarely. Unfortunately, many doctors tend to prescribe the newer, stronger, and more toxic antibiotics first, rather than the old standbys, like penicillin, that have fewer side effects.

The wisdom of using antibiotics in spite of their hazards might be arguable if they were truly necessary to get rid of an ear infection, but they're not. One double-blind study looked at 171 children with otitis media—a total of 239 affected ears. The children were divided into four different treatment groups: one had neither myringotomy (a procedure that is widely used in Europe that involves making an incision in the eardrum through which fluid can drain) nor antibiotics, one had myringotomy only, one had antibiotics only, and one had both myringotomy and antibiotics. There was no significant clinical difference in the course of the disease (pain, temperature, duration of the discharge, otoscopic appearance of the eardrum, sensitivity of hearing, or recurrence rate) among the four groups.[7] Another study looked at 4,680 children who were treated with nose drops and analgesics for otitis media; more than ninety percent recovered within a few days.[8] In yet another study, 149 children with acute otitis media were divided randomly into two groups, one of which was treated with penicillin and the other with a placebo. After one day of treatment the majority of both groups experienced a significant decrease in pain (as measured by the amount of analgesic taken for pain relief), although a slightly higher percentage of those on antibiotics were pain-free at this time. The overall course of the disease was unaffected by the use of antibiotics. There was no difference in the appearance of the eardrum; measurements of fluid after one week, one month, and three months; relapses (one week to one month); or recurrences (one to three months) between the two groups. The authors of this study concluded that antibiotic treatment is not necessary in most cases.[9]

Nevertheless, this is not an idea that has taken hold in the medical community, and the subject of antibiotic use for ear infections remains highly controversial, with most doctors strongly favoring their use. One of the justifications frequently cited for using antibiotics is the risk of developing mastoiditis, an infection of the mastoid bones that are located behind the ear. Mastoiditis was a major concern from the early 1900s until around the 1930s. At that time the only treatment for the disease was surgery, which carried with it a significant mortality rate. Mastoiditis is now relatively rare. In the study of 4,680 children cited above, only 2 developed mastoiditis, and these were easily recognized and responded promptly to antibiotic treatment. (No other complications were noted in this study.)

This decrease in mastoiditis is often attributed to the introduction of antibiotic therapy. However, one group of researchers who has studied otitis media has noted that "children of today appear less susceptible to such serious complications as mastoiditis. . . . However, factors other than antibiotics appear to be concerned. Better nutrition and general care made available in this section of North America may be responsible for improved natural resistance."[10]

Aside from antibiotics, the other frequently prescribed treatment for recurring infections is to place small plastic tubes in an incision in the eardrum. The tubes allow the existing fluid to drain and then prevent further accumulation, at least until the tubes fall out or are removed. This procedure is known as a tympanostomy. While the tubes do help the fluid to drain, I object to their use for several reasons. To begin with, the operation has a relatively high failure rate. In one study, twenty-three percent of the tympanostomy patients required more than one surgical procedure in order to get the tubes in place. Thirty-seven percent of that group went on to have between three and eight procedures.[11] This means that not only is the child exposed to general anesthesia several times, but the repeated puncturing of the eardrum leads to an increased risk of hearing loss.

A study that measured the function of the eardrum with a test called a tympanogram found that there was a direct correlation between the rate of abnormalities and the number of myringotomies.[12] In other words, the more often an eardrum had been operated on, the more likely it was that the eardrum did not function properly (and hence, that the hearing had been decreased). Since tubes cause more scarring than a simple incision does, it seems likely to me that their use poses an even greater threat to the hearing.

Another study evaluated children with chronic fluid in both ears. For each child, a tube was placed in one ear only. When the hearing was tested several years later, it was found that the ears with the tubes had greater hearing loss than those that had been left alone.[13]

Ironically, the medical community often justifies tympanostomy tubes on the grounds that fluid in the middle ear may cause a hearing loss that can lead to developmental delays. It is true that a *temporary* hearing loss will occur as long as there is fluid behind the eardrum, but once the fluid has drained the eardrum will function normally again. This is more or less the same effect that you would get if you filled a bass drum with water. As long as there's water in the drum, it won't sound right. Once you empty out the water and dry out the heads, however, the sound quality returns.

Whether or not this temporary hearing loss leads to a developmental delay is still open to question. Studies in animals have suggested that this is the case, but no studies in human beings have adequately addressed the topic,[14] and the degree and duration of a hearing loss required to produce these delays is unknown.[15] The theory behind this concern is that a child who is at a stage of rapid language development will permanently lose ground and may never catch up again if his hearing is significantly impaired for any length of time. I don't

mean to suggest that you can take this possibility lightly, but to put it in perspective by noting that it has not ever been proven to occur. Since there is evidence that placing tubes in the ears results in a hearing loss, I feel that tympanostomy presents the greater danger. Note, too, that I am not suggesting that you can just ignore persistent fluid in your child's ears; the problem should be dealt with, but surgery isn't the answer. (I'll get to how you *should* get rid of the fluid momentarily.)

Permanent hearing loss from otitis media occurs only in children who have had recurrent ear infections for many years, so that it is rarely seen in a child younger than eight. Sometimes called "glue ear," this type of deafness is caused by a hardening of the fluid in the middle ear, and can be corrected only through surgery. Long before glue ear has a chance to develop, you should be able to identify and eliminate the source of your child's repeated infections.

Doctors who favor the use of tubes also try to scare parents into having the operation done by telling them that there is a danger that the eardrum will rupture from the pressure produced by the fluid. This is true, but while a ruptured eardrum is not desirable, neither is it dangerous. It is simply nature's way of dealing with the problem of excessive fluid behind the eardrum. The eardrum must be punctured to place the tubes anyway. In either case the eardrum will heal eventually. With tubes, however, it cannot heal completely until the tubes have fallen out or been removed, which may lead to more scarring (and hence, decreased hearing). In contrast, an eardrum that perforates naturally will probably heal within a week. The other difference between an eardrum that nature ruptures and one that is opened for a tympanostomy is that the surgery must be done under general anesthesia.

My main objection to both tympanostomy and antibiotics, however, is that neither really gets to the root of the problem of recurrent ear infection. They are both means of treating the symptoms—the overgrowth of bacteria and the fluid behind the eardrum—but they do nothing about the conditions that allow the fluid to accumulate and the bacteria to proliferate in the first place. As you may remember from the introduction, I see these treatments as measures that may temporarily take the child from a state of sickness to unsickness, but do nothing to help him reach "wellness."

In my experience, an allergy, usually to a certain food or foods, is at the root of almost every case of chronic otitis media, except in those rare instances when a severe anatomic defect (such as a cleft palate) is a factor. Now, this is my theory, and I'll readily admit that it is not widely accepted among doctors. I've seen the connection between allergy and ear infection over and over again, however, both in families I have treated and in three of my own children. In the vast majority of cases tracking down and eliminating the offending food from the child's diet (or the mother's, in the case of a breast-fed baby), has permanently cleared up the infection. (See chapter 12 for more information.)

I have not always treated ear infections this way. Up until about 1979, I prescribed antibiotics for otitis media. Persistent cases were referred to an ear, nose, and throat specialist (ENT), and not a few of my patients ended up with tubes in their ears. I first began to seriously question the wisdom of these practices when my son Jared developed recurrent ear infections. He was less than three months old when the first infection started, and for the next year he was on antibiotics almost continuously. Finally we had tubes put in Jared's ears, and the infections did subside temporarily. As soon as the tubes fell out, however, the problem returned. The ENT recommended another operation to place a second set of tubes in Jared's ears, plus more antibiotics. Pat and I were very unhappy about the idea of subjecting him to more surgery, particularly since he had developed an infection following the first operation, and left the hospital much sicker than he was when he went in.

So we set out on a round of visits to specialists to try to find an alternative. Every ENT we saw made the same recommendations: more tubes and antibiotics. Finally, as we were literally halfway out the door of one doctor's office, he mentioned in an offhand way that some physicians felt that chronic otitis media was caused by allergy. This doctor was obviously scornful of the idea, but I seized it and ran with it, researching the topic in medical journals and reading everything I could get my hands on on the subject. (This was how I first learned about the elimination diet described in chapter 12.) We finally found that eliminating three foods from Pat's diet (since she was breast-feeding him) took care of the ear infections. Jared is now thirteen, and hasn't been on antibiotics since we altered his diet. Up until about the age of six he would still get an occasional ear infection if he ate something he shouldn't. This did sometimes happen, since we did not follow him around at friends' houses or birthday parties, watching every morsel of food that went into his mouth. As soon as he got off the offending foods, however, the infection cleared up.

While the allergy-otitis connection is not a popular concept, several researchers have noted it.[16] More attention has been paid to the connection between inhalant allergies and ear infections, and this is also a factor that should be considered. As I noted in chapter 12, allergic individuals tend to have more than one type of allergy. Food allergies may aggravate inhalant allergies, and both may be responsible for chronic or recurrent ear infections.

How to Diagnose and Treat Ear Infections

Except in unusually severe cases, it is not necessary to take your child to a doctor to diagnose and treat an ear infection. This is something that can be done at home with an otoscope and two medications that you should keep on hand.

The only sure way to diagnose an infection of the middle ear is to look at the eardrum with an otoscope. However, there are several symptoms that should lead you to suspect an ear infection in your baby or child, although they may also be seen in a teething baby or a child of any age who has an upper respiratory infection or virus. The most common of these are the following:

1. Pulling on the ears.

2. A sharp, piercing cry.

3. Congestion in the nose or postnasal drainage.

4. A cough.

5. Refusing to nurse because of pain while sucking, or gnawing at the nipple in an attempt to "pop" the pressure in the ear.

6. Redness of the external ear (probably from pulling on it).

7. Drainage from the ear (this indicates that the eardrum has ruptured).

8. Fever.

9. Biting or chewing on objects—again, an attempt to pop the pressure in the ear.

10. Tilting of the head, or wanting to nurse on only one breast (this is an attempt to lessen the pressure in the ear).

11. Hearing loss, indicated by the child talking louder, turning up the volume on the television, or failing to hear you when she normally would.

12. Restless sleep; waking more often than usual.

13. Loss of appetite.

14. Pain: An older child will complain of pain in the ear, but a younger child may not be able to locate the source of the pain accurately, and so may complain that her head hurts.

If your child has some of these symptoms, use your otoscope to examine her eardrums (see chapter 3). If the eardrum is reddened, or if you can see blood vessels on its surface, there is some degree of infection present. If you also see a horizontal line across the eardrum or bubbles behind it, there is fluid in the middle ear. (Fluid may also be present even if you are unable to identify it.) The intensity of the redness of the eardrum does not necessarily correlate with the severity of the infection; I've seen very red eardrums in children who have no other symptoms of an infection. In order to judge just how bad the infection is, you must take into account all of the child's symptoms (once again, you have to evaluate the whole child). If one or both eardrums are red, however, you will know that there is, at least, a mild infection.

If your child does have an ear infection, you shouldn't rush to the doctor for antibiotics, of course, but you can take steps to decrease the pain and hasten the end of the infection. Prescription ear drops such as Auralgan will numb your child's eardrum and ease the pain, if necessary. (If the pain is not too bad and your child can be comforted with TLC, you can and should forgo the drops. Because they are oily, it may be more difficult to assess the condition of the eardrum after using them.) Your doctor should be willing to give you a prescription for these so that you can keep them on hand, especially if your child has had ear infections in the past. The drops will do nothing to clear up the infection, but they should instantly ease the pain. If you don't have the drops when you need them, you can also use warm garlic oil, moulin oil (available in health food stores), or even olive oil, as long as you are careful not to overheat it. These will not be as effective as prescription ear drops, but they will help.

To clear up the infection, you should also start the child on a decongestant. This will open up the eustachian tube and drain the fluid. To get back to the stagnant pond analogy, this process is like removing the dam so that the water can flow freely again. Once you get the water moving, you no longer have to keep dumping chlorine into it to keep your pond free of organisms. Once you get the fluid moving through the eustachian tube, you no longer need antibiotics to keep bacteria from proliferating.

The use of decongestants and antihistamines to treat otitis media is another controversial topic in the medical community, and some studies have indicated that they are of little or no use in treating this condition.[17] However, other researchers have suggested that these studies are seriously flawed in several respects.[18] Furthermore, even studies that concluded that decongestants were not effective in treating otitis media did note that the drugs had a positive effect on the opening of the eustachian tube, and that this effect was more pronounced after the children had received four doses of the drug.[19]

My own theory as to why decongestants and decongestant/antihistamine combinations have sometimes been shown to be clinically ineffective is that the dosages used are often too small. I arrived at this conclusion when we were working with Jared's ear infections. We found that the recommended dose for a child his age had little effect, but that a higher dose cleared up the problem.

The medication I prefer to use for this purpose is Ryna, a nonprescription antihistamine/decongestant formula that contains no sugar, dye, or alcohol (ingredients to which a child might be allergic), although it does contain sorbitol (supposedly not absorbed by the body) and artificial flavor. The chart below gives the dosages I use according to age:

0–3 months	¼ teaspoon
3–6 months	½ teaspoon
6–9 months	¾ teaspoon
9–18 months	1½ teaspoons

Another, more accurate way to figure the dosage is by the baby's weight. For this, I base my calculations on the ingredient pseudoephedrine (a decongestant), of which there is thirty milligrams per teaspoon of the medication. I give 3.75 milligrams per pound per day (divided into four doses), so that for a twenty-pound baby, the dosage would be two and a half teaspoons per day, or slightly more than a half-teaspoon four times a day.

If you are unable to find Ryna, I have also found the nonprescription formula Demazin to be effective, although it does contain some additives. A child who is old enough to swallow pills could also take Sudafed in pill form, another product that contains no alcohol and can be made free of sugar and dye by scraping off the red coating.

Although a decongestant and ear drops will help your child recover, you should keep in mind that this, too, is merely symptomatic treatment. While preferable to antibiotics and tympanostomy tubes, they should not be considered a "cure." The decongestant and ear drops may be all your child needs to become healthy again if the infection is of the once-a-year variety, but if the problem recurs, you still need to track down the allergy and deal with it. This takes time, though, and the decongestant/ear drops therapy will help you through any infections that occur while you're playing detective.

Your child may feel noticeably better after one to two days on the decongestant and ear drops, or it may take three to four days, depending on how quickly your child's body is able to fight off the infection. As long as his condition does not worsen, you can continue the therapy, allowing time for the body's natural defenses to work. If the child's condition worsens (i.e., he becomes more lethargic, continues to run a fever, and seems generally sicker), more aggressive treatment is necessary. With my own children, I have found a combination of two homeopathic solutions, Preparations 510 and 526, and Immuno-klenz (derived from echinacea, goldenseal, and other roots) to be effective. Since these preparations are probably not available at your local drug store, I recommend that you keep them on hand if your child develops chronic otitis media. (They can be purchased at some health food stores, or by mail from Lewis Gitomer Labs, 139 Haven Ave., Port Washington, N.Y. 11050. Call 800-645-6016 for ordering information.) If the child's condition still does not improve, or if these medications are not available, you will then have to resort to treatment with an antibiotic.

If antibiotic treatment does become necessary, plain penicillin, the mildest antibiotic, should be used first. When my practice was at its peak (and before I began teaching parents to recognize an ear infection themselves) I saw between forty and fifty ear infections a week, yet I was only forced to resort to antibiotic treatment about four times per year. In those cases, I would start the child on penicillin, and it usually eradicated the infection. Only rarely was it necessary to use a stronger antibiotic, such as ampicillin or amoxicillin. Because of the excessive use of antibiotics, however, there are strains of bacteria that are resistant to penicillin and some of the other lesser antibiotics. Your doctor may suggest putting your child on a stronger, more toxic antibiotic right from the start. This is a judgment call, and may be best viewed in light of where and how you live. If you live in a city and your child is frequently exposed to other children—particularly ill children—he may have picked up one of the stronger organisms. If you live in a rural area and your child has a fairly limited circle of playmates, you're probably dealing with a bacteria that will respond to penicillin. It has been noted that middle ear infections due to pneumococcus bacteria are more often characterized by a sudden onset of fever over 101°F and severe pain than are those due to other organisms.[20] Since pneumococcus responds well to penicillin, this is another reason to make it the first choice when antibiotic therapy is necessary. If a child does not respond to penicillin after forty-eight hours, a stronger antibiotic should then be used.

A very small percentage of children with chronic otitis media may not respond to control of their allergies or even to antibiotic therapy, leaving parents feeling that they have little choice other than surgery. If you find yourself in this position, there are a few things you should consider. First, the child should have a very thorough physical exam to rule out the possibility of an abnormality (such as a submucous cleft palate or a tumor in the upper respiratory system) or condition (such as sinusitis) that is contributing to the problem. Also, you may want to consider obtaining a tympanogram, which can identify the presence of fluid in the middle ear more accurately than observation with an otoscope. A series of tympanograms might help you to determine that the level of fluid in the middle ear is decreasing over time, indicating that the therapy is actually more successful than previously thought.

Finally, if you are dealing with a newborn with otitis media (which is rare), a child who is critically ill or immunologically deficient, or one who has had an unsatisfactory response to antibiotic therapy or an onset of otitis while already on antibiotics, you may want to consider tympanocentesis. This test involves inserting a needle through the eardrum and drawing out some of the inner ear fluid so that the bacteria can be cultured and identified. Identifying the bacteria in these cases will allow the doctor to determine which antibiotic will be most effective. In all likelihood, however, I don't think you'll have to resort to these measures.

As I noted at the beginning of this chapter, my approach to ear infections is unorthodox, and I don't expect your doctor will necessarily agree with it. Since I first started treating ear infections as outlined above, I have talked to many other doctors about the subject and have always been surprised at the resistance I encounter to any deviation from the standard medical practice, especially in light of some of the very good research that has been done refuting the effectiveness of antibiotics and tympanostomy tubes. One possible reason for this was pointed out to me by a young pediatrician I met several years ago at a La Leche League convention. When he first learned of my methods of treating ear infections, he was very excited about them. As our conversation continued, though, he suddenly underwent a complete change in demeanor. I thought perhaps I had offended him and asked what was wrong. He answered, very quietly, "One-third of my practice is ear infections." If his patients no longer needed his antibiotics and advice, his practice would decrease by one-third. I don't believe

this doctor had an unusually high percentage of his practice devoted to ear infections, and he certainly wasn't alone in his hesitancy to see his business cut substantially. I believe parents will have to take the lead in changing the way the medical community handles ear infections.

This is something I firmly believe parents both can and should do. As we've seen, most middle ear infections can be effectively treated with ear drops and decongestants. Those that recur or become chronic can almost always be permanently eliminated by dealing with the allergies that cause them. Taking this approach to otitis media could save your child from unnecessary medications and surgery, with all their attendant risks, not to mention money for doctor's visits and drugs you don't need. While not popular in the medical community, my methods have strong scientific support and they *work*.

Summing Up: Middle Ear Infections

1. Infection of the middle ear is the disease that most commonly prompts parents to take their children to the doctor.

2. The most helpful distinction between types of ear infections is between those that occur infrequently and those that recur frequently or become chronic.

3. In the majority of cases, there is no need to use antibiotics to treat an ear infection.

4. Parents can learn to diagnose and treat middle ear infections at home with an otoscope, ear drops, and a decongestant.

5. The placing of tubes in the ears to control middle ear infections is not highly effective and may lead to hearing loss.

6. Chronic or recurring middle ear infections are almost always due to a food allergy and should be treated by identifying and eliminating the offending food or foods from the child's diet.

Notes

1. David W. Teele, M.D., et al., "Chapter 2: Epidemiology of Otitis Media in Children," *Annals of Otology, Rhinology and Laryngology*, Supplement 68, Vol. 89, No. 3 (May–June 1980): p. 5.

2. Philip Fireman, M.D., "Otitis Media and Its Relationship to Allergy," *Pediatric Clinics of North America*, Vol. 35, No. 5 (Oct. 1988): p. 1076.

3. Charles D. Bluestone, M.D., "Otitis Media in Children: To Treat or Not to Treat?" *The New England Journal of Medicine*, Vol. 306, No. 23 (June 10, 1982): p. 1399.

4. Frederick W. Henderson, M.D., et al., "A Longitudinal Study of Respiratory Viruses and Bacteria in the Etiology of Acute Otitis Media with Effusion," *The New England Journal of Medicine*, Vol. 306, No. 23 (June 10, 1982): p. 1382.

5. W. J. Doyle, "Functional Eustachian Tube Obstruction and Otitis Media in a Primate Model," *Acta Oto-Laryngologica* Supplement, Vol. 414 (1984): p. 52.

6. Charles D. Bluestone, M.D., "Recent Advances in the Pathogenesis, Diagnosis, and Management of Otitis Media," *Pediatric Clinics of North America*, Vol. 28, No. 46 (Nov. 1981): p. 727.

7. F. L. Van Buchem et al., "Acute Otitis Media: A New Treatment Strategy," *British Medical Journal*, Vol. 290, No. 6474 (Apr. 6, 1985): p. 1035.

8. Van Buchem et al., p. 1033.

9. J. Thomsen et al., "Penicillin and Acute Otitis: Short- and Long-Term Results," *Annals of Otology, Rhinology and Laryngology*, Supplement 68, Vol. 89, No. 3 (May–June 1980): p. 271.

10. Oliver E. Laxdal, M.D., F.R.C.P., F.A.A.P., et al., "Treatment of Acute Otitis Media: A Controlled Study of 142 Children," *Canadian Medical Association Journal*, Vol. 102 (Feb. 14, 1970): p. 268.

11. W. Draf et al., "Insertion of Ventilation Tubes into the Middle Ear: Results and Complications in a Seven-Year Review," *Annals of Otology, Rhinology and Laryngology*, Supplement 68, Vol. 89, No. 3 (May–June 1980); p. 303.

12. Ibid.

13. M.J.K.M. Brown, F.R.C.S., S. H. Richards, F.R.C.S., and A. G. Ambegaokar, "Grommets and Glue Ear, a Five-Year Follow-Up of a Controlled Trial," *Journal of the Royal Society of Medicine*, Vol. 71 (1978): p. 353.

14. Ralph D. Feigin, M.D., "Otitis Media: Closing the Information Gap" (editorial), *The New England Journal of Medicine*, Vol. 306, No. 23 (June 10, 1982): p. 1418.

15. Bluestone, "Otitis Media in Children: To Treat or Not to Treat," p. 1403.

16. L. H. Hansen et al., "Immunoglobulin Sub-Class Deficiency," *Pediatric Internal Disease Journal*, Supplement 17 (May 1988): p. 7.

17. Erdem I. Cantekin, Ph.D., et al., "Lack of Efficacy of a Decongestant-Antihistamine Combination for Otitis Media with Effusion ('Secretory' Otitis Media) in Children," *The New England Journal of Medicine*, Vol. 308, No. 6 (Feb. 10, 1983): p. 297.

18. Ellen R. Wald, M.D., "Antihistamines and Decongestants in Otitis Media," *Pediatric Infectious Disease*, Vol. 3, No. 4 (July 1984): p. 388.

19. Erdem I. Cantekin, Ph.D., et al., "Effect of Decongestant With or Without Antihistamine on Eustachian Tube Function," *Annals of Otology, Rhinology, and Laryngology*, Supplement 68, Vol. 89, No. 3 (May–June 1980): p. 294.

20. Laxdal et al., p. 264.

Chapter 14

Immunizations and Infectious Diseases

Ask any doctor why infectious diseases such as whooping cough, polio, and diphtheria are so much less common now than they were in the 1800s, and he will almost inevitably tell you that immunizations are responsible for their decline. The medical profession has been presenting this view for so long that nearly everyone believes it, including most doctors. A close look at the history of different infectious diseases and vaccines makes it abundantly clear that this isn't true. One of my goals in this chapter is to show you some of that history and perhaps change your perspective on vaccines. This background will undoubtedly raise questions in your mind—as it has in mine—about whether it is wise for every child to receive every vaccine.

The viewpoint that we have successfully eradicated or diminished many of the once deadly infectious diseases through the use of vaccines (as well as other medical ad-vances) seems at first glance to be easily supported. Life expectancy and general health have improved dramatically in the Western world since the early 1800s. Prior to this time only three of ten children lived to the age of twenty-five. Two out of the ten did not reach their first birthday, and five died before the age of six. By contrast, in developed countries today, fewer than one child in twenty dies before reaching adulthood.[1] The reason for this decline in the death rate is that fewer children die of infectious diseases.

It is easy to assume that more and better medical care account for this increased life expectancy. In reality, however, the decrease in the death rate was mostly due to other factors. In fact, approximately ninety percent of the decline took place *before* the advent of significant medical advances. Up until the early 1900s, most of the decline was probably attributable to better nutrition.

"Better" nutrition means simply that

there was more food, so that fewer people were undernourished. Prior to this time, the quality of the food itself was undoubtedly good, but many people simply did not consume enough calories. With the increase in food supply, people became relatively well-fed and so were better equipped to resist infectious diseases. We can see this effect even today in developing countries, where malnourished people contract more infections than those who are adequately fed, and suffer more complications when ill. As has been noted by the World Health Organization, the best vaccine against common infections is an adequate diet.[2]

Around the early 1900s, improvements in sanitary conditions, such as the purification of drinking water, better sewage disposal, and the pasteurization of milk, as well as further nutritional gains, were probably responsible for the continued drop in the death rate. It was not until the 1930s that medical science had much to offer in the way of treatment for most infectious diseases. Sulfa drugs, which prohibit the reproduction of certain types of bacteria, were discovered around this time, followed shortly thereafter by the first antibiotics in the mid-1940s. Even if we give full credit to these treatments for the decline in the death rate after 1900 (and clearly they weren't responsible, since they were not discovered by 1900), they would still account for only a fraction of the decline in the death rate, most of which took place before 1900.

To better evaluate the contribution of vaccines and other measures to the decline of infectious diseases, let's look at the individual histories of the diseases. There was a substantial decline in the death rate from tuberculosis between 1838 and the mid-1960s, but nearly all of this decline took place prior to 1947, when the first effective treatment for TB came into use (graph 1). It has been estimated that medical advances contributed only about 3.2 percent of the total decline.[3] Deaths from pertussis (whooping cough) declined steadily from the mid-1860s to 1970, with only a small portion of the decline occurring after the vaccine was generally available in the early 1950s (graph 2). Measles has a similar history, although the decline started later (graph 2). From about 1915 on, the death rate from measles fell steadily, and was at a very low level long before the vaccine was even available. Deaths from scarlet fever, for which there has never been a vaccine, also declined substantially decades before any sulfa drugs or antibiotics were available, and the same is true for pneumonia, bronchitis, and influenza (graph 1). Deaths from tetanus, too, dropped substantially before the vaccine came into widespread use, although the decline was not proportionately as great as with other diseases (graph 3). The vaccine, which is highly effective, undoubtedly contributed substantially to the further decline of the disease.

Both the case rate of polio (graph 4) and the death rate from smallpox (graph 5) dropped dramatically after the introduction of the respective vaccines. The polio vaccine was discovered in 1898, first used in 1920, and came into widespread use during World War II. Widespread use of the Salk vaccine (IPV) began in 1955. Around 1962 the Sabin vaccine (OPV) came into wide-

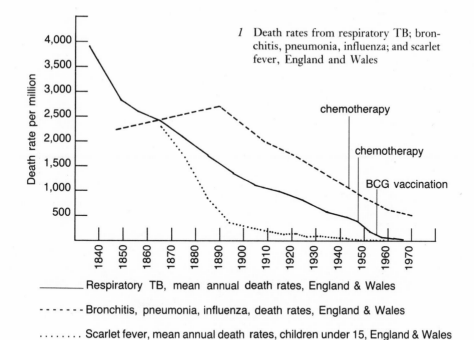

1 Death rates from respiratory TB; bronchitis, pneumonia, influenza; and scarlet fever, England and Wales

_____ Respiratory TB, mean annual death rates, England & Wales

- - - - - - Bronchitis, pneumonia, influenza, death rates, England & Wales

. . . . Scarlet fever, mean annual death rates, children under 15, England & Wales

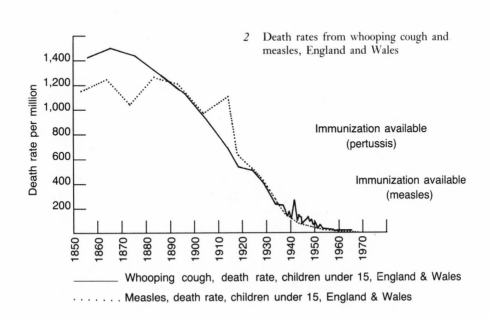

2 Death rates from whooping cough and measles, England and Wales

_____ Whooping cough, death rate, children under 15, England & Wales

. . . . . . Measles, death rate, children under 15, England & Wales

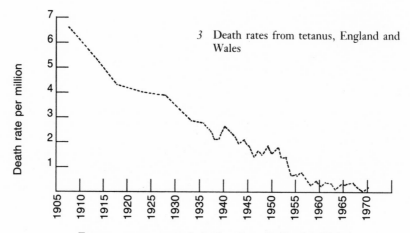

3 Death rates from tetanus, England and Wales

Tetanus, mean annual death rates, England & Wales

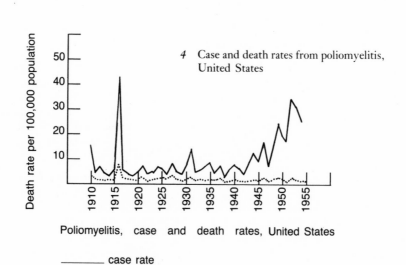

4 Case and death rates from poliomyelitis, United States

Poliomyelitis, case and death rates, United States

——————— case rate

. . . . death rate

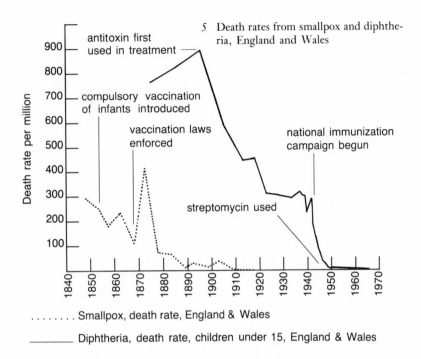

5 Death rates from smallpox and diphtheria, England and Wales

Death rate per million

900 — antitoxin first used in treatment

700 — compulsory vaccination of infants introduced

vaccination laws enforced

national immunization campaign begun

streptomycin used

1840 1850 1860 1870 1880 1890 1900 1910 1920 1930 1940 1950 1960 1970

.... Smallpox, death rate, England & Wales

_____ Diphtheria, death rate, children under 15, England & Wales

spread use. However, smallpox-related deaths in England and Wales steadily declined until 1872, when compulsory vaccination laws began to be rigorously enforced. In spite of a high vaccination rate, there was a major epidemic between 1882 and 1887. Although no one can be certain of the cause, one not unlikely theory is that some deaths were actually due to cases of smallpox contracted from the vaccine. After 1887, parents increasingly took advantage of a conscientious objection clause in the law, and by 1948, fewer than half the children were vaccinated. Nevertheless, the disease continued to decline, probably, again, because of improved nutrition and sanitation, and has since been declared extinct. I do not doubt that smallpox immunization was a significant factor in the total eradication of the disease, but clear-

ly it does not deserve full credit for the disease's decline.

Polio seems to run in rough cycles (graph 4). There was a major epidemic of polio in this country in the 1950s, which ended around the time the vaccine was introduced. Interestingly, though, there was also an epidemic around 1917 that reached a higher level than the one in the fifties, yet the rates for cases and deaths fell spontaneously to their previous low levels even though there was no vaccine at that time.

Treatment and immunization appear to have had more effect on the course of diphtheria (graph 5) than on any other disease, since the death rate was on the rise until around the time that the antitoxin came into use. It fell rapidly then, and went into an even sharper decline after immunization was begun. Once again, though, deaths had already fallen substantially before the vaccine was discovered.

As these histories demonstrate, although medical science has made some positive contributions to our generally improved health, it is essentially a secondary factor in the determination of our health. We live longer than our ancestors did not so much because of measures taken when we are ill, but because we are ill less often. And we are ill less often not because doctors have eradicated disease, but because improved nutrition, sanitation, and general living conditions have made us less susceptible to disease.[4]

I have arrived at my recommendation regarding each of the vaccines after careful consideration of the historical context described above, and after extensive reading of the medical literature on the subject. My conclusions may not be the same as your own, however, and I urge you to study carefully the information provided below regarding the effectiveness of the vaccines, the frequency and severity of side effects, the incidence of the diseases, and their possible complications. I hope you will read other sources, too, and reach your own conclusions, rather than blindly following my recommendations. Remember, there are risks involved no matter what route you decide to take in regard to vaccinating your child. These are important decisions, and ones in which you should be a full participant.

Before we look at the individual vaccines and the diseases they are intended to prevent, let me clarify a few terms:

Vaccines are suspensions of killed or weakened live bacteria or viruses that are used prophylactically, usually before exposure to a disease. Vaccines made from killed organisms or from certain components thereof are given in sufficient quantities to stimulate antibody production. In contrast, weakened live bacteria or viruses are given in smaller quantities but reproduce in the recipient, producing a mild infection that stimulates antibody production. Vaccines may contain a single agent (e.g., polio) or a combination (e.g., diphtheria/pertussis/tetanus).

A *toxoid* is a type of vaccine that consists of a weakened toxin that, when introduced into the body, stimulates antibody production and provides immunity to the disease caused by the toxin. Toxoids are used to prevent or treat diseases in which the symptoms are actually caused by toxins produced by the bacteria that causes the disease (e.g., tetanus and diphtheria).

Antiserums are used both preventively and therapeutically to provide temporary immunity against infectious agents, toxins produced by bacteria, and snake and insect venoms. Antiserums provide protection by the transfer of antibodies produced in another party. This protection may be specific for a particular disease (as with tetanus and diphtheria antiserums) or general in nature (as with gamma globulin). Antiserums are made from either human or horse serum. Those made from horse serum are much more likely to cause serious hypersensitivity reactions. Horse antiserums stay in the blood only for about seven to ten days, while human antiserums last approximately three to four weeks. Human antiserums are usually referred to as *immune globulins. Antitoxins* are types of antiserums that work against specific toxins excreted by an organism (as with tetanus, diphtheria, and botulism bacteria), rather than against the organism itself.

Tetanus

....

THE DISEASE

Tetanus is a disease caused by a bacterium that produces a toxin that attacks the spinal cord nerve cells that control muscle activity, resulting in rigid muscles and painful spasms.

TRANSMISSION. The bacterium that causes tetanus is anaerobic (that is, it cannot grow unless there is a lack of oxygen) and exceptionally resistant. When tetanus bacteria are exposed to oxygen, they ball up into spores that lie dormant until they're exposed to conditions conducive to growth. Because they are extremely hardy, the bacteria are found almost everywhere: in the soil, in people's homes, even in operating rooms. The most common source of tetanus bacteria is animal feces, particularly that of horses. The disease is contracted when tetanus bacteria enter a wound that provides anaerobic conditions, allowing the bacteria to become active.

The Public Health Services Advisory Committee on Immunization Practices of the Centers for Disease Control (CDC) categorizes a wound as very tetanus-prone if it has been exposed to a high level of contamination (examples of highly contaminated sources are barnyards and sewers); if it is over twenty-four hours old at the time of treatment; or if it contains unremovable debris or dead tissue. (For this reason it is important to clean all wounds thoroughly with water only. Antiseptics will not kill tetanus bacteria, and they will result in more dead tissue.) A wound is considered moderately tetanus-prone if it has been exposed to a moderate level of bacterial contamination (from wood, pavement, most industrial areas); if it is a crush injury or puncture wound; or if it extends into muscle. Although wounds from human bites contain a lot of bacteria, they are considered only moderately tetanus-prone because tetanus is not part of the oral flora. All other wounds are considered not tetanus-prone, and most household objects are considered to have a low level of bacterial contamination.[5]

INCIDENCE. There are approximately one hundred cases of tetanus a year in the United States, usually in people who are less than one year old or over sixty. Most tetanus cases are seen in the warmer climates, in people with no immunization or incomplete immunization. Virtually all babies who contract tetanus have been born to mothers who have never been immunized against the disease. (Babies whose mothers have been immunized acquire antibodies from their mothers, which protect them in the newborn period.) Infants who contract tetanus almost invariably become infected through an unhealed, improperly cared-for umbilicus, and are generally from homes where living conditions are unsanitary.

Females contract tetanus more often than males. The disease is twice as common among blacks as whites, perhaps a reflection of lower socioeconomic conditions rather than an inherent susceptibility to the disease.

COURSE OF THE DISEASE. The incubation period for tetanus is generally between two weeks and two months. The more quickly symptoms appear, the more severe the illness will be. The incubation period also depends in part on the location of the wound, because the toxin produced by the tetanus bacteria must travel from that site to the brain. This will take longer if the wound is on the foot, for example, than on the face.

Painful muscle spasms can occur in just about any part of the body once the toxin reaches the brain. Often, the area that is first affected is the jaw or neck muscles, which is why tetanus was originally called "lockjaw." The site of the wound may also be affected first (a wound that is infected with tetanus will not turn red and ooze pus, but will appear to be healing normally). In infants the first symptoms may be difficulty in sucking, irritability, excessive crying, and stiffness. Once the muscle spasms begin, they can be set off by noise, a cold wind, or even a full bladder—virtually any kind of disturbance. Symptoms are most severe in the first two weeks, and taper off during the next three to four weeks, if the patient survives.

DIAGNOSIS. Tetanus is usually diagnosed by looking at the history and following the course of the disease, although there are some sophisticated methods of diagnosing it biochemically.

TREATMENT. There is no treatment available that has any effect on the toxin once symptoms have begun. However, if a person is unvaccinated, antitoxin is usually given at the time of a tetanus-prone injury to provide temporary immunity and neutralize any toxin that may be free-floating in the system. (Once the toxin is in a fixed site, it is not affected by antitoxin.) There are two types of tetanus antitoxins, one made from horse serum (usually referred to as tetanus antitoxin) and one made from human serum (tetanus immune globulin). Because the immunity provided by tetanus antitoxin is of much shorter duration, and because the antitoxin is much more likely to cause a hypersensitivity reaction ("serum sickness"), it should only be used if tetanus immune globulin is not available or if the patient has a known allergy to immune globulin. Tetanus immune globulin does have possible side effects, too, however, although they are relatively minor. The American Academy of Pediatrics does not recommend the use of tetanus immune globulin for postexposure prophylaxis in patients with clean minor wounds, regardless of their immunization status, or in patients with tetanus-prone wounds who have previously received three or more doses of tetanus toxoid.

In addition to administering tetanus immune globulin or antitoxin, supportive care, including muscle relaxants, oxygen, and a tracheotomy (if necessary to assist breathing) may also be undertaken. The disease will eventually subside on its own and the survivors generally do not suffer long-term consequences. The survival rate is about seventy percent, although it is only twenty percent for infants. Tetanus infection does not provide future immunity to the disease.

COMPLICATIONS. There are no complications from tetanus, if the disease is survived.

THE VACCINE

There are two types of tetanus toxoid vaccine: the tetanus toxoid fluid and the tetanus toxoid adsorbed. The tetanus toxoid adsorbed contains an aluminum compound that is thought to make it more effective.

EFFECTIVENESS. There is no doubt that tetanus toxoid is an effective vaccine. During World War II, when most of those serving in the armed forces were vaccinated, there were only 12 cases of tetanus in a series of 2,734,819 hospital admissions for wounds and injuries.[6] The vaccine is considered to be approximately ninety-five to ninety-six percent effective.

REACTIONS, SIDE EFFECTS, COMPLICATIONS. Serious reactions to both tetanus toxoid vaccines are considered relatively rare, but mild reactions appear to be fairly common. It is difficult to assess just how often reactions do occur. Most estimates in the medical literature on the subject are approximately one to two percent, with a higher percentage of local reactions than systemic ones, although some studies have found much higher rates. One likely reason for the discrepancy is that side effects are vastly underreported, both by patients and physicians. In fact, a survey done in Alaska found that only 0.5 percent of the people who experienced a reaction—less than a third of the total of serious reactions—bothered to see a doctor about it.[7]

There is a great range in the possible side effects of the tetanus toxoid vaccines. Those seen most frequently are a sore arm, swelling at the site of the injection, and itching. Other possible reactions include blisters at the site, fever, irritability, unusual tiredness, swollen glands in the armpit, headaches, seizures, vomiting, difficulty in breathing, and swelling around the face.

Complications involving the nervous system occur very infrequently, on the order of 0.4 cases per one million doses of the vaccine.[8] There have been a handful of reports of temporary paralysis of one or more extremities.[9,10,11,12] In nearly all of these cases the patients eventually recovered completely. There are no reports of deaths due to the tetanus toxoid.

The one factor that is repeatedly correlated with reactions to the tetanus toxoid is receiving too many doses of the vaccine, although some do occur in people receiving their first dose.[13]

RECOMMENDATIONS. Considering the high level of effectiveness, low level of reactions, and relatively strong potential for exposure to tetanus bacteria, I recommend you do have your children receive tetanus toxoid. It is usually given at two, four, and six months of age, with a booster at eighteen months and five years, and then every ten years thereafter. However, studies have found repeatedly that antibody levels remain at levels high enough to afford protection for very long periods of time even without booster shots; several have noted that World War II veterans still had protective levels up to twenty-one years after vaccination.[14] A study done in Denmark concluded that primary vaccination in infancy and a booster shot five years later will secure continuous protection until about the age of twenty-five, and that more frequent boosters increase the risk of hyperimmunization[15] (and hence, reactions).

For this reason, I recommend having the initial course and the five-year booster, and then a booster at the age of twenty-five. If your child sustains a tetanus-prone injury after the age of fifteen (so that it has been more than ten years since his last booster), you may want to have an additional booster at that time, just to be safe. If your child has a reaction to one of the initial shots, it has been found that you can successfully continue immunization by lowering the dose.[16]

If you are an expectant mother and have never been immunized against tetanus yourself, it is safe to be vaccinated during pregnancy to confer passive immunization to your newborn. Note, too, that proper care of the umbilicus can greatly reduce the chances of your baby's contracting tetanus.[17]

Whether you have your child immunized against tetanus or not, there is a significant risk that he will receive improper care if treated for a tetanus-prone injury in a hospital emergency room. Twenty-three percent of patients treated with open soft-tissue injuries in six different emergency rooms received improper care with tetanus toxoid or tetanus immune globulin. More patients were overtreated than undertreated, probably because doctors realize that the potential outcome of this mistake (a reaction to the vaccine) is less serious than the potential outcome of undervaccination (the patient's contracting tetanus).[18] Though this position is certainly defensible, your child shouldn't have to be subjected to either risk. If you keep accurate records of his immunization history, you can determine for yourself whether or not your child is adequately protected against tetanus. I think it is also wise to educate the child as to his history, so that he will be able to convey the proper information if you aren't available. This won't necessarily protect him from an unnecessary booster from an overzealous doctor, but it will ensure that the physician is at least working with the facts. This may be particularly important if you choose not to have your child immunized against tetanus. Treatment errors have been found to be most likely in those who had wounds that were moderately or very tetanus-prone and who were not protected by active immunization—in other words, those who were at greatest risk of contracting tetanus.[19]

CONTRAINDICATIONS. Tetanus toxoid is contraindicated during a polio outbreak and in children with febrile illnesses, those with acute respiratory disease, and patients who already have tetanus.

Pertussis (Whooping Cough)

....

THE DISEASE

Pertussis is an extremely contagious, long-lasting disease that strikes children more frequently than adults. It is characterized by paroxysmal spasms of severe coughing that are frequently followed by vomiting. Because a coughing spell often ends with a characteristic "whoop," pertussis is commonly known as "whooping cough." In early America, it was also often called "the hundred-day fever," a reference to the persistence of the low-grade fever that comes and goes throughout the course of the disease, usually lasting for approximately one hundred days.

TRANSMISSION.   Pertussis is caused by bacteria that are transmitted through respiratory droplet (i.e., being coughed on or sneezed on by someone who has the disease). The person transmitting the disease will almost always have a cough and other symptoms, although their condition may be relatively mild, and so may not be recognized as pertussis. Asymptomatic carriers are rare.[20]

INCIDENCE.   More than half of all pertussis cases occur in babies under one year of age, and more than three-quarters in children under the age of five. Only about five per-cent occur in persons older than fifteen. Pertussis is more common in the summer and early fall and strikes females more often than males. The disease is cyclic in nature, with attack rates rising and falling at approximately three- to four-year intervals.[21]

COURSE OF THE DISEASE.   Once transmitted, the bacteria attach themselves to cells of the trachea and bronchi, causing inflammation and rotting. The incubation period is six to twenty-one days, after which the disease progresses through three stages. The first of these is the catarrhal stage, which lasts for one to two weeks, and is symptomatically indistinguishable from a cold.

The paroxysmal stage, which lasts approximately two to four weeks, is characterized by coughing fits that increase in severity and number. Typically, the child will cough forcefully five to ten times with just one exhalation, and then, in a sudden massive effort to bring air into the lungs, will produce a "whoop." While coughing, the child's face will turn blue, the eyes will bulge, and she may drool. It is very common for children with pertussis to cough so hard they vomit. Between coughing spells, the child will be exhausted and lethargic, but will otherwise seem well. Coughing may be triggered by attempts to eat or drink, yawning, sneezing, or physical exertion.

During the convalescent stage, which lasts for one to two weeks, there is a decrease in the number and severity of the coughing spells. However, they may continue to occur infrequently for several months, possibly after exertion or sudden exposure to cold air or some other trigger, or when the child has another, unrelated upper respiratory infection.

DIAGNOSIS. When pertussis is in the paroxysmal stage and the characteristic whoop is present, diagnosis is straightforward, especially if there has been a known exposure. The whoop may be absent in as many as fifty percent of the infants who contract the disease[22] and for many cases there has been no known exposure. When this is the case, the disease can be much harder to identify. During the catarrhal stage it is possible to culture and identify the bacteria, but pertussis is rarely suspected at this point. As the patient enters and progresses through the paroxysmal stage, a culture is increasingly difficult to obtain. Further complicating the diagnosis is the fact that the pertussis bacteria will not show up on a routine culture, but only when a certain type of culture plate is used. If it never occurs to the doctor to look for pertussis, it is highly unlikely that the correct diagnosis will be made. Because pertussis is relatively rare today, and because both parents and doctors erroneously assume that it cannot occur in a child who has been immunized, the disease may not be looked for. When errors are made, the disease is most likely to be mistaken for bronchiolitis or pneumonia.

TREATMENT. Treatment for pertussis is largely supportive. Antibiotics do not affect the course of the disease once it is in the paroxysmal stage, although they may lessen the duration and severity of the cough if given during the catarrhal stage. The drug of choice is erythromycin, and the current recommendation is that it be taken for two full weeks, although studies have shown that the organism is eliminated within three to four days, [23,24] so there is probably no point in giving the drug for longer than four days. Antibiotic therapy is also often recommended to prevent secondary infections such as bacterial pneumonia. There is a pertussis immune globulin, but it is not effective and should not be used.

In recent years, hospitalization has been necessary for approximately half of all reported cases, and seventy-seven percent of those occurring in babies under six months.[25] Supportive care may include administering oxygen, preventing dehydration and malnutrition, and, in some cases, suctioning out the trachea to help reduce the accumulation of fluid. Because this last treatment may trigger a coughing spell, it must be used with discretion. Cough medicines are sometimes used, but they may do more harm than good by making it more difficult for the child to cough up mucus.

COMPLICATIONS. The most common complication of pertussis is pneumonia, although this seems to occur most frequently in children whose nutritional status is poor before they become ill. Malnutrition and dehydration are also common, particularly in those under a year old. Because attempting to swallow can provoke a coughing attack, and because the attacks are often followed by vomiting, an infant can lose a significant amount of weight in a short period of time. This is not as great a problem in older children, who are generally better able to tolerate the weight loss. Another common complication that primarily affects infants is middle ear infection. Pertussis does not result in permanent lung damage (although it did at one time); however, children who have had pertussis tend to be more susceptible than others to upper respiratory infections, although this susceptibility actually may precede the pertussis infection.[26]

Complications involving the central nervous system are by far the most serious that result from pertussis. It is difficult to calculate how often these occur, and estimates in the literature vary greatly. Of the cases reported in this country from 1982 to 1983, 0.3 percent resulted in encephalopathy (brain disease) and 1.9 percent in seizures, with slightly higher rates for babies under the age of one year.[27] These figures are for reported cases only, however, and as such are undoubtedly inflated. Many cases of pertussis go unreported and even unrecognized,[28] and it is reasonable to assume that those that are reported are the most severe. Of the children who do develop encephalopathy, one-third will die, one-third will survive with permanent damage, and one-third will survive with no long-lasting effects.[29] The disease does seem to convey immunity from future infections, although recurrences have been noted.

The overall death rate from pertussis in this country is approximately 0.5 percent of all reported cases, and 1 percent for babies under one year of age.[30]

THE VACCINE

The pertussis vaccine is given in combination with tetanus and diphtheria vaccines. The pertussis component of the vaccine is made from the whole, killed organism, which is added to the tetanus and diphtheria components.

Even within the medical community, the pertussis vaccine is considered crude, and there is a lot of controversy over whether or not its benefits outweigh its risks. Because the vaccine uses the whole cell of the bacterium, it causes more side effects than other vaccines, and is thought to be responsible for the vast majority of reactions to the DPT immunization. Several countries, including Japan and Sweden, no longer use the whole-cell vaccine, and in others, such as England and Wales, acceptance rates have dropped dramatically. Though acceptance rates in this country remain relatively high, there has been a tremendous increase in the number of lawsuits brought against pharmaceutical companies by parents of children who allegedly have been harmed by the vaccine, some resulting in large settlements. To spare pharmaceutical companies million-dollar lawsuits and ensure future production of the vaccine, the Vaccine Compensation Act was passed in 1986. It provides for monetary awards to the parents of children who have died or suffered neurologic damage due to a vaccine. The act is also designed to keep these cases out of court, thereby reducing negative publicity and encouraging high acceptance rates.

EFFECTIVENESS. Part of the difficulty in assessing the pertussis vaccine's worth lies in reaching a reasonable estimate of its efficacy. Various estimates in the medical literature rate the vaccine from zero to ninety percent effective, with medical textbooks citing figures between seventy and ninety percent. In 1987 a review of several vaccine efficacy studies was done, with particular attention given to methodological flaws that might influence the rates.[31] The authors noted several reasons efficacy rates may be erroneously high. They also pointed out so many biases that affect efficacy estimates that it appears we may never really pin down one unequivocally correct rate.

Clearly, though, the vaccine is at least somewhat effective, as has been demonstrated in those countries where, for one reason or another, the acceptance levels went from very high to very low. In Japan in the early 1970s, the acceptance rate was very high, and they had an average of only three pertussis deaths per year between 1971 and 1975. In 1975, following two vaccine-related deaths, acceptance rates fell dramatically.[32] The incidence of pertussis increased, reaching a peak in 1979, when forty-one deaths were attributed to the disease.[33] A similar series of events occurred in England and Wales.

However, there is also substantial evidence of vaccine failures. There was a marked increase in the number of cases of pertussis in Maryland in 1982, in spite of a vaccine acceptance rate of ninety-six percent.[34] In one study of a 1962 outbreak in Michigan, fifty percent of the people in whose family pertussis was confirmed had been vaccinated with three or more doses, and forty-six percent of those contracted the disease.[35] One study done in England showed that during the pertussis epidemic in the late seventies, thirty-five to forty-six percent of the reported cases were in children who had received three or more doses of pertussis vaccine.[36]

There are other points concerning the vaccine's effectiveness that should be taken into account. The period of protection it offers seems to be relatively short. A ten-year study found that the efficacy of the vaccine dropped to less than fifty percent within seven years after immunization.[37] It should also be noted that the vaccine does not seem to have had as great an effect on the number of deaths due to pertussis as it has had on the number of cases of the disease. At the peak of the Japanese epidemic, the death rate was at approximately the same level as in 1963—not the prevaccine era, but thirteen years after routine immunization began.[38] In Sweden, there were no deaths from pertussis at the peak of an epidemic that occurred between 1971 and 1980.[39] This seems to indicate that the severity of the disease has declined, an idea that is supported by an English study of children hospitalized for the disease.[40]

REACTIONS, SIDE EFFECTS, COMPLICATIONS. The problem of determining the vaccine's effectiveness is perhaps surpassed only by the difficulty in ascertaining the extent and frequency of its side effects. One study that looked at reactions to 15,752 DPT injections found (in decreasing order of frequency) the following minor side effects: pain at the injection site and fretfulness; local swelling and redness; fever; drowsiness; weight loss; vomiting; and persistent crying.[41] While these are disturbing, the major adverse effects are downright frightening. The following have all been temporally associated with the DPT vaccine: unusual high-pitched cry, convulsions, hypotonic/hyporesponsive state (collapse and shock), encephalitis, encephalopathy, infantile spasms, Reye's syndrome, Guillain-Barré syndrome (temporary inflammation of some nerves, resulting in pain and paralysis), inflammation of the spinal cord, loss of coordination due to a disturbance of the cerebellum, sudden infant death syndrome (SIDS), anaphylaxis, thrombocytopenia (abnormally low blood platelet count, resulting in bleeding and easy bruising), and hemolytic anemia (premature destruction of red blood cells).

How often do these side effects occur? No one knows for certain, although there have been several different studies of the issue. One of the difficulties in estimating the rates of serious side effects is that some of these events—SIDS, seizures, and some neurological problems—have their peak incidence or onset during the same time frame in which the pertussis vaccine is given. SIDS primarily occurs in babies under the age of one year, and some insults to the central nervous system, such as those manifested in cerebral palsy and infantile spasms, are generally not apparent until sometime between the age of two months and one year. Damage to a specific area of the brain, even if it has occurred at birth or before, may not become apparent until the child has matured to the point at which that area is called upon to function. It is not surprising, then, that a certain percentage of these events should occur within hours, days, or weeks of the primary series of pertussis immunizations, which is usually given at two, four, and six months. In fact, although many experts believe there is a

specific neurological risk to the vaccine, some have concluded that many of the cases of damage or death attributed to the vaccine are events that would have occurred regardless of immunization. At least one study has also concluded that certain neurological illnesses are not usually caused by pertussis immunization, but may occur earlier than they might have without immunization.[42]

There have been many reports of deaths following pertussis immunizations. In some cases the deaths appear to have had a probable cause other than the vaccine, and as such have been considered only coincidentally linked to pertussis immunization. Sometimes, however, no other cause can be found, and occasionally deaths have been attributed to anaphylactic shock due to the vaccine. There is also controversy over whether or not the pertussis vaccine may precipitate SIDS. In a 1979 cluster of four SIDS deaths in Tennessee, a weak statistical connection was found with one lot of the vaccine.[43] A recent investigation into twenty-nine SIDS deaths in Washington over the course of twelve years found that four had taken place within three days of immunization, suggesting a causal link with the vaccine.[44] Other studies, including a large case-control study done in this country, have not found a link between the vaccine and SIDS.[45] It is my opinion that the pertussis vaccine may be a factor in some SIDS cases, but SIDS also occurs in babies who have not been vaccinated.

Estimates on the occurrence of neurologic complications, including permanent brain damage, cover a wide range of figures. In the late seventies, a study in Great Britain found that the DPT-immunized child is two to five times more likely to have neurologic disease than the nonimmunized child.[46] The same study reported an overall incidence of serious neurological disorders in 1 in 110,000 immunizations (approximately 1 in 27,500 children immunized). One English author has suggested that the rate of encephalopathy (with or without permanent brain damage) might be as high as 1 in every 750 children.[47] Most estimates of permanent neurological complications range from 1 child in every 53,000 vaccinated[48] to 1 incidence in every 310,000 doses of the vaccine given[49] (approximately 1 child in every 77,500 vaccinated.) Since 1978, the CDC has monitored adverse reactions to the DPT and other vaccines. Between 1978 and 1981, severe neurologic reactions (though not necessarily permanent damage) were reported in 1 in every 230,000 doses of DPT administered[50] (approximately 1 in 57,500 children). One extensive review found that of children with neurological complications from DPT, approximately fifteen percent died, approximately thirty percent were left with permanent damage (seizures, retardation, weakness, or paralysis), and fifty percent recovered. (The outcome was unclear in the remaining patients).[51]

Of the more serious reactions, seizure appears to be the most common. Estimates of frequency range from 1 in 2,200 immunized children to 1 in 800,000 immunizations[52] (1 in 20,000 children). One of the more disturbing studies was done at the UCLA Emergency Medical Center in the late seventies. For 15,752 DPT immunizations given to children less than a year old to six years old, 9 children developed convulsions within forty-eight hours, for a rate of 1 seizure for every 1,750 immunizations.[53] Unfortunately, the report does not state how many children were involved, although it notes that seventy-five percent received more than one shot. If you assume that twenty-five percent received one dose and that the remaining seventy-five percent received an average of three doses, this works out to 1 seizure in every 875 children immunized.

The same study also reported that 9 children had hypotonic/hyporesponsive episodes. This side effect has also been well documented, although its significance is not fully understood. A hypotonic/hyporesponsive episode usually occurs within twelve hours after immunization, with the child becoming pale, limp, and unresponsive. The breathing becomes shallow, and the child may have signs of cyanosis. The episode may last only a few minutes or may persist for up to a day or more. If you include the 9 children who had hypotonic/hyporesponsive reactions in the UCLA study in calculating the number of children who had neurological problems, the frequency increases to 1 in every 437 children.

An additional seventeen children in this study were reported to have had an unusual, high-pitched cry within forty-eight hours after immunization. This type of reaction usually begins within eight hours after immunization, with the child becoming inconsolable for an hour or longer, and possibly having intermittent crying bouts throughout a twenty-four-hour period. Parents typically describe this reaction as a pain cry of an intensity and pitch they have never heard from their child before. Though the significance of this reaction is not known, some physicians feel that it is related to central nervous system damage.[54] If you assume that they are correct, the incidence of neurological problems in this particular study increases to 1 in every 218 children.

This is a far cry from most of the statistics in the literature on the risks of pertussis immunization, even though this study only looked at reactions that occurred within the first forty-eight hours following vaccination. Other researchers have found evidence of reactions occurring much later on, so that there may have been even more problems that weren't considered.

Surprisingly, the authors of this study concluded that the risk of pertussis immunization was still less than the risk from the disease itself. To understand how they reached this conclusion, let's look at the assumptions on which their calculations are based. Because eight of the children who had convulsions were subsequently examined by a pediatric neurologist who found each of them to be normal, the seizures and hypotonic/hyporesponsive events were not considered serious neurological problems, but transient occurrences.[55] However, considering that the median age of the children was eighteen months, it would hardly have been possible to make a reliable determination of normal neurologic function at that point in their development. Perhaps permanent damage occurs during some of these reactions but is not detectable

until much later in the child's life, at which point no one thinks to relate it to a vaccine given in infancy. I think it is interesting to note that the vaccine is not given to anyone over the age of seven, because of the high rate of reactions and neurological damage associated with it. It may be that the vaccine is no less dangerous for younger children but that we fail to recognize much of the damage it does. For example, some of the learning disabilities we see in children of school age may actually be signs of neurological damage suffered during a vaccine reaction.

Because the neurologic events seen in this study were not considered serious problems, the figures the authors used to calculate the damage from the vaccine in their risk/benefit analysis came from a Swedish study that estimated that 1 in every 170,000 children would suffer from encephalopathy, and that 1 in 510,000 children would suffer permanent brain damage.[56] Compared with figures from other studies, these seem extremely optimistic. If you take a broader view of what may constitute neurological damage and use the results of the UCLA study, an entirely different picture emerges.

The majority of DPT reactions occur with the first or second dose; however, reactions can occur with any dose.[57] If your child does have a reaction, your doctor may suggest a half-dose for subsequent immunizations on the assumption that it will convey some immunity while reducing the chance of another adverse reaction. Alternatively, some doctors also recommend giving the full amount of the DPT vaccine, but broken down into several small doses. Neither of these practices has been shown to reduce the number of serious reactions to the disease, and both may decrease the amount of protection conveyed.[58]

Another practice that some doctors advocate is giving the child acetaminophen (Tylenol) immediately prior to or after the vaccine to prevent some of the minor reactions such as local tenderness and irritability, and possibly seizures that are fever-related. Others, myself included, feel that this practice may mask reactions such as a high fever (and possibly a convulsion precipitated by the fever) that would normally lead to withholding future doses of the vaccine. In addition, routine use of acetominophen might mask fever due to a bacterial infection, possibly leading to a delay in appropriate treatment.

RECOMMENDATIONS. I am opposed to the use of the pertussis vaccine now on the market. Unquestionably, pertussis is a terrible disease for anyone to endure; however, the severity of the disease has declined, so that the incidence of mortality is no longer very significant. If and when the vaccine is scrutinized as carefully as it should be—with mandatory reporting of all reactions over a period of time longer than the usual twenty-four to forty-eight hours—I believe the vaccine will be found to cause more death and permanent damage than the disease itself.

CONTRAINDICATIONS. If you do decide to have your child vaccinated against pertussis, you should be aware that there are several contraindications to the vaccine that

are recognized by the Department of Health and Human Services and the American Academy of Pediatrics. It should not be given to a child who has had any of the following reactions to a previous dose: allergic hypersensitivity, fever of 105°F or higher within forty-eight hours post-immunization, hypotonic/hyporesponsive episode within forty-eight hours post-immunization, persistent or inconsolable crying lasting three hours or more or an unusual high-pitched cry occurring within forty-eight hours postimmunization, convulsions with or without fever occurring within three days postimmunization, and encephalopathy occurring within seven days postimmunization. These contraindications are based on the presumption that children who experienced such reactions are more likely to have similar reactions of equal or greater magnitude upon subsequent immunization. This concept appears to be sound: In one review of 108 cases of vaccine-related encephalopathy, 7 children were found to have been reimmunized. Of these, 2 died, 4 were left with permanent neurological damage, and only 1 recovered.[59]

It is important to realize that these recommendations are a policy statement, not a pronouncement of scientific fact. If your child screams uncontrollably for two and a half hours, there is no guarantee that he will be less likely to have a severe reaction to the next pertussis vaccine than the child who screams for three hours. Encephalopathy occurring on the eighth day postimmunization or a convulsion that occurs on the fourth day postimmunization cannot immediately be assumed to have a cause other than the vaccine. There are no magic numbers that allow us to predict precisely who will have a severe reaction and who will not. For this reason, *if* you decide to have your child immunized against pertussis and *if* she has a reaction that is a little less severe than those listed above, don't assume reimmunization is safe because your doctor says it is.

In addition to the above contraindications, the Department of Health and Human Services and the American Academy of Pediatrics also both recommend delaying vaccination against pertussis in an infant or child who has a personal history of seizures until the possibility of an evolving neurological disorder can be ruled out. A CDC study found that children who had a postimmunization seizure with DPT were 7.2 times more likely to have had a prior seizure unassociated with immunizations than were children who had severe nonneurologic reactions.[60] This same study also found that children with a family history of seizures were several times more likely to have a postimmunization seizure. Because five to seven percent of the child population has a family history of convulsions, the authors felt that withholding the vaccine from these children would significantly lower the currently high immunization levels and might lead to an increase in pertussis. If your child is one of those who has a family history of seizures, I think you would be wise not to study this question from the point of view of whether or not immunization is the best thing for the country as a whole; instead, I suggest you look at which course seems wisest for your individual child.

Diphtheria

THE DISEASE

Diphtheria is an acute, potentially life-threatening bacterial disease. A diphtheria infection most commonly occurs on the skin or in the respiratory tract, although it may also rarely be seen in the mucous membranes of the genitals or the eyes. As the bacteria grow, they produce a potent toxin. When the infection is located on the skin, the toxin does not invade the body, and complications are quite rare. When the infection is located in the respiratory tract, however, the toxin is carried throughout the body by the bloodstream, and may damage any of the organs or tissues.

TRANSMISSION. Diphtheria is transmitted by respiratory droplet or through dust or objects with which an infected person has come in contact. Humans are the only host.

INCIDENCE. The incidence of respiratory diphtheria is only about four cases per year,[61] most of which occur in unimmunized children from poor families with limited health care.

COURSE OF THE DISEASE. Diphtheria has an incubation period of one to six days. Infections of the respiratory tract are usually located in the throat, and symptoms may include fever, a rapid pulse, hoarseness, a cough, and a sore throat. The distinguishing characteristic is a membrane that forms at the site of the infection. Initially, it is thin and whitish in color, resembling the exudate often seen with a strep infection, and is easily removed. As the disease progresses, the membrane grows thicker and more deeply rooted, varying in color from gray to black, and cannot be removed without causing substantial bleeding. Depending on the location of the membrane, or if a section of it pulls loose, it may obstruct the airway, hampering breathing or causing suffocation.

Less commonly, the infection may also occur in the nasal passages. Most often seen in infants, nasal diphtheria is generally milder than that which occurs in the throat. It resembles a common cold, but with a membrane forming on the septum of the nose.

DIAGNOSIS. Diagnosis is usually made through clinical findings, particularly observation of the characteristic membrane. The bacteria can be isolated and cultured, but, like pertussis, require a specific culture medium in order to grow.

TREATMENT. Treatment for diphtheria consists of administration of an antitoxin to neutralize any toxin that is not in a fixed site. (Unlike the tetanus antitoxin, diphtheria antitoxin can be used in both immunized and unimmunized victims of the disease.) Because the antitoxin does not affect toxin that has become attached to cells, the earlier in the course of the disease the antitoxin is used, the better the prognosis. The antitoxin, which is made from horse serum, does carry a risk of anaphylactic reaction or serum sickness. Antibiotics are not very effective at the infection site, but may help to limit the spread of the disease and prevent secondary infections. Supportive treatment may include bed rest, even for mild cases (because of a danger of cardiac complications), suctioning of secretions, and tracheostomy, if necessary, to relieve respiratory obstruction.

COMPLICATIONS. The major complications that result from diphtheria infection are caused by absorption of the toxin. While any tissue or organ may be affected, the heart, kidneys, and peripheral nerves appear to be most susceptible. Inflammation of the heart, sometimes leading to heart failure, is the most serious complication, and can result from either a mild or a severe infection. Clinically significant cardiac abnormalities are present in approximately twenty percent of diphtheria patients,[62] with a smaller percentage experiencing serious impairment that may lead to cardiac failure.

The death rate from diphtheria is approximately five to ten percent. Mortality is generally highest among the unimmunized, particularly the very young.

THE VACCINE

The diphtheria vaccine is a toxoid that is usually given in combination with the tetanus and pertussis vaccines.

EFFECTIVENESS. There is no doubt that the vaccine is obviously at least partially effective. However, studies done in this country have found that thirty to fifty-five percent of those tested were not immune, and a study done in Sweden, where acceptance rates are also high, found that nineteen percent of the children were not immune.[63] One explanation for these findings is that childhood vaccination does not incur lifelong immunity, so that in some recipients the effects of the vaccine have simply worn off over time. Lack of immunity in children, on the other hand, clearly indicates failure of the vaccine. One reason for these failures may be that the vaccine does not provide protection against all strains of the bacteria.[64]

REACTIONS, SIDE EFFECTS, COMPLICATIONS. Because the diphtheria vaccine is nearly always given in combination with the pertussis and/or tetanus vaccines, it is particularly difficult to assess the severity and frequency of reactions to it. Reactions to the combined vaccines are almost always attributed to the pertussis or tetanus components, although there is rarely proof that the diphtheria component is not responsible. There have been few studies, if any, that looked at reactions to the diphtheria vaccine alone, although there are various case histories in the medical literature. These are mainly of reactions that are neurologic in nature, similar to those caused by the pertussis vaccine. One source estimates that permanent neurological damage due to the combined tetanus/diphtheria vaccine and the diphtheria vaccine alone occur at the rate of 1 case per 771,000 vaccinees.[65] From the available medical literature, it seems reasonable to conclude that reactions to the diphtheria vaccine do occur, but are much less common than reactions to the tetanus or pertussis vaccines.

RECOMMENDATIONS. Although the diphtheria vaccine does not seem to be as unqualified a failure as the pertussis vaccine, I also do not recommend its use. Considering the rarity of the disease, I believe that the vaccine has outlived its usefulness. This is an example—like the smallpox vaccine, which was administered for years after smallpox was eradicated—of medicine continuing a course of action out of habit rather than need. Once again, I feel that a true accounting of reactions to the vaccine would result in the discovery that it is more harmful than the disease it prevents.

If you decide to use the diphtheria vaccine anyway, three doses (usually given at two, four, and six months of age) are necessary to ensure immunization, but the series need not be restarted in the event of an interruption in the schedule, no matter how much time passes between doses. Boosters are recommended at eighteen months and five years of age and then every ten years thereafter. Make certain that your child does not receive booster shots more frequently, since the diphtheria vaccine also seems more likely to cause reactions when too many doses are given.[66] Be particularly cautious if your child receives emergency treatment for a tetanus-prone wound, since he may receive Td (tetanus/diphtheria toxoid) rather than the plain tetanus toxoid. Even if you agree that a tetanus booster is in order, you should object to the unnecessary use of the combined vaccine.

CONTRAINDICATIONS. The diphtheria vaccine should not be given to a child who has experienced neurological symptoms or signs following administration, and should be deferred during a febrile illness or acute infection. Routine immunization should also be deferred during a polio outbreak.

Polio

THE DISEASE

Polio is a viral disease that ranges in severity from asymptomatic infection to paralysis and death.

TRANSMISSION. There are three types of poliovirus, all of which reproduce in the intestines and are spread by respiratory droplet and fecal content.

INCIDENCE. There are approximately eight reported cases of polio per year in this country, virtually all of which can be attributed to the oral polio vaccine (see page 259). In general, polio infections are more common in the warmer months and in temperate climates. In developed countries, all age-groups are affected, with the highest rate of paralytic disease occurring in young adults.

COURSE OF THE DISEASE. Approximately ninety to ninety-five percent of those who contract the virus remain completely symptom-free. Another four to eight percent have abortive polio, which results in mild symptoms such as a low-grade fever, malaise, sore throat, muscle aches, and, occasionally, abdominal pain and vomiting, followed by complete recovery. One to two percent come down with nonparalytic polio, which is clinically indistinguishable from nonbacterial meningitis. Patients with nonparalytic polio nearly always recover fully. Finally, one to two percent of those who contract the virus come down with paralytic polio.

Paralytic polio begins with the same sort of vague symptoms as abortive polio. However, two to five days into what appears to be the recovery period, the patient's temperature will shoot up and the previous symptoms will return along with a severe headache and muscle pains. Within one to two days partial or complete paralysis of some muscles occurs. This paralysis usually affects the legs and lower back, although any area of the body, including the centers that control breathing and heart function, may be involved. If the paralysis affects respiration or the heart, sudden death may occur. The extent of the paralysis is usually evident within one to two days. Over the next several months, slow recovery from the paralysis may take place, and in some cases will be complete. If there is no evidence of recovery within the first six months, the paralysis is probably permanent.

The incubation period for the virus is usually seven to twelve days, although it may be as long as three weeks. Those infected become contagious several days before symptoms develop.

DIAGNOSIS. Paralytic polio is usually diagnosed through clinical means but must be confirmed by isolation of the virus, since other viruses may also rarely produce poliolike symptoms.

TREATMENT. There is no effective antiviral treatment for polio. The management of paralytic polio depends largely on the extent of the paralysis. At the very least, bed rest is strictly required, and analgesics may be prescribed to alleviate the pain. In severe cases, respiratory and cardiovascular support may be undertaken in an attempt to prevent death.

THE VACCINE

There are two types of polio vaccine: the live, attenuated oral vaccine (OPV) and the inactivated, or killed vaccine (IPV) that is given by injection. Although IPV was the first polio vaccine developed and used in this country, it was essentially replaced by OPV in 1961. At that time OPV had some significant advantages over IPV. It was easier to administer and conferred long-lasting immunity with four doses (as opposed to the five required for the IPV in use at that time), facilitating high acceptance rates. In addition, the IPV available then was contaminated with a monkey virus, which, though it did not appear to affect humans, was a cause for concern. There were also concerns about the safety of IPV because of a one-time production failure that resulted in a number of cases of vaccine-related paralysis in its first year of use.

While OPV is still easier to administer

than IPV, the other disadvantages of IPV have been eliminated over the years. It no longer contains the monkey virus, and there have been no cases of vaccine-related paralysis due to IPV in the world since the 1955 incident, in spite of widespread use in other countries. In addition, a new, enhanced IPV has been developed which is as effective as OPV[67] but requires only three doses.

EFFECTIVENESS. Both IPV and OPV have been shown to be highly effective. Their efficacy—as well as their limitations—has been demonstrated in various outbreaks of the disease around the world. For example, two small epidemics occurred in this country in 1972 and 1979, one among Christian Scientists and the other among the Amish, both of whom refuse vaccination. In each outbreak, despite close contacts with the general public, no one outside these groups contracted the disease.[68] Similar occurrences have been documented in the Netherlands, where IPV is used exclusively, with no spread of the disease outside the nonvaccinated subgroups.[69]

It has also been shown that vaccine failures do occur, if infrequently. During an epidemic in Taiwan in 1982, eight percent of the cases of paralysis occurred in children who had had two or more doses of OPV.[70] After a polio outbreak in Finland, it was determined that the cause was a slightly different strain of the virus than that used in the vaccine.[71] To prevent a major epidemic, mass immunization was undertaken with a new vaccine. Although 100,000 persons were estimated to have been infected, the outbreak was halted with no further cases.

This incident shows that the vaccines may fail if new strains of the disease appear, but also that they can effectively prevent an epidemic.

REACTIONS, SIDE EFFECTS, COMPLICATIONS. Despite the fact that IPV and OPV are now comparably effective, OPV is still the recommended vaccine in the United States. This would be understandable if it were as safe as IPV, but it isn't. Each year, approximately eight people in the United States suffer from paralysis caused by OPV. The victims are either children who have received the vaccine or their close contacts. The reason vaccine-related paralysis occurs is that the weakened live virus reproduces in the intestines and is then shed and passed along to contacts. In most cases this simply results in passive immunization of unvaccinated contacts (the "spread vaccine" effect). In certain rare instances, however, the vaccine virus reverts to its former strength and may then cause paralysis in the recipient or one of those unimmunized contacts. That these cases occur is unsurprising, since "it was known even before licensing that the virus excreted by vaccinated children was less attenuated than the vaccine itself."[72]

It is impossible to determine precisely the risk of contracting polio from the vaccine, but the most reliable figures are in the range of one to three cases per million.[73,74,75] There are physicians who believe that the rates may actually be much greater, however. One group of doctors reported four cases of vaccine-related paralysis in Indiana with-in a fourteen-month period, each of which had been misdiagnosed by the patient's doctor.[76] The university physicians suggested that doctors fail to recognize such cases because most of them have no previous experience with polio. They calculated the risk at 1 in every 37,000 patients immunized in Indiana during that fourteen-month interval and suggested that more active surveillance would probably reveal a higher incidence of vaccine-related polio overall.

Even if those who calculate the risk to be very low are correct, the number of victims of paralysis due to the vaccine is significant when compared with the number who are paralyzed by wild poliovirus. Why then, have policymakers not recommended a return to the inactivated vaccine to eliminate all cases of vaccine-induced polio? The primary reason is the spread vaccine effect of OPV. This process has often been given credit for the low levels of polio in this country, since presumably the vaccine reaches even those population groups in which immunization levels are low.

This assumption may well be erroneous. Several countries have chosen to use IPV exclusively and have been successful in virtually eliminating polio. In fact, the decline in the incidence of paralytic polio due to wild poliovirus was strikingly similar in Finland, Sweden, and the United States, despite the use of IPV in Finland and Sweden and OPV in the U.S.[77] For that matter, in this country the rate of the decline did not increase when IPV was replaced by OPV, in spite of the spread vaccine effect.

RECOMMENDATIONS. Because there is no polio in the United States other than that caused by the OPV, I do not feel that immunization against polio with either vaccine is necessary. However, if an outbreak were to begin, I would probably feel it was wise to vaccinate children with IPV, since it is both safe and effective. You may also want to consider vaccination with IPV if you are particularly worried about polio, or if your kids are often exposed to children who have received OPV, putting them at a small but real risk of contracting vaccine-related polio.

If you do decide to use IPV, the current recommendation is to give it at two, four, and fifteen months. However, Dr. Jonas Salk, who developed the vaccine, feels that it should not be given before six months, since until this age most babies have maternal antibodies that still protect them and may interfere with immunization.[78] If your child has had two or more doses of OPV, there is probably no sense in switching to IPV, since the risk declines with each dose.

If for some reason your child does receive OPV, make sure that it is not given at the same time as an injection (e.g., of DPT, as is the current accepted practice) since there is some evidence in a European study that "simultaneous intramuscular injections may increase the incidence of paralytic poliomyelitis."[79]

CONTRAINDICATIONS. The only contraindications to IPV are severe febrile illness or a sensitivity to neomycin or streptomycin.[80]

Measles, Mumps, and Rubella

· ·

The vaccines for measles, mumps, and rubella are virtually always given as a combined vaccine (although they are available individually), commonly known as MMR. Since the vaccines are frequently treated as one unit in the medical literature, and since I do not consider any of them either more beneficial or more dangerous than the others, I will discuss the vaccines as one unit. The diseases are described separately.

Measles

· ·

THE DISEASE

Also known as rubeola, red measles, hard measles, and five-day measles, measles is a highly contagious viral disease mainly characterized by fever and a red, raised rash.

TRANSMISSION. Measles is spread by respiratory droplet. Humans and monkeys are the only hosts of the measles virus, and there are no asymptomatic carriers.

INCIDENCE. In unvaccinated populations, measles is primarily a disease of young childhood. In countries like ours, where immunization levels are high, measles occurs primarily in preschool children, adolescents, and young adults, with about half of all cases occurring in ten- to nineteen-year-olds.[81]

COURSE OF THE DISEASE. Measles has an incubation period of approximately ten to twelve days, followed by a prodromal stage characterized by fever, malaise, a runny nose, a barking cough, and conjunctivitis. Bluish white spots, as small as grains of sand and surrounded by redness (Koplik's spots), may appear on the insides of the cheeks. The child may complain that light hurts his eyes and may have swollen lymph nodes, particularly at the angle of the jaw and the back of the neck. Two to four days later, a red, raised rash appears, usually starting on the face and at the hairline and then spreading to the trunk and extremities. The rash itches little or not at all. After five to seven days it begins to fade, disappearing in the order in which it appeared. The disease lasts between ten days and two weeks, with the contagious period beginning with the onset of symptoms and lasting until three to four days after the appearance of the rash. Except in rare cases, infection with measles conveys lifelong immunity.

A second, rare type of measles infection, known as atypical measles, has been recognized since 1965. Between 1963 and 1965 the measles vaccine in use was a killed virus vaccine. Atypical measles occurs in some people who have received this vaccine and are then exposed to natural measles, and, in some cases, among those who receive the live virus vaccine now in use and, even more rarely, in recipients of the live virus vaccine who are exposed to natural measles. Atypical measles is characterized by high fever, muscle aches, headache, pneumonia, abdominal pain, extreme weakness, and a rash. The rash may resemble that of typical measles, or it may be characterized by small, flat reddish or purplish spots (petechiae) or chicken pox–like blisters. Unlike a typical measles rash, it begins on the extremities and progresses inward, finally involving the trunk, and may itch.

DIAGNOSIS. The diagnosis of measles is usually made on a clinical basis. Atypical or modified measles may be harder to diagnose, but can be confirmed through blood tests or virus isolation.

TREATMENT. Treatment is symptomatic, consisting mainly of bed rest and increased fluid intake. A vaporizer and an expectorant cough medicine may be helpful, but cough medicines containing narcotics or sedatives should be avoided. Secondary bacterial infections can be treated with antibiotics, but the bacteria should first be isolated and tested to determine which antibiotic will be most effective. The prophylactic use of antibiotics is not recommended and may actually increase the risk of severe, difficult-to-treat infections.[82]

Human immune globulin, given within six days of exposure, can prevent the disease or modify it so that it is less severe. If the disease is prevented no permanent immunity is acquired, but modified measles infection is believed to provide lifelong immunity. Human immune globulin is considered safe for pregnant women.

COMPLICATIONS. Although measles has a high mortality rate in underdeveloped countries, in this country, it is relatively benign in the vast majority of cases. The most common complications are middle ear infection (five to nine percent of cases) and pneumonia (one to five percent). Measles encephalitis occurs in 0.01 to 0.02 percent of cases, usually from one to seven days after the onset of the rash. It is rare in children under the age of two, and most common in those between the ages of two and four. Approximately half of the children with measles encephalitis recover fully, about thirty-five percent are left with permanent neurological complications, and five to ten percent die.[83]

The most serious complication of measles is an extremely rare degenerative disorder of the central nervous system, subacute sclerosing panencephalitis (SSPE), that does not become apparent until approximately seven years following measles infection. The disease is characterized by increasingly severe neurological problems, including personality changes, seizures, impairment of motor skills, coma, and eventually death, which occurs months to years after symptoms first appear.

Other complications include thrombocytopenic purpura, a temporary blood disorder characterized by easy bruising and petechiae; transient changes in EEG readings; and keratitis, an inflammation of the cornea. (In underdeveloped countries keratitis sometimes leads to bacterial infections that can cause blindness, but this is not a concern here.) Children whose immune systems are compromised are at a much higher risk of complications from measles.

Measles infection during pregnancy significantly increases the risk of miscarriage, particularly in the first trimester, and premature birth, but there is no evidence that it causes birth defects. Most infants are born with immunity to the disease from the transfer of maternal antibodies, which last until approximately six to fifteen months of age. Infants of mothers who have acquired immunity through natural infection are probably protected longer than those who have been immunized.

Mumps

THE DISEASE

Mumps is an acute, generalized viral disease characterized by swelling and pain of the salivary glands.

TRANSMISSION. Humans are the only known host for the mumps virus, which is primarily spread by respiratory droplet but may also be spread through handling of objects contaminated with saliva or urine.

INCIDENCE. Most cases of mumps occur among school-age children, but approximately fifteen percent are seen in adolescents, and cases do occur in both newborns and the elderly.[84] The disease is more prevalent during the winter and spring, although cases can occur at any time of year.

COURSE OF THE DISEASE. The mumps virus has an incubation period of about sixteen to eighteen days. Approximately one-third of mumps cases are asymptomatic. In the remainder, there may be a prodromal period of fever, aching muscles, and loss of appetite, although this is less common in children. The parotid glands—located at the sides of the face below and in front of the ears—then begin to swell. In most cases both parotids are affected, but the swelling may also be unilateral. The swelling usually peaks in one to three days, but may progress so rapidly that it peaks within a few hours. It subsides slowly over the next three to seven days or so. The swollen area is tender, and the pain is particularly intense when tasting something sour, such as vinegar or lemon juice. In some cases the salivary glands located about halfway between the angle of the jaw and the chin on the underside of the jaw may also swell, and in a few cases, they alone may be affected. Less commonly, the glands located under the tongue are involved, with swelling in the floor of the mouth.

Though swelling of the salivary glands is the most common manifestation of mumps, it is a systemic disease that may involve other glands and parts of the nervous system. If fever persists or returns after the swelling goes down, additional organs may be affected.[85]

A person with mumps is contagious approximately from twenty-four hours before parotid swelling to three days after it has subsided. Patients with asymptomatic infection are also contagious. Mumps infection nearly always conveys lifelong immunity to the disease, even if asymptomatic, although some second cases have been reported.

DIAGNOSIS. A diagnosis of mumps can usually be made on the basis of symptoms, especially if there is a known history of exposure. If necessary, blood tests can confirm the diagnosis.

TREATMENT. Treatment is symptomatic. Cold packs may reduce parotid swelling.

COMPLICATIONS. The most well-known complication of mumps is swelling of the testicles accompanied by inflammation of the tubes in which sperm mature (epididymoorchitis). This is rare in prepubescent boys, but relatively common in adolescent and adult males. The swelling usually begins abruptly about eight days after the swelling of the salivary glands, along with a rise in temperature, chills, headache, nausea, and lower abdominal pain. In about a third of cases, both testicles are affected. Of affected testes, approximately a third atrophy, and in about thirteen percent of these cases fertility may be impaired.[86] Absolute sterility, even when both testicles are affected, is extremely rare.[87]

The female counterpart to epididymoorchitis, inflammation of the ovaries (oophoritis) is less common. Symptoms are the same as in males, minus the testicular swelling, of course. Oophoritis does not impair fertility.

Aseptic meningitis is the most common complication of mumps in childhood, occurring in approximately ten percent of cases, usually seven to ten days after swelling has subsided. It is two to three times more common in boys than girls, and may occur even in the absence of parotid swelling.[88] The symptoms are similar to those of other forms of aseptic meningitis and the course is usually benign. Encephalitis occurs in about 1 in 6,000 cases,[89] and is, again, more common in boys. Permanent neurological complications or death are rare, but do occur.

Permanent nerve deafness, usually unilateral, is an uncommon complication of mumps, occurring in about 1 in every 15,000 patients. Transient deafness may occur during the illness in as many as four percent of cases.

Infection of the pancreas, from mild to severe, may also occur as a result of mumps infection, even in the absence of other symptoms of the disease. The infection usually clears up in about a week, although it may persist for up to two weeks.

Mumps infection during pregnancy increases the likelihood of miscarriage if it occurs in the first trimester, but does not cause birth defects. Infants are protected by maternal antibodies (if their mothers have immunity to mumps) for the first six months of life.

Rubella

....

THE DISEASE

Also known as German or three-day measles, rubella is a moderately contagious, generally mild viral disease characterized by swollen lymph nodes and a rash.

TRANSMISSION. Rubella is spread by respiratory droplet.

INCIDENCE. Before the rubella vaccine came into use, most cases occurred in children between the ages of five and fourteen. The majority of cases now occur in teenagers and young adults. There is a slight rise in rubella cases in the spring.

COURSE OF THE DISEASE. Rubella has an incubation period of fourteen to twenty-one days. There is sometimes a brief prodromal stage similar to but less severe than that seen with measles. In other cases the first sign of rubella infection may be enlargement and tenderness of the lymph nodes at the back of the head. One to five days later, a pink, raised rash consisting of discrete lesions will usually appear. It most often begins on the face (but may start on any part of the body) and spreads quickly down over the trunk and extremities. By the end of the second day, the rash on the trunk may be nearly continuous. It generally disappears within three days, usually in the order of appearance. In severe cases there may be fine peeling of the skin, but this usually does not occur on the hands and feet. Approximately a third of rubella infections are asymptomatic.[90]

The contagious period for rubella begins about one week before the rash appears and lasts until about four days after its onset. Overt and asymptomatic rubella infection both usually provide lifelong immunity to the disease.

DIAGNOSIS. Rubella can be difficult to diagnose on the basis of clinical symptoms, and in its more severe forms may be confused with measles or scarlet fever. The presence of enlarged lymph nodes at the back of the head strongly suggests rubella infection. Rubella can be definitively diagnosed with a blood test.

TREATMENT. Treatment for rubella is symptomatic. There is a human immune globulin that is occasionally used in pregnant, nonimmune women exposed to rubella, but its efficacy has not been established.

COMPLICATIONS. The most significant complication of rubella occurs when a pregnant woman contracts the virus. Whether the mother's infection is overt or asymptomatic, the virus can pass through the placenta and infect her unborn baby. Congenital rubella syndrome (CRS) causes a wide range of birth defects, from heart problems to mental retardation to diabetes to deficiencies of the immune system, and it may cause death. The danger to the fetus is greatest in the first three months of pregnancy, gradually decreasing over time, until it becomes almost nonexistent by the twentieth week. In one study of 1,000 pregnant women with rubella infections, defects occurred in all infants infected before the eleventh week of pregnancy.[91] As many as fifty to seventy percent of infants with CRS appear normal at birth, but develop problems months and even years later. Babies born with CRS may continue to be infected with the virus and are contagious for months after birth.

Other complications from rubella are rare. Encephalitis similar to that seen with measles occurs in approximately 1 in 6,000 cases, becoming evident one to seven days after the appearance of the rash. Although the mortality rate from rubella encephalitis is relatively high (twenty percent), children who recover rarely have permanent neurological damage.[92] Transitory arthritis or joint pain occurs in approximately a third of women who contract rubella, but it is uncommon in children and men.

THE MMR VACCINE

The MMR vaccine contains live, attenuated measles, mumps, and rubella viruses, and is administered in one dose. Although the diseases are potentially the most dangerous to young infants, the vaccine is usually not given until fifteen months of age. If administered earlier, maternal antibodies, which have been shown to persist for as long as fifteen months, may render it ineffective.

EFFECTIVENESS. Although one dose of MMR is still considered to provide lifelong immunity to all three diseases, there is mounting evidence that protection may be less durable than we believe. More cases of each of the diseases now occur in older teens and adults than in young children, perhaps indicating that vaccine immunity declines over time. One study compared antibody levels in children who acquired immunity to rubella through the vaccine with those of children who had had the disease. Three to five years later, the vaccinated group had much lower levels of antibodies, and a quarter of this group had no detectable antibodies at all.[93] Similar studies of measles and mumps antibody levels showed failure rates of eighteen percent and nine percent, respectively.[94]

While some vaccine failures are undoubtedly due to declining antibody levels, in other cases immunity may never have been achieved in the first place. The MMR vaccine is sensitive to both heat and light, so that improper handling can easily render it ineffective. Secondary vaccine failures, in which antibodies are produced but fail to prevent clinical disease, have also been documented.[95]

Some vaccine failures do result in disease. Thirty-eight percent of the total reported cases of measles in the United States in 1986 occurred in people who had been properly immunized.[96] In an outbreak in upstate New York in 1982, fifty-four percent of the people who contracted measles had a history of adequate immunization,[97] as did fifty-five percent of the students who came down with measles in an outbreak in Pennsylvania around the same time.[98] Similarly, in an outbreak of mumps in a Nashville high school, forty-three percent of the students who came down with the disease had been immunized.[99]

REACTIONS, SIDE EFFECTS, COMPLICATIONS. Several different types of complications have been reported in association with the MMR vaccine. One Swedish study of 174 children found that eighty percent had some sort of reaction.[100] Fever and irritability were the most common, with the peak incidence for fever occurring on or around the ninth day following vaccination. Other reactions included a cough, a rash, diarrhea, conjunctivitis, and local redness and/or pain.

Most medical texts report a much lower rate of reactions to MMR. The higher rate seen in the Swedish study may be a result of the close monitoring of these children. Parents were asked specifically to report any reaction for twenty days following vaccination, so that reactions that might have been otherwise overlooked or attributed to other causes were included.

There are also reports of various reactions to each of the different components of the vaccine. The measles vaccine occasionally causes encephalopathy. The reported frequency is once in every million doses administered,[101] but in all probability the actual rates are higher; as the study above demonstrates, careful monitoring can result in higher rates than expected. One review of fifty-nine cases of encephalitis or encephalopathy following measles vaccination found that fifty-two percent recovered fully, ten percent died, and the remaining thirty-eight percent had permanent neurologic damage.[102] The measles vaccine has also been reported to cause SSPE, although this is extremely rare.[103] Other reported complications are Guillain-Barré syndrome,[104] hearing loss,[105] and immediate reactions of vomiting, fever, rash, and cyanosis.[106]

The mumps vaccine occasionally causes allergic reactions such as rash and itching at the immunization site. Rare complications include meningitis, diabetes mellitus, and unilateral deafness. It has been suggested that deafness due to the mumps vaccine may occur more frequently than is realized, since deafness can be difficult to detect in young children. By the time hearing loss is found several years after immunization, it may be difficult to prove a connection with the vaccine.[107]

The rubella vaccine has been estimated to cause neuropathy (nerve problems such as pain and loss of sensation) in 1 of every 1,000 recipients. A study of a rubella immunization program in Nashville in 1970 turned up 32 children with such problems. Sixty-two percent had one episode with no further symptoms, thirty-one percent had continuing minor complaints, and six percent had major recurrences over the two-and-a-half-year observation period.[108] Once again, I am struck by how many children develop complications when vaccine reactions are monitored closely. If 32 children can be found in one community over the course of one year, how many are there across the country that are not associated with the vaccine or reported?

The rubella vaccine is also known to cause arthritis or arthralgia (joint pain), most commonly in adolescent girls or women, and rarely in children. Symptoms generally first occur three to twenty-five days after immunization. Though these conditions are usually transient and of short duration, in rare instances they may become chronic and persist for years. Additional adverse reactions include fever, rash, and swollen lymph nodes.

RECOMMENDATIONS. Because measles, mumps, and rubella themselves are usually mild and uncomplicated in childhood and because the vaccines appear to be often in-effective and of short-term duration, I don't believe vaccination with MMR is justified. If in fact the immunity conferred by the MMR vaccine is not long-lasting, there will continue to be a rise in cases of these diseases in teenagers and adults. (The American Academy of Pediatrics and the CDC are now recommending a second dose of MMR for adolescents to prolong immunity, a course of action that also will double the rate of vaccine reactions.) In the long run, the result of this short-term immunity will be protection from the diseases during childhood, when the risks are lowest, with greater susceptibility occurring during adolescence and adulthood, when complications tend to be more serious.

This scenario is particularly troublesome with regard to the rubella vaccine. If immunization prevents the disease in early childhood but wears off in adolescence or early adulthood, there will be an increase in women who are susceptible to the disease in their childbearing years. In my opinion, it is wiser to skip the vaccine and allow children to gain immunity by contracting the disease. If you choose this course of action with your daughter and she does not acquire natural immunity to rubella (this can be determined with a blood test), you may want to reconsider vaccination when she reaches puberty, to prevent the possibility of damage to a fetus, should your daughter become pregnant.

CONTRAINDICATIONS. The MMR vaccine should not be given to children with untreated malignant disease or impaired immunity due to X-ray therapy or steroids; those who have received another live vaccine injection within the past three weeks; those with allergies to neomycin or kanamycin or a history of anaphylaxis due to any cause; children who have a fever, or pregnant women or those who are likely to become pregnant within a month.

The Hib and Other New Vaccines

There is not enough information available at present to be able to intelligently evaluate the new hemophilus influenza type B (Hib) vaccine, although I have seen studies that question its efficacy,[109,110] and one that shows that children who receive the vaccine actually seem to be more susceptible to the disease than those who do not.[111] My approach to this and other new vaccines (such as the chicken pox vaccine, which may soon be approved for general use) is one of extreme caution. Until these vaccines have been in use for many years, it is impossible to predict their long-term consequences, and hence to determine their safety.

No matter how much you have learned from this chapter (and will learn from other sources), the decisions you must make regarding immunizations for your child are by no means simple ones, and I realize that your decisions will not necessarily concur with

my recommendations. Ultimately, your choices will have to be based, at least partially, on your particular belief system. Where you place your faith—whether in good nutrition and a healthy life-style or in medical science and technology—will have a lot to do with the direction in which you decide to go. As I have made clear throughout this book, my own approach has been to emphasize overall good health, not medicine.

Should you ultimately decide to reject some or all immunizations for your child, you may fear that you will encounter problems with the authorities when your child is ready to attend school. Although most states require immunization records when registering a child, there are ways around these regulations. One option is to obtain a written exemption from a physician. In some states, such an exemption must be received from an M.D., but in others, an exemption from an alternative healing practitioner is acceptable. All states, except for Mississippi and West Virginia, also grant religious exemptions. In the recent past, these exemptions applied only to Christian Scientists and Jehovah's Witnesses, but several states have now rewritten their laws so that the belief does not have to be part of your church's doctrine, but simply a personal religious belief. For more information on laws as they vary from state to state, consult the National Vaccine Information Center/Dissatisfied Parents Together, 204-F Mill Street, Vienna, VA 22180.

Summing Up: Immunizations and Infectious Diseases

··

1.   The decline of infectious diseases up until the early 1900s had more to do with improvements in sanitation and nutrition and less to do with improved medical care than most people realize.

2.   Most of the vaccines currently available are less effective and cause more side effects than is commonly believed.

3.   Parents should evaluate each vaccine on an individual basis with regard to its dangers and incidence of the disease it prevents, the dangers of the vaccine itself, and its effectiveness.

4.   There are no easy answers to the question of whether or not to immunize, so parents should make their own decisions based on their life-style and belief system rather than the blanket recommendations of any doctor or health authority.

Notes

1. Thomas McKeown, "Determinants of Health," *Human Nature*, (Apr. 1978): p. 60.

2. Ibid.

3. Thomas McKeown, *The Role of Medicine: Dream, Mirage, or Nemesis?* (Princeton, N.J.: Princeton University Press, 1979): p. 93.

4. McKeown, "Determinants of Health," p. 60.

5. Donald A. Brand, Ph.D., et al., "Adequacy of Antitetanus Prophylaxis in Six Hospital Emergency Rooms," *The New England Journal of Medicine*, Vol. 309, No. 11 (Sept. 15, 1983): p. 637.

6. Wesley Furste, M.D., "Four Keys to 100 Per Cent Success in Tetanus Prophylaxis," *The American Journal of Surgery*, Vol. 1218 (Nov. 1974): p. 617.

7. Joseph P. Middaugh, M.D., "Side Effects of Diphtheria-Tetanus Toxoid in Adults," *American Journal of Public Health*, Vol. 69, No. 3 (Mar. 1979): p. 246.

8. Patti L. Holliday, M.D., and Raymond B. Bauer, M.D., "Polyradiculoneuritis Secondary to Immunization With Tetanus and Diphtheria Toxoids," *Archives of Neurology*, Vol. 40 (Jan. 1983): p. 56.

9. W. Baust et al., "Peripheral Neuropathy After Administration of Tetanus Toxoid," *Journal of Neurology*, Vol. 222, No. 2 (1979): p. 131.

10. G. K. Schlenska, "Unusual Neurological Complications Following Tetanus Toxoid Administration," *Journal of Neurology*, Vol. 215, No. 4 (Dec. 1977): p. 299.

11. George I. Blumstein, M. D., "Peripheral Neuropathy Following Tetanus Toxoid Administration," *Journal of the American Medical Association*, Vol. 198, No. 9 (Nov. 28, 1966): p. 1030.

12. L.T.C. Elias Deliyannakis, M. C., "Peripheral Nerve and Root Disturbances Following Active Immunization Against Smallpox and Tetanus," *Military Medicine* (May 1971): p. 459.

13. W. G. White et al., "Reactions to Tetanus Toxoid," *Journal of Hygiene*, Vol. 71, No. 2 (June 1973): p. 283.

14. Furste, p. 618.

15. Ole Simonsen et al., "Evaluation of Vaccination Requirements to Secure Continuous Antitoxin Immunity to Tetanus," *Vaccine,* Vol. 5 (June 1987): p. 115.

16. White, p. 295.

17. Furste, p. 619.

18. Brand, p. 636.

19. Ibid.

20. James D. Cherry, M.D., et al., "Report of the Task Force on Pertussis and Pertussis Immunization," *Pediatrics* Supplement, Vol. 81, No. 6 (June 1988): p. 951.

21. Paul E. M. Fine and Jacqueline A. Clarkson, "Reflections on the Efficacy of Pertussis Vaccines," *Reviews of Infectious Diseases,* Vol. 9, No. 5, (Sept.–Oct. 1987): p. 867.

22. Centers for Disease Control, "Leads from the MMWR," *Journal of the American Medical Association,* Vol. 252, No. 21 (Dec. 7, 1984): p. 2951.

23. Ralph D. Feigin and James D. Cherry, "Pertussis," *Text Book of Pediatric Infectious Disease* (Philadelphia: W. B. Saunders, 1987): p. 1231.

24. Cherry et al., p. 950.

25. Centers for Disease Control, p. 2951.

26. H. P. Lambert, M.D., "The Enigma of Pertussis, The Marc Daniels Lecture 1984," *Journal of the Royal College of Physicians of London,* Vol. 19, No. 2 (Apr. 1985): p. 67.

27. Centers for Disease Control, p. 2951.

28. Juan Sotomayor, M.D., et al., "Inaccurate Diagnosis in Infants With Pertussis," *American Journal of Diseases of Children,* Vol. 139 (July 1985): p. 724.

29. Cherry et al., p. 946.

30. Centers for Disease Control, p. 2951.

31. Fine and Clarkson, p. 866.

32. Tatsuo Aoyma, M.D., et al., "Efficacy of an Acellular Pertussis Vaccine in Japan," *The Journal of Pediatrics,* Vol. 107, No. 2 (Aug. 1985): p. 181.

33. Cherry et al., p. 956.

34. Centers for Disease Control, "Leads from the MMWR," *Journal of the American Medical Association*, Vol. 250, No. 2 (July 8, 1983): pp. 159–160.

35. Harold J. Lambert, M.D., D.P.H., "Epidemiology of a Small Pertussis Outbreak in Kent County Michigan," *Public Health Reports*, Vol. 80, No. 4 (Apr. 1965): p. 369.

36. Gordon Stewart, "Whooping Cough in Relation to Other Childhood Infections in 1977–1979 in the U.K." *Journal of Epidemiology and Community Health*, Vol. 35, No. 2 (June 1981): p. 139.

37. Fine and Clarkson, p. 876.

38. Cherry et al., p. 956.

39. Cherry et al., p. 957.

40. I.D.A. Johnston et al., "The Severity of Whooping Cough in Hospitalized Children—Is It Declining?" *Journal of Hygiene*, Vol. 94, No. 2 (1985): p. 151.

41. Christopher L. Cody, M.D., et al., "Nature and Rates of Adverse Reactions Associated with DPT and DT Immunizations in Infants and Children," *Pediatrics*, Vol. 68, No. 5 (Nov. 1981): p. 650.

42. Cherry et al., p. 965.

43. Cherry et al., p. 976.

44. Cherry et al., p. 967.

45. Ibid.

46. Feigin and Cherry, p. 1233.

47. Ibid.

48. Ibid.

49. Cherry et al., p. 963.

50. Feigin and Cherry, p. 1233.

51. William A. Altemeier III, "Pertussis and Parapertussis," *Infections in Children*, Ralph J. Wedgwood, ed. (New York: Harper and Row, 1982): p. 728.

52. Cody, p. 656.

53. Cody, p. 650.

54. Cody, p. 656.

55. Cody, p. 653.

56. Cody, p. 658.

57. Altemeier, p. 729.

58. Centers for Disease Control, "Diphtheria, Tetanus and Pertussis: Guidelines for Vaccine Prophylaxis and Other Preventive Measures," *Journal of the American Medical Association*, Vol. 254, No. 8 (Aug. 23, 1985): p. 1009.

59. Altemeier, p. 728.

60. Harrison C. Stetler, M.D., et al., "History of Convulsions and Use of Pertussis Vaccine," *The Journal of Pediatrics*, Vol. 107, No. 2 (Aug. 1985): p. 175.

61. Edward W. Brink, Steven G. F. Wassilak, and Kenneth J. Bart, "Diphtheria," *Public Health and Preventive Medicine*, 12th ed., John M. Last, ed. (Norwalk, Conn.: Appleton-Century-Crofts, 1986): p. 206.

62. Paul D. Hoeprich, "Chapter 25: Diphtheria," *Infectious Diseases*, 4th ed., Paul D. Hoeprich and M. Colin Jordan, eds. (Philadelphia: Lippincott, 1989): p. 322.

63. Rino Rappuoli, Maria Perugini, and Enevold Falsen, "Molecular Epidemiology of the 1984–1986 Outbreak of Diphtheria in Sweden," *New England Journal of Medicine*, Vol. 318, No. 1 (Jan. 12, 1988): p. 12.

64. Ibid.

65. S. Dittman, "Chapter 34: Immunobiological Preparations," *Side Effects of Drugs*, Annual 11, M.N.G. Dukes, ed. (New York: Elsevier Science Publishers, 1988): pp. 282.

66. Ibid.

67. A. M. McBean et al., "A Comparison of the Serologic Responses to Oral and Injectable Trivalent Poliovirus Vaccines," *Reviews of Infectious Diseases*, Vol. 6, Supplement 2 (May–June 1984): p. 552.

68. Lawrence B. Schonberger et al., "Control of Paralytic Poliomyelitis in the United States," *Reviews of Infectious Diseases*, Vol. 6, Supplement 2 (May–June 1984): p. 424.

69. Henk Bijkerk, "Surveillance and Control of Poliomyelitis in The Netherlands," *Reviews of Infectious Diseases*, Vol. 6, Supplement 2 (May–June 1984): p. 451.

70. Robert J. Kim-Farley et al., "Outbreak of Paralytic Poliomyelitis, Taiwan," *The Lancet* (Dec. 8, 1984): p. 1322.

71. T. Hovi et al., "Outbreak of Paralytic Poliomyelitis in Finland: Widespread Circulation of Antigenically Altered Poliovirus Type 3 in a Vaccinated Population," *The Lancet* (June 21, 1986): p. 1427.

72. Joseph L. Melnick, Ph.D., "Vaccination Against Poliomyelitis: Present Possibilities and Future Prospects," *American Journal of Public Health*, Vol. 78, No. 3 (Mar. 1988): p. 304.

73. Pearay L. Ogra, M.D., and Howard S. Faden, M.D., "Poliovirus Vaccines: Live or Dead," *The Journal of Pediatrics*, Vol. 108, No. 6 (June 1986): p. 1032.

74. Neal Nathanson and John R. Martin, "The Epidemiology of Poliomyelitis: Enigmas Surrounding Its Appearance, Epidemicity, and Disappearance," *American Journal of Epidemiology*, Vol. 110, No. 6 (Dec. 1979): p. 687.

75. Alan R. Hinman, M.D., et al., "Live or Inactivated Poliomyelitis Vaccine: An Analysis of Benefits and Risks," *American Journal of Public Health*, Vol. 78, No. 3 (Mar. 1988): p. 291.

76. John W. Gaebler, M.D., et al., "Neurologic Complications in Oral Polio Vaccine Recipients," *The Journal of Pediatrics*, Vol. 108, No. 6 (June 1986): p. 878.

77. Darrell Salk, M.D., "Polio Immunization Policy in the United States: A New Challenge for a New Generation," *American Journal of Public Health*, Vol. 78, No. 3 (Mar. 1988): p. 297.

78. Jonas Salk, "One-Dose Immunization Against Paralytic Polio Using a Noninfectious Vaccine," *Reviews of Infectious Diseases*, Vol. 6, Supplement 2 (May–June 1984): p. 444.

79. Thomas Mertens and Hans J. Eggers, "Vaccine-Associated Poliomyelitis," *The Lancet* (Dec. 15, 1984): p. 1390.

80. Centers for Disease Control, "Leads from the MMWR," ("Poliomyelitis Prevention: Enhanced-Potency Inactivated Poliomyelitis Vaccine—Supplementary Statement") *Journal of the American Medical Association*, Vol. 259, No. 3 (Jan. 15, 1988): p. 346.

81. Christopher J. Sullivan and M. Colin Jordan, "Chapter 94: Measles," *Infectious Diseases*, 4th ed., Paul Hoeprich and M. Colin Jordan, eds. (Philadelphia: Lippincott, 1989): p. 875.

82. Sullivan and Jordan, p. 883.

83. Sullivan and Jordan, p. 880.

84. Claire Pomeroy and M. Colin Jordan, "Chapter 82: Mumps," *Infectious Diseases*, 4th ed., Paul Hoeprich and M. Colin Jordan, eds. (Philadelphia: Lippincott, 1989): p. 798.

85. Pomeroy and Jordan, p. 799.

86. Carol F. Phillips, "Viral Infections and Those Presumed to Be Caused by Viruses," *Nelson Textbook of Pediatrics*, 13th ed., Richard E. Behrman, M.D., and Victor C. Vaughn III, M.D., eds. (Philadelphia: W. B. Saunders Co., 1987): p. 674.

87. Stephen R. Preblud and Walter A. Orenstein, "Mumps," *Public Health and Preventive Medicine*, John M. Last, ed. (Norwalk, Conn.: Appleton-Century-Crofts, 1986): p. 168.

88. Pomeroy and Jordan, p. 800.

89. Ibid.

90. Kenneth J. Bart, Stephen R. Preblud, and Alan R. Hinman, "Rubella," *Public Health and Preventive Medicine*, John M. Last, ed. (Norwalk, Conn.: Appleton-Century-Crofts, 1986): p. 888.

91. Bart, Preblud, and Hinman, p. 163.

92. S. Michael Marcy and M. Colin Jordan, "Chapter 95: Rubella," *Infectious Diseases*, 4th ed., Paul Hoeprich and M. Colin Jordan, eds., (Philadelphia: Lippincott, 1989) p. 890.

93. D. M. Horstmann, "Controlling Rubella: Problems and Perspectives," *Annals of Internal Medicine*, Vol. 83, No. 3 (Sept. 1975): p. 412.

94. Henry H. Balfour, Jr., M.D., and Don P. Amren, M.D., "Rubella, Measles and Mumps Antibodies Following Vaccination of Children," *American Journal of Diseases of Children*, Vol. 132 (June 1978): p. 573.

95. Marco Antonio Reyes et al., "Measles Vaccine Failure After Documented Seroconversion," *Pediatric Infectious Disease Journal*, Vol. 6, No. 9 (Sept. 1987): p. 848.

96. Sullivan and Jordan, p. 883.

97. Disease Control Board, New York State Department of Health, *Annual Summary*, Vol. 13, No. 14 (May 20, 1982).

98. Steven G. F. Wassilak et al., "Continuing Measles Transmission in Students Despite a School-Based Outbreak Control Program," *American Journal of Epidemiology*, Vol. 122, No. 2 (Aug. 1985): p. 211.

99. Melinda Wharton et al., "A Large Outbreak of Mumps in the Postvaccine Era," *The Journal of Infectious Diseases*, Vol. 158, No. 6 (Dec. 1988): p. 1257.

100. Timo Vesikari, M.D., "Clinical Trial of a New Trivalent Measles-Mumps-Rubella Vaccine in Young Children," *American Journal of Diseases of Children*, Vol. 138 (Sept. 1984): p. 844.

101. Anne S. Yeager, "Measles," *Infections in Children*, Ralph J. Wedgwood et al., eds. (New York: Harper & Row, 1982): p. 1112.

102. P.J. Landrigan and J.J. Witte, "Neurologic Disorders Following Live Measles-Virus Vaccination," *Journal of the American Medical Association*, Vol. 223, No. 13 (Mar. 26, 1973): p. 1459.

103. W. Edwin Dodson, Joseph Pasternak, and John L. Trotter, "Rapid Deterioration in Subacute Sclerosing Panencephalitis After Measles Immunisation" (letter), *The Lancet* (Apr. 8, 1978): p. 767.

104. Charles Grose, M.D., and Ilya Spigland, M.D., "Guillain-Barré Syndrome Following Administration of Live Measles Vaccine," *The American Journal of Medicine*, Vol. 60 (Mar. 1976): p. 441.

105. Linda Brodsky and John Staneivich, "Sensorineural Hearing Loss Following Live Measles Virus Vaccination," *International Journal of Pediatric Otorhinolaryngology*, Vol. 10, No. 2 (Nov. 1985): p. 159.

106. P. P. Van Asperen, J. McEniery and A. S. Kemp, "Immediate Reactions Following Live Attenuated Measles Vaccine," *The Medical Journal of Australia*, Vol. 2, No. 7 (Oct. 3, 1981): p. 331.

107. J. Nabe Nielsen, M.D., and B. Walter, M.D., "Unilateral Deafness as a Complication of the Mumps, Measles and Rubella Vaccination" (letter), *British Medical Journal*, Clinical Research Edition, Vol. 297, No. 6646 (Aug. 13, 1988): p. 489.

108. William Schaffner, M.D., et al., "Polyneuropathy Following Rubella Immunization," *American Journal of Diseases of Children*, Vol. 127 (May 1974): p. 684.

109. Michael T. Osterholm, Joan H. Rambeck, Karen E. White, "Lack of Efficacy of Haemophilus B Polysaccharide Vaccine in Minnesota," *Journal of the American Medical Association*, Vol. 260, No. 10 (Sept. 9, 1988): p. 1423.

110. Edward A. Mortimer, Jr., M.D., "Efficacy of Haemophilus B Polysaccharide Vaccine: An Enigma," *Journal of the American Medical Association*, Vol. 260, No. 10 (Sept. 9, 1988): p. 1454.

111. Ibid.

The Sick Child

Recognizing a Sick Child

I have found that parents, and new parents in particular, sometimes find it difficult to tell when their child is ill and to judge just how sick he is. For this reason, I have compiled a list of symptoms that are commonly seen in sick children. Parents who have taken my course and used the list have told me that they have found it helpful. If you are uncertain whether or not you should do the physical exam, comparing the symptoms on this list with your child's may help you decide whether or not he is ill. When you use the list, though, keep in mind that it is by no means complete, so that your child may have symptoms that do not appear here. Remember, too, that these symptoms are only helpful if they represent a deviation in your child's normal behavior. You may, for example, notice a "symptom" on the list that is always present in your child, such as paleness or wanting to be held a lot. The true tip-offs to illness are *changes* in your child's behavior or appearance.

Symptoms of Illness

1. Change in nursing or eating pattern: A child who is breast-fed will nurse more; a child on table food or a bottle will eat less.

2. Change in behavior: Inappropriate crying, with a change in tone and an increase in volume and amount; fussiness, irritability, or restlessness; feeling tired at a time of day when the child is usually energetic; wanting to be held; unusual calmness.

3. Fever, chills, or increased pulse rate.

4. Changes in the color, odor, consistency, and/or regularity of the stool.

5. Changes in the skin: It may feel warm, moist, or cool, or appear unusually flushed or pale. There may be rashes or lesions, or the child may feel itchy without any sign of a rash. The skin may even take on a peculiar odor as the body rids itself of toxins.

6. Somatic signs: Pulling on the ear; watery eyes; touching a limb or complaining of pain in a limb; a glassy-eyed look, or "looking sick"; walking differently; changes in the texture of the hair; stomachaches; loss of coordination, especially in babies and younger children; new lumps, such as swollen glands or hernias; dizziness; light sensitivity, etc.

7. Changes in the pitch or quality of the voice, or a regression in language patterns.

8. Vomiting.

9. Runny nose.

10. A coated appearance to the inside of the mouth or tongue and/or a peculiar odor to the breath.

11. Pain.

12. Changes in the breathing, such as congestion, coughing, an increased respiratory rate, flaring of the nostrils, and/or retraction of the muscles between the ribs.

13. Bed-wetting or toilet-training accidents during the day, especially in a child who has been reliably trained for several months or longer.

Your Child's Physician

Regardless of the measures taken to ensure your child's health, you will undoubtedly also need the services of a physician at some point. The purpose of this chapter, then, is threefold: First, to teach you how to choose the physician who will provide the primary medical care for your children and perhaps for yourself as well. Second, to show you how to communicate effectively with your doctor, to ensure that he gets the information needed to treat your child to the best of his ability. And finally, to give you some guidelines to use in evaluating how well that doctor meets your needs. This doctor may be a pediatrician or a family practitioner, or you may choose to go outside the realm of traditional medicine and consult a chiropractor, homeopath, osteopath, naturopath, or other health professional. As a family practitioner, I feel you will get the best care

from a doctor in family practice, whatever discipline he chooses to follow, since he will come to know every member of your family and will be familiar with each one's medical history. Whatever your choice, the approach described here will help you to find a health care provider—for yourself and/or your children—to turn to when you have reached the limits of your knowledge, and will help you to get the best possible care from him.

Choosing a Family Doctor

The first step in finding a doctor who will meet your child's needs is to get some referrals that you can investigate. If you are moving to a new area and are happy with your child's present doctor, it may be helpful to ask if she knows of a good physician in your new town. In the medical profession, birds of a feather truly do flock together, so that your doctor may know others in different locations who share her philosophy and approach.

Another good way to get referrals is to conduct your own private poll. Ask your neighbors, relatives, and friends whom they use and how they feel about him. Medical professionals such as nurses, residents, interns, midwives, and medical social workers are also good people to question, as are La Leche League leaders and members of birthing groups such as Informed Home Birth or Association for Childbirth at Home International.

As you poll people, you must take into account their value systems. Medical professionals tend to be most impressed with doctors who are highly knowledgeable about modern technology and are inclined to use that technology often, while you may prefer a doctor whose philosophy is to intervene only when absolutely necessary. Similarly, your next-door neighbor's idea of a great pediatrician may be one who handles her son's ear infection by taking a quick look in his ear, handing over a prescription for amoxicillin and then rushing him out the door, telling the mother to bring him back for a recheck in a couple of days. If you happen to want a doctor who won't bother you with details like discussing options for treatment and preventing future problems and who would be appalled at the thought of you as an equal partner in your child's health care, then your neighbor's doctor is just the physician for you. If you want some input into your child's care, however,

obviously this doctor is not going to meet your needs.

If you have the time and inclination to do volunteer work, you can also learn a great deal about local doctors by joining the hospital auxiliary. This way, you can observe the doctors in action and see how they treat their patients first-hand. Alternatively, joining the local volunteer ambulance corps or rescue squad will allow you to see how they respond in stressful situations.

The yellow pages of your telephone book may also offer you some clues as to which doctors in your area might suit your child's medical needs. As the number of M.D.s has increased, doctors have begun to advertise more to attract new patients. These advertisements can be helpful in locating a doctor who performs a particular service or who takes a certain approach to health care. Don't believe everything you read, however. Doctors have learned that there are certain catchwords, such as "holistic" or "alternative," that can help attract new patients. I know of one "holistic" doctor whose definition of the term seems to be that he is entitled to your whole bankroll. Another physician in our area claims to offer "alternative" births. This seems to mean that he will cheerfully spend nine months talking you out of giving birth the way you want to, so that your alternative is to do it his way. Make sure you check up on any doctor through other avenues before you decide that he is the one to whom you will entrust your family's medical care.

If there happens to be a consumer's guide to doctors in your area, you are in luck. These are usually published by organizations as fund-raisers, and consist of a survey done by sending out questionnaires about individual doctors to a sampling of each one's patients. The responses are then compiled and printed, sometimes with a reaction to the questionnaire from each doctor, too. The nice thing about these guides is that they allow you to see a range of opinions on several different doctors without having to do a lot of leg work.

One avenue I recommend you do not follow in tracking down a doctor is to get a referral from a medical society. These referrals are given out based solely on who is next in line, and they are essentially worthless.

Once you have the name of a doctor who seems like she might be right for your children, schedule an appointment to interview her. When you speak to the receptionist, tell her that you've heard good things about the doctor. It can't hurt to get on her good side, and she probably thinks highly of the doctor. Make it clear that you want to come in to talk about becoming a patient, and request at least half an hour (preferably a full hour) of her time, so that you know you won't be sneaked into a five-minute slot. Try to make the appointment in the late afternoon, when the doctor will probably be tired and anxious to finish for the day. That way, you'll see her at her most hurried and impatient, and you'll get an idea of the kind of treatment you can expect under these circumstances.

Whether or not you will have to pay for this service will depend on the doctor-patient ratio in your area. If you live in an area where there are so many doctors that they must compete for patients, the interview may be free. On the other hand, in an area with a sparse physician population, there will most likely be a charge. Some doctors charge for the service regardless of the local doctor-patient ratio. Personally, I can't fault them, since I believe it shows a high self-regard and a belief that their services are valuable. So that you won't encounter any surprises later, ask the receptionist about the charge when you call to make the appointment.

Before your visit, take a little time to consider the role you want your doctor to play in your child's health care. Go through the list of questions below and star those that pertain to your particular needs. To get the most complete picture of the doctor, you should ask all of the questions, but emphasize those that are most important to you. Keep in mind that there are some very real pressures on him that will influence how well he is able to meet your child's needs. Those pressures might include state rules, hospital requirements, quality control, and the threat of malpractice, among others.

On the day that you interview the doctor, I strongly suggest that you bring your children with you. If you have only one or two, borrow a couple from a friend. After all, if this doctor is going to be treating your children, you want to be sure that she really likes kids, and can deal with them good-naturedly, even under stress. Surprisingly enough, many pediatricians *don't* like children. They've gone into pediatrics mostly to get away from adults, not to get closer to kids. (Unfortunately for them, each child comes with at least one adult of her very own.)

Before you even get to the questions you want answered, watch how the doctor interacts with your children. Does she talk to them, touch them, hold them on her lap? Also, take note of how the office is set up. If it's filled with priceless objects, you'll know that children aren't really welcome.

Now, the questions. I've divided these up into two categories: questions most doctors will not mind answering and those that will put on a little heat. The answers to the questions in the first group will give you a good idea of the doctor's background and credentials and the way the practice is set up. The answers to those in the second group will give you clues to his attitudes toward some of the more important aspects of children's health care.

BASIC QUESTIONS

1. What is your specialty? You may think you know the answer to this one already, but it is a good idea to ask, just in case there are any surprises.

2. Do you have a subspecialty? His subspecialty may never be important to you, but if your child has (or develops) a special problem, it would be helpful to know whether or not it is in an area of particular interest to the doctor.

3. Are you board-certified or board-eligible? If the doctor is board-certified he has completed a residency and, at the end, passed a test. If he is board-eligible, he has completed a residency but not passed the test, either because he was unable to or because he has not yet taken it. Some specialties require a doctor to practice for two to three years after his residency before taking the boards, although this is not the case with pediatricians or family practitioners. Board certification may not be very significant, especially for a doctor who has been in practice for many years, since many specialties only require doctors to pass the boards once. In order to remain board-certified, family practitioners must retake their exams every seven years. The same holds true for pediatricians who were certified after May 2, 1988. Those who received their certification earlier are certified for life, although they are encouraged to retake the exam every seven years. The recertification process ensures that specialists periodically bring their knowledge up to the level of those who are just graduating from their residencies.

4. What type of practice do you have (group or solo)? The question of whether a group or solo practice is preferable will vary from person to person and from doctor to doctor. There are a few considerations to keep in mind, however. A doctor who is in practice alone may tend to be overworked, have a limited exchange of ideas, and have little formal evaluation of his practice. On the other hand, I have found that doctors who go into solo practice tend to be their own harshest critics and to set very strict standards for themselves, so that they may be less inclined to need the kind of monitoring that occurs in a group practice. In addition, solo practitioners face the problem of who will cover for them when they are unavailable. Those doctors who, as I do, advocate treatment that is sometimes out of the mainstream may have difficulty finding another physician in their area who shares their views. In any event, if you choose a physician in solo practice, there may be times when you will end up taking your child to a doctor you don't know. To minimize surprises, find out in advance who covers for him and how much that doctor charges.

A group practice comes with its own set of disadvantages. Depending on how the practice is set up, you might not see the same doctor twice in a row, which makes it difficult to establish a relationship with any one doctor. Each of the physicians on the team may also be very specialized, so that which doctor your child sees depends on what the particular complaint is. When this happens, you're liable to find your child being treated as a collection of different parts rather than as one whole person. Granted, this is less likely to happen with doctors who treat children than those who treat adults exclusively, although you may still encounter the problem to a lesser extent, since even pediatricians and family practitioners may have subspecialties. Also, in a group practice the welfare of the group must always come before that of any one patient. For example, let's say that your child has a sore throat, and you take her to Dr. A, who tells you that it's nothing serious. You wait several more days, perhaps giving your daughter medicine Dr. A has prescribed, but her condition does not improve. You take her in again, and this time you see Dr. B, who discovers a serious condition or complication that Dr. A missed. Dr. B won't find fault with Dr. A for the mistake. Instead, it will be covered up, or you will be blamed instead, since the welfare of the group must always come first.

5. Do you have any postgraduate education (internship, residency, or fellowship)? A residency would generally be done in a specialty, a fellowship in a subspecialty. Pediatricians, in particular, often take fellowships in such areas as allergy, adolescent medicine, cardiology, and gastroenterology, and it may be helpful for you to know if your doctor has an interest in any of these areas.

6. With which hospital(s) are you affiliated? If there is only one hospital in your area, this question may have no relevance for you. On the other hand, if there are several, it is important to know which hospital you would go to if the need arose. If one hospital is significantly better than the others, you may wish to choose a doctor affiliated with the best hospital.

7. Do you have any teaching appointments? A "yes" to this question should be considered a plus. Since teaching appointments are usually available only in cities with residencies at the larger hospitals and even then are very limited in number, you can't really hold a negative answer against the doctor. If she happens to have a teaching appointment, however, you can be fairly certain she keeps up with the advances in her field. You may also find that she has

more patience than the average doctor for questions, since she must constantly deal with interns and residents who stay up all night trying to come up with one she won't be able to answer.

8. Do you have any professional memberships? These memberships aren't significant in terms of the quality of the doctor's work, but they will give you some idea of his particular interests both within his field and outside it.

9. Do you participate in continuing medical education? All doctors do, but, again, the types of seminars the doctor has attended are clues to his interests.

10. Do you make house calls, and if so, under what conditions? Some doctors, even in this day and age, will tell you that they make house calls in certain instances. If you know what the conditions are in advance, you should be able to reasonably request a house call if they arise.

11. Do you accept Medicare or Medicaid? The answer to this question may be of no significance to you personally, but it will clue you in to the doctor's attitude about social responsibility and helping those who are less fortunate.

12. Does your office have the equipment to do X rays and lab tests such as cardiograms, EKGs, Pap smears, throat cultures, and urinalysis? Doctors who are able to do these tests in their offices may tend to use them more often, since there is a certain amount of pressure to pay for the machines and facilities. On the other hand, it is very convenient for you to be able to have X rays

or tests taken care of right at your doctor's office. If you are willing to take some responsibility for monitoring the doctor in this area and feel confident in refusing tests that seem unnecessary, the convenience of a lab on the premises is a real advantage. If the doctor does offer these services, ask if he subscribes to a private lab service that spot-checks his results for accuracy. If he does, you can be sure that he is concerned about maintaining a high level of quality.

13. What sort of medical records do you keep? There is a system called the Problem-Oriented Medical Record that I think is especially good. There's no point in explaining how it works here, but you can give the doctor an extra point if he uses it. Give him extra points for typed records also, since they tend to be more complete and are certainly easier to read. You can even ask to be shown a copy of an old record so that you can see how thorough it is.

14. Do you see patients by appointment or on a first-come, first-served basis? Nearly all doctors now see patients by appointment only, but you will certainly want to know if this doctor is one of the few who uses a different system.

15. How long do you allot for a patient visit? The answer to this question will help you to gauge whether or not you will be able to get all the information you need from the doctor on any particular visit. If you know you are going to need twenty minutes to discuss your child's problem and the doctor schedules patients every ten minutes, you can ask for extra time when you call for the appointment. On the other hand, if he tells you that each patient is allotted thirty minutes and you need that much time to discuss what's on your mind, you will know that you need not feel guilty for taking up the doctor's precious time. You might also want to question the receptionist about how long patients usually have to wait before seeing the doctor. If it is an average of forty-five minutes and you're unwilling to spend that much time in the waiting room with your four children, you should make this clear from the beginning. The receptionist may make other arrangements for you, or you may need to consider another doctor.

16.   What do you charge? What are your fees for new patients, a new visit, and a return visit? If the doctor has a lab on the premises, you may also want to inquire about the cost of various lab tests that you may need in the future, such as X rays or a urinalysis.

17.   Do you have phone hours? Many doctors schedule a time during the day, usually early in the morning, when patients can call and speak to him directly rather than having to go through the receptionist and then wait for a time when he can call them back. This service can save you time and money, since it may help to eliminate unnecessary trips to his office.

18.   Do you expect payment at the time of the visit? If you prefer to make payments with a credit card, you should also ask if the doctor accepts them.

19.   How do you handle insurance claims? Some offices will fill out the insurance forms for you, while others expect you to handle them yourself.

CONTROVERSIAL QUESTIONS

1.   How do you feel about breast-feeding? How long were your children breast-fed? Almost all doctors in practice today will tell you that they favor breast-feeding. The answer to the second part of this question will give you a better idea of how committed to nursing the doctor really is, so you shouldn't feel hesitant about asking. Most of what I know about the practical aspects of breast-feeding I learned from my wife and her experiences nursing each of our eleven children, not from what I've read on the subject, and certainly not from medical school. Obviously, not every doctor is going to have this much family experience with breast-feeding, but if the answer is that each of the doctor's three children was nursed for six weeks, you'll know that "breast is best" is a handy slogan, not a statement of personal conviction. Should you run into problems with breast-feeding, you won't be able to count on this doctor for support (or even, possibly, accurate information) to see you through. Once you have opened up this can of worms, the doctor may volunteer information about involvement with La Leche League or offer other evidence of a commitment to breast-feeding, which you will be able to consider.

2.   How do you feel about vitamins and nutrition? If these are areas that are especially important to you (and I think they should be), you will want to know that your doctor shares at least some of your views.

3. Do you practice any preventative medicine? If so, what and how?

4. Do you do any patient education? If so, what and how?

5. How do you feel about jaundice in the newborn? The answer to this question will give you some idea as to how current the doctor is on this subject. (For my views on jaundice, see chapter 2.)

6. Can you summarize in a few words how you feel about discipline? Undoubtedly, you have your own ideas about how to discipline your children, and your doctor's methods don't really matter to you. However, the answer to this question may give you some indication of how the doctor will deal with *you*. If he's a strong authoritarian who believes there is little room for negotiation, he may very well expect you to adhere to the letter of his law when it comes to medical care.

7. How would you feel if I chose not to follow your advice or give my child a medication you prescribed? This is probably the single most important question you can ask. Again, the response will tell you whether or not the doctor would have an adult-adult or adult-child relationship with you. She should express a willingness to discuss medical matters with you on an equal basis and respect your wishes. Don't just listen to her words, however, since her facial expressions and body language will tell you at least as much about her true feelings as what she says.

8. How would you feel if I wanted to get a second opinion? If the doctor answers this question defensively, saying something like, "Don't you trust me?" or "Aren't you going to rely on my judgment and skill?" beware. He should be confident enough to not feel threatened by the prospect of having his work subjected to the scrutiny of his peers.

If you move frequently and prefer to carry your medical records with you rather than having to have them mailed to your new physician later, this is the time to let the doctor know. The original records are the doctor's to keep, but you are entitled to a copy of them. Personally, I feel that the medical records you keep for your children will be more complete and informative than your doctor's records, but it is within your rights as a patient to have your records travel with you if you so choose.

Since it is unrealistic to expect that any doctor will be able to meet all of your needs, a contract may help both you and the doctor in arriving at a mutual understanding of your expectations. Of course, if you are for some reason unable to negotiate a contract that satisfies you both, you should not enter into a relationship with that doctor.

Evaluating Your Doctor

If you already have an established relationship with a doctor and want to evaluate the care you are receiving, you have a tricky task before you. Several studies have attempted to pin down the qualities that make a good doctor, but since the view of any doctor differs from one patient to the next, the results are usually vague. No single criterion has ever been established to define the "good" physician. Furthermore, there does not seem to be any correlation between such factors as whether or not the doctor attended top schools and/or graduated at the top of his class and whether or not he is considered a good doctor by his patients. However, a study conducted by Dr. Gordon Deckert of the University of Oklahoma has found that four basic qualities set the best doctors apart from the rest.[1] These are:

1. He is skilled at getting the patient involved in the healing process. Ultimately, you are the only one who can make yourself well, not your doctor. If he recognizes this and treats you accordingly, he will be more effective. While not essential, it's also nice if your child's doctor is sufficiently tuned in to children to be able to help your child feel that she is a participant in the healing process, too. This might be as simple as explaining to the child—in terms she can understand—why she needs to take a particular kind of medicine, or what she needs to do to get well.

2. He explains the disease process in a way that the patient understands. Interestingly enough, it may not even matter whether the doctor provides the correct information, as long as he takes the time to explain what is going on in the body so that the patient feels he understands. No one knows for certain why this is so important, but perhaps understanding what is happening helps to marshal one's mental faculties to combat the disease, which in turn speeds recovery. If your child is the patient, it is helpful if the doctor explains the disease process so that both of you feel you understand.

3. He is appropriately nurturing. Family practitioners have been accused of being overly nurturing: we put our arms around you, give you advice even when you aren't looking for it, and are happy to discuss anything that's on your mind. I'm not convinced this is a negative quality, but you have to find the level of closeness that is most comfortable for you. At the very least, the doctor should listen attentively to your concerns, try to understand your viewpoint and answer your questions. He should also be generally supportive of you as a parent and able to reassure you when you are worried. A doctor with whom you have little rapport or communication is not nurturing enough.

4. The doctor himself is healthy, both physically and mentally.

I think you also should consider the following factors:

Does he speak in a language you understand? If his conversations are full of medical jargon you are not familiar with, you won't get the information you need. It's fine for him to use technical terms if you can effectively communicate on that level, but otherwise, he should use terms you understand.

Is the doctor forthcoming with helpful information on the problems that you need help with? You will undoubtedly have questions that relate to your child's growth and development that are not strictly about medical problems. For example, you may want your doctor's advice on nutrition, toilet training, or sleep habits, and it may be important for you to know that he'll take the time to discuss these things with you. I think you should also realize, however, that your doctor is probably not an expert in these areas, and he may have ideas that clash with your own. If his advice on any particular topic seems inappropriate to you, reject it and find your own way. After all, your doctor cannot possibly know your family and your child the way you do, so he cannot know what is right for you in every instance.

Does the doctor emphasize a natural approach to healing? As I've noted before, the vast majority of childhood illnesses will cure themselves. Many times all you really need from your doctor is reassurance that this is indeed one of those times. You *don't* need a physician who relies heavily on *unnecessary* drug therapy and lab tests.

Does he tend to treat symptoms or to look for the underlying disease that causes the symptoms? If you want to get at the root of a problem but your doctor is only interested in controlling symptoms, he's not the doctor for you.

There may come a time when your physician, even if he's very good, makes a mistake. Unless he makes repeated errors or shows an obvious lack of knowledge, this is not necessarily a reason to leave his care. After all, doctors are subject to human error just like everyone else. If you expect him to be perfect, you may end up hopping from one physician to the next for the rest of your life. Like any other relationship, the one between physician and patient takes time and a certain amount of effort to build. I know that in my own practice, some of the patients I am closest to are ones with whom I made a mistake. Because they were open-minded enough to come back and tell me about it, I was able to learn from them, and I appreciated that. I think they, in turn, appreciated my willingness to be open and honest about being wrong. So while you can't expect perfection, you should expect your doctor to handle himself well in the event that you do confront him with a mistake. He should be willing to consider the facts of the case as you present them and to apologize and learn from the mistake. If he becomes defensive or tries to put the blame for the error on you, he is not the doctor you should entrust with your family's care.

If your child's doctor ever treats you condescendingly or implies that you are incapable of understanding a diagnosis or treatment, beat a quick path to the exit. Watch out for these key phrases: "Leave it to me," "Don't you trust me?" "What medical school did you go to?" "Are you an R.N.?" and (when giving you a consent form to sign) "Don't worry about that." They're a sure sign that the doctor has no intention of treating you as an equal partner in your child's medical care.

How to Get What You Want from Your Doctor

Consider, for a moment, your part of the doctor-patient relationship. You seek out the doctor, take the time to see him, pay him well, and then take on the responsibility of following through on his advice. You put a great deal into this exchange, and you have the right to get what you want from it. That said, let me also point out that accomplishing this will take some assertiveness on your part. You have to be able to communicate effectively the information the doctor needs from you and to extract from him the knowledge you need to help your child get healthy.

The information you give your doctor about your child's physical condition is of paramount importance. Remember, a full ninety percent of the knowledge used to make a diagnosis comes from the information the patient (or the patient's parent) gives the doctor. Keeping this in mind, look at the following doctor-parent dialogue:

DOCTOR: "What seems to be the problem?"
Parent: "Well, Susie has been complaining about her stomach hurting."

DOCTOR: "Tell me about it."
Parent: "She keeps saying she has a tummy ache. It got a little better after we moved, but now it's worse again."

DOCTOR: "Was the move recent?"
Parent: "No, two months ago. I took her to a doctor in New York before, and he did some tests."

DOCTOR: "Do you know what the results were?"
Parent: "I'm not sure, but he gave me some pills to give her. They don't help much, though."

DOCTOR: "Do you know what they were called?"
Parent: "No, but they were those little white ones."

What has the parent told the doctor? Almost nothing. There's no accurate description of the condition, no information about previous tests, and not even an identification of the medication the child was given. This doctor has her work cut out for her, and it's going to be unnecessarily difficult to make an accurate diagnosis. Now take a look at the following exchange:

DOCTOR: "What seems to be the problem?"
Parent: "Susie has been complaining about her stomach hurting off and on for the past two months."

DOCTOR: "Tell me about it."
Parent: "Well, the first time it happened, we were standing in line at the grocery store. The color drained out of her face and she got very faint and then she broke out in a sweat. I immediately took her home and put her to bed. She was very thirsty, but after about an hour she felt all right again. Since then she's had three more episodes. Two of them happened before we moved, one just before dinner one night and then again around bedtime another night. Right after that we moved here from New York, and she was fine at first. But then yesterday it happened again, after dinner, so I called your office. Before we left New York I took her to our family doctor there. He thought the problem was excessive stomach acid, and prescribed Gaviscon."

DOCTOR: "Did your doctor do any tests?"

Parent: "Yes, he checked for blood in her stool and did an upper GI series, but everything was negative."

DOCTOR: "Has she been taking the Gaviscon?"

Parent: "No, because it doesn't seem to help anymore."

Now the doctor has some information to work with: a detailed description of the child's symptoms and when they occurred, the tests that have already been done and the results, and the name of the medication the child has taken for the problem. He'll be able to arrive at a correct diagnosis and proper treatment much more quickly than the doctor who's been given almost no helpful information.

GIVING YOUR CHILD'S MEDICAL HISTORY

To make sure your child's doctor gets the information he needs, keep these points in mind:

Tell him what the child's symptoms are, not what you think the diagnosis is. If you provide him with a handy, logical-seeming diagnosis before he has a chance to reach his own conclusions, he may not examine the problem as closely as he should. Don't assume he'll ferret out the information he needs, either: Tell him anything that you think might be relevant.

If your child has had a significant medical problem in the past or any condition that you think might be related to the current problem, give specific details. These should include the name of the illness and any drugs the child has taken, as well as information about any other therapy the child may have had. Don't assume that the doctor can send for medical records from another doctor; this may be too time-consuming to be worthwhile, and the records may arrive virtually unreadable. This is a time when the health record you keep for your child will prove invaluable, since everything you need to remember should be written down there.

When you are giving your child's medical history, it may be helpful for you to know that doctors divide it into these six categories:

1. Chief complaint: a short statement of your child's main symptom—whatever brought you to the doctor today.

2. Present illness: the full story concerning your child's illness, including symptoms he had last week or even last month that may be related. Try to keep this short, though; the doctor needs only relevant information, not a travelogue.

3. Past history: any of his prior illnesses, whether or not they are related to the present problem.

4. Family history: any significant health problems in either side of the child's family among parents, siblings, and/or grandparents.

5. Social history: likes, dislikes, school activities, hobbies, etc.

6. Review of systems: the history of any problem with each of the "systems" of the body: skin, head, eyes, ears, nose, throat, mouth, neck, heart and lungs, abdomen, kidneys, urinary tract, reproductive organs, extremities. These are symptoms, not findings from a physical exam. For example, a sore throat (noted in the patient's history), not enlarged red tonsils with pus on them (found through a physical exam).

Do your homework: Know enough of the language doctors use so that you can describe a condition accurately. Is your child's cough moist, so that there is some phlegm produced, or dry? Does his pain seem sharp, so that he doubles over when it occurs, or intermittent and dull? Be sure you use only medical terms of which you are sure, however. Not every severe sore throat is a strep throat, nor is every bad headache a migraine.

Be prepared to answer the following questions as clearly and succinctly as possible: (1) How long has your child had this problem? (2) What makes the condition worse? (3) What makes it better? (4) Has the problem changed, and if so, how? (5) What have you done about it and why? (6) Does anyone around you have the same problem?

GETTING THE INFORMATION YOU NEED

Whenever you see a doctor for a specific problem, you will undoubtedly have questions you want answered. Take in a written list, so that you don't forget them during your visit. By the time you leave the doctor's office you also should have the answers to these questions:

1. What is my child's problem? If it's a broken arm or a concussion, the answer to this question might be obvious. Some di-

agnoses, however, can be ambiguous, such as a "nervous stomach" or a "weak bladder." What, exactly, does that mean?

The answer may legitimately be "I don't know." If it is, the doctor should outline a course of action, such as lab tests or watching the child for other symptoms (in this case the doctor should tell you what to look for).

2. What caused the problem and how can I prevent a recurrence? Again, if your child has broken her arm falling down the stairs, the answers might be obvious. On the other hand, if the diagnosis is something like anemia, you need to hear the doctor's responses.

3. What should I do about it? This question is a doctor's whole reason for being, and you can rest assured that your doctor will answer it before you have a chance to ask. To make sure you get the answer right, take notes. If you're trying to concentrate on the doctor's instructions while your baby is climbing into the trash can and your three-year-old is screaming to go home, you're bound to miss something important. Write down what the doctor says, and you won't be left with incomplete instructions.

If the doctor uses a term with which you are unfamiliar, ask him to spell it out (write it down!) and explain what it means. *Your written notes are invaluable to your self-education and understanding of the disease and healing processes.* Don't neglect them, and don't be afraid to ask questions that will clarify anything that you do not understand. Without written notes, you may think you understand what the doctor is saying while you are in his office, only to realize later that for some reason you haven't retained the information.

4. When should the child's condition improve, and what should I do if it doesn't? Knowing the answer to these questions can save you unnecessary worry and expense. For example, let's say your child is in a car accident. She's been examined by your doctor, and possibly X-rayed, but no serious injuries have been detected. The next morning, however, she's feeling worse, and by nightfall, she's complaining so much about the pain that you are certain the doctor missed something. You take her to the emergency room, where she is subjected to another examination and possibly more X rays, but still no injuries are found. What your doctor neglected to tell you is that it is normal to feel progressively more sore for a day or two after an accident, and then to get better. Had you known this, you would have saved yourself worry and money, and—perhaps—exposing your child to unnecessary X rays.

5. What are the signs or symptoms that indicate that the problem is growing worse, and what should I do if they appear?

6. Do you want to see me again for this problem? Even if you don't really need to be seen again, the doctor may expect you to come back. This happens partly because return visits are considered good medical practice, partly because doctors are under some economic pressure to meet their overhead and keep their incomes up, and largely because doctors assume that you will want

to come back, if for nothing other than reassurance that your child is well. For some conditions, return visits are truly necessary, but many times they are not. If you ask him whether or not your child needs to be seen again, he will have to justify a return visit, both to himself and to you, and you will also have a chance to convey whether or not you feel you need one. He may conclude that it isn't really necessary, or that any follow-up could be easily handled over the phone.

7. Does my child really need this prescription? The drug your doctor prescribes may have have nothing to do with curing what ails your child. Doctors have learned that people hate to leave without something that shows they really needed to visit the doctor and that prescriptions are a good way to ensure that patients come back. Let's say, for example, that you take your child to the doctor for an upper respiratory infection. She suggests that you give the child vitamin C, and sends you home. The next time your child has a similar infection, you won't bother to go to the doctor, because you don't need her to get vitamin C. Prescriptions help bring in those patients who don't really need medical attention, and this, in turn, keeps the doctor's practice healthy. If your doctor prescribes a decongestant or cough syrup for that upper respiratory infection, you'll be more likely to return the next time your child is ill.

Often the drug your doctor prescribes will relieve the child's symptoms but do nothing to cure the disease. This symptomatic relief is not necessarily undesirable;

in some instances it's very important, like when your child is in pain or has a severe cough. Before you give him a drug, however, you need to know just what it will do and whether or not it is truly necessary to make your child well again. If it is intended just for symptomatic relief, you may want to try something else, even just tender loving care, if that seems sufficient. In addition, if money is a problem and you cannot afford the prescription, knowing that it will not affect the course of the disease will make you feel better about not having it filled.

8. Do you have any patient education materials available for this condition? Doctors nearly always have patient materials available, but we often forget to use them. The material is usually supplied by one of the pharmaceutical companies, but advertising is kept to a minimum, and the information can go a long way to helping you understand what is wrong with your child.

If at any time the doctor suggests that he would like to have a medical test done on your child, you will need to know the answers to these questions:

1. Where will the test be done, and by whom?

2. What is it for?

3. Do I need to do any preparation for the test?

4. What is the exact procedure for the test?

5. What do you expect the results to be?

6. How will the results change the treat-

ment? If they won't, why is the test being done?

7. When will the results be in and how will I be notified? The doctor may say that he will call you, or he may prefer that you call, but some arrangements to discuss the results should be made. He may tell you that he will only call if the results are positive, so that no communication from him can be interpreted as a negative result. This is unacceptable, however, as test results do get lost, even under the best circumstances. If this happened, your doctor might not realize that he never received the results, while you simply assumed they were negative.

8. What are the percentages of false positives and false negatives with this test? In other words, what percentage of normal people have results that indicate that there is a problem (false positive) and what percentage of people who do have a problem receive results that indicate that they do not (false negative)? These are important considerations. If your doctor does not know the answer, he should find out before the test is done.

Ideally, the doctor should provide the answers to all of the above questions without your ever having to ask them. Realistically, however, doctors are human, and we don't always function perfectly. If your child happens to be the fifteenth patient of the day with a sore throat and a cough, your doctor may be tired of reciting his sore throat/cough routine, and you may get the abbreviated version. So step right in and ask what you need to know. Your interest will snap the doctor back to attention, and you'll get the full story. Should you ever run into a doctor who refuses to answer your questions or is downright rude, I suggest you refuse to pay for the visit. You have come to him for information, and you have the right to get it.

There is one simple thing you can do that will ensure that you get better treatment from your child's doctor: Always take another adult with you for consultations. If your spouse cannot accompany you, bring a friend. No one really knows why, but in repeated studies this practice has been shown to result consistently in more thorough and humane treatment by the doctor. If you have ever brought another adult into the examining room with you, you've probably noticed this effect. Dr. Lowell S. Levin of the Department of Public Health in the Yale Medical School has noted the following advantages of this practice:[2]

1. A friend's presence helps you stay relaxed and focused so you can get what you want out of the consultation.

2. Standing up for your desire to bring a friend into the examining room lets your doctor know that you intend to stay in charge of the situation. You'll be less likely to feel intimidated, and your doctor may well take more time and communicate more clearly.

3. A companion can bring up concerns that you had discussed earlier.

4. A friend may be able to raise considerations neither you nor your doctor thought of (for example, your life-style,

your work environment, or the way a current family problem may be affecting your health).

5. A friend can help you recall the details of what the doctor said and what you agreed to do.

6. A friend can remind you of the practical aspects of your plans and decisions (who takes care of the kids, who drives you to the hospital to have a needed test, how to obtain the special heating pad your doctor recommends, etc.).

If it's absolutely impossible for you to bring a friend to the office with you, take a tape recorder and record what the doctor says. If he objects (but I doubt he will), just tell him you're making sure you don't miss anything important.

No matter how carefully you follow the above guidelines, you may find that you get home from a visit with the doctor and suddenly come up with questions you didn't think to ask. To prepare for this possibility, it's a good idea to tell the doctor that you may have more questions after you've had a chance to think over what she has told you, and ask when it would be convenient to contact her.

Handling Your Anxiety

When you're trying to get the best possible medical care for your child, you should be aware that doctors sometimes have a tendency to overtreat a child because one of the parents is exceptionally anxious about the child's health. The doctor who is confronted with an anxious parent has the choice of either subjecting the child to more tests and treatment than necessary or instantly becoming a psychoanalyst and trying to work through the parent's anxiety on the spot. Since it is easiest to order an additional X ray or blood test or write another prescription, doctors often take that route. If you know you're an anxious parent—either in general or in any one instance—make sure your physician doesn't base his recommendations on your feelings rather than your child's needs. Don't be afraid to admit you are anxious; even the most calm and reasonable parent can get disproportionately worried when a child is ill. I got anxious when my daughter Nina had strep throat and didn't recover as quickly as I thought she should. I was alone with her for the day, and when she fell into a deep sleep for several hours, I imagined the impossible and thought she had rheumatic fever and was slipping into a coma. My fears were completely unfounded, but even my training and experience didn't keep me from worrying. Let your physician know that you are willing to deal with your feelings separately and that you do not want him to treat your child on the basis of your anxiety.

Handling Disagreements with Your Doctor

Even in the best doctor-patient relationship, you're bound to run into an occasional disagreement. The way you handle these disagreements may affect both your future relationship with the doctor and your child's health, so they deserve consideration before problems arise.

Should you disagree with a course of treatment your doctor recommends, let him know. One of a doctor's worries is patient noncompliance, which often occurs because a patient doesn't agree with his recommendations. (The other reason for patient noncompliance is not understanding the doctor's instructions, but this should not be a problem if you have followed the suggestions in the previous section.) If you disagree with a particular therapy, voice your objections openly and promptly. It won't do you any good to go home with a prescription you won't have filled or instructions you have no intention of following, and the consequences could be serious if your child is truly ill. If you are worried about the side effects of a particular medication, or if the doctor is asking you to do the impossible, like give your squirmy, obstinate two-year-old a vile-tasting medicine four times a day, let him know. He may be able to allay your fears or prescribe a drug that needs to be given less often. There may also be times when you're doubtful about the doctor's suggested course of action but are willing to give it a try. If that's the case, tell him so, ask what you should do if you are not successful, and find out when you should get back in touch with him if things aren't working out.

Make sure you voice any disagreements calmly and reasonably. Don't attack the doctor; remember, you're trying to build a good relationship with him, not turn him into an adversary. Be prompt in your disagreement, too. One of my particular pet peeves is the parent who lets me ramble on about giving her child an antibiotic, and then, as I've got my hand on the door, informs me that her family never takes antibiotics. That's fine, but I need to know before I've covered the entire topic, so that I can suggest an alternative treatment without first wasting her time and mine.

There are two sets of circumstances under which you may decide you need a second opinion. The first of these is when your doctor comes up with a diagnosis that just doesn't seem right to you. If you feel comfortable with whatever health field that doctor belongs to, you should see another doctor within the field to see if the diagnosis is the same. On the other hand, if you have confidence in the doctor's evaluation of the problem but do not feel comfortable with the suggested course of treatment, you should seek out an opinion from another type of health care practitioner (such as a naturopath, chiropractor, osteopath, acupuncturist, etc.) who is trained in a different method of treatment. Let's say, for example, that you take your two-year-old to your pediatrician for his fourth ear infection in three months, and the doctor suggests that it is time to see Dr. Smith, an ENT (ear, nose, and throat specialist). Dr. Smith puts the child on another course of antibiotics, and when that still doesn't clear up the problem, tells you that he wants to schedule your son for surgery to place tubes in his ears. You get this funny look on your face, and he says, in his best Dr. Welby voice, "I understand. You want a second opinion." You admit that, yes, you do, and

he gives you the name of Dr. Jones, another ENT across town.

What's going to happen when you visit Dr. Jones? She's going to tell you it's time to put tubes in your child's ears. Dr. Smith wouldn't have sent you to someone who was likely to disagree with him, but more to the point, Dr. Jones is going to have the same exact orientation to the problem as Dr. Smith. Consult with virtually any ear, nose, and throat specialist in this country for chronic middle ear infection, and the recommended treatment will be surgical placement of tubes in the ears, because that's what they are trained to do. On the other hand, if you take your child to a chiropractor, he's going to have a different approach to the problem. He might suggest a series of chiropractic adjustments, massaging of the eustachian tubes, and a change of diet, which will give you an alternative therapy to consider. A naturopath will have a different approach, and a homeopath, yet another. (I have my own views on the cause of chronic middle ear infections, which are discussed in chapter 13.)

When you do seek out the opinion of a doctor in another field, keep in mind that as a general rule of thumb, his approach should be more or less accepted by others in his field. If it is not, you may be dealing either with someone who is practicing shoddy (and possibly harmful) health care or with someone who is one step ahead of the establishment. The trick is in telling the difference, and I think the key here is whether or not he is able to explain the treatment in such a way that the rationale behind it makes sense to you. If he cannot, or if his treatment involves a high degree of risk, find another source for your second opinion.

In her book, *The New York Times Guide to Personal Health,* Jane Brody sensibly lists five situations in which you should always get a second opinion: (1) the doctor is unable to make a definite diagnosis after three visits, and the symptoms persist; (2) the doctor says you have a serious, chronic, or potentially fatal illness, such as diabetes or cancer; (3) the diagnosis is a rare illness; (4) the doctor says the illness is on an emotional basis; or (5) surgery is recommended.[3]

If you're hesitating about giving your consent for a particular treatment, a doctor may use scare words to bulldoze you into doing things his way. At the top of the list of these scare words is "die," or "death," followed by others such as "totally irreversible," "brain damage," "rupture," and "hemorrhage." Doctors learn this handy little technique in training, when the surgery and procedures a resident gets to perform— and therefore learns to do—depend on what he is able to convince people to have done to them. As you can imagine, those scare words come in very handy. Now, I certainly don't mean to imply that either residents or doctors in practice con people into having surgery for which they have absolutely no indication. Many cases are borderline, however, and even in instances when surgery is clearly indicated, patients may be reluctant to consent to it. A doctor's powers of persuasion and those scare words are very useful at these times. Once a doctor is in practice, he no longer needs to talk his patients into certain treatments to learn how

to do them, but by then the habit is well ingrained and those terrible words are very effective in getting patients or parents to do things his way.

Before you condemn any doctor for resorting to such tactics, put yourself in his place for a moment. He's not trying to talk you into a course of action that he sees as potentially harmful, but just the opposite. He's sure he knows how to make your child well again, and the only obstacle in reaching that goal is convincing you that he's right. He wants to win you over as quickly as possible, not spend thirty minutes discussing the pros and cons of different treatments. He knows that if he tells you that your child has pneumonia and must be hospitalized immediately or else he might *die,* you're going to rush him right to the hospital. You are certainly not going to sit and argue, telling him you'd like to try large doses of vitamin C first.

Don't go flying out the door to the hospital, however, until you repeat what the doctor has said back to him, very slowly and with particular emphasis on that scare word: "You mean, if I don't take Tommy to the hospital right now, he's going to *die?*" Doctors don't like to hear those words either, and you may bring him up short. There's a chance he'll modify his position somewhat: "Well, no, he probably won't die, but he needs to be put on antibiotics and have his temperature and pulse carefully monitored to keep him out of danger." At this point you'll get a better idea of the care the child really needs, and whether or not a hospital stay is absolutely indicated. Forced to consider carefully what he is saying, your doctor may come up with an alternative that would be better for both you and your child.

If you do end up at the hospital after all, remember that the consent form you sign does not give your doctor or the hospital staff permission to do anything they like to your child. You don't lose your right to a say in your child's health care just because he's been admitted to the hospital. To make sure your doctor and hospital staff understand that you want to be fully informed, write a line on the form stating that your consent must be received before performing any further tests or procedures.

At the far extreme of doctor-parent disagreement is the rare case that gets taken to court because the parents refuse a treatment that the doctor considers essential to the child's well-being. From what I have seen, the times parents lose these cases is when they have refused any type of recognized medical intervention on behalf of their child. When the child is seriously ill or has a life-threatening condition and there is a strong possibility of a good outcome with the treatment, the court will almost always find in favor of the doctor. On the other hand, if the parents have found a second licensed physician who will render care that

they consider acceptable, the court rarely intercedes on behalf of the doctor bringing the suit. If, by some chance, you find yourself in the unenviable position of fighting over your child's medical care in court, remember that you are always entitled to a second opinion from a physician of your choice, although it will be hard, at this stage of the game, to change medical fields. In addition, keep in mind that the more knowledgeable you are about the condition and the more evidence you have that supports your viewpoint, (e.g., studies from medical journals) the more receptive the courts will be to your arguments.

The standards I've set forth here are probably too high for any individual doctor to meet in total. Bearing this in mind, I suggest you use these criteria as guidelines, not absolute necessities, whether you're shopping around for a new doctor or rating the one you've already got. You'll have to take your own priorities into consideration, decide which points are most important to you and which ones you can be flexible about. Don't ever settle for a doctor who fails to meet your needs, though. There *are* good doctors out there. With a little effort you can find one with whom you are comfortable and can work effectively.

Summing Up: Your Child's Physician

....

1. Always interview a doctor before you decide whether or not your child (or you) will become his patient, asking both basic questions and controversial ones.

2. In addition to having the proper credentials, your doctor should be appropriately nurturing, explain the disease process in a way that you understand, and get you involved in the healing process.

3. When you visit the doctor, be prepared to give him the information he needs and to ask questions (refer to your written list!) to get the information you need.

4. Write down what the doctor tells you about a disease or condition and treatment.

5. Take another adult into the examining room with you if at all possible.

6. Voice disagreements with your doctor promptly and reasonably.

7. Get a second opinion when you need one.

Notes

1. Personal telephone conversation with Gordon Deckert, M.D., University of Oklahoma School of Medicine, Oklahoma City, Jan. 24, 1992.

2. Charles Inlander, M.D., Lowell S. Levin, M.D., and Ed Weiner, M.D., *Medicine on Trial,* (Englewood Cliffs, N.J.: Prentice Hall, 1988): p. 57.

3. Jane Brody, *The New York Times Guide to Personal Health* (New York: Times Books, 1982): p. 437.

Medications

How to Read a Prescription

On the occasions when your doctor prescribes a drug for your child, it is helpful to
be able to read the prescription. Because we
like to preserve the mystique of our profession, we write out prescriptions in what
appears to be an unintelligible code (and
often in notoriously unreadable handwriting). They are really not difficult to de-
cipher, however, once you're familiar with
a few abbreviations and symbols.

On page 306 are two examples, one for a
drug dispensed in tablet or capsule form
(fig. 1) and the other for a liquid medication
(fig. 2). In both cases, the patient's name
and date appear at the top, with the name of
the drug directly below. You should be able
to read the name of the drug. If the doctor's
handwriting is illegible, ask him to spell the
name for you, so that you can write it out
on another piece of paper. You may also
want to write it out phonetically, if the pro-
nunciation is difficult.

Some doctors use the metric system for
prescriptions. If yours does, then you want
to ask her to explain it to you, too. In either
case, don't be afraid to ask for help! You
should know exactly what your child will
be taking as medication.

In figure 1, the milligram strength of the
pill appears next to the name. This information is useful only if you know in what
dosages that drug is available, since you
cannot compare milligram sizes from one
drug to the next. However, if you are aware
that the drug comes in two-, five-, and ten-
milligram sizes, you'll know that a prescription for the ten-milligram pills is the
strongest dose.

Below the milligram size is the number of
pills or capsules to be dispensed. You
should always count how many the
pharmacist has given you. I think you'll be
surprised at how often mistakes are made.

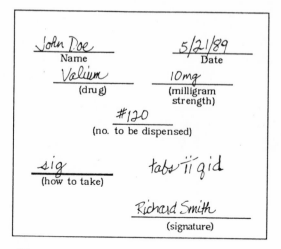

Fig. 1

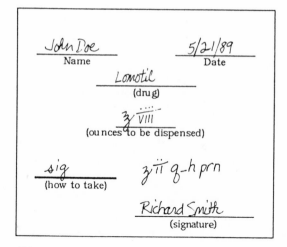

Fig. 2

These are written in abbreviations that follow "s.i.g.," which stands for the Latin for "take thou of." The abbreviations and their meanings are as follows (note that these can be written in either lower case or capital letters, as the doctor prefers):

qd	every day	q	every
bid	two times/day	h	hour
tid	three times/day	℥	ounces
qid	four times/day	ʒ	drams (1 dram = 5 cc = 1 teaspoon)
hs	before bedtime		
ac	before meals	tabs	tablets
pc	after meals	caps	capsules
prn	as necessary		

The prescription in figure 1, for example, is to be taken in a dosage of two ($\ddot{\text{ii}}$) tablets (tab), four times a day (qid). In figure 2, it is to be taken in a dosage of one ($\dot{\text{i}}$) teaspoon (ʒ) every two hours (q2h) as necessary (prn).

The prescription form also has a space for the number of refills you can get without having to see the doctor again. If you know that you are going to need the drug for an extended period of time, or feel that you will need a refill for some reason, ask the doctor for it while you are in his office. There are drugs for which your doctor will be justifiably unwilling to prescribe refills without seeing you again, but you are entitled to know this in advance and the reason behind the need for a return visit. For some drugs, the doctor is prohibited by law to refill the prescription, although he is

In figure 2, the amount of the drug to be dispensed appears under its name. The symbol for ounces (℥) is followed by a strange-looking Roman numeral that, as far as I know, is used only by doctors ($\dot{\text{i}}$ = 1, $\ddot{\text{ii}}$ = 2, $\dddot{\text{iii}}$ = 3, $\ddddot{\text{iv}}$ = 4, etc.)

Next come instructions on the dosage and how frequently the drug is to be taken.

allowed to write the patient a new prescription for the same drug.

Know Your Medications

You should learn as much as you can about any drug before using it. Every medication your pharmacist purchases comes with a package insert which contains information on its uses and contra-indications as well as any side effects it may have. These inserts are mandated by the FDA, and are fairly accurate, although not perfect. Since the pharmacist receives only one copy of the insert for each bottle of the drug he buys, whether it contains ten units or a thousand, he may not always have the information to give out. When this happens you can look up the drug in the *Physicians' Desk Reference* (PDR), which is a compilation of the inserts for all recent prescription drugs. (Some older prescription drugs are no longer in the PDR; your pharmacist has information on them.) The PDR is available in every library. I've found that in some communities the librarians will even read you the information on a particular drug over the phone, which can be very helpful if you're housebound with a sick child.

You should be aware of any interactions a drug might have with other medications. This is especially important if your child is seeing two different doctors (such as your family physician and a specialist), since one doctor may not be familiar with a medication the other has prescribed. (Your child's doctor should always be informed of medications another doctor has prescribed,

though, to minimize the chance of drug interactions.) Many pharmacies are now taking the lead in this area, with computerized records that automatically alert the pharmacist to a possible interaction between the drugs a person is taking. Often the computer programs used to maintain these records are also capable of keeping track of any drug allergies a person has and of any adverse reactions to a drug, provided you notify the pharmacist of them. If your pharmacy does not have such a service, be sure to ask the pharmacist about possible interactions if your child is taking more than one medication. Since the PDR tends to be inadequate in this area, your pharmacist is the best source for information.

There is also the possibility of interactions between prescription medications and over-the-counter drugs. Once again, your pharmacist is a good source of information, as are the package inserts and labels. If your child is taking a prescription medication, never give her an over-the-counter drug without first making sure that there are no interactions between the two.

In addition, you should get the answers to the following questions from your doctor or your pharmacist for any drug your child must take: What is the medicine's name and what does it do? How much do I give, how often, and for how long? Are there any special instructions (e.g., take the medication after meals, keep it refrigerated, shake it vigorously)? Are there common side effects or rare, adverse risks I should be aware of? (Don't rely solely on your doctor's or pharmacist's answer to this question; look it up yourself, since no one can remember everything about every drug.) If my child has a known allergy, might she be allergic to this medicine? Does my child really need this medication? Do the benefits outweigh the risks and the cost?[1] How much does this prescription cost? (If the drug is expensive and money is a problem, there may be a less expensive alternative.)

You might also want to ask your doctor or pharmacist whether the medication can be purchased without a prescription, particularly if your health insurance plan does not cover the cost of prescription drugs. Many medications that were once available only by prescription can now be purchased over the counter at substantial savings. These include some antihistamines, decongestants, cough medicines, pain relievers, antifungal agents, antidiarrheal agents, hemorrhoid preparations, and drugs to treat motion sickness.

When you take a prescription to your pharmacist, it's a good idea to ask him whether or not the dosage seems appropriate for your child. For many drugs, there's a wide margin of error in dosage amounts, but this isn't the case for every medication, and mistakes *are* made. In one study of 1814 prescriptions written by twenty physicians, twenty-one percent contained at least one error.[2] In another study done in a hospital just prior to the implementation of a new medication-dispensing system, 31.2 percent of the dosages were in error.[3] While your pharmacist will not know exactly how much of the medication your pediatrician feels your child should have, he will be able to double-check the dosage to be sure that it is within safe limits for your child.

You should also ask your pharmacist to label the medication with an expiration date as well as the name of the drug. Many drugs are good for years and can be saved for future use. In fact, if you have a medicine cabinet full of half-used prescriptions, it would be wise to sort through them, discarding any that have expired (if they are so labeled). Make a list of those you decide to keep, their dosages, the amount you have, and the date the prescription was filled. If you are given a prescription for any of these medications in the future, ask your doctor if you can use what you already have on hand. Since many drugs do have a very long shelf life, there is no reason to spend money on a new prescription if your old medications are still good.

As a doctor and a parent, I have tried to refrain from using any drug until after it has been on the market for at least two years. My reason for doing so is that some drugs that have been found to be "safe" in testing have later been found to have serious side effects occasionally. For example, the drug bupivacaine was marketed as an obstetrical anesthetic but its use was later restricted to nonobstetrical cases when it was discovered that some pregnant women experienced respiratory arrest, cardiac arrest, and even death after being given the drug. When tested on a relatively small group of people the drug seemed safe, but when used on a much larger scale, it was found to be potentially dangerous. Since the benefits of some new drugs seem to outweigh the risks, I have not always been able to stick to my two-year rule. However, it is something to think about if you are prescribed a medication that is new to the market.

How to Choose a Pharmacist

Since a pharmacist can be very helpful in providing you with information about the medications your family uses, it is worth putting some thought into which pharmacist you use and then making the effort to develop a relationship with him. Whether you use your local neighborhood pharmacy or one of the larger chain stores, there are several things to consider. Is the pharmacy conveniently located, is it open at convenient times, and are the prices competitive? Do they accept third-party payment, credit, or bank credit cards? Do they provide emergency after-hours or delivery service? Is the pharmacist informative and accessible? (If considering a large pharmacy, keep in mind that there may be several pharmacists.) Does he explain drug uses, dosages, and storage conditions? Are the prescription medications clearly labeled with instructions for use and, when appropriate, any special instructions or warnings?[4] In addition, of course, you should consider whether or not the pharmacy has the computerized files mentioned above, and if not, whether or not the pharmacist supplies you with information concerning drug interactions.

Generic vs. Nongeneric Drugs

There is no one, simple answer to the question of whether generic or brand-name drugs are preferable, and I'm not going to make a case here for one over the other. Instead, I'd just like to present you with a few things to think about and perhaps raise your level of awareness about the quality of the drugs you may buy.

When a new drug is approved by the FDA, the company that developed it has exclusive rights to produce and market it for seventeen years. After that period of time, other pharmaceutical companies can manufacture and market the drug. For this reason, most drugs that have been on the market for more than seventeen years are manufactured by a number of different pharmaceutical companies, and the products may vary from one company to the next. In an effort to find out whether or not medications manufactured by different companies are comparable, investigators at Columbia University conducted a study of the drug digoxin, a heart medication that is made by approximately 130 different companies, including the original manufacturer.[5] The investigators looked at several different brands of digoxin, and found that, depending on the manufacturer, the amount of the drug contained in each pill could vary from as little as 12 percent to as much as 276 percent of the amount specified on the label. With this in mind, picture this scenario:

Mrs. Smith's doctor determines that her child, Tommy, has a cardiac irregularity and should take the drug digoxin to control his symptoms. Mrs. Smith takes the prescription to her local pharmacy, and the pharmacist fills it with a generic digoxin that contains only .125 milligrams of the drug in each pill, even though the tablet is marked 0.25 milligrams. Several weeks later Mrs. Smith brings Tommy in for a follow-up evaluation. The doctor decides to increase the dosage to two pills, since Tommy's condition has not significantly improved.

Mrs. Smith's supply of the drug is a little low, so the doctor gives her a new prescription. Because it is more convenient for her on this particular day, Mrs. Smith has the prescription filled at a pharmacy close to the doctor's office, rather than at her usual drugstore. This pharmacy happens to stock a generic digoxin that actually contains .5 milligrams per pill. Since Mrs. Smith is doubling the number of pills she is giving her son, as per the doctor's instructions, Tommy's dosage will now suddenly increase *eightfold*. The consequences could be severe, even life-threatening. If Mrs. Smith had been given the brand-name digoxin, she would be assured of getting the same amount of the drug no matter what drugstore she used. But because she's buying generics, there's no way she can be certain she's receiving the same dosage of the drug in each prescription she buys. And even if she used the same drugstore every time she had Tommy's prescription refilled, there's no guarantee her pharmacy won't switch to a different manufacturer of generic digoxin at some point.

In addition to the problem of drug potency, there is the question of the variation in the other ingredients that make up any given medicine, such as the fillers, binders, dispersing agents, flavorings, coloring matter, and the capsule. Generics are not required to use the same inert ingredients as the original brand-name product, but these ingredients can have an effect on how well the drug works. In order for a medication to be of any use, it must disintegrate and be absorbed into the bloodstream. A major drug company will usually have done tests to ensure that this is the case. Some of the smaller generic houses may not go to the expense of doing so, however. As Drs. Milton Silverman and Philip R. Lee noted in *Pills, Profits and Politics*, there have been antibiotics that were combined with "inert" ingredients that actually blocked the absorption of the active ingredient, and some drug manufacturers have used formulations that quickly decomposed on the pharmacist's shelf, or have mixed up labels so that drugs have been distributed under the name of a completely different medication. Even more disturbing, there have been cases of drugs contaminated with dangerous or even lethal ingredients.[6]

Obviously, then, there can be some serious problems with the quality control of generic drugs. The FDA is trying to address this problem and has introduced criteria that generic drugs must meet before they are marketed. These include requirements that the drug contain the same active ingredient as the original drug (inert ingredients may vary, however); be the identical strength and dosage form and have the same route of administration; have the same indications, precautions, and labeling instructions; be bioequivalent (have the same rate and extent of absorption); meet the same batch-to-batch requirements for identity, strength, purity, and quality; and be produced under the same good manufacturing practice regulations of the FDA as the original drug. While these guidelines should help to standardize generic products, they are no guarantee that generic drugs will be exact reproductions of the pioneer drugs nor do they ensure that generic houses will have good internal quality control.

It should also be noted, however, that most generic drugs are *not* manufactured by small, fly-by-night companies that must cut costs at every opportunity. In fact, approximately eighty percent of generic drugs are produced by the fifty-nine major pharmaceutical companies that bring us brand-name medications. Finding out the manufacturer of a generic from your pharmacist may help you to decide whether or not to use it. A large, reputable company will in all likelihood produce a safe, effective product that may be considerably cheaper than the brand-name medication.

Cost, in fact, is the major argument in favor of buying a generic drug. Using a generic can save you, on the average, about seventy percent of the cost of a brand-name drug. This is not a hard-and-fast rule, however, since you will sometimes find more variation between the cost of a drug from one pharmacy to the next than between the cost of a generic and a brand-name at any one pharmacy. For example, a pharmacy might use a particular high blood pressure medication as a loss leader (pricing it low to bring in customers), so that it is as cheap—or even cheaper—than their generic version of the same drug. At another pharmacy, another drug may be used as a loss leader. For this reason, you can't assume that the generic is always the least expensive choice, nor, for that matter, that

a pharmacy's low price on one brand-name drug will mean they have similarly low prices on others. (Most pharmacies will quote prices over the phone, so that it is possible to shop around for the best deal.)

It is also entirely possible that the "generic" drug and the brand-name drug at any one pharmacy are exactly the same, except in price. For example, consider this scenario: One of the major drugstore chains decides that it needs to buy ten million capsules of tetracycline for its stores across the nation. They send a letter to the pharmaceutical companies asking for a bid on this order, and the company that wins comes in with a price of ten cents per capsule. Because the cost is so low, the chain's pharmacists use the drug to fill prescriptions that call for generic tetracycline and then price them lower than prescriptions that call for the drug by brand name. Obviously, you'd benefit from requesting the generic in this case, since you'd be getting the same drug as you would if you asked for the brand name, but at a lower price.

There is, then, no simple answer to the question of whether you are better off using a generic or brand-name medication. In some cases buying a generic may mean getting a product of inferior quality—with the possibility of serious consequences—and in others it may simply mean saving money. One thing you may want to consider is the drug's purpose. If it's a pain reliever or cough suppressant or other medication that relieves an annoying but nonserious symptom, you may be willing to buy the generic and take the small chance that the drug will be ineffective. On the other hand, if the drug is essential to the life of the person it was prescribed for, you don't want to take any chances. Another consideration may be how long the drug is going to be used. If it's a short-term, one-time prescription, the extra two or three dollars you pay for the brand name might not be significant. If the drug is one that you'll be purchasing for several months to several years, it might be worth the time and effort required to seek out a good-quality generic. (Another way to save money on a drug that you'll be using this way is to buy it in large quantities—assuming it has a long shelf life—since the more you purchase at a time, the lower the cost per unit will be.)

You should also be aware that most physicians are biased in favor of brand-name drugs. This is due in part to the influences of the pharmaceutical companies, who put a lot of effort into promoting their brand-name products. Their sales pitches to physicians may include insinuations that any generic on the market is of inferior quality (whether or not this is the case), and since doctors do want to prescribe the best product, they usually play it safe and go with the brand-name drug. In addition, by the time a generic is available, a doctor has been writing the brand name for so long that it is simply habit to continue doing so. Your financial situation is not a major consideration for the doctor, so she takes the easiest course and prescribes the product with which she is most familiar.

Pharmacists are biased toward brand-name drugs for reasons of their own. They too are influenced by the extensive advertising and promotion done by the pharmaceutical companies, and they have the added incentive of a higher mark-up on brand-name drugs in many cases. Nevertheless, your pharmacist can help you make an educated decision on whether to use a generic or not, by telling you the manufacturer of the drug, the difference in cost, and any other pertinent information he may have. If you are a regular customer and have established a relationship with him, it will be in his best interests to serve your best interests.

Giving a Child Medication

Your child is ill, you've seen the doctor and received a prescription that you're satisfied really will do more good than harm, and you've had it filled at the pharmacy of your choice. Now comes the hard part: getting the medicine into the child. If you're lucky, the medicine will be something your child finds delicious and is happy to swallow without protest, but more often than not, he'll react as though you are trying to poison him. My wife and I have found that the easiest way to get medicine into our children is with a plastic oral medicine syringe (available at drugstores). Assuming the child is old enough to cooperate, we first give him the option of taking the medicine in a normal, reasonable way. If that doesn't work, we lie the child down on his back, place the syringe far enough into one side of his mouth so that he can't push it out with his tongue, and gently squirt the medicine in. (If you squirt it in too quickly, the child will choke, so don't be too forceful.) If you are using a regular teaspoon, place the medicine on the spoon, lie the child down, and then put the spoon on his tongue and hold it there until the medicine has dripped off and been swallowed. Your child will undoubtedly squirm and cry throughout this process, but it will take only about seven seconds. If you try to use reason and your powers of persuasion, all you will do is prolong your child's anxiety. I've seen parents spend an hour and a half trying to convince a child to take medicine, and it just doesn't work. If you lie to the child and tell him it tastes good, you'll erode his trust in you. Telling him the medicine is good for him will convince your child of nothing; it doesn't taste good and it doesn't immediately make him feel better, so how can it be good for him? If you try to disguise the taste of the medicine by adding it to fruit juice, you'll make the juice taste bad and may even compromise the effectiveness of the medicine, depending on how it interacts with the juice. Your best bet is to simply give him the medicine over his protests and get the process over with so that you can both get on with your other activities.

Dr. Edward M. Friedman, Jr., of Mt. Kisco, New York, has passed along this tip for getting eyedrops into a child's eye: Have the child close her eyes and tip her head back. Place the drops in the small depressions adjacent to the nose, and then have her open her eyes. The drops will slide down into the eyeballs, just where you want them.

Medications and Supplies

The following is a list of medications and supplies that are helpful to have on hand when treating the minor illnesses and injuries of childhood.

1. Chlorpheniramine Maleate (Chlor-Trimeton, Dristan) or Benadryl: Antihistamines that are available in various dosages and in liquid and pill form. Good for bee stings, itching from poison ivy or chicken pox. Cause drowsiness.

2. Vitamin C: When using as a drug (e.g., for colds or lung infections), I generally recommend about fifty-seven milligrams per pound of body weight per day. Since no toxic amount of vitamin C has been identified, I sometimes use much higher dosages.

3. Vitamin B_6: For relief of headaches. Start with half a twenty-five milligram tablet, gradually increasing by half a tablet every 30 minutes until you reach 100 milligrams or the headache disappears. This dosage is for a 50-pound child, and would have to be adjusted accordingly for a heavier child or an adult.

4. Allergy remedy:

Pantothenic acid	400 mg.
Calcium	1300 mg.
Vitamin C	4000 mg.
Bioflavinoids	4000 mg.
Betaine HCL	1 tablet

The dosages for the first four ingredients are the amounts a 100-pound child should take over the course of twenty-four hours. You should divide each amount so that the child receives a dose every four hours, since the body excretes vitamin C, pantothenic acid and bioflavinoids approximately this often. The amount you give in each dosage will depend on how many waking hours your child has each day. For example, if your 100-pound daughter sleeps eight hours, you would divide the dosage over the remaining sixteen hours of the day, so that she receives one-quarter of the total dosage every four hours. If your child weighs 50 pounds and is awake twelve hours a day, divide the dosages in half, and then split that amount into three parts, to be given every four hours. The last ingredient, Betaine HCL, should be given three times a day, with meals.

Both bioflavinoids and large doses of vitamin C are natural antihistamines; the other ingredients help them work. Once again, these dosages are calculated for a 100-pound child, so you will have to make appropriate adjustments for smaller children. The allergy remedy is good for relieving the symptoms of hay fever, bee stings, hives, asthma, or any other allergic reactions, and is safe for use by pregnant women and nursing mothers.

5. Peppermint tea or drops: Good for stomach upsets and cramps. When giving peppermint drops to a child, dilute them in water so that they will not burn the tongue.

6. Chamomilla: A homeopathic preparation for pain relief.

7. Hyland's Teething Tablets (see chapter 3).

8. Phenergan suppositories: For severe cases of vomiting (see chapter 5). Available by prescription only.

9. Ear drops (Auralgan): For pain associated with middle ear infections (see chapter 13). Available by prescription only.

10. Fluorescein strips or dye: For assessing eye injuries (see chapter 18).

11. Ipecac syrup: To induce vomiting after ingestion of certain poisons. Ipecac syrup works both by irritating the stomach and by acting on the part of the brain that controls vomiting. There has been some concern that ipecac syrup itself might be poisonous. However, the reported cases of poisoning due to ipecac have largely been attributed to accidental injection of fluid extract of ipecac, which is fourteen times more potent and is considered a poison. Syrup of ipecac may be poisonous also if used on a chronic basis over a long period of time. (See chapter 18 for information on administering syrup of ipecac.)

12. Antiseptic solution (Betadine): Good for specialized situations (e.g. impetigo, or when an obvious infection is present) when more than water is required to wash out a wound.

13. Burow's solution (e.g., Domeboro): A solution that is similar in composition to the body's tissue excretions. May be used to flush out the ears or, again, in specialized situations when more than water is needed to clean a wound. Also good for wounds that must be flushed out repeatedly.

14. Antiseptic ointment (such as bacitracin, Neosporin, or Polysporin): For use on

cuts or scrapes that are not healing well on their own, or impetigo that has not responded to treatment with Betadine. I do not recommend this type of ointment for routine treatment of cuts or scrapes, since it does cause minor tissue damage. However, in cases where healing is not progressing as it should, an antiseptic ointment will help.

15. Mild steroid ointment (Cortaid): Good for poison ivy, chemical irritations, and other skin rashes.

16. Assorted adhesive bandages (Band-Aids).

17. Sterile gauze pads or nonstick pads: For dressing scrapes and cuts.

18. Butterfly bandages: For holding cuts together as they heal. See chapter 18 for specific instructions on use.

19. Nonallergenic tape: This type of tape will cause fewer allergic reactions than regular first aid tape, although it is still possible to be allergic to it.

20. Ace bandages: These stretchy bandages come in two-inch, four-inch, and six-inch widths, and are usually used to wrap sprained limbs. They are also very handy for putting over another dressing on a child, so that he'll have something to pull and pick at other than the dressing that covers the wound.

21. Kerlex or Kling: A stretchy gauze bandage that is good for wounds on the head or ears, joints such as elbows and knees, or on the fingers.

22. Magnifying glass, tweezers, and a light: For removing splinters.

23. Three-ounce blue rubber ear syringe.

24. Stethoscope.

25. Otoscope.

Summing Up: Medications

• •

1. Learn as much as possible about any drug that is prescribed for you or your child, especially whether or not it interacts with any other medications.

2. Choose your pharmacist carefully and then build a relationship with him.

3. Generic drugs may not be of the same potency as brand-name drugs, and they may not be manufactured with the same quality control.

4. In some cases, the only difference between a generic drug and a brand-name drug may be the price.

5. A good relationship with your pharmacist may help you in determining which generics you shouldn't purchase and which you should.

6. Keep your medicine cabinet supplied with the list of medications and first-aid items listed in this chapter.

Notes

1. Robert H. Pantell and David A. Bergman, M. D., *The Parent's Pharmacy*, (Reading, Mass.: Addison-Wesley, 1982): p. 22.

2. A. F. Shaughnessy, PharmD., and Ronald O. Nickel, Ph.D., "Prescription-Writing Patterns and Errors in a Family Medicine Residential Practice," *Journal of Family Practice*, Vol. 29, No. 3 (Oct. 1989): p. 290.

3. Eric W. Martin, Ph.D., *The Hazards of Medication*, 2nd edition (Philadelphia: J.B. Lippincott, 1978): p. 93.

4. Pantell and Bergman, overleaf.

5. John Lindenbaum, Mark H. Mellow, Michael O. Blackstone, et al., "Variations in Biologic Availability of Digoxin from Four Preparations," *New England Journal of Medicine*, Vol. 285, No. 4 (Dec. 9, 1971): p. 1344.

6. Milton Silverman and Philip R. Lee, *Pills, Profits and Politics*, (Berkeley and Los Angeles: University of California Press, 1976): p. 139.

Chapter 18

Emergencies

*I*f your child (or you, for that matter) is to receive acceptable care from an emergency room, there are two things you must be aware of before ever setting foot in the door. The first is the mind-set of the emergency room personnel and the second is their legal responsibility to you once you have placed yourself or your child in their care.

Emergency room personnel may well be the brightest on the American medical scene: They are exceptionally well trained with their own residency programs and board-certification process, and they have their own journals and conventions to keep them current in their field. When it comes to snatching people from the clutches of death, they shine. It is little wonder, then, that these professionals are less than impressed with those who treat emergency rooms like clinics, coming to them with a sprained ankle, a crushed toe, or depres-

sion. They've been trained to perform miracles, not execute mundane medical duties.

As a result, you may find the emergency room staff a little condescending should you make the mistake of coming to them with what they consider minor problems. You know you're an intelligent, responsible person, but you can expect emergency room doctors and nurses to assume you must be dumb, irresponsible, and unreliable. You're dumb because you should have realized you were sick during regular doctor's hours, you're irresponsible because you don't have someone to take care of you in this particular situation, and you're unreliable simply because you're an unknown quantity and have never had the opportunity to build any sort of rapport with them.

Pair this attitude with the medical/legal obligations of a hospital emergency room and a disturbing picture emerges. The hospital is legally responsible for your care—

the diagnosis of your complaint, your treatment, and follow-up. The accepted procedure for your particular condition is not based on what is healthiest for you (as you might expect), but on whatever is required to cover them in the event of a malpractice suit. These requirements are a combination of medical protocol plus tests the malpractice lawyers have deemed important in that situation. In the case of a head injury, for example, most doctors are capable of clinically assessing whether or not a skull X ray is necessary. In the emergency room, that skull X ray is going to be done regardless of the doctor's clinical assessment, just to be sure the hospital is covered in the unlikely event the doctor is wrong and the patient decides to sue. The result is unnecessary tests that are possibly detrimental to your health.

Let's say, for example, that your six-year-old is experiencing abdominal pain with no apparent cause. Perhaps he has an intestinal virus. On the other hand, he may have appendicitis—I'm just not sure. If your child were my patient and you brought him in for an office visit, I might suggest that we watch the situation for the next eight to ten hours to evaluate it further. Because I know you, I'm reasonably sure I can point out any danger signs and feel confident that you'll call me later, at which time we can arrive at the appropriate course of action. If you're being treated in an emergency room, however, this kind of doctor-patient cooperation can't happen.

Instead, your child will be subjected to a urinalysis, blood test, abdominal X ray, and possibly an ultrasound to ensure that the proper diagnosis is made on the spot. The hospital can't take the chance that you'll take your child home and let his appendix rupture. Because you're an unknown—and very possibly not terribly bright or responsible—you might just do so, and they have to be legally covered in that event. If you doubt that you could be so misjudged, just think back on the last time you were in an emergency room. How were you treated?

It *is* possible to visit an emergency room and escape unnecessary testing and procedures. In order to do so, however, you have to be prepared to take back some of that legal responsibility. In the example above, you would want to question the reasons the doctor wants to perform the various tests to see if the results will alter either his diagnosis or the treatment he will recommend. If it becomes clear that any of the tests will simply confirm what he already knows, you should refuse them because he is only covering himself legally, not guarding your health.

Should you decide that some or all of the tests are medically unnecessary, you can sign a release refusing them and absolving the hospital of the responsibility for not having done the tests.

Bringing a child to the emergency room presents added complications. The hospital may try to separate you from your child on the grounds that your presence during treatment will upset the child. This makes no sense at all; your child will fare better if you are there to comfort him and ensure that he is treated with respect. Just look at it from your child's point of view: He's hurt, maybe bleeding, and has just been sped to the hospital. You rush in and hand him over to a complete stranger who takes him to a room he's never seen before, straps him to a table, and begins poking around right where he already hurts. He's terrified, and no wonder. Your presence in the waiting room is not doing him any good at all. He needs you to comfort him.

Nevertheless, many hospitals persist in this unenlightened policy. If you object to the separation, the emergency room personnel may try to intimidate you with claims that it is against state law, or at least against hospital policy, for you to accompany your child. No state has a law that calls for separating a parent from a child undergoing medical examination and treatment. It may be against hospital policy for you to stay with your child, but that policy can be changed on the spot, if necessary.

Should you find yourself confronted with a particularly obstinate hospital official, conjure up a tear, clutch your baby in your arms and ask in a loud voice, "You mean I have to take my baby home to *die*?" The word "die" will send everyone scurrying around for permission to bring you into the examining room. If they are still unwilling to change their rule, you can be certain that the hospital personnel have evaluated the situation enough to satisfy themselves that whatever the problem is, it is not truly an emergency. They are confident that no harm will come to your child if you simply wait until you are able to arrange for care by your regular doctor.

If drama isn't your style, you can turn up the heat another way. Ask for a signed release stating that your child is being refused medical treatment because you won't agree to separation. Only the hospital administrator can authorize such a release, and it is highly unlikely that any doctor or nurse will go to this extreme simply to keep you away from your child during medical treatment. If by some chance they do, and the hospital is willing to sign the release, you can rest assured that your child does not require immediate care. Remember, the hospital is legally responsible for your child's care from the moment you set foot in that emergency room. If they choose to refuse treatment, they are obviously sure that doing so won't land them in court. No hospital is going to run the risk of a lawsuit because they refused care to a child who needed it, particularly if the only thing preventing them from giving treatment was a desire to separate the child from the parent.

As a parent, you have the responsibility to ensure that your child receives compassionate care from the medical personnel. Your child's physical and emotional well-being depend on fulfilling that responsibility, particularly in an emergency situation. Don't let yourself be intimidated.

Another thing you should realize about a hospital's legal responsibilities is that any public hospital is required by law to accept you as a patient, regardless of your ability to pay. Public hospitals must display a sign saying that you may apply to the Hill-Burton Act if you're unable to pay (there won't be any such sign in a private hospital). Private hospitals have the right to refuse care for any reason they choose, if they are so inclined.

The remainder of this chapter will deal with conditions that commonly send parents speeding to the emergency room. Most of them are not life-threatening nor do they pose a danger of long-term negative consequences. People have come to view some situations as emergencies because they do require some medical attention and a visit to the emergency room may seem like the only way to get that care. This is especially true when accidents occur or conditions arise after regular doctor's hours. You may understandably feel you have no choice but to dash to the hospital when your child smashes his finger in the car door or slices his leg open at nine P.M. However, in these two cases and many others, there are alternatives. You can effectively treat some conditions entirely at home, while others can be dealt with at home initially and followed up with a visit to the child's doctor.

Of course, sometimes you or your child may need the services of an emergency room. I hope you never confront a true medical emergency, but if you do, the advice that follows should help you to minimize the trauma to you and your child and afford your child the best medical care.

ANIMAL BITES. Children get bitten by dogs more often than by any other animal, and the major worry with dog bites is rabies. However, in this country it is relatively rare to contract rabies from a dog bite, although it is more common in some parts of the country than others. The major offenders in transmitting rabies are bats, followed by skunks, foxes, opossums, and rodents.

If your child is bitten by an animal, you should try to catch the animal. While it may be unrealistic for you to chase after some small creature when your child is hurt and upset, if someone can catch the animal, it can be examined for rabies. Whether or not you are able to do this, call your local county health officer. The officer will be able to provide you with statistical information on the frequency of rabid bites by that particular animal in your area. If it has been twenty-five years since anyone in your town was bitten by a rabid dog, you may decide to forgo the rabies shots.

You must make a decision very soon after the attack on whether or not to have your child receive the vaccine. The rabies virus is injected at the location of the bite. The virus must then travel from that site up the nerves to the spinal cord, and up the spinal cord to the brain. Once the virus reaches the brain and signs of rabies are apparent, it is too late for treatment. The location of the injury will determine how quickly the virus will travel to the brain; a bite on the face must be treated more quickly than a bite on the foot.

The treatment for rabies consists of five to six shots in the arm or leg, rather than the old dosage of twenty-one shots in the stomach. While it still has some side effects, the vaccine is not nearly as toxic as it once was. Health authorities feel that it is safe enough to give the series to one official in each county on a preventative basis, so that this person can become the rabid-animal handler.

Animal bites often become infected because of bacteria in the animals' mouths (in this respect, human bites tend to be among the worst). Whatever type of bite you are dealing with, the best treatment is to wash it out with *lots* of water (i.e., several gallons). If the bite is relatively small, you can give it a chance to heal on its own. If it is a large bite, you should see a doctor and start antibiotic treatment without waiting to see how the bite heals.

BEE STINGS. The sting of a bee, wasp, hornet, or yellow jacket can be potentially fatal for the individual who is allergic to them. There can be no allergic reaction the first time a person is stung, however; the allergy only becomes apparent with subsequent stings. If your child is stung by a bee, you should be aware that there is a significant difference between a reaction and an allergic reaction. A reaction occurs only at the site of the sting, but an allergic reaction will affect other parts of the body as well. If a child is stung on the hand and it swells to the size of a basketball, he is experiencing a reaction. If his throat closes up, he has trouble breathing, or he breaks out in hives on the rest of his body, he is having an allergic reaction.

If you suspect that your child is allergic to bee stings, it would be wise to have him desensitized. Your doctor may first want to do a skin test to determine whether or not the child is truly allergic; however, there are a significant number of people who do not react to the test but who do react to the actual stings. For this reason, a negative result cannot completely rule out the possibility of an allergy. In addition, approximately thirty to forty percent of those who test positive will not react when stung.

The newer methods of desensitization are much less dangerous and more effective than those used in the past. Until the process is complete, the child should wear a Medic Alert bracelet identifying him as being allergic to bee stings. He (or his parent or babysitter) should always carry a bee sting kit called EpiPen, an injectable dose of epinephrine, which will block the immediate reaction. The EpiPen is simple to use: The drug is premeasured, so that all you do is hit the leg of the affected child with the pen, and it will automatically inject the right amount of medication, blocking the reaction. It is usually recommended that an antihistamine be taken at the same time, since the epinephrine wears off fairly quickly. After using EpiPen, you should take the child to an emergency room for observation over the next few hours. He may need further doses of the drug to control the reaction completely.

EpiPen is available by prescription only, so you will have to ask your child's doctor for it. Make sure it is always available. If for some reason the kit is not available when your child needs it, an antihistamine such as Chlor-Trimeton or Benadryl will help control the reaction until you can get to an emergency room.

If your nonallergic child is stung by a bee, you can reduce the pain by wetting the area around the sting and rubbing an aspirin on it. When the analgesic effect has worn off, it can be reactivated by moistening the skin once again. Meat tenderizers containing the enzyme papain, when applied topically, also help to relieve pain and itching from bee or insect stings.

BURNS. There are three degrees of burns. First-degree burns are characterized by reddened, slightly swollen skin, and are usually caused by a very brief exposure to something hot, such as steam or a hot iron. Sunburns are also considered first-degree burns. Second-degree burns are characterized by blisters, swelling, and weeping. If they are deep, the skin may be a whitish color. Scalds from hot food or liquid, which are usually second-degree burns, are the most common type of burn seen in children.

A first- or second-degree burn should be treated immediately with ice, or, if no ice is available, cold water. This will reduce the heat in the skin. If you are treating a first-degree burn—the skin is dry, no weeping or blisters—there is no need to apply a dressing. Aloe from an aloe plant, not an aloe-containing cream or lotion, may be helpful. Second-degree burns should be treated with Silvadene, a cream that reduces the pain and speeds healing. Since Silvadene is available only by prescription, you will have to contact your doctor to obtain it. Both first- and second-degree burns should be carefully watched for signs of infection (increased swelling, pain, and redness; pus; fever). Break the blisters on a second-degree burn; this will help protect against infection by getting rid of the tissue fluid, which is a good place for bacteria to grow. Many people recommend applying vitamin E to first- or second-degree burns, but this is not a good idea. Vitamin E, or any other oily substance, such as butter or cocoa butter, will seal the skin, allowing anerobic bacteria to grow and increasing the risk of infection. Once the burn has healed, however, vitamin E may be helpful in reducing the scar.

Third-degree burns are characterized by dry, hardened, and sometimes blackened skin, such as occurs with flame, grease, or electrical burns. When a child has a third-degree burn, some parts of the skin will also have first- and second-degree burns. Third-degree burns usually involve a fairly large area of the body and always require professional medical attention. You will obtain the best treatment at a burn center, which is staffed with professionals trained in the care of burn victims, a medical specialty in itself. Emergency room personnel are generally not trained or equipped to deal adequately with third-degree burns. You should locate the nearest burn center now, so that you will not waste time looking for it if you do need it. If the closest burn center is far away, the center can probably arrange for transportation of the victim by helicopter.

Another type of burn that you should be aware of is scorched lungs. This condition, though uncommon, may occur if a child is exposed to a substantial amount of smoke or hot air. When the lungs are scorched, the tissue will ooze fluid just as burned skin does. This fluid can collect in the lungs and actually cause drowning. Scorched lungs are not easy to recognize, and treatment is difficult. If your child is in a situation where he may have inhaled a lot of smoke and toxic fumes (e.g., a large fire, or even a small one in a contained area), observation in a hospital is probably wise. If the condition does not develop over the few hours following the fire, no damage to the lungs has occurred.

For information on electrical burns, see "Electric Shock" on page 329.

CHOKING. As long as the child is coughing or making noise, don't interfere. If she becomes silent and unable to breathe, do the Heimlich maneuver. To do this on a child, place your fist in the inverted V just below where the ribs meet at the breastbone, then place the child face down across your lap and solidly whack his back with your other hand. This should dislodge the object that is stuck in the trachea.

Objects such as sticky caramel, a piece of paper, a balloon, or peanut butter eaten by itself will not be loosened by the Heimlich maneuver. In these cases, you must reach in and dig the object out. Sweep deeply into the mouth along the check with a hooked finger so that you do not force the object further down.

One study has shown that eighty-five percent of serious choking incidents involve peanuts,[1] which are just the right size to lodge in the trachea of a child under the age of about six. Pieces of balloons, paper, and other foods such as hot dogs, grapes, and candy are also common offenders. Larger objects that often worry parents more (such as coins) are much less of a problem. They may make the child gag, but anything that is much larger than a peanut is too big to lodge in the trachea, which is about the size of the child's little finger.

CONVULSIONS. Once your child (or anyone else, for that matter) has begun to have a convulsion, there is nothing you can do to stop it, whether the cause is epilepsy or some other condition. While the convulsion runs its course, you should put the child on one side to prevent him from choking on or inhaling saliva or anything else that may be in his mouth. Don't try to put anything in his mouth; the teeth are already clenched, and the only thing you will accomplish is to damage them or damage yourself if you let your fingers get in the way. You can loosen the child's clothing to make it easier for him to breathe, but beyond these simple measures, there is nothing you can or should do. The convulsion will last three to five minutes, which will seem like an eternity.

Once it is over, the child should be evaluated by your doctor, who may very well refer you to a neurologist to determine whether the convulsion was caused by seizure disorder (epilepsy) or another, more serious condition. I recommend that you consult a neurologist. He will probably be inclined to do fewer tests than your pediatrician or family doctor, since he will have a clearer idea of exactly what he is looking for. His first concern will be to rule out the possibility of a more serious cause for the seizure, such as a lesion on the brain or a tumor. A CAT scan, EEG, and blood test will be required to do this. Your family doctor or pediatrician may also be inclined to do a skull X ray, but it will only duplicate the information available from a CAT scan.

Most likely the doctor will come back to you with a diagnosis of seizure disorder and will want to put the child on medication. Before you make this decision, you should do some research on the drugs involved. Most of the drugs used to control seizures have numerous side effects. These medications and their side effects are listed in detail in the PDR. Whether or not you decide to put your child on medication will depend on the type and frequency of the seizures, your life-style, and how you feel about drug therapy, but regardless of what you choose to do, you should be as informed as possible before making your decision.

While drug therapy for seizure disorder is the accepted practice within the medical community, many alternative practitioners disagree strongly with this approach, arguing that seizures can be controlled through changes in the diet or environment. Chiropractors, homeopaths, naturopaths, and some nutritionists all have their own treatments for seizure disorder. While you are considering your options, keep in mind that drug therapy controls the symptom—the seizures—but does nothing about whatever is causing them. Since most medical doctors, once a diagnosis of seizure disorder has been made, do not bother to look further for a cause of the seizures, this is an area where a parent can make a tremendous difference by learning as much as possible about her child's disease. If you are able to identify the cause, you may be able correct the problem without drugs. To be fair, I have to admit that a good percentage of children who have seizures do need medication to control them, either because the cause cannot be identified or because it cannot be treated. If this turns out to be the case for your child, you will at least have the satisfaction of knowing that you have investigated the possibilities and taken the best course of action available.

CUTS. First, stop the bleeding by applying pressure directly to the cut. It is best to use a clean towel or rag, but your hand will do if nothing else is available. It will take from five to fifteen minutes to stop the bleeding.

Once you've stopped the bleeding, the most important thing you can do is to calm yourself down. Most cuts are not initially very painful. Your child will react with dis-

tress, however, if you are upset. Take a few deep breaths, fix yourself a cup of herbal tea, and review the information below. When your child sees you relaxed, even though her blood has just been spilling out in what seemed to be great quantities, she will realize that things aren't so bad after all, and she will calm down too.

Once you've regained your composure, take a good look at the injury. Wootan's theory of lacerations states that a cut shrinks by about seventy-five percent once the bleeding has stopped, and you will undoubtedly notice that the cut seems considerably smaller than it did when your child first entered the room, bleeding profusely.

Next, clean the cut by washing it with tap water. The force of the water will probably start the bleeding again, but unless a major artery has been severed (indicated by blood spurting from the wound), you can ignore the bleeding until the cut is clean. Don't be stingy with the water—again, it will take *gallons* to clean the laceration thoroughly. Your goal is to get out all the dirt in the wound. If there is ground-in dirt or gravel, you can even scrub it out with a clean, unused toothbrush, although your child will not be happy about this. You may be tempted to use an antiseptic solution such as Betadine or Mercurochrome instead of water. Resist the urge; water is the best cleaning solution for a cut. Antiseptic solutions damage the tissue cells as well as killing bacteria, which results in more debris in the wound, providing more places for the bacteria to hide and grow and, ultimately, an increased risk of infection. If you simply wash the cut with water and allow the body's own defense mechanisms to work, healing will be faster and more complete. Once the cut is clean, apply more pressure with a cloth to stop the bleeding again.

Most lacerations can be effectively closed at home by following the instructions below, which will allow you to forgo the trauma and expense of stitches. If you can't stop the bleeding, if there's a large amount of skin missing, or if the laceration is in a location such that it continually reopens, stitches are required. In these cases, it is preferable to sew up the cut within two to three hours, although this can be done any time within twelve hours. This is not an emergency situation. You have time to make the necessary arrangements and proceed calmly.

A clean cut on the face will usually heal very nicely if it is treated as described below with butterfly bandages. However, if you are concerned about scarring or feel that the cut should be stitched, you may want to have it done by a plastic surgeon. He will be able to stitch the tissue under the skin so that the scar is very fine and does not have the track marks normally caused by stitches.

If the cut is on the scalp, the wound often can be closed by taking a strand of hair from each side of the cut and tying them two to four times (fig. 1.) Longer cuts may require tying the hair in several places. Granted, this method will not leave as clean a scar as stitches would, but since it will be covered with hair, a rougher scar will not matter.

If the cut is on the tongue or the inside of the mouth, stitches will probably not be attempted. We generally choose not to stitch these cuts, since working inside the mouth (particularly the mouth of a small child) is extremely awkward, and because the sutures there dissolve too quickly to hold the tissue long enough for it to heal effectively. You can save yourself a visit to the emergency room or even your doctor's office and just let the cut heal on its own. (The exceptions to this would be if there are very large pieces of tissue hanging out of place or excessive bleeding. In these cases, stitches may be helpful.)

Cuts on the tongue or inside the mouth turn green and ooze pus as they heal (even if the cut has been stitched). Because of the normal bacteria in the mouth, these cuts always get infected. While the sight may be quite alarming, the infection will clear up without treatment in about four days.

Cuts on other parts of the body can be held together with butterfly bandages (see fig. 2). Butterfly bandages are sticky all over, so, like stitches, they hold the edges of the wound together as it heals. To apply a butterfly bandage properly, stick one side of the bandage to one edge of the cut, pull the cut together so that the edges of the skin are just touching—*not* overlapping—and apply the other side of the bandage on the opposite edge of the cut (fig. 3). The most common mistake people make with butterfly bandages is to overlap the skin slightly, which will leave a raised scar. Use as many butterfly bandages as you need to close the wound.

If your house is like mine, you may find that there is never a butterfly bandage around when you need one. My solution to

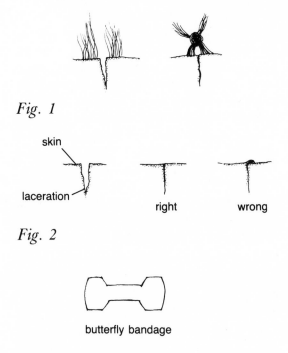

Fig. 1

Fig. 2

butterfly bandage

Fig. 3

this has been to take a regular adhesive bandage, cut out the center, and use only the sticky ends to close the cut. If you're really desperate, any kind of tape will do the job, although something designed to stick to skin, such as adhesive tape, will work best.

Once you have closed the cut, put a clean bandage or cloth over the butterfly bandages, so the child will have something to pick at other than the bandages that are actually closing the wound. Change this second bandage whenever it gets dirty, but do not disturb the butterfly bandages until the cut has healed. This will take about three to five days if the cut is on the face, or about seven days on other parts of the body. If the cut is over a joint, leave the bandage on for ten days. When the cut has healed

and it is time to remove the butterfly bandage, gently pull it down the length of the cut (not across), so that you don't tear the wound apart again.

Even large cuts can be treated with butterfly bandages instead of stitches, although they will not heal quite as quickly. As long as you are able to close the cut and stop the bleeding, it will heal. If you are treating a large, deep cut on a limb, you should wrap the affected area with an ace bandage after following the procedure above.

If the cut becomes infected, the skin will feel hot and turn red, and the wound will hurt and ooze pus. This should not happen if the cut has been adequately cleaned with water, but if it does, enclose the affected area of the body in a plastic bag and immerse it in hot—not scalding—water. If this is not possible because of the location of the cut, wet a washcloth with hot water, lay a piece of plastic wrap over it and place it on the cut. Put a heating pad over the bag to keep the washcloth warm, and a large towel over that to keep the heat in. This will increase the circulation to the cut without wetting the dressing. If the infection persists, you will need to follow up with a visit to the doctor for antibiotics.

Cuts on the hand or foot should be checked for severed tendons or nerves. To determine whether or not there is nerve damage, press a sharp object, such as a pin, lightly against the skin in several places around the affected area. If the child cannot feel the object, a nerve has been damaged. To check for severed tendons, have the child attempt to move the affected hand or foot in every possible direction. An inability to move the extremity in all directions may signal tendon damage. The child should be able to move each joint of the fingers separately. To test the top joint of a finger, hold the second joint as the child attempts to bend the tip. If he can bend the first joint only when the second joint is also bent, the tendon may be cut. Should you suspect nerve or tendon damage, or have any doubts in this regard, take the child to the emergency room and have the wound evaluated immediately.

DISLOCATED ELBOW. Dislocated elbows are fairly common in children between the ages of one and four, and are easily treated. The dislocation usually occurs when an adult is holding the child's hand, and the arm is somehow jerked, perhaps because the child trips or the adult is a little too forceful in pulling the child along. A child with a dislocated elbow will hold the arm close to the body and not want to move it, and may hold the shoulder very stiff, so that you might think that the shoulder is dislocated. To correct the problem, shake hands with the child, giving a little tug and rotating the child's hand outward, away from the body. You may feel a small click as the bone slips back into position. The child probably will refuse to move the arm for another thirty to forty minutes, but after this time he should not have any discomfort. There is no need to place the arm in a sling, unless the problem occurs repeatedly. If the elbow does become dislocated repeatedly, consult your doctor.

DISLOCATED FINGER OR THUMB. A dislocated finger or thumb may occur in older children, usually as a result of a finger or thumb being bent back or jammed in toward the hand. To correct the problem, grab the finger or thumb and tug on it to straighten it out. Once the dislocation has been corrected, check to make sure no tendons have been torn by having the child move the finger or thumb in all directions, and by moving each joint separately (see "Cuts" on page 325). The dislocation will result in torn ligaments, which will heal without treatment. However, the ligaments will thicken as they heal, so that you may notice that the affected finger or thumb appears broader than its counterpart on the opposite hand.

DISLOCATED SHOULDER. Dislocated shoulders are not common in children, although they do sometimes occur in older kids and teenagers. Should your child complain of pain in his upper arm, gently feel around the area to see if you can locate any sharp or rough spots. If you do, the problem is probably a fracture (see "Fractures" on page 331). If not, compare the two shoulders; with a dislocated shoulder there will be an indentation at the end of the clavicle. If your child is not too uncomfortable, you can wait for a day to see if the condition improves. If it does not, the child should be seen by his doctor.

DROWNING. There are about five thousand deaths a year in the United States due to drowning, and it is a major cause of accidental death among children. Deaths among older babies and toddlers make up a disproportionately large number of these deaths, probably because they can get into trouble in relatively small amounts of water, such as in the bathtub, or even in a bucket. The only real "cure" for true drowning is, of course, prevention. However, if your child suffers a near-drowning, the first thing you should do is clear the trachea of any debris by performing the Heimlich maneuver once. Don't waste precious time trying to clear the throat by hanging him upside down, rolling him over a barrel, or other extreme (and ineffective) measures; doing the Heimlich maneuver one time will be sufficient. Then resuscitate the child using cardiopulmonary resuscitation (CPR). There have been documented cases of children who have been submerged for as long as forty-five minutes who have been resuscitated and then recovered without damage. Even if the child has been under water for a long time, try to resuscitate him.

When the child is breathing again, take him to the emergency room even if he seems fine. If he has ingested a great deal of water (and this is likely), he will probably have to be admitted for observation. If the accident took place in fresh water, the water will be absorbed into the blood. This causes an abnormality in the surface tension of the lungs, allowing fluid to leak into the alveoli and resulting in fluid in the lungs. If, on the other hand, the child has ingested a lot of salt water, the body will secrete fluid into the lungs in an attempt to dilute the salt content. In either case, the child can actually drown in his own secretions. Observation in a hospital is absolutely necessary to recognize these reactions and to treat them as quickly as possible.

ELECTRIC SHOCK/BURNS. First disconnect the child by pulling or knocking him away from the source of electricity with something that will not conduct electricity (e.g., a rubber glove or broom handle). Once the child is disconnected, administer CPR to restore breathing.

Electrical burns are very different from thermal burns. A thermal burn covers a large surface area on the skin and gets narrower as it goes deeper into the tissue. An electrical burn affects only a small area on the surface of the skin, but grows wider below the surface. As a result, an electrical burn can appear insignificant at first, but the skin may turn black and begin to rot over the course of several days. It is important to observe the point of contact with the electricity for about a week. If the child's skin begins to turn black, arrange to have the burn examined by a doctor. Another sign that the burn needs medical attention is that the child's urine turns red. This happens because there has been significant muscle damage, causing excretion of a substance that produces the red color.

One type of burn that is seen only in children is an electrical burn at the corners of the mouth. This occurs when a child chews on an electrical cord or puts his mouth on the socket itself. You should contact your doctor to have this type of burn evaluated.

EYE INJURIES. The most common eye problem in children is a foreign object in the eye. To deal with these incidents, you should have on hand fluorescein, which is available in drop or strip form at pharmacies. When you place fluorescein in the eye, it stains any objects or scratches so that you will be able to see them. Simply shine a bright light in the eye and look at it through a magnifying glass or otoscope. A yellowish green area indicates a foreign object or a scratch. (You will be able to tell the difference easily.)

If there is something in the eye, the best thing to flush it out with is breast milk, but water will also do nicely. Once you have flushed out the eye, restain it with fluorescein to be sure the object has been washed away. If the object is gone but you are still able to see a fluorescein stain, the eye may be scratched. Put a patch over it for twenty-four hours, then check it again. If there is any redness or discomfort after this time, see an ophthalmologist.

If your child gets something large in the eye such as a stick or piece of wire, the first and most important thing to do is to calm your child. It is absolutely essential that you arrange to have an ophthalmologist remove the object. Don't dash off to the emergency room without making arrangements with an ophthalmologist first. A doctor who is not a specialist in eye problems is no more qualified to perform this delicate procedure than you are, and permanent damage may result if it is not done properly.

Eye injuries are often overlooked when a child suffers an injury to the face, particularly if the eyelid is swollen shut. There are instruments that can be used to open a swollen eyelid and examine both the surface of the eye and deep inside it, but they must be used by an ophthalmologist. Never try to force open eyelids that are swollen shut or allow a doctor other than an ophthalmologist to do so. If the eyeball has been lacerated, forcing the lids open may push the fluid in the center of the eye out through the laceration, damaging the eye beyond repair.

There are seven ways in which the treatment of eye trauma may be mishandled: (1) failure to examine the other eye; (2) failure to check the vision in the injured eye; (3) failure to consider perforation of the eye with external injury; (4) prescription of topical anesthetics; (5) prescription of steroid preparations if the diagnosis is uncertain or if herpes infection is possible; (6) use of any ointment when the eyeball is perforated; and (7) failure to ensure proper follow-up with an ophthalmologist.[2] If your child suffers an eye injury, make sure the doctor who treats your child avoids these.

FAINTING (SYNCOPE).   This sudden, brief loss of consciousness is not common in young children, but occasionally happens in older kids and teenagers. Fainting occurs when most of the blood suddenly drains out of the brain and rushes to the extremities. The loss of consciousness causes the person to fall, which puts the head and the heart on the same level. Circulation to the brain is restored, quickly bringing the person back to consciousness. Fainting may be caused by excitement, fear, exhaustion, nervousness, overheating, hyperventilation, and other emotional or physical upsets. In adolescents and some adults, fainting or dizziness may occur when they lie or sit for a long time and then stand up too quickly.

The only real danger posed by fainting is an injury from falling. A person who feels faint can quickly restore blood flow to the brain by getting his head down to level of the heart, which is accomplished by sitting down and putting the head between the knees. Once a person has fainted, you do not need to use smelling salts to arouse him; he will quickly regain consciousness on his own. An occasional episode of fainting is nothing to worry about, particularly if you are able to determine a probable cause. Unexplained, repeated fainting may be a sign of an illness, however, and should be reported to your doctor.

FRACTURES.   Fractures can be dealt with initially in the home. First, splint the bone with something soft, such as a pillow, by tying it onto the limb with a piece of cloth (you'll still need to support it with your hands when moving the child). Some people recommend using cardboard or a piece of wood, but a soft splint will conform to the bend in the bone. You don't want to straighten the bone, just support it. Most of the pain from a fracture is caused by a tearing of the muscles or a stretching of the periosteum, the layer of tissue that surrounds the bone and contains the nerve fibers; there are no pain fibers in the bone itself. Supporting the bone will reduce the strain on the periosteum and help tremendously in relieving the pain.

You should also check the neurovascular status of the limb, that is, the status of the nerves (neuro) and circulation (vascular). The circulation is easy to evaluate by checking for a pulse, making sure the limb is warm (or at least is not colder than the other, unaffected limb), and making sure the limb is not turning a bluish color. (If the circulation appears to be cut off, make sure the splint you've applied is not too tight.) To check the nerves, have the child close his eyes while you go up and down the limb, touching it with a straight pin and alternating between the point and the dull end. The child should be able to tell you which end of the pin he feels. If there appears to be a circulatory problem or nerve damage, you should seek immediate treatment.

Once you have splinted the limb, checked the neurovascular status and made the child comfortable, sit down, have a cup of tea, and review the information that follows. You have time to make some decisions. A fracture does not have to be set immediately. When I was in training, there was a hospital in the eastern part of the United States that set fractures every Tuesday. If you broke your arm on Wednesday, they would splint it and send you home until Tuesday. So that's how quickly you need to get to the emergency room: by Tuesday.

Granted, you probably won't want to wait around a week to have the bone set, but you do have plenty of time to call your doctor. Most likely he will refer you to an orthopedist, who will undoubtedly be unavailable for the next several hours because he's in surgery replacing a hip or performing some other delicate operation. You and your child will both be much more comfortable spending that time at home than in the hospital. There's no reason to rush off to the emergency room before the orthopedist is ready to see you.

There are two exceptions to the "set-it-by-Tuesday" rule. Fractures of the elbow and fractures of the thigh may require immediate attention. Problems of the elbow result because it is an enclosed space with blood vessels and nerves running through it. When the bone is fractured, very often a blood vessel will also tear, resulting in bleeding in the enclosed space, which puts pressure on the nerve. This pressure, combined with compressed blood vessels, can cut off the blood supply to the hand and cause permanent damage. Fortunately, you will be able to determine if this is happening when you check the circulation. If the hand is cold and blue and you cannot feel a pulse, the blood supply has been cut off. If this is the case, seek immediate medical attention.

Fractures of the thigh can pose special problems if torn blood vessels result in hemorrhaging into the thigh muscles. Because we usually wear clothing that covers the thigh, a hemorrhage in this area may go unnoticed, and, left untreated, can lead to shock and even death. Again, however, it is easy to detect this problem, simply by leaving both thighs uncovered so that you are able to observe them. If the fractured thigh begins to swell and becomes visibly larger than the unaffected thigh, or if the patient begins to show signs of shock (increased pulse, feeling faint or dizzy, becoming very pale) seek immediate treatment.

Once you do get to the doctor, the first thing he will want to do is an X ray to assess the fracture. While I urge you to strenuously resist all unnecessary X rays, in the case of a fracture there are some X rays that need to be done if the bone is to be properly treated. Preliminary X rays will provide the doctor with essential information. Fractures can sometimes be difficult to diagnose, if, for example, there is a hairline fracture or if the growth center (the epiphyseal plate) at the end of the bone has been fractured or knocked out of place. Fractures in children rarely require an operation to be set; how-

ever, if these growth centers have been affected, surgery may be necessary, and only an X ray will provide this information. (In an adult the epiphyseal plates are no longer significant, since growth has stopped.) Since each child differs slightly from all others, in some cases it may be difficult for the doctor to assess whether or not the epiphyseal plates have been affected, and he may want to X-ray the unaffected limb also in order to compare the two. This is a reasonable request, and you should consent to it. (If it turns out that the epiphyseal plates are involved, arrange to have a pediatric orthopedist set the bone if at all possible.) The joints above and below the painful area may also need to be X-rayed, since the pain from the fracture may mask damage to these joints. Once the bone has been set, another X ray will be required to determine that the bone is in the proper position.

After these initial X rays, the doctor may very well want to do more to confirm that the bone is healing properly. If he has good reason to be concerned about a particular problem and can specify to you exactly what he is looking for, you should certainly consent to the X ray. If he simply wants to see how the bone is healing, you should probably refuse it, provided there are no signs of infection and you are confident that your child's general health status is good. If your child is also recovering from an illness or other injuries, you may feel that further X rays are justified. There are no hard and fast rules in this situation, so you will have to evaluate your child's case on an individual basis.

When dealing with fractures in children, there a few additional points that should be kept in mind: (1) Incomplete or "greenstick" fractures (so called because the bone is split only on one side, in much the same way as a green tree limb would break) are the most common. (2) Bone healing is more rapid in children than adults, primarily because the covering over the bone grows faster in children. (3) The bones do not have to be set perfectly straight, because as the young skeleton grows, it tends to straighten itself out. (4) The increased blood supply and disrupted periosteum (the membrane that covers the bones) stimulate longitudinal growth, so that length inequalities will tend to correct themselves.[3]

Broken ribs are rare in children, but they do occur. In the average child, a fall or blow to the chest will not fracture a rib unless the trauma is unusually severe. If a rib is broken, you should be able to feel a rough spot on it, and it will be tender. We no longer wrap or "strap" the ribs, because this tends to cause lung problems, but the child should be seen by a doctor as soon as possible to determine whether or not the rib is fractured. This may require an X ray. If the bone is fractured, there is a possibility that the rib could puncture a lung, and only a doctor will be able to ascertain whether or not there is a danger of this.

Broken collarbones are generally treated by putting the patient in a harness that keeps the shoulders back and makes the injury more comfortable. The harness can be taken on and off by the parent as needed. Broken collarbones heal in two to three weeks. Broken tailbones do occur, but they cannot be set, and are best left to heal on their own.

FROSTBITE.   Frostbite is not common in children, since they usually have excellent circulation and are not often out in severe cold for long periods of time. However, if the child does suffer from prolonged exposure to extreme cold, frostbite can occur. Much like a burn, frostbite can destroy the circulation to an area. It most commonly affects the nose, ears, fingers, and toes, and will cause the skin to turn numb and hard. The most common mistake in dealing with frostbite is to thaw the skin too quickly. When the skin is frozen, it has no need for oxygen or other nutrients. If it is thawed quickly, however, the skin will suddenly need these nutrients again, but the blood vessels that supply them will still be frozen, since they lie beneath the skin. Deprived of these nutrients, the skin will die.

To bring a frostbitten area back to normal without causing damage, place the affected area in warm water (104°F to 108°F) or warm it with your body heat. If the area is thawed slowly, it will have a greater chance of returning to normal undamaged. As it returns to normal it will get red, and blisters will appear. If the frostbite is severe, it can cause the blood vessels to form clots, so that blood flow cannot be returned even when the area is warmed. The result can be gangrene, which is evidenced by the skin turning black. To help prevent gangrene, give the child 125 milligrams of aspirin (325 milligrams for adults) every six hours for three days. I do not normally recommend the use of aspirin, but it is justified in this case, as it will prevent the blood from clotting. You can also help the skin heal by applying an aloe cream every six hours. (I recommend Dermaid Aloe, available from Dermaid Research Corp., P.O. Box 562, Palos Heights, IL. 60463.)

HEAD INJURIES. A fall resulting in a blow to the head is one of the accidents that most frequently befalls children and one of the most common reasons parents seek emergency-room treatment. Their concern is, of course, concussion. It is important to realize, however, that a concussion is nothing more than a bruised brain. It won't show up on X rays, EEGs, brain scans, ultrasound of the brain, or any other type of test, except perhaps a CAT scan, and then only in very severe cases. This makes it extremely difficult to diagnose a concussion definitively, and even if it is somehow diagnosed, there is no treatment for it. Like any other bruise, a concussion will heal itself, given time.

So why do people get so upset about head injuries? Because a blow to the head can lead to cerebral hemorrhage, a life-threatening condition that occurs when a blood vessel inside the brain has been broken. The blood vessel will bleed into the brain cavity, which is already filled with the brain and the cerebral fluid. Since there is no room for the blood, the resulting pressure can force the brain down into the opening at the base of the skull where the centers for controlling breathing and heart rate are located. When pressure is placed on these areas they cease functioning, and the child may die.

A child with a head injury needs to be watched closely for signs of cerebral hemorrhage. While a headache is not uncommon with any concussion, a headache that persists and increases in intensity is cause for alarm. Similarly, a child may vomit with a concussion, but persistent vomiting is a sign of real trouble. Other signs of cerebral hemorrhage are a stiff neck, abdominal pain, fever, blurred vision, pupils of unequal size, confusion or abnormal behavior, unusual drowsiness, dizziness, stumbling or other problems with coordination, numb patches on the skin, bleeding or fluid draining from the ear, and seizures.

Children invariably seem to hit their heads just before bedtime or naptime, and the usual advice is to keep the child awake so that you can watch for signs of hemorrhage. In some cases the doctor may suggest putting the child in the hospital so that he can be watched closely. You can take him home, however, and even let him sleep, as long as you wake him every twenty minutes for the eight hours following the injury to check for signs of cerebral hemorrhage. Remember, though, that if you are waking the child from a sound sleep, some confusion, drowsiness, and even lack of coordination is to be expected and may be perfectly normal. This frequent waking will be inconvenient for you and annoying to the child, but it is preferable to staying in the hospital, where the child will have to be wakened frequently anyway and may be separated from you.

Most signs of cerebral hemorrhage will occur within eight hours after the injury, but they may not show up for as long as two weeks, although this is extremely rare. The more quickly signs appear after the injury, the more serious the bleeding is. If you suspect cerebral hemorrhage, take the child to the emergency room immediately. A doctor *can* treat a cerebral hemorrhage, if it is caught in time. The procedure involves putting burr holes in the skull, clamping the bleeding blood vessel, and suctioning out the blood to relieve the pressure. This process is not nearly as bad as it sounds, and once the bleeding has stopped, the crisis is over. In most cases the patient will recover completely.

If you take your child to the doctor for a head injury, he may tell you that the child has a skull fracture. While this sounds very serious, skull fractures do not usually require treatment and are rarely an emergency. A skull fracture is not necessarily an indication of an injury to the brain (nor is the lack of a fracture a guarantee that the brain has not been injured). If your doctor feels that your child may have sustained a brain injury, a CAT scan, not a skull X ray, is in order to determine the extent of the injury.

If the child has been knocked unconscious and is not breathing, you must administer CPR. You should be very careful about moving the child's head and neck if the injury is the result of a fall. Most CPR instructors will teach you to bend the head back, but this is not really necessary, and it may cause more damage if the spinal cord is injured. If the child must be moved, do so as gently as possible. Keep in mind the ABCs of resuscitation: airway (make sure it is clear), breathing (make sure there is respiration), and circulation (make sure there is a pulse).

NECK INJURY. Before you move a child who has had a bad fall, make sure he can move his arms and legs. If he cannot, or if he is unconscious, you must be very careful about moving him, because the neck and/or spinal cord may be injured. If the neck or spine is hurt, improper handling could cause further damage. In these cases the child should not be moved except by trained professionals, unless absolutely necessary. Call an ambulance and have the rescue squad put the victim on a stretcher and take him to the emergency room. Once at the hospital, make sure the child is moved as carefully as he was before. If it took four trained people to move him properly the first time, it will take four trained people to move him again; one X-ray technician won't be able to handle it. Stay with the child throughout the process to ensure that no one gets careless.

PAIN. Pain must be evaluated in terms of the whole child. While it is difficult to make any broad generalizations about pain, my basic premise is that a child who is sick enough to be experiencing a significant amount of pain will also have other symptoms. Other signs to watch for in a child who is not feeling well can be found in chapter 15.

When you are trying to determine the cause of pain, there are a few possibilities to consider. Head pain in children is usually due to an injury. Chronic headache is not a common symptom in children, and can have a variety of causes, from an allergy to a brain tumor. Chest pain in children is rarely a life-threatening problem, although parents do worry that it may signal a heart problem. If your child has chest pain that concerns you, you can reassure yourself by checking his vital signs and listening to his lungs. If the vital signs are normal, you can be fairly certain that neither the heart nor the lungs is involved. Chest pain is most often due to an acute respiratory illness and is usually secondary to a cough. It may also be caused by an injury to the muscles or bones of the chest. Another possibility is an injury to the esophagus caused by something the child has swallowed, or an object lodged just above where the esophagus and stomach join (if this is the case, the child may complain of chest and/or throat pain). If the child has abdominal pain, think of constipation first, or an allergic reaction to a food, gastroenteritis, or a trauma to the abdominal region. Babies may have colic, and children ages two to five, a urinary tract infection. In teenage girls, menstrual cramps, ovulation or pregnancy may cause abdominal pain. In teenage boys, testicular problems may be the cause. (See chapter 5 for more on abdominal pain).

POISONING. The most commonly ingested poisonous substances are plants, followed by soaps, detergents and cleansers, cold medicines and other medications that might be around the house, perfume, vitamins and minerals, aspirin, and household cleaners and products. If your child has swallowed a poison, the first thing you must do is determine what it was. *Do not induce vomiting* if the substance was lye

(oven cleaner, drain opener, dishwasher detergent, hair straighteners, some laundry detergents) or acid (battery acid, muriatic acid, Clinitest tablets). These substances will burn on the way up as well as on the way down, causing twice as much damage to the stomach and esophagus. Give the child one half to one cup of water or milk to dilute the ingested substance and then call a poison control center. Do not give anything else by mouth, and do not attempt to neutralize an ingested alkali by giving vinegar or citrus juice.

I always tell parents to rid their homes of lye or acid substances because they are simply too dangerous to keep on hand. Some of the newer alkalis, such as granular drain cleaners, are particularly bad, since they can lodge in the esophagus and do a great deal of damage. If you need to use drain opener or oven cleaner, buy a container and use it all or immediately dispose of the unused portion *safely*. The amount of money you might save by conserving a small amount of oven cleaner is not worth the damage it could do to your child. If you have an automatic dishwasher, keep the detergent out of reach of your child, preferably in a locked cabinet.

For information about other poisons, contact your poison control center. The number of your local poison control center should be posted on or by your phone so that you do not have to go searching for it when you need it. The poison control center will be able to tell you the recommended treatment for whatever it was your child swallowed. In most cases of accidental poisoning, you will need to induce vomiting with syrup of ipecac (available at any pharmacy), which you should always have on hand. Syrup of ipecac will cause the child to vomit, but only if there is something in the stomach in addition to whatever it was the child just swallowed. If his stomach is empty, he will be unable to vomit up the poison, so you must give him water or some other liquid first. (It's best not to give the child a red juice, since it will turn everything he vomits red, too, making it hard to see what's coming up.) Consider how long it has been since your child has eaten before you try to give him the syrup of ipecac. You can give the child a second dose if necessary, but when he sees you coming at him with another spoonful of that vile stuff, he'll undoubtedly muster his considerable forces of resistance.

The recommended dosage for syrup of ipecac is as follows:

| 1–10 years | 1 tablespoon |
| 11 and up | 2 tablespoons |

(The dosage for infants between one month and one year of age has not been established, but should probably be two teaspoons.) If vomiting does not occur within thirty minutes, you can repeat the dose one time *only*. After giving syrup of ipecac to a baby, you should hold the infant up on your shoulder or face down across your lap so that he does not inhale vomit into his lungs. Babies under the age of six months do not have a fully developed gag reflex, so you must be especially careful when inducing vomiting. (Luckily, babies of this age are usually not mobile enough to get into trouble with poisons.) Ipecac should not be given to a child of any age who is not fully

conscious, because, again, there is the possibility that the child will inhale vomit into his lungs.

If you do not have ipecac on hand and cannot obtain it within thirty minutes, you can substitute six teaspoons of dishwashing liquid (such as Ivory or Dove), which will also induce vomiting, although not as effectively as ipecac.

In addition to ipecac, you should also have epsom salts and USP activated charcoal powder on hand. The epsom salts may be needed if it is desirable to force the poison through the child's system as quickly as possible. The charcoal may be needed to absorb as much of the toxin as possible while it is still in the stomach. Your poison control center will direct you as to the appropriate dosages of these substances in the event that you need them.

Once you have followed the poison control center's preliminary instructions, you will probably be told to contact your doctor. When you speak to her, you should be prepared to provide the following information: What the substance was and/or what it was used for, how long ago it was purchased or obtained, when food was last eaten and how much food was ingested, and the amount of substance ingested. If the substance is uncommon, the doctor will want to know the name and address of the manufacturer. If it was a prescription drug, she will also need the prescription number and the name and address of the store where it was purchased. Your doctor may then call the center to receive the most up-to-date information on the poison involved. Depending on the seriousness of the situation, she will decide whether it is necessary to see the child, or if you can simply observe him at home, watching for warning signs the doctor will give you.

PUNCTURE WOUNDS. Puncture wounds on the arms or legs do not present much of a problem and do not require a visit to the emergency room. The depth of a puncture wound can be difficult to assess, however. Such an injury to the chest or abdomen can result in complications if the wound is deep enough to affect an artery or internal organ. A child with a puncture wound on this part of the body should therefore be evaluated at an emergency room.

If the child has a puncture wound in the chest that produces a sucking sound, air is being pulled into the chest cavity. This will cause one lung to collapse, pushing it onto the second lung and eventually causing that lung to collapse, which will suffocate the child. You must seal off the wound, either by covering it with your hand or with a piece of gauze or cloth smeared with petroleum jelly. This will keep the child out of danger until you are able to reach an emergency room for help.

SEVERED LIMB. The very first thing you must do in the case of a severed limb is to control the hemorrhage with a tourniquet. Then, if possible, retrieve the limb, place it in a plastic bag and pack it in ice. Don't place the limb directly in the ice. Still warm, it will cause the ice to melt and will then become waterlogged, making it much more difficult to reattach. (If the limb is hanging by a thread of flesh, make sure you preserve that thread, as it may contain the nerve, which is key to successful reim-plantation.) Once you have done these two things, call the nearest Reimplant Center and arrange to have your child taken there. If the nerve damage is not too severe and circulation can be reestablished within four hours, it may be possible to reattach the limb.

SMASHED FINGER OR TOE. Another injury that commonly befalls children is to smash a finger or toe in a car door, a drawer, or door inside the house. This causes a large blood clot to form under the nail, so that it turns black and throbs painfully.

Elevating the affected limb will help to relieve the pain temporarily, but to eliminate it substantially, you must relieve the pressure caused by the blood collecting under the nail. Assemble alcohol, a cotton swab, a candle and match, pliers, and a paper clip. Swab the nail with alcohol and allow it to dry (so that you do not ignite the nail in the next step). When the nail is dry, unbend the paper clip and light the candle. Holding the paper clip with pliers, place it in the flame until red-hot, and touch it to the nail. The paper clip will melt a hole in the nail, allowing the blood to escape. As the blood comes up through the hole, it will cool the paper clip, so there is no danger that you will burn the skin under the nail. Once the blood has drained, the pressure will be released and the pain will stop.

You may be a little nervous about performing this procedure, but it is actually quite easy to do. If you take the child to the hospital, they will do essentially the same thing, but it will cost you a lot more time, trouble, and money.

If the child continues to complain of pain in the finger after you have made a hole in the nail, the tip of the finger may be broken. If this is the case, put a finger splint (available in drugstores) on the finger. It will heal nicely in approximately two weeks.

SNAKEBITE. Fortunately, we do not have many varieties of poisonous snakes in the United States. The four types that do pose danger to people are rattlesnakes, coral snakes, copper snakes, and water moccasins. The coral snake is by far the most poisonous snake found in this country and poses the greatest threat to children. Because coral snakes do not have fangs, they chew into the skin and hang on, rather than biting and releasing as other snakes do. If a child is too young to have the presence of mind or the strength to remove the snake, a great deal of venom can enter the system and may cause death. Adults, who will automatically remove the snake, rarely die from coral snake bites.

It is a good idea to learn to identify poisonous snakes, so that if a member of your family receives a snakebite, you will know whether or not it is dangerous. The treatment for snakebites is to administer antivenin, which is made from horse serum. Some people are allergic to horse serum, and may die from a reaction to it. For this reason, it is important to ensure that antivenin be used only when absolutely necessary.

If someone in your family is bitten, kill the snake if possible so that it may be positively identified. If the snake gets away, there are a few signs that can help determine whether or not it was poisonous. Venomous snakes usually leave puncture wounds, while nonvenomous snakes leave scratch marks or tooth marks. Venomous bites tend to be very painful, surpassing the amount of pain you would expect for the damage done. The pain starts immediately, and is not relieved by pressure or ice.

Several factors influence the danger involved in any snakebite: the degree of penetration, the length of contact, how recently the snake has eaten, and the victim's body size. Since it can be difficult to determine some of these factors, you do need to seek immediate treatment at an emergency room. In most areas only one hospital will stock the antivenin, so you should find out which hospital in your area is able to treat snakebites before you head for an emergency room.

In the meantime, it is important to keep the victim calm and quiet. Excitement or exertion will speed up the circulation and spread the venom more quickly. You can also apply a tourniquet between the heart and the location of the bite, just loose enough to allow one finger beneath it. (If the bite is on a finger, apply the tourniquet to the hand or arm rather than on the finger, or the finger may be lost.) Leave the tourniquet in place (do not apply and remove it intermittently), and loosen it as swelling increases. You should also clean the fang wounds and cut lines through the skin at the site (do not make X-shaped cuts), cutting only one-quarter inch deep. Squeeze out as much of the venom as possible with your fingers, but do not attempt to use oral suction. Rest the extremity horizontally at the level of the heart until the victim reaches the emergency room.[4]

Most snakebites can be prevented by using a little caution and common sense. Don't hike or camp in snake-infested areas, and be careful where you sit or step when in areas that snakes might inhabit. Teach children not to reach into holes or onto hidden ledges, and never to tease or disturb snakes, even small ones. If you hike and camp out regularly, carry with you a snakebite kit with a supply of antivenin and learn now to use it before you need it.

SPIDER BITES. Most spider bites are not poisonous. If there are poisonous spiders in your area, such as the black widow spider, the brown recluse spider, or scorpions, teach your child to identify them and to stay away from then. If your child is bitten by a poisonous spider, take him to the emergency room immediately. There are antivenins for some poisonous spider bites.

Other spider bites, while not truly dangerous, can result in the sloughing off of large patches of skin in the area of the bite. This can be prevented by applying a poultice of tobacco mixed with water to the bite and covering it with a piece of plastic or a gauze pad. The tobacco will prevent the center of the bite from rotting out.

SWALLOWING A FOREIGN OBJECT. Swallowing a foreign object generally poses no risks to a child, as even sharp objects will usually pass through the system without causing damage. You will, however, want to check the child's bowel movements for several days until the object reappears, so you can be sure it has passed through the system safely. Foreign objects travel through the body more slowly than food, so this may take up to six days. A child who has swallowed a sharp object should also be watched carefully for signs of illness until the object has been passed.

To illustrate the body's ability to deal with foreign objects, I often relate the following story from my medical school days. Four times a year, at class parties, a fellow medical student would collect two dollars each from the rest of us, and for that amount of money, eat an entire glass. He never cut his mouth and never had any internal injuries. (In addition to showing you what you can ingest and get away with, there is a lesson here about some of the people who enter the medical profession.)

Occasionally a child will partially swallow something that will get stuck in the throat or the esophagus. When this happens, the object will usually be just below the neck muscle, at the level of the aorta, or just above the diaphragm where the esophagus and stomach join. The child will continually swallow in an attempt to work the object down, and may drool or complain that it hurts to swallow. Swallowing may bring on an attack of coughing or choking. If the child's symptoms are limited to the sensation of having something stuck in the esophagus, the problem may be a muscle spasm, which will usually disappear overnight. If the child's symptoms are severe or persist longer than this, a foreign object is probably the case, and you should arrange to have the child seen by her doctor.

TOOTH, KNOCKED-OUT. If at all possible, place the tooth in the socket and hold it there as you proceed immediately to the dentist. The more quickly you are able to get the tooth back into place, the better chance it has for survival. Ninety percent of the tooth replacements done within thirty minutes of an accident are successful. Beyond four hours, there is really no chance the tooth can survive, although it may still be possible to reimplant it. Should it be impossible to hold the tooth in place, store it in lukewarm milk (breast milk is best) until you can get the child to a dentist.

Even if the tooth does not survive, the dentist may want to put it back in place by bonding it to the teeth next to it in order to maintain proper spacing. He may also push to do a root canal immediately, especially in an older child. It is not necessary to rush into a root canal, however. The tooth can be bonded back in place and further evaluated later on.

UNCONSCIOUSNESS. If you find your child unconscious for no apparent reason, first check the ABCs of respiration: airway (make sure it is clear) breathing (check for respiration), and circulation (check for a pulse). Resuscitate the child if necessary and then take him to the emergency room immediately. If you must wait for an ambulance or other transportation, you can also count the rate of respiration to see if the child is hyperventilating or hypoventilating, and you should check to see if the pupils are dilating. When the doctor examines your child, your observations will help him to assess whether or not there has been a change in the child's condition. The causes of unconsciousness vary from trauma to strokes, tumors, and some diseases, and can only be properly evaluated by a doctor.

VOMITING BLOOD. Vomiting blood is another situation that requires immediate attention at an emergency room. Again, without certain equipment and skills, it is impossible for you to determine why and how much the child is bleeding.

These are the emergency situations you are most likely to encounter in raising children, and, as you have seen, not many of them truly require risking life and limb to speed to the emergency room. The most important thing you can do in any of these situations is to stop and think before you act.

Another story from my training, this time a sad one about something that occurred when I worked in an emergency room: One afternoon a woman came in carrying a child and yelling for help, saying that he had been hit by a car. The boy was badly shaken up, and had a fairly large laceration on his head. As we proceeded to stitch him up, the woman suddenly screamed and rushed out. We later learned that at the time the accident had occurred, she had been bathing her baby. In her panic, she left the child alone in the bathtub. The baby drowned.

Don't act without thinking. In the overwhelming number of emergency situations, you should take time to stop, think, and even have that cup of tea. Keep your cool. The quality of care you receive—and even your child's life—could depend on it. *Have a cup of tea!*

Summing Up: Emergencies

1. Emergency room treatment is not necessarily dictated by what is best for the patient, but rather by what is legally necessary to protect the doctor and the hospital.

2. If you bring your child to an emergency room, you should not allow him to be separated from you for examination or treatment; he needs your presence for comfort and reassurance.

3. Many of the injuries or conditions that parents commonly consider emergencies can be effectively treated at home (in some cases with a follow-up visit to the doctor).

4. Always stop and think before you act in an emergency situation.

5. *Have a cup of tea!*

Notes

1. Gayle Gatch, R.N.; Laura Myre, M.D.; Richard Eugene Black, M.D.; "Foreign Body Aspiration in Children: Causes, Diagnosis and Prevention," *Association of Operating Room Nurses Journal*, Vol. 46, No. 5 (Nov. 1987): p. 850.

2. Gary R. Diamond, "Ophthalmic Emergencies," *Textbook of Pediatric Emergency Medicine*, Gary Fleisher, M.D., and Steven Ludwig, eds. (Baltimore: William and Wilkins, 1983): p. 879.

3. John A. Ogden, M.D., "Chapter 17: The Injury to the Immature Skeleton," *Pediatric Trauma*, Robert J. Touloukian, ed. (New York: John Wiley & Sons, 1978): p. 473.

4. Clifford C. Snyder and Robert P. Knowles, "Snake Bites," *Postgraduate Medicine*, Vol. 83, No. 6 (1988) p. 52.

Suggested Reading and Other Sources of Information

Chapter 5: The Abdomen, Genitalia, and Rectum

For helpful information on fiber write to James W. Anderson, H.F.C. Diabetes Foundation, P.O. Box 22124, Lexington, KY 40522.

Dietary Fiber: Fiber-Depleted Foods and Disease, edited by Hugh R. Trowell, Denis Burkitt, and Kenneth Heaton (Academic Press, New York, 1985).

The Management of Diarrhea and Use of Oral Rehydration Therapy, 2d ed., A Joint WHO-Unicef Statement (World Health Organization, Geneva, 1985).

Medical Aspects of Dietary Fiber, by Gene A. Spiller and Ruth M. Kaye (Plenum Publishers, New York, 1980).

Chapter 6: The Spine and Extremities

Further information on scoliosis can be obtained from the Scoliosis Association, Inc., Dept. WD, 1 Penn Plaza, New York, NY 10019, or from the Scoliosis Research Society, 444 North Michigan Ave., Chicago, IL 60611.

Information on LESS can be obtained from Neuromedics, Inc., Scolitron Project, 1-800-231-2330 (in Texas, 1-800-392-3726).

The Neurological Examination of Children with Minor Nervous Dysfunction, by Burt C. L. Tousen and Heinz F. R. Prechtl, Clinics in Developmental Medicine, No. 38 (Lippincott, Philadelphia, 1970). Available at medical libraries.

The Neurological Examination of the Full-Term Newborn Infant, 2d ed., by Heinz F. R. Prechtl, Clinics in Developmental Medicine, No. 63 (Lippincott, Philadelphia, 1977). Available at medical libraries.

Soft Neurological Signs, edited by David E. Tupper and Robert W. Johnson (Grune & Stratton, Orlando, 1987). A good book if your child is having problems in school that may be developmental or neurological.

Chapter 7: Breast-Feeding, Weaning, and Nurturing

Biology of Human Milk, edited by Lars A. Hansen, Nestlé Nutrition Workshops Series, Vol. 15 (Raven Press, New York, 1988).

Breasts, Bottles and Babies: A History of Infant Feeding, by Valerie A. Fildes (Columbia University Press, New York, 1985).

Human Milk and Infant Nutrition and Health, edited by R. Rodney Howell, Frank Morris, Jr., and Larry K. Pickering (Charles C. Thomas, Springfield, Ill., 1986).

Out of the Mouths of Babes: The Infant Formula Controversy, by Fred D. Miller, Jr. (Transaction Publishers, New Brunswick, N.J., 1983).

Chapter 9: Communication and Discipline

How to Really Love Your Child, by Ross Campbell (NAL, New York, 1982).

How to Really Love Your Teenager, by Ross Campbell (Victor Books, Wheaton, Ill., 1982).

How to Talk So Kids Will Listen and Listen So Kids Will Talk, by Adele Faber and Elaine Mazlish (Avon, New York, 1982).

Oneness and Separateness, by Louise J. Kaplan (Touchstone Books/Simon & Schuster, New York, 1978).

Raising Your Child, Not by Force but by Love, by Sidney Craig (Westminster/John Knox, Louisville, Ky., 1982).

Without Spanking or Spoiling: A Practical Approach to Toddler and Preschool Guidance, by Elizabeth Crarey (Parenting Press, Seattle, Wash., 1979).

Chapter 10: Marriage, Sex, and Family

Caring, Feeling and Touching, by S. Simon (Argus Communications, Niles, Ill., 1976).

Touching, by Ashley Montague (New York Perennial Library, New York, 1971).

Chapter 12: Allergies

Allergy: Principles and Practice, edited by Elliot Middleton, Jr., et al. (C.V. Mosby, St. Louis, Mo., 1988). Available in medical libraries.

An Alternative Approach to Allergy, by Theron G. Randolf and Ralph W. Moss (Lippincott, Philadelphia, 1979).

Detecting Your Hidden Allergies, by William G. Crook (Professional Books/Future Health, Jackson, Tenn., 1988).

Chapter 14: Immunizations and Infectious Diseases

Ideas in Progress: Medical Nemesis: The Expropriation of Health, by Ivan Illich (Pantheon, New York, 1976).

An Introduction to Social Medicine, 3d edition, by Thomas McKeown and C. R. Lowe (Blackwell Scientific Publications, Oxford, 1984).

The Reality Behind the Myth, by Walene James (Bergin & Garvey, Granby, Mass., 1988).

The Role of Medicine: Dream, Mirage or Nemesis? by Thomas McKeown (Princeton University Press, Princeton, N.J., 1979).

Chapter 17: Medications

Goodman and Gilman's The Pharmacological Basics of Therapeutics, by Louis Sanford Goodman (Macmillan, New York, 1980).

The Medicine Show, by the editors of *Consumer Reports* (Consumer's Union, Mount Vernon, New York, 1974).

The Parent's Pharmacy by Drs. Robert H. Pantell and David A. Bergman (Addison-Wesley, Reading, Mass., 1982).

Index

Note: Page numbers in boldface type denote major discussions of index entry.

About the Authors

GEORGE WOOTAN, M.D., is a board-certified family practitioner and a medical associate of La Leche League International. For the past thirteen years he has traveled across the country holding seminars for parents on basic pediatric care, and has spoken before hundreds of groups on the subject of children's health care and related topics. Dr. Wootan and his wife, Pat, are the parents of eleven children and the grandparents of seven. They live with four of their children in Hurley, New York.

Dr. Wootan is available for seminars nationally. He can be reached by writing to Box 270, Hurley, New York, 12443, or by calling 1-800-635-2126.

SARAH VERNEY is a free-lance writer who has worked with Dr. Wootan for several years on materials related to his seminars. She lives in Orange, Connecticut, with her husband, Robert Fink, and their three children.